PURSUING CUSTOMERS

Volume 171   Sage Library of Social Research

RECENT VOLUMES IN . . .
SAGE LIBRARY OF SOCIAL RESEARCH

PURSUING CUSTOMERS
An Ethnography of Marketing Activities

Robert C. Prus

Volume 171
SAGE LIBRARY OF
SOCIAL RESEARCH

SAGE PUBLICATIONS
The Publishers of Professional Social Science
Newbury Park   London   New Delhi

For information address:

SAGE Publications, Inc.
2111 West Hillcrest Drive
Newbury Park, California 91320

SAGE Publications Ltd.
28 Banner Street
London EC1Y 8QE
England

SAGE Publications India Pvt. Ltd.
M-32 Market
Greater Kailash I
New Delhi 110 048 India

Printed in the United States of America

Library of Congress Cataloging-in-Publication Data

Prus, Robert C.
     Pursuing customers : an ethnography of marketing activities / by
Robert C. Prus.
          p.   cm. — (Sage library of social research ; 171)
     Bibliography: p.
     ISBN 0-8039-3407-6.   ISBN 0-8039-3408-4 (pbk.)
     1. Marketing.   I. Title.   II. Series: Sage library of social
research ; v. 171.
     HF5415.122.P78 1989
     658.8—dc19   88-27623
                                                                   CIP

FIRST PRINTING 1989

DEDICATION

To my mother, Jean Eva, for her love, sacrifices, and un-
wavering confidence over the years. . . .

And in memory of Erving Goffman, whose works on
self-reflectivity and impression management not only
brightened up the social sciences but also made them more
social in their essence.

CONTENTS

FOREWORD

Pioneering in his subject matter, novel in his approach, Robert Prus has broken new ground with this two-volume study of marketing behavior. In his previous books, *Road Hustlers* and *Hookers, Rounders, and Desk Clerks,* Professor Prus has provided us with an insider's portrait of the worlds of traveling rings of professional card and dice cheaters, and the colorful underside of deviant roles in the rougher hotel scene. Now he brings life to the activities of buyers, sellers, and merchandisers in the respectable community of the marketplace.

In many ways, this project represents a more difficult undertaking. We are all consumers, customers, clients, patients, and buyers, and for that reason, the scenes Prus describes here are ones that we find familiar. While describing the exotic may sometimes be inherently more interesting, to provide a sociological understanding of a mundane arena of everyday life requires a different and more sensitive type of "sociological optic." In these two volumes, we see how sellers (retailers, wholesalers, manufacturers, and promoters) do their business, develop clients, purchase and price products, and generally negotiate the world of mercantile exchange.

In focusing on mercantile exchange, Prus pursues a thread that has run constant throughout his work. His occupational studies, whether of professional criminals, the boundary between the deviant and the respectable, or of legitimate business, are all marked by descriptions of people making human responses to the structural features of their scenes. As such, they tell us about how people go about solving the same problems under very different circumstances. They also all involve, at their base, a pervasive human concern: money. The most symbolic of human media, money provides a key for the insightful and detailed observer of human life to grasp both bold and subtle nuances of human relations, motivations, actions, organization, and, ultimately, social structure. Like Simmel, Prus has chosen to look into the social forms and social relations surrounding money to learn about human behavior generally. By diversifying the focus of his work between legitimate and illegitimate marketplaces, Prus has further created a foundation of knowledge and insights from which to make comparative analysis.

Through his cumulative life's work, and with this set of books in particular, Prus has made a significant and lasting contribution to the vastly underaddressed field of *social economy*. Falling on the cusp between sociology and economics, this area of inquiry has been largely neglected. Those who have looked at human economic behavior have focused mostly on macro dimensions of the economy, or on micro aspects of the psychology of human finance. Both of these have been extremely rationalistic in their approach, and little attention has been focused on the way humans, in groups, or as individuals within groups, make economic decisions. This particularly sociological problem is taken up by Prus in these volumes. In them, he extends our knowledge of human behavior, from the interactionist perspective, to show how people reach for, draw upon, and manipulate human communication, symbolic meanings, relationships, and the norms of the moral order, to accomplish their goals.

In so doing, he also adds to our understanding of symbolic interactionist theory and shows its major advantages over other social psychological theories. His depiction of human group life as socially constructed, perspectival, reflective, negotiable, relational, and processual, combines all of the major tenets of interactionism, and illustrates for the reader its appropriateness for analyzing any kind of setting, behavior, or interaction. Not only are we provided with a view of buyers and sellers, but of organizations, interactions, stratification, relationships, and social psychological processes.

These volumes are also especially welcome because of the paucity of ethnographic work in this arena. Prus goes into fascinating detail about the world of "marketing and sales." It is ironic that, despite its omnipresence in our lives, this area has received short shrift in the sociological literature. Although a number of books exist that tell us the "hows" of marketing, few exist that phenomenologically describe and explain the subtle nuances, the behind-the-scenes dramas, and the interactional dimensions of selling behavior. To social scientists, the everyday marketplace has remained a rather conspicuous, but under-studied, phenomenon. Perhaps too afraid to enter into worlds so close to home, most social scientists have apparently considered the inter-actional dynamics of marketplace behavior unworthy of study. Prus's penetration beyond the fronts, deceptions, schemes, sales pitches, and dramaturgical presentations that are so characteristic of these scenes has yielded a plethora of consumer commerce. After reading these books, sociological understanding of the marketplace will advance well beyond the mostly formulaic laws laid down by economists, or the attempts at understanding the psyche of the buyer that is so evident in pop psychological treatments of this area, to the inner fabric and underlying, dynamic processes that occur between buyer and seller.

Prus could not have provided such a picture without employing a methodology that remained true to the everyday world he studied. Shunning the standard methods often employed in (largely market research) studies of selling behavior, these books reveal an ethno-graphic approach that accentuates the richly diverse and contoured reality of marketplace behavior. Prus is searching for generic concepts and features that characterize all selling behavior, drawn from a variety of settings and participants, to provide the reader with a theory that will go beyond the particularistic features of a single type of marketing. He is not satisfied by merely describing the activities, but wants to take us beyond them to show how they sociologically represent a range of interactional procedures. The marketplace, in many ways, is for Prus a metaphor for the daily exchanges we enter into in all walks of life. We, the readers, get the benefits of a wide sampling of sellers, hear them tell us, in their own words, how they do their business, and we are then permitted, along with Prus, to step back and assess these in light of sociological theory and research.

Two volumes may seem a lot to devote to a single work, but with the paucity of information we have had on this behavior, and the relevance it holds to us on a daily basis, the following pages will touch a sensitive nerve in all. These descriptions ring true to our understanding of these scenes. After reading these books, we will obtain a new perspective, the fresh look and unique viewpoint that only a sociological grounding can provide. Dive in, enjoy, learn, and react, for reading these books, like the scenes they describe, should be an interactional process, where reader and author, like buyer and seller, negotiate their ways together and build on the knowledge that we all have as participants in the mercantile exchanges of human behavior.

Patricia A. Adler
University of Colorado

Peter Adler
University of Denver

ACKNOWLEDGMENTS

During the eight years that I've been studying the marketplace, I've been fortunate in having had the opportunity to discuss this project with a great many people in North America and, to a lesser extent, scholars around the world.

My acknowledgments take two forms. First, I would like to thank all of the people in marketing and sales who have so generously shared their life experiences with us. I undertook the task of gathering and assembling the material and trying to present it in a manner that accurately portrays their activities, dilemmas, and adjustments, but their contributions were vital and this book is very much their product. They remain anonymous, but they are most heartily thanked for their input and the education that they have collectively provided for us.

My second set of acknowledgments goes to a rather extensive set of colleagues and other benefactors. After completing a book on card and dice hustlers (Prus and Sharper, 1977), and another on the social organization of the hotel community (Prus and Irini, 1980), I had expected to have completed the present study in two to four years. It's been eight years since I started. Part of the time was spent working on other projects and part of the time was spent developing papers around some of the activities depicted in these volumes. But I also hadn't anticipated the overall complexity of the marketplace vis-à-vis social processes and how much time I would have to spend pursuing and sorting out information gathered in this setting. In addition, although I only sporadically pursued a publisher for this material, it took considerably longer to find a publisher willing to brave new territory (a new area for the social sciences, a new approach for marketers) than I had expected. Fortunately, a process orientation to the study of group life has a rather timeless quality to it, which means that the material presented herein should long continue to be relevant to a consideration of exchange and human relations. An appreciation of this aspect of the project was helpful in sustaining my own enthusiasm over that time. Nevertheless, I am very much indebted to all those who provided assistance and encouragement along the way. During this time, a great many people have taken an interest in this project. I know that any listing I might assemble will inevitably miss some to whom I am grateful, so I offer my apologies in advance. With that caveat in mind, allow me to extend my thanks to Cheryl and Dan Albas, Paul Anderson, Eleen Baumann, Russ Belk, Herbert Blumer, David Booth, Craig Boydell, Dick Brymer, Janet Burns, Dorothy Counts, Carl Couch, Jim Curtis, Donna Darden, Mary Lou Dietz, Robert Emerson, Frank Fasick, Augie Fleras, Wendy Frisby, Mary Gallant, Julie Gigante, Scott Grills, Ed Gross, Jack Haas, Nancy Herman, John Johnson, Ron Lambert, Ed Lemert, Jean Langdon, John Lofland, Stan Lyman, Nancy Mandell, Jim Marks, Barabara Mitchell, Rich Mitchell, Tom Morrione, Al Olmstead, Trevor Pinch, Howard Robboy, Julius Roth, Susie Russell, Clint Sanders, Marvin Scott, Bill Shaffir, John Sherry, Charlie Smith, Bob Stebbins, Anselm Strauss, John Swan, Graham Tomlinson, Melanie Wallendorf, Robert Whitehurst, Audrey Wipper, and Lou Zurcher.

I have also benefited from opportunities to use earlier drafts of this statement in a course on the sociology of marketing and sales. We've run the course seven times now, and with enrollments comparable to those in our deviance and social psychology courses. Not all of these classes were equally stimulating, but the forums and feedback they generated were helpful in developing this material into its present form.

I would also like to thank Mitch Allen of Sage for his willingness to brave new frontiers and for his recognition of the necessity of building a social science on the lived experiences of people. Finally, I would like to express my gratitude to Peter and Patti Adler for writing forewords to these volumes. I have been immensely impressed with both their written work and the depth they possess vis-à-vis the interpretive social sciences. I also value the interest that they have taken in my work over the years and very much appreciate the time they have taken from their own highly demanding schedules to share their insights with us.

—Robert C. Prus

Chapter 1
MARKETING IS . . .
SOCIALLY CONSTRUCTED ACTIVITY

> The store is a great theatre, the customers are the audience, the selling force the actors, the nonselling force and the managers are the stage hands and the scene-shifters. As in the theatre, not many get behind the scenes and yet it is these hidden recesses, these unseen openings, that are the most interesting [Donovan, 1929: 188].

Viewing the marketplace as a theatre and an "action spot," this book examines the ways in which vendors prepare for and pursue contacts with prospective buyers. The marketplace is a great theatre in the sense that there is much drama, suspense, and adventure. As an arena in which people put their money down, the marketplace is clearly an action spot. Thus there is desire, sacrifice, commitments, competition, and uncertainty. It is, further, an interactive theatre. Both buyers and sellers assume roles as tacticians and targets as the scenes unfold. It is an emergent theatre. The marketplace involves considerable planning, scripting, and orderliness, but it contains much ambiguity, and allows for much creativity, persuasion, and resistance.

Reflecting what Goffman (1959) would term the "drama of everyday life," the marketplace is most fundamentally a realm of people activity. It is a setting of human contrasts; of haste and indecision, of boredom and excitement, of confidence and stage fright, and of success and failure. Thus we may ask not only what we can learn about the marketplace from this immediate inquiry, but also what we can learn of other settings and people's relationships and activities therein from a close, intimate examination of the dynamics of the marketplace. This volume does not instruct people on how to play roles or to make their millions.

Rather, it is an attempt to provide a careful, grounded account of how vendors assemble their activities in anticipation of customer encounters. In developing this material we have drawn upon the experiences of people involved in the marketing of a wide range of products (and services). So far as possible, we let the participants speak for themselves. They portray their worlds in terms that they find appropriate in describing their dilemmas and disappointments, and their successes and exciting times. Activity by activity, and piece by piece within, they show us how their world is constructed and indicate the sorts of ongoing adjustments they make to customers, competitors, co-workers, suppliers, and others with whom they associate. In the process, they take us through the back regions, share their strategies and dilemmas with us, and still manage to provide us with front row seats.

The central thesis is that business is a social activity, and is best understood by considering the processes by which people do business on a day-to-day basis. Our interest is in people selling everything from ice cream and candy, to clothing and jewelry, automobiles, insurance, real estate, computer systems, industrial goods, and advertising. Thus the material contained herein focuses on the ways in which people *actually* do business and builds fundamentally on their lived experiences.

Pursuing Customers is organized around the *activities* included in preparing for buyer encounters. It considers such things as setting up and managing businesses, buying goods, setting prices, and recruiting prospects through the media, deploying sales agents in the field, and utilizing showrooms and other exhibits.[1]

This volume should be of interest to everyone who buys or sells goods, as well as to every student of human interaction, for it is in the marketplace that people put their money down. It is here that we have an opportunity to gain much insight into the uncertainties, the dilemmas, the frustration, and the excitement that people experience as they endeavor to gain control of their lives in a world they jointly experience with others of potentially diverse and often competing interests. Rather than giving advice or prescriptions for "how to sell a million," the objective is to provide a thorough, balanced, and intimate view of marketplace activity; to show how people go about preparing for exchanges with others. Thus the strategies and excitement of marketplace activities are depicted, but so are the risks, frustrations, and dilemmas of doing business.

A Generic Activity

Sales are sales. . . . If you learn something in one place, you are going to use it in your next job as well. You use it every place. You use it in your everyday life [mixed sales].

In contrast to those who suggest that each type of product or level of sales requires a different approach, this book considers the similarities and differences of doing business within and across product areas and levels (e.g., manufacture, wholesale, retail) of sales. While the reader will be better able to judge the value of this strategy at the conclusion, it is suggested that as people read the material following, they assess it relative to any and all marketing contexts with which they are familiar.

In addition to providing a rather unique framework from which to view marketing activity, this book is "grounded" (Glaser and Strauss, 1967) in the experiences of those doing marketplace activity. Those never having been in business are likely to find that they will be better able to make sense of the marketplace, as well as their own experiences with vendors. Those having been in business should find the material even more rewarding as they can readily compare their situations with those of people selling products in a number of diverse settings. An attempt will be made to draw parallels across sales arenas, and to note differences in styles of selling where appropriate. It is intended, how-ever, that the material developed herein be viewed not just as a state-ment on the marketplace, but as material relevant to a more general understanding of group life. It is hoped that by examining the dynamics of the marketplace, we may learn more about the ways in which people work out their activities with others more generally.[2]

A People Activity

You have to be very self-disciplined to make a success at sales. It's difficult to keep the momentum, the motivation, where you've worked hard and don't get a return. . . . Some of the people are difficult. We're all different, and we all think differently, and I think any business would be very successful if they didn't have to content with people! It makes life interesting, but it also makes life very confusing, and very difficult sometimes. It's a people business [real estate]!

Business involves the exchange of goods and services, but it is fundamentally social activity. Not only are all exchanges best seen as denoting relationships among the parties involved, but even the meanings of the objects being exchanged reflect emergent group interactions. These notions will be developed further as the book unfolds, but it means that vendor activities need to be examined in reference to their preparations, direct customer contacts, and their postcontact behaviors, as together these constitute the social activity of sales. While direct vendor-prospect interaction is most obviously subject to negotiation, all vendor activities pertaining to those exchanges (before, during, and after) are of significance for understanding those encounters and any subsequent vendor-prospect encounters.

It is also crucial that the meanings of the *objects* (representing the content) considered in the exchange be seen in reference to their social natures. The *value* of objects arises not from any inherent properties or objective worths. *Worth* is the value attributed to objects by prospective buyers (a valuing which may be shaped by the vendor and others). Thus central significance will be given to the symbolic nature of exchange; to the meanings of objects as attributed to them by those engaged in exchange.

While the emphasis is on marketing as experienced by vendors, the perspectives of buyers will also be considered. For although there may be but one exchange, any exchange may be seen in several different ways by the participants and any other observers—in anticipation of the exchange, as the encounter develops, and in retrospect. Both buyers and sellers may plan and expect certain outcomes, but marketplace exchanges entail cooperative behavior as the participants (jointly) shape the directions of their encounters.

A Multifaceted Activity

Selling is your attempt to make sales, but it's all the things that go on there. How you relate to the people you're trying to sell on something, your desire to make the sale, their resistance, them trying to work you for a deal. And, everyone's different, so even if they want the same thing, they're going to come at you from different angles [manufacture—industrial].

Sales might be most basically defined as exchanges of goods, but like all social behavior, marketplace exchanges often entail a great deal of anticipation, assessment, and ongoing adjustment on the part of those involved. Exchanges involve commitments on behalf of all participants, and the resultant alterations in goods can significantly affect the subsequent experiences of those involved in the exchange. As such, one finds the weighing of resources, the assessment of options, the anticipation of consequences, and the emergence of strategies designed to enhance one's position. With some experience also comes the recognition of similar concerns on the part of others, mutual capacities for deception, and the possibilities of misunderstanding and disappointment.

Exchanges (and the activities involved thereof) can be challenging, reflecting adversity, excitement, risk, and failure. Likewise, they can be entertaining, stimulating, refreshing, and creative, as well as dull, uninspiring, and boring. Exchanges afford opportunities for persuasion, diplomacy, deception, and pressure, but they may also entail inquiry and assessment, honesty, and trust. Marketplace exchanges are far from a simple (and very misleading) matter of supply and demand.[3] Denoting social activity, marketplace exchanges are as multifaceted as those in any other area of group life. In class, for instance, I've suggested that buyer-seller relationships might be paralleled to dating relationships. Thus while one may encounter some uncertainty and stage fright (Lyman and Scott, 1970: 159-188) in both settings, so might one also find strategies and gaming, impression management (Goffman, 1959), and attempts to play the field, as well as stabilize relationships. In both instances, one also notes the role of the competition, concerns with loyalty, breakups, and sometimes reinvolvements. And, while many contacts may be fleeting, others may involve considerable commitment, concern, and the organization of one's routines around the other.

An Interdependent Activity

> There are so many things you can do, and it's hard to tell how much any of the business you get is due to this, or this, or this. You don't know if it's because of your advertising, your staff, your displays, your service, or what. All these things are there, and they're all happening at once, more or less [mixed clothing].

As will become more apparent as the material unfolds, marketing (and sales) consists of a plurality of activities,[4] each of which is dependent on the others for overall effect.[5] Thus how one "structures" one's business will have implications for styles of management, buying supplies, pricing, recruiting customers, presenting products, developing loyal customers, and vice versa. The same is true in reference to the other activities. How one buys can affect the prices one charges, the ways customers are recruited, how products are presented, and so on. Changes in any aspect of one's marketing procedure can affect the significance of each of the other components. The effect of any marketing program is not, however, a direct function of the ways in which vendors define their activities. Since sales are contingent on the cooperation of the buyers, any changes in the prospective buyers' interests or options can dramatically affect the effectiveness of all these activities.

From the larger project from which this monograph was derived, 15 areas of activity had emerged as central to a more comprehensive understanding of marketing and sales. These 15 activities subsequently have been organized around two more basic themes: vendor preparations (in the pursuit of customer contact) and interpersonal selling practices.

The present volume, *Pursuing Customers,* examines the preparations that vendors make in anticipation of customer encounters. These stage setting activities not only reflect vendor anticipations of the activities of both the competitors they envision on the horizon and the customers with whom they expect to deal in the future, but these preparations also reflect vendors' ongoing adjustments to both the customers with whom they have previously dealt and their appraisals of their competitors' activities to date. Thus these activities assume a dialectic, processual quality. While vendors act in the present, they are acting in reference to their past experiences, and mindful of the (rather unpredictable) future. Further, they live in an interactive world, a world in which their outcomes not only reflect their own enterprises, but are also shaped by the activities of all of those whose lives intersect with those of the vendors.

In contrast to the more direct interpersonal encounters dealt with in the companion volume, *Making Sales,* the present volume, *Pursuing Customers,* is very much a study of the anticipation of "the generalized other" (Mead, 1934). While most people seem much more sensitive to the drama (i.e., their dilemmas, sacrifices, risks) entailed in direct interpersonal encounters with vendors, vendors most acutely experience their dilemmas, investments, and gambles in setting the stage for their encounters with the generalized other. This is not to imply that vendors do not experience pressure and tactical dilemmas in dealing with the specific people they encounter in the course of doing business or that these individual encounters are not consequential to the overall success of that business. However, it is in the activities involved in preparing for these (necessarily ambiguous) encounters that vendors are most cognizant of the dramatic nature of their undertakings.

Pursuing Customers
  Setting Up Business
  (options, formats, ownership dilemmas)
  Doing Management
  (responsibilities, staffing, performance)
  Purchasing Products
  (concerns, gaming, relationships)
  Setting Prices
  (price, value, profit)
  Using the Media
  (tasks, formats, dilemmas)
  Working the Field
  (prospecting, calls, pressures)
  Exhibiting Products
  (location, displays, assessments)

Making Sales
  Presenting Products
  (approach, qualification, interest)
  Generating Trust
  (integrity, quality, obligations)
  Neutralizing Resistance
  (skepticism, price, loyalties)
  Obtaining Commitments
  (closings, groups, dilemmas)
  Encountering Troublesome Customers
  (carelessness, rudeness, returns)
  Developing Loyalty
  (service, signification, contact)
  Holding "Sales"
  ("bargains," action, dilemmas)
  Maintaining Enthusiasm
  (pressures, slumps, support)

The Literature

In order to locate the present statement within a broader context, it seems advisable to consider the efforts to date of other researchers in marketing and sociology (as a representative of the social sciences).[6]

THE MARKETING TRADITION

There is a very large marketing and sales literature. This literature is also quite diverse. It ranges from "quick and slick ways to sell a million . . . ," and popular-applied business, characterized by practical advice on all sorts of business matters, to "scientific" attempts to better predict and control the business world, generally by using experimental and survey data. Mixed between and variously reflecting these emphases is a wide selection of textbooks presenting elementary and advanced statements on the art and science of marketing. While these texts generally have a chapter or two on the social sciences, this material is very limited. The desirability of incorporating sociology and psychology into marketing schemes is often emphasized, with general references to Maslow's (1954) vague statement on the "hierarchy of needs,"[7] Hyman's (1960, generally uncited) concept of "reference groups," Festinger's (1957) theory of "cognitive dissonance," and Warner and Lunt's (1941) and Warner et al.'s (1949) analysis of "social class." In large part, this material seems intended to provide insight into customer motivations. These themes are sometimes supplemented with material indicating the desirability of conducting demographic (e.g., age, class, gender, ethnic compositions) analyses of prospective populations of customers; the implication is that certain categories of persons would be more apt to have certain interests in making purchasing decisions. This material, which largely focuses on consumers, is then left behind as marketing and sales procedures are discussed. In discussing the role of the vendor, the emphasis is extensively on definitions and technical prescriptions with the seeming inference that good technicians would do the proper thing at the right time in the appropriate degree. Scant attention is paid to vendors as persons in situations that remain to be worked out with others (prospective customers).

As Bagozzi (1979), Enis (1979), and Lutz (1979) so aptly note, marketers have spent a great deal of time developing models and giving advice, but have given minimal consideration to the actualities of marketplace activities, interactions, and the relationships emerging therein.[8] Unfortunately, their observations have not been heeded by most academic practitioners. Long-standing traditions and (the related) gatekeepers of the major journals in this area have largely disregarded these notions. This is even more ironic in light of the practitioner backgrounds of many of those in marketing schools. Insofar as they, themselves, have run businesses, engaged in saleswork, tried management, and the like, one would expect to see more evidence of their own lived experiences in their depictions of the marketplace. Instead, it is as though they operate with two largely nonintegrated sets of knowledge—their own lived experiences and what might be termed *academic positivism*.[9] Given their own stocks of knowledge (Schutz, 1971), these people are quite able to provide illustrations of (and insights into) the very sorts of processes examined in this study. To date, however, the marketing literature has evidenced little direct appreciation of the extent to which business is fundamentally social activity. And even less concern has been directed toward studying business in its naturalistic settings.

The American Marketing Association recently defined *marketing* in the following manner:

> Marketing is the process of planning and executing the conception, pricing, promotion, and distribution of ideas, goods, and services to create exchanges that satisfy individual and organizational objectives [*Marketing News:* March 1, 1985].

This (revised) view of marketing as a process, subject to planning and implementation, is very consistent with the material presented herein. However, in contrast to the more traditional marketing literature, our emphasis is on the ways in which marketing practices are actually accomplished. It is here, by drawing attention to the social nature of all marketing and sales activity, and by depicting the ways in which these activities are worked out by the parties involved, that this study can make a contribution to what is already an immense literature.

SOCIOLOGY ET AL.

For their part, the social sciences have given very little attention to the study of marketing and sales. This is not to say that there is no theory that could be applied to this activity, only that there has been little work done in this area by social scientists. Most applications of social science concepts to this realm reflect the initiatives of marketing people. Without going into much detail, the work in sociology seems typical of the social sciences more generally.[10]

Despite the centrality of the marketplace for urban society, one finds relatively few sociological studies of this phenomenon. While purporting interest in all facets of society, this very significant aspect of group life has been largely neglected by sociologists. The bases of this oversight are unclear, but may reflect some combination of the following: (1) the stigma attached to crass and commercial activities by social scientists,[11] (2) a tendency to see business as consisting of mundane exchanges,[12] (3) a perception that business people (and/or economists) have already done this or are more adequately equipped to study marketing activity, (4) minimal personal contact and/or familiarity with this setting, (5) an anticipation of resistance to sociological inquiry on the part of business people, (6) a lack of government funding for sociological research in this area, (7) an anticipated lack of interest on the part of other sociologists and/or limited opportunities for publishing in this area,[13] (8) a lack of conceptual tradition in this subject matter,[14] and (9) a definition of some sociologists as "their mission being that of critics of capitalist society." [15]

There is a sociological literature pertinent to business, but much of this material has remained subterranean relative to the discipline, and very little integrative work (or even cross-referencing) exists. As a result, this literature is very uneven in character and emphasis. Other than the present project, there has been little attempt on the part of sociologists to approach systematically the larger field of marketing and sales.

For those wishing to familiarize themselves with the range of this literature, the following listing is provided:

In brief reviews of the literature, Lazarsfeld (1959) and Foxall (1974) lament the neglect of business and consumer behavior by sociologists; while Tucker (1964) posits that there is a "social base to economic behavior."

Among the inquiries into the retail sector, some consideration has been given to department and other store settings (MacLean, 1899; Donovan, 1929; Lombard, 1955; French, 1958, 1960; Sofer, 1965; Caplovitz, 1973; Greenberg, 1980), mall life (Jacobs, 1984), automobile sales (Miller, 1964; Browne, 1973; Valdez, 1984), real estate operations (Angrist, 1955, 1984; House, 1977), and time-sharing programs involving vacation accommodations (Katovich and Diamond, 1986).

Other retail endeavors sampled by sociologists include antiques (Maisel, 1966), flea markets (Maisel, 1974), street markets (Pinch and Clark, 1986), auctions (Clark and Halford, 1978; Olmstead, 1986; Smith, 1986), ghetto merchandising (Sturdivant, 1969), home party plans (Peven, 1968; Prus and Frisby, 1989), door to door sales (Bogdan, 1972; Stets-Kealey, 1984), hippie enterprises (Cavan, 1972), art markets (Levine, 1972; McCall, 1977; Becker, 1982), and "race horse sales" (Lilly and Ball, 1979).

As well, attention has been directed toward a variety of service-related exchanges such as those involving junk dealers (Ralph, 1950), watch repairers (Strodtbeck and Sussman, 1956), cab drivers (Davis, 1959; Henslin, 1968), milkmen (Bigus, 1972), contractors (Glaser, 1972), doctors (Hayes-Bautista, 1976; Kasteller et al., 1976), and lawyers (Darden et al., 1981).

Also noteworthy in the retail setting are materials focusing on consumer behavior (Stone, 1954; Caplovitz, 1963, 1974, 1979; Glock and Nicosa, 1964; Nicosa and Mayer, 1976; Wallendorf, 1978; Wiseman, 1979), fashions (Kaiser, 1985; Sanders, 1985, 1988; Solomon, 1985), "troublesome customers" (Roth, 1965; Siporin, 1967, Eaton, 1980; Karikas and Rosenwassen, 1980), and debt collection practices (Rock, 1973; Bass, 1983). Additionally, some attention has been directed toward market research (Jacobs, 1979) and advertising (Schudson, 1984).

At another level, sociologists have also tapped into buyer-supplier relations (Kriesberg, 1956; Macaulay, 1963), purchasing departments (Strauss, 1962, 1964), and franchisee-franchisor relations (Sklar, 1973, 1977). While much neglected, Simmel (1900, 1978) provides a most valuable statement on the "philosophy of money" and the relative relationships of price, value, and supply and demand. Nevertheless, some of these themes have been explored in studies of financial markets (Glick, 1957; Adler, 1981; Smith, 1981; Adler and Adler, 1984) and the setting of rental fees (Gilderbloom, 1985). Some consideration has also been given to the "selling of communities" to corporate investors (Prus and Fleras, 1987). Others have studied self-images and status problems of salespeople (Howton and Rosenberg, 1965; Ditz, 1967), elements affecting success (French, 1960), vendor-seller traits (Evans, 1963), and the professionalization of real estate (Hughes, 1979) and insurance (Bain, 1959; Ross, 1970) sales-related groups. As well, while the term *(informal economy)* appears to be much more troublesome (i.e., very nebulous, confusing, and value-laden) than it may be worth, some attention has been recently given to what is purported to be some alternative ways of doing business (see Ferman et al., 1987).

Finally, albeit involving "disrespectability," some valuable insights into the practice of business may be gleaned from the deviance literature. Relevant in this respect are studies of black market operations (Clinard, 1969), fencing (Klockars, 1975; Walsh, 1977), fiddling and pilferage (Ditton, 1977; Henry, 1978), bookmaking (Hindelang, 1971; Lesieur, 1977; and Prus and Sharper, 1977), drug dealing (Carey, 1968; Adler and Adler, 1983; Fields, 1984; and Adler, 1985), and the sales of sexual and related entertainment commodities (Cressey, 1932; Velarde, 1973; Hong et al., 1975; Rasmussen and Kuhn, 1976; Miller, 1978; Prus and Irini, 1988; and Luckenbill, 1984). Additionally, one finds some consideration of trust violations within legitimate businesses (Sutherland, 1949; Cressey, 1953; Quinney, 1963; Leonard and Weber, 1970; Farberman, 1975; and Clinard and Yeager, 1980).

Despite the seemingly impressive array of sources just cited,[16] and the value of each item included in the preceding listing, it is important to recognize the limited forays of sociologists into the interaction dynamics characterizing the marketplace. The marketplace may be seen to epitomize human interchange, but we have learned little of the social dynamics of exchange from this setting. Insofar as any theme may be seen to dominate the literature, it reflects the desirability of studying the marketplace in ethnographic (observations, participation, interviews) terms. Even here, however, one finds relatively little attempt to locate these studies within the broader dimensions of the marketplace. Accordingly, by focusing on activities generic to a wide range of products and marketing formats, it is hoped that the present undertaking will also serve as an integrative frame.

Rather than attempting to speak for all of sociology, this statement more specifically indicates the relevance of symbolic interactionism or an interpretive social science for the study of marketing and sales activity. This approach is grounded in the everyday, lived experiences of people and focuses on the ways in which they work out (construct) their associations with others.

Group Life as Socially Constructed Activity

Somewhat like a group of people building a house or people putting on a play, marketplace exchanges may be seen as socially constructed activity. The parties negotiating an exchange may be much less "scripted" than the house builders (blueprints) or the actors on stage. Likewise, the parties in exchanges may be less interested in achieving shared objectives than are the others. But, just as one may consider the processes by which a house is assembled, a play is produced, a game is played, or a medical operation is performed, so may one also examine the ways in which people involved in business exchanges assemble (and negotiate) their activities with those with whom they interact.

Building on "symbolic interactionism" (Mead, 1934; Blumer, 1969), the "dramaturgical" metaphor (Goffman, 1959, 1963), and "reality construction theory" (Berger and Luckmann, 1966),[17] one may delineate five premises central to understanding how people work out their interests and activities with one another on a day-to-day basis.

These premises or base-line assumptions are: the world can have multiple meanings to people (people act toward objects in terms of the meanings they have for them); people have capacities for taking themselves (and others) into account when developing lines of action toward objects (including self and others); meanings are shaped by people's interaction with others, people develop particular bonds with others; and human life has an emergent nature. In short, human behavior is seen as perspectival, reflective, negotiable, relational, and processual. This approach is concerned with studying and analyzing human behavior mindful of the perspectives of the people involved, the ways in which these people interpret situations, the ways in which they influence one another's actions, the particular interconnections people establish with others, and the ways in which the participants actively (in process) construct their activities. Given their centrality for the approach undertaken in this volume, each of these points will be examined in greater detail.

INTERACTION AS PERSPECTIVAL

Part of the problem is that everybody sees things differently. So things you might like, or think are good ideas, other people may see them quite differently. And that goes for everything, pretty well, your stock, your prices, your displays, even your staff and the way they approach people. What one will like, the next one may find disgusting or ridiculous. As a department store, we try to go more middle-of-the-road, but even there, you have problems trying to predict what people will want [department store].

As this suggests, it is important not to presume an objective or stimulus reality that everyone will experience similarly. Objects (people, products, concepts, scenes, sounds, odors, and so on) do not have inherent meanings for humans. It is essential, therefore, that we recognize the multiple (symbolic) realities (Schutz, 1971) within which people construct their activities.

Humans attribute meanings to objects and these meanings reflect the perspectives (i.e., frames of reference, viewpoints, world views, stocks of knowledge) to which those people have been exposed and presently operate. One can find all sorts of variations in meanings attributed to objects (e.g., sex, religion, and politics) in our own society,[18] and one has only to watch the socialization of the young to realize that meanings (and valuings) of objects are learned. Objects become meaningful when located within a group's symbolic system. Thus parents may buy children "toys" that they (the parents) find attractive only to find the children more interested in the packaging than the toy. To play appropriately, children have to acquire perspectives on how to play with toys; that a toy gun is not a hammer, or that a doll is not a projectile, for instance. Likewise, a wooden chair may be seen as something to be sat upon, but this phenomenon can also be used as a weapon (in barroom brawls for example), a means of defense (from a lion), a stand for giving speeches, or for a flower pot, a door jamb, kindling for a fire, an eyesore, an antique, and so on.

Consistent with this discussion of the chair, we can intend or presume objects to have specific meanings, but we are always dependent on the interpretations of others for the confirmation of our reality. Clearly, the same objects can have different meanings to different audiences at the same time. They can also have different meanings to the same audiences at different times, and even to the same audience at the same time. Orrin Klapp's (1962, 1971) analysis of "heroes," "villains," and "fools" is illustrative here. From Klapp's discussion of the processes by which people become known as "social types," it becomes readily apparent that one audience's villain may be another audience's hero, and yet be considered a fool by a third audience. In the sales setting, this suggests that each customer may view the same product differently, and that products thought to be attractive or good buys by a vendor may be perceived in similar or different ways from one customer to the next.

It is also evident that the same audience can attribute quite different meanings to be same object over time. A person earlier defined as a hero (as a result of a particular activity) may later be redefined as a fool or a villain by the same audience when it is reconsidering the very same event. Formerly stylish clothes (once much desired) may be given away to obtain closet space when newer styles are popular. Similarly, customers happy with purchases at one time may, upon further reflection, decide to return the goods. These goods need not have changed in any way for these people to now define them as inappropriate, too costly, and such.

People may also attribute different meanings to the same object at the same time. For instance, one may define another as a villain, but simultaneously admire his resourcefulness, defiance, courage, and so on. An attractive item may also be defined as costly, fragile, dangerous, and the like. These multiple and potentially shifting definitions have important implications for understanding the valuing of goods by prospects and their willingness to enter transactions with particular vendors. They are critical for vendors as they endeavor to assess prospects, do presentations, attempt to complete sales, and build a repeat clientele. From the vendor's perspective, it means coming to terms with multiple and shifting sets of meanings that prospects (and existing customers) attribute to and/or associate with themselves, the items under consideration, and the vendors involved.

While the meanings of objects are audience-specific and reflect the perspectives of those audiences, one also encounters a sense of objectivity in reference to object definitions. Thus, although I may never have met the reader, I presume that the reader will have somewhat shared interpretations of the symbols (letters and words) printed on this page. A sense of objectivity seems evident. It should be noted, however, that our sense of objectivity in this instance (and in all others) rests on the presumption of shared perspectives (those with which others would agree). People unfamiliar with the English language may be able to make little (if any) sense out of this material. People unfamiliar with books may view this phenomenon in untold ways, possibly using it as a window prop, a projectile, an object on which to stand, material for starting a fire, and so forth, *ad infinitum.* What is considered objective seems better recognized as reflecting "intersubjective consensus"

(Schutz, 1971); an affirmation of shared perspectives and definitions on the part of communicating parties.

This sense of objectivity, however, is prompted from first contact with a group. Thus, for instance, newborns enter a social world, but one that has no immediate meaning for them. As they acquire rudiments of the symbolic realities of others, and begin to internalize the perspectives to which they are exposed, we may speak of them becoming "minded beings." They will be taught to identify and label objects in manners approximating those with whom they have contact. They will be taught value systems and shown techniques for doing things. They will be given perspectives for interpretation and communication. And, unless this knowledge about the world is challenged, it is apt to be considered natural and objective, denoting paramount reality.

INTERACTION AS REFLECTIVE

You're always trying to anticipate them (customers). What would they like? How much would they be willing to spend for an item like this? How would this style look to them? How can you make it more interesting to them, more attractive, more appealing [shoes]?

As perspectives are internalized, they represent frames of reference (Shibutani, 1961) for the actor's behavior. The world becomes known through (and acted toward in terms of) these perspectives. It is in this respect that we may speak of people as having minds or as engaging in minded activity. Mind develops through interaction with others, as persons acquire perspectives for interpreting and conceptualizing the world they encounter. Although minded activity takes place within the brain, the two are not synonymous. The brain is the physiological locus of mental activity, but the mind denotes the ongoing process of acquiring perspectives, interpreting, and conceptualizing the phenomena one encounters.

Especially significant in the acquisition of perspectives is the *definition of oneself as an object* in a world of other objects. The capacity of humans to be "self-reflective," to be "objects unto themselves," to have a self-identity is one of the most crucial elements in the understanding of human behavior. It means that humans can communicate or converse with themselves, about themselves. People thus not only interpret all phenomena from certain perspectives, but they can fit themselves into their interpretations and their anticipated lines of action. They are recipients of action, but they are also planners and doers. As entities capable of making self-indications and fitting themselves into anticipated lines of action, humans not only live on the past but also invoke images of the future ("What if . . . ?") as they work their way through the present. People interpret (define, assess) their situations on an ongoing basis, and they can act back on (plan, maneuver, accept, resist) those acting toward them as their encounters take place.

Another aspect of minded behavior is the recognition that others also operate from particular perspectives and have the capacity for self-reflective behavior. These realizations seem to occur on a variety of levels, but (regardless of levels) have important implications for one's interpretations (and behaviors). One may take others into account in both specific and general ways. The term *role taking* is used by the interactionists (Mead, 1934) to refer to situations in which people try to define the perspectives from which another (specific) person is operating (i.e., achieve some understanding of the other's concerns, interests, values, meanings). Denoting role taking on a more extensive basis, the "generalized other" (Mead, 1934) signifies a sensitivity to the perspectives of people more generally (i.e., What would they think?).

The value of these concepts (mind, self-reflectivity, and role taking) for understanding marketing and sales activity seems indisputable. Both vendors and buyers have perspectives on the marketplace and both may take themselves and others (generally or specifically) into account in interpreting the activities of others and developing strategies of their own. Both may also attempt to manage the impressions they give off to each other. As objects unto themselves, people not only interpret the activity of others, they can intentionally construct their own activities in an attempt to promote selective interpretations of the part of others. While they need not be accurate in their predictions of others' definitions of them, actors can endeavor to "present themselves" (Goffman, 1959) in ways they feel would most facilitate their interests (i.e., exercise control over how they present themselves to others); and may assess one another in terms of strategy and sincerity.

INTERACTION AS NEGOTIABLE

In selling, you're dependent on the other person. You can promote a sale all you want, but you still have to obtain the buyer's consent [mixed clothing].

Notions of persuasion and resistance are also central to an analysis of human behavior. While people may define objects in an infinite number of ways, and can engage in conversation with the self, these capacities are predicated on persons actively participating in a world of other people. Through those with whom they associate, people not only develop their preliminary symbolic systems (language) and their senses of self (as symbolic essences), but it is with other people that they work out their lived experiences on an ongoing (day-to-day, moment-to-moment) basis. Thus we attend to the manners in which these minded, reflective beings shape their realities in conjunction with others.

By depicting objects (regardless of whether they are so-called tangibles or intangibles) in certain ways, people may be able to alter the meanings others hold for those items. Similarly, by providing alternative perspectives, actors may dramatically affect the ways in which others interpret the same situations. In all cases, however, the success of attempted redefinitions of symbolic significances is dependent on acknowledgment by the other party or parties. Negotiations may be largely promoted by one party, but both parties to an exchange may attempt to redefine the significance of any exchange. And both parties may be somewhat successful in doing so, all the while realizing that they may both be doing this. The participants to an exchange may also find their objectives (relative to one another) shifting considerably as the interaction sequence unfolds. Likewise, actors may intensify or reduce the significance of their interests (those of self and/or others) as they interact.

People may invoke a wide variety of strategies (sequentially or simultaneously) as they attempt to work out their interests (preexisting and emerging) in an interactive context. Beyond ongoing interpretations, comparisons, and evaluations, people may (for instance) reveal, conceal, stall, hedge, joke, and bluff. Likewise, they may exhibit enthusiasm, surprise, skepticism, condemnation, become intimate or distant. They can seek support from others as well as make compromises to others. In the process of interacting with one another, people may move far and in unexpected directions from their earlier anticipations. This means, for example, that an agreement on the purchase of a particular item is much more a conclusion of an exchange than the embodiment of the exchange. Similarly, settlements or agreements to exchange specific items need not signify the end of exchanges in which buyers and sellers are involved. Were one to focus only on the actual changing hands of goods, one would miss the large substance of doing business.

INTERACTION AS RELATIONAL

> When you're in business, you're dependent on all these other people. You may own the business, but they own you! Your fate is in their hands. Your customers, your suppliers, your staff, everyone you deal with. It's all part of the package. All these people, they're very important to whether you have a good day or a bad day in your business, or whether you survive or you don't [manufacture—giftware].

Insofar as people tend to develop particularistic bonds or affiliations with others and take these relationships into account in developing their activities, these interconnections represent additional elements to which we would want to attend in developing a more complete awareness of human behavior.

In discussing relationships, we would not only want to recognize the capabilities of people to become involved in multiple (and possibly conflicting) relationships on an overlapping basis, but also the unfolding or processual nature of these relationships, the abilities of people to redefine the viability of these relationships over time, and the precarious nature of people's relationships with others. These associations may vary greatly along several dimensions (e.g., fleeting versus enduring, limited versus unlimited choices, specific versus multicontext). But insofar as people take these associations into account in formulating and implementing their lines of action, these relationships emerge as exceedingly central to an understanding of human behavior.

Given both the immediate impact of sales relationships on buyers' purchasing commitments and the significance of repeat patronage to the success (or demise) of most businesses, a consideration of relationships is most consequential to a fuller appreciation of buyer-seller exchanges. This seems especially important in view of the alternatives buyers have in "free choice" markets. Thus, for instance, while buyers seem most amenable to vendor influence (negotiation) when they experience higher levels of ambiguity and urgency, vendors who are accorded higher levels of trust seem especially effective in this regard. Not only do the suggestions of vendors with whom buyers have established trust relationships seem more likely to be accepted, but these vendors are also more likely to be sought out when these buyers feel more uncertain of their options. Representing a collage of competitors and an ever-shifting assortment of customers, combined with vendor concerns for both immediate purchases and long-term buyer loyalty, the marketplace is a most exciting arena in which to consider the dilemmas and processes that relationship work entails.

INTERACTION AS PROCESSUAL

You're never going to know all there is to business. Every day, you seem to learn something new, and that's one of the nice parts of being in business, the new people you meet, the new situations, new problems and that's what makes it interesting [grocery].

The preceding concepts of perspectives, interpretations, negotiations, and relationships are best understood in the dynamic context of interaction. Focusing on the processes by which interaction emerges, one finds that exchanges are built up over time, with participants more or less continually interpreting other people, themselves, and other objects in the ongoing situations in which they find themselves. By viewing interaction as a dynamic quality, one becomes aware of the ongoing definitions, decisions, and selected lines of actions leading to (or away from) exchanges. While more aspects of new situations remain to be interpreted and considered in developing one's line of action, all situations are problematic in their outcomes. Each and every situation needs to be interpreted anew (if only as a confirmation of earlier expectations). This is not to suggest that situations may not become considered routine and predictable by the participants; but that all routines presume consistent (and cooperative) behavior on the part of all participants.

As outcomes are predicted on the basis of past experiences, frequently encountered situations (or types thereof) tend to be defined as more routine. Over time, people tend to develop somewhat standardized ways of assembling these encounters. In this sense, recurrent situations tend to acquire a normative quality. Others develop ideas of our interactional styles and we do the same with them, all parties anticipating activities accordingly. As patterns or routines become more firmly established among the interactants, we may speak of a "taken-for-granted" reality (Schutz, 1971), in which participants assume that others will maintain existing arrangements and understandings. Thus, for instance, one may find that store hours in an area are 9:00 a.m. to 9:00 p.m., Monday through Saturday. There is nothing intrinsically objective about these hours. They can, however, define shopping times and will take on an objective appearance (so long as all abide by these hours). However, as Schutz (1971), Berger and Luckmann (1966), and Garfinkel (1967) note, reality is quite precarious. Our notions of reality are dependent on ongoing acceptance by others for their continued validation. Generally speaking, the more widespread a practice becomes, and the longer it persists, the less vulnerable it is to successful challenge. And, in the interim, all practices in line with the prevailing style serve to affirm its reality (appearances thereof). However, each time that situation is encountered, the possibility of alternative forms of exchange exists. And, as any alternative becomes more widespread, it threatens the earlier practice. It challenges the integrity or objectivity of the earlier routine.

Whenever two or more people come together, they do not know how their encounters will end. Each may have certain objectives and may plan for certain conclusions. However, as minded beings, continually assessing incoming information relative to self and other, participants may find that their eventual outcomes take them some distance from the original anticipated outcomes. While one person may anticipate another (with considerable accuracy in some cases), each action of the other remains to be interpreted (and potentially negotiated) within an emergent context.

METHODOLOGICAL IMPLICATIONS

The methodological implications for those accepting these premises are as follows. First, researchers should at the outset and throughout the entire research and analysis stages of the study exhibit a fundamental concern with uncovering, elaborating upon, and conveying the meanings (of objects) of those they are purporting to study. The emphasis is on providing an account of the world of the participants as defined by those participants in as careful, thorough, and representative a manner as possible.

Second, researchers should be profoundly sensitive to people's capacity for reflectivity. If researchers can think, experience dilemmas, develop strategies, selectively present themselves to others, and make ongoing adjustments through internal conversations, would it not also make sense to see if other people could be likewise? Thus we would ask questions around issues such as the following. How do the participants make sense of their worlds? How do they envision their situations, their activities, their relations with others? This means not only recognizing people's main viewpoint(s), but centrally attending to the interpretations that people make as they do their activities. These interpretations are individualized and personalized, but they should not be dismissed as subjective, peripheral, or epiphenomenal. Since people know the world only as they experience it, these meanings are as objective, central, and basic as any other piece of information we may possess about the world. The meanings that people attach to things may vary greatly in longevity and the extent to which they are shared by others at this or that point in time. But this does not make these meanings any less consequential for understanding the production of human behavior.

Third, recognizing that people's behaviors cannot be reduced to their individual properties, researchers would want to examine the ways in which people interact with others. As reflective entities (objects unto themselves), people can take themselves into account not only in developing their own lines of action, they can also endeavor to shape the ways in which others define, experience, and act toward the world. As well, they may attempt to resist the possible influences of others. Here we would want to ask about any preparations people make in anticipation of encounters with others, their styles of approaching others, the ways in which they attempt to understand (i.e., take the role of) others, the practices they employ to shape meanings (and interests) on the part of others, and the ways in which they deal with resistances and pursue commitments from others. Viewed thusly, we ask about influence as practical, ongoing accomplishment on the part of people interacting with one another.

Fourth, researchers in this tradition would not only acknowledge people's tendencies to form particularistic bonds with others, but would also ask about the short-term and long-term implications of these relationships for people's activities more generally. It is not simply a matter of asking who interacts with whom, but rather attending to the developmental aspects (i.e., initial involvements, continuities, disinvolvements, and reinvolvements) of people's relationships with others, as well as acknowledging the ways in which people take these particular others into account in formulating their own lines of action.

Fifth is the focus on process. While the concept of process implies an ongoing, emergent, or unfolding dimension to human behavior, its relevance is much greater for students of human behavior. Not only does process cut across notions of perspectives, reflectivity, negotiation, and relationships—insofar as all of these elements assume a temporal quality (however short-lived or fleeting some instances may be), but process also offers us a comparative, transsituational feature on which to build as we work toward a theory of human behavior. The methodological implication is that researchers would want to attend to the sequencing or natural history of each episode that they encounter, seeing how people formulate their activities in process. And, indeed, this is central. For it is only by examining the ways in which particular instances of human behavior take their shape that we can more fully appreciate the significance of people's perspectives, reflectivity, negotiations, and relationships. Then, by focusing on parallel occurrences across situations, we may begin to arrive at a fuller appreciation of the more basic processes of which each case is but an instance. In this way, we may be better able to develop a theory of human activity.[19]

As may be quickly surmised, survey (standardized questionnaires, administered by interviewers or oneself) and experimental research do not generate very much depth along these lines. These modes of research may be useful in other respects, but they are much too presumptive, decontextualized, and cursory to shed much light on the lived experiences (and emergent practices) of human beings. We need a methodology that will provide us with greater levels of intimate familiarity with the life worlds and activities of those we are purporting to study.

No technique will give us a perfect representative of the data one would wish (mindful of these premises), but participant observation (researcher as participant) and open-ended interview formats seem especially valuable in this respect. These materials may be supplemented by a variety of other procedures, such as direct observation, audio-visual recordings, and the use of diaries and other documents. In each case, however, the task remains that of obtaining a full account of the situation examined, being especially mindful of the perspectives, reflections, negotiations, relations, and processes experienced by the people we are purporting to study.

Buyer Behavior

In discussing interaction as socially constructed activity, we have been considering the formulation of what Blumer (1969) terms "joint activity." Examining interaction as perspectival, reflective, processual, negotiable and relational, it becomes apparent that the behavior of individuals cannot be adequately understood without reference to the social settings in which people find themselves and the ongoing adjustments that minded, reflective beings make in the process of interacting with others. If sales are viewed as two-way exchanges, then every model of marketing activity implicitly assumes a model of buyer behavior and vice versa. Thus, while necessarily brief, it seems instructive to provide a statement on buying activity.[20] Given the relative emphasis of the present project on vendor activities, this statement on buyer behavior should be regarded as more tentative. It relies on a model derived from research on people's involvements in a wide variety of other settings. These include studies of union organizers (Karsh et al., 1953), check forgers (Lemert, 1972), delinquency (Matza, 1964), religious recruitment (Lofland and Stark, 1965; Prus, 1976), collective behavior (Klapp, 1969); and hustlers, thieves, hookers, entertainers, violence, drinking, and bar life (Prus and Sharper, 1977; Prus, 1978; Prus and Irini, 1988).

One might ask what relevance these studies have for buying behavior. My answer is this. Unless we require a separate theory for buyer behavior versus other involvements, we should be able to learn about buying behavior by examining the participation of people in other settings and the relationships these people develop therein.[21] Indeed, if one looks past the content to the processes of interaction, extensive similarities emerge. For instance, whether one focuses on the activities of clergymen, hookers, or businesspeople, one typically finds that all are concerned about building up clienteles; location is important to their overall success; all not only find themselves in competitive contexts, but are also highly dependent on the cooperation of others; all have their better customers and their troublesome characters; all engage in public relations work; all develop reputations within their communities relative to the notions of morality prevailing within these settings; and all are subject to the problems of sustaining enthusiasm. This is not to suggest that these people share the same belief systems, only to draw attention to the fundamentally social nature of people's involvements.

Thus, while the contexts of people's involvements may vary greatly, the studies on which this model is based are exceedingly relevant to buyer behavior. They focus on the processes by which people become initially involved in situations, they continue (and intensify) other involvements, they become disengaged from these involvements, and they become reinvolved in earlier situations. The buyer analogues are first-time purchases, customer loyalty, dropping products (brands, suppliers); and revitalizing patronage.

The model outlined appreciates the perspectival, reflective, processual, negotiable, and relational nature of group life. Judging from its applicability across other settings, it should have considerable generalizability to the marketplace.[22] Consistent with earlier work (Prus and Sharper, 1977; Prus and Irini, 1988), the term *career contingency model* (or *involvement theory*) is used to refer to the general model introduced here.[23]

CAREER CONTINGENCIES (INVOLVEMENT THEORY)

Denoting a history of people's involvements in particular settings, we may envision persons as having "careers" in each of the situations in which they participate. Thus one might have a "career" as a drunk, a thief, a parent, a purchaser of clothing or a buyer of Brand X office supplies, for instance. It should however be noted, in reference to the aforementioned processes (initial involvements, continuities, disinvolvements, and reinvolvements), that not everyone will experience each of these processes for each possible involvement. For instance, many will not become involved initially in particular situations; while others, once involved, may never become disinvolved from particular situations. Likewise, some will leave particular involvements never to become reinvolved in these situations again.

We should also recognize that each involvement is likely to be only one of several that people experience at any given time. Thus the existence of multiple involvements should be noted, for it is within the context of one's other involvements that each single involvement is located. Multiple involvements are not only commonplace and inevitable, but each involvement may interfere with a person's other involvements. Thus disinvolvement from B may be significantly related to an earlier involvement in A, a later involvement in C, or even a chance to become involved in D. With this notion of multiple involvements in mind, we may consider the career contingency model in reference to purchasing situations.

Initial Involvements (First-Time Purchases)

Reflecting people's participation in a wide variety of contexts, the literature suggests three basic routings by which involvements may occur: seekership, recruitment, and closure.[24] When people pursue situations they define as attractive, interesting, enjoyable and the like, the concept of seekership is applicable. When their involvements are promoted by others who solicit their participation in situations, that constitutes recruitment. Closure comes into play when people engage in activities as a means of realizing pressing obligations. While one of these routings may clearly dominate in any given case, many involvements reflect combinations of these. Thus, for example, a young man may want to own a car (seekership), find his employer requires him to have access to ready transportation (closure), and be approached by a friend now in the car business (recruitment).[25] It is most important to view involvements as perspectival, reflective, processual, and negotiable.

Involvements presume some contact of the person with others involved in the situation, but involvements are also affected by the perspectives (viewpoints, frames of reference, ideologies) from which persons interpret their situations. In addition to the other ways (seekership, recruitment, closure) in which people define situations, perspectives are also important with respect to any reservations persons may have in reference to particular involvements; the restraints (moral, financial, physical safety) persons experience at particular times.[26] To follow the car example further; while the young man may buy a car from his friend, he may also buy elsewhere. For example, although he may consider the price of his friend's line reasonable, he may define the safety features of his friend's cars to be inadequate (for him, a noteworthy reservation). His friend may or may not be successful in moving him past these concerns by stressing the images associated with style and performance.

An issue of considerable significance to those involved in marketing, is the question of how people initially make product purchases. The following four points are central to this process.

Seekership. Prospective buyers (purchasing agents, dealers, consumers, and so on) may pursue particular products/brands on their own. Products do not have inherent meanings, but are defined within the prospects' frames of reference. These assessments of desirability may occur prior to, or after contact with particular products (or their representatives).

Recruitment. As part of their promotional effort, vendors may attempt to define products as more favorable to their prospects by relating products to these people's situations. Indicating how their products would help prospects realize their interests, solve their problems, and the like, vendors may generate relevance, establish worth, and justify purchases of their products. Should the prospects not be initially inclined to view products favorably, vendors may also attempt to shape the ways in which prospects envision products by suggesting alternative viewpoints and interpretations. Other modes of recruitment reflect the initiative of third parties, such as friends, relatives, and other associates.

Closure. Albeit reluctantly, people may also consider involvements that they would not have chosen when they envision these as meeting their obligations. Thus, for instance, vendors may carry lines that they personally despise in attempts to generate profits. Or many people may buy sump pumps to maintain dry basements rather than because of any particular interest in their inner workings or exterior appearances. Likewise, many products are purchased at Christmas because someone needed "something" to meet their familial obligations. Recognizing these sorts of obligations, vendors may attempt to promote purchases more generally and immediately by creating closure. To the extent that vendors can intensify existing (product-linked) obligations, indicate urgency, and provide more exclusive routings to solve pressing problems, they increase the likelihood of obtaining target investments.

Reduced reservations (drift). Even when prospects are inclined to make purchases, they may still consider the implications of particular purchases for other aspects of their situations. Recognizing that prospects have other commitments (obligations), vendors may be concerned that these other commitments not interfere with the present transactions. To the extent that vendors can eliminate or minimize the significance of other obligations, they increase the likelihood of obtaining investments in the products being promoted. Should prospective buyers be skeptical of vendors (products, warranties, and so on; thereby reflecting concerns about losing money, making unwise commitments, and such), then notions of trust become more central to the purchasing decision. Recognizing concerns of this nature, vendors may attempt to promote definitions of themselves (and products) as sincere, knowledgeable, reliable, and such; thereby potentially reducing people's reservations concerning particular purchasing commitments.

Continuity (Buyer Loyalty)

Once people have become involved in situations, the question of when and how they are likely to continue (and intensify) their involvements becomes prominent. Continuity may reflect earlier routings of involvement, but persons may continue to participate in situations on bases other than that related to their initial involvements. Since repeat customers represent the basis of most successful businesses, it is essential to ask how this repeat patronage comes about.

Assuming that repeat purchases represent feasible options, we can ask about the elements affecting continuity of the buyer-seller relationship. The earlier cited literature suggests that customer loyalty would depend on the extensiveness of the patron's involvements in the use of the vendor's product. In this regard, customer loyalty seems largely contingent on: developing more comprehensive perspectives (justifications) for continued use and patronage of particular products; achieving more extensive and exclusive identification as buyers of particular products; making larger, irretrievable investments in particular products or getting involved in more comprehensive product programs; incorporating particular products more fully into their routines (activities); and becoming more fully involved in ongoing relationships with product-supportive others (vendors and/or loyal patrons). To the extent that vendors recognize these bases of continuity, they may endeavor to generate loyalty by providing justifications, fostering identification, obtaining commitments, facilitating patterns of use, and promoting supportive associations. Finally, although buyers in pluralist societies typically have a number of product and vendor options from which to choose, it should be noted that there may be cases in which people may continue making particular purchases when they fail to perceive a lack of feasible alternatives (i.e., continuity by default).

Disinvolvement (Dropping Products/Brands/Suppliers)

As with initial involvement and continuity, it is important to envision disinvolvement in process terms. While any reassessment of one's current situation may generate definitions conducive to disengagement, the multiple involvements (and other options) in which people find themselves are especially consequential for disinvolvement from particular situations. Given the existence of competition and the shifting situations in which buyers find themselves, it is important to ask when buyers are likely to switch products (brands, suppliers). While some terminations of purchasing involvements reflect the lack of applications, other instances denote opportunities for purchases elsewhere. However, these alternative involvements are most likely when combined with apprehensions regarding present perspectives; discomfiture with current identities; reassessments of existing commitments; re-evaluations of product-related activities; and redefinitions of product-related associations. Although disenchantment may arise on any of these bases, it should be noted that its significance may be offset by positive definitions of involvements in other respects. And, insofar as disenchantment need not result in disinvolvement, in itself, the timing and nature of buyer contacts with vendors representing alternatives can be critical for determining subsequent involvements.

Reinvolvement (Revitalizing Patronage)

Should disinvolvement (and any alternatives) be defined as unsatisfactory, reinvolvement becomes a viable option. As former customers are familiar with the routines and styles of vendors with whom they have dealt in the past, reinvolvement in these earlier relationships becomes more likely when current situations are deemed inadequate. Reinvolvement presupposes (re)acceptance of buyers by the vendors to whom they return. And, as with initial involvements, reinvolvements may be sought out by buyers (seekership), be promoted by vendors (recruitment), or reflect buyers' assessments that these involvements are the best or only ways to meet pressing obligations (closure).

Reinvolvement seems most likely when former relations were dissolved on a more congenial level, patrons experience some disenchantment with their new products, and some changes have taken place on the part of either the buyers or vendors considered that could be used to justify renewed contact.

Some attention will be given to this model in the chapters following. However, the material is focused primarily on the recruiting activity (preparations, presentations, strategies, dilemmas, and so on) of vendors rather than on the involvements of buyers.

The Data Base

This project began as an examination of retailer activity. As the study developed, however, it became evident that in order to better understand this realm of activity, it was necessary to learn more about the retailers' suppliers and their relationships with the retailers. Subsequent visits to trade shows and ongoing interviews with suppliers and buyers confirmed the value of this strategy. As a result of attending these trade shows, and talking with the people involved, the base of the project was expanded considerably. The retail element remained central to the project, but it was now located within the more general realm of sales activity. Thus, in addition to retail sales, the participants include those involved in wholesale, manufacture, and promotional (advertising agencies and mediums; premiums and incentives programs) trade.

While questions may be raised about including both a wide range of products and multiple levels of enterprise in the analysis, these strategies have considerable merit. Once one moves past the mystique surrounding particular products and levels of merchandising, the parallels are striking. For example, vendors can sell candy in a wide variety of ways, but others can also sell clothing, appliances, and automobiles in similar ways (and vice versa). Likewise, manufacturers, wholesalers, retailers, and those involved in promotional trade all deal with suppliers, face pricing decisions, rely heavily on repeat trade, face troublesome customers, and so forth. Qualifications will be made as these seem appropriate (e.g., regarding organizational complexity), but once one looks past the "content" to the "forms" of association (Simmel, 1950), it becomes readily apparent that one does not need a separate theory for each product, industry, or level of sales. The advantage of this wider scope is considerable. It provides invaluable comparisons and contrasts across a wide range of products and styles of marketing. The result is a much more balanced statement, and one that sheds considerable light on marketing and sales activity in a variety of settings.

COLLECTING DATA

Three modes of data collection were used in this study: interviews with businesspeople, observations of trade shows, and participant observation in a craft enterprise.

Interviews

The (118) interviews were obtained largely on an individual basis and reflect a variety of contacts with vendors. These ranged from a few preexisting personal contacts with vendors to a majority of people encountered as relative strangers at their places of business, at trade shows, and in other settings. Despite adages such as "Time is money," the businesspeople encountered were generally quite receptive to the study. While some were "too busy" to be bothered with the research (no particular pattern emerged herein), most of the vendors encountered were willing to assist me with the project. As a result, I was able to locate many more willing participants than I was able to interview (geographical accessibility, mutual schedules).

As is the case with all interview research, some participants were more helpful than others. Some were willing to explain situations more fully and candidly than others, some were more informed about more areas of activity than others, and some had broader bases of experience upon which to draw. Overall, more attention was given to the retail market than to other categories of sales, but the emphasis was on marketing as a process rather than on any given product or realm of sales. Thus, while most of the participants worked primarily in retail sales (n = 71), others pursued trade in wholesale (n = 12), manufacture (n = 21, and promotional (n = 14) sectors at the time of interviews. Given the multifaceted nature of salespeople's careers, however, these numbers considerably underrepresent the effective base of the study. These multiple involvements consequently afforded a much greater base of comparison and information than the numbers of interviews indicate. Most people had worked for more than one company by the time they were interviewed, and of these, a large proportion had worked for companies selling different products. Salespeople often remain within the same realm of sales (e.g., retail versus manufacture), but it is not uncommon to encounter people who have worked at several realms of trade (e.g., retail, wholesale, and manufacture) on a simultaneous and/or concurrent basis. To this end, statements from the participants have been coded in accordance with the categories of sales that participants referenced at particular points in the interview. Although vendors' activities are not so sharply defined, participants were placed in the following categories as a result of their primary activities in order to provide readers with a sense of the sample:

Retail: those who sell directly to the public. While primarily retailers, some of these vendors also have significant wholesale ventures in their enterprises.

Wholesale: those who sell (pre)manufactured goods to other vendors.

Manufacture: those who construct, process, or assemble products to sell to others. It should be noted that many manufacturers also serve as distributors (e.g., wholesalers, retailers) for products manufactured by others.

Promotions: those involved in the sales of advertising and other promotional materials (e.g., media, packaging, incentives, premiums).

These categories are further qualified in the extracts (quotations/observations) in reference to the products (e.g., shoes, real estate) involved. While references will be made within the text relative to both company size and participant position within organizations, neither the size of organization nor the positions of the participants are indicated in the extracts.[27] Table 1.1 shows how the sample distributed itself, relative to the position and category of sales the participants found themselves in at the time of their interviews.

Trade Shows

In addition to providing further insight into buyer-supplier relations, the trade shows (32 attended) were especially valuable in providing firsthand material on large scale and international levels of trade. Featuring items such as giftware, clothing, luggage, hardware, computers, office supplies, and a wide range of industrial supplies, these exhibitions were extremely important for: generating sources of interviews; making observations of multiple levels and areas of trade; providing opportunities to make related inquiries of vendors, albeit generally on a more fleeting basis; suggesting new realms of inquiry; providing opportunities to observe ongoing buyer-supplier exchanges; and assessing the validity of materials that emerged in other contexts. Thus, in addition to providing innumerable specifics, the trade shows have been invaluable for developing a more complete understanding of the marketplace.

TABLE 1.1

Participants' Positions at Time of Interview

Category	Manager (owner)	Salesperson	Total
Retail	41 (12)	30	71
Wholesale	6 (3)	6	12
Manufacture	10 (4)	11	21
Promotions	5 (2)	9	14
Total	62 (21)	56	118

NOTE: Since the owners interviewed were also managers, it was decided to include these in the general category of managers (the numbers of owner-managers are indicated in brackets).

Craft Enterprise

The interviews and trade show materials were supplemented by three years' involvement in a craft enterprise. This business microcosm not only generated insider contact with a number of craft show vendors, and provided opportunities to experience most aspects of marketing (from product design, purchasing, and manufacture to completed sales, repeat patronage, and doing exhibits), but it also provided practitioner access to a number of suppliers in several different product lines and facilitated access and acceptance at trade shows. Like other small businesses, craft enterprises provide limited insight into the internal organizational exchanges characterizing larger businesses. However, since small operations involve the same basic marketing activities as larger companies, and those participating in small businesses are more likely to experience all these elements themselves, the craft enterprise generated a more holistic sense of marketing than that commonly achieved by individual functionaries in larger operations. Nevertheless, it was most valuable as an analytical device when my experiences therein were assessed relative to the experiences of the vendors encountered in other contexts.

An Overview

Pursuing Customers considers vendor activity conducted in anticipation of customer contact. As a means of providing readers with a fuller, more holistic sense of the ensuing discussion, a brief chapter-by-chapter overview is provided.

Following this introductory statement, Chapter 2 examines the ways in which businesses may be organized. The objective is to facilitate understanding of basic features of business structures and to indicate some of the uncertainties characterizing business ventures. Thus organizational formats such as proprietorships (including partnerships), corporations, chains, and franchises are discussed to provide a clearer understanding of business similarities and differences. Likewise, those calling themselves manufacturers, wholesalers, and retailers (and others) are contextualized within their roles as merchants, indicating basic commonalities and differences in their approaches to marketing activities. This chapter also examines the routes of involvements and dilemmas experienced by those entering businesses as hands-on owners. Although necessarily brief, this chapter provides valuable background understandings for sales and marketing activity.

Chapter 3 focuses on the doing of management activity. Following a brief discussion of owning and managing perspectives, the emphasis shifts to the central responsibilities of those managing marketing activities. Managerial concern with accountability and efficiency are portrayed, as are the problematics of hiring staff, providing training, salary arrangements, and generating performance. In developing this material, an attempt is made to indicate both management and staff perspectives, showing how these interests intersect in reference to the management of marketing activities. It is clear, however, that the following chapters are exceedingly relevant for a fuller appreciation of management and staff concerns, activities, and relationships.

Chapter 4 examines the purchasing of products on the part of businesses—those items used for resale, manufacture, or as supplies. Since one's ability to market products can be significantly affected by the particular products one obtains (and otherwise uses), purchasing becomes a critical feature in the marketing package. This chapter considers the activities of vendors (or their purchasing agents) as they attempt to obtain better lines at better prices in an area punctuated by competition, potential deception, and cooperation. Attention is also given to buyer-supplier relationships and the problematics of obtaining winning numbers or hot items.

Assuming that one has stock, the next marketing activity of concern (Chapter 5) is that of setting prices. Although pricing can have very precise referents (e.g., $29.98), prices are subject to much assessment and negotiation as vendors attempt to establish prices favorable to their interests within a shifting and competitive marketplace. Pricing is a dynamic, social aspect of marketing; one that affects and is affected by other aspects of marketing activity.

Subsequently, we examine the ways in which vendors endeavor to make contact with their prospects. Thus attention is directed toward the three major avenues of customer contact: using the media, working the field, and exhibiting products. Highlighting media promotions (advertising and so on), Chapter 6 depicts the use of "nonpersonal" messages to create product awareness, interest, obtain orders, and the like. Here, the various tasks expected of the media are examined, as are the formats that media promotions assume and the dilemmas media promotions represent for vendors.

Chapter 7 ("Working the Field") focuses on the practices of vendors approaching prospects in attempts to secure orders for their merchandise (e.g., door to door, business account sales). In the process, attention is given to activities such as prospecting, dealing with organizational gatekeepers, and managing stage fright and the other pressures field sales agents may experience.

Denoting situations in which vendors establish settings where prospects may approach them to purchase goods, Chapter 8 ("Exhibiting Products") considers both showroom and exhibit sales settings. While addressing showplaces more generally, this chapter also features a discussion of trade shows. This is an arena in which media, field, and showroom selling frequently intersect. While vendors may rely totally on any one of these formats, all may be used by any given company on a concurrent and/or sequential basis. In a general sense, the implementation of any particular format promotes some stability within vendors' marketing programs as other elements (e.g., ordering goods, setting prices) are incorporated into those styles of promotion. However, changes in promotional formats are possible whenever vendors reassess the relative feasibility of their present strategies (and the cost/inconvenience of change) relative to their immediate and long-term objectives and the shifting marketplace in which they find themselves.

The conclusion (Chapter 9) affords us an opportunity to locate some of the themes developed in this book in broader contexts. Beyond attending to some questions commonly encountered while doing the research, consideration is given to the significance of mystique in the marketplace, the commitments that vendors make in the pursuit of success, purchasing involvements as dynamic two-way processes, and some possible directions for future inquiry.

Providing background material on vendor preparations, *Pursuing Customers* considers the ways in which vendors prepare for prospect encounters. Thus attention is given to the processes and problematics of setting up businesses, doing management, purchasing stock for eventual resale, price setting, and attempts to make customer contact via the media, agents in the field, and exhibiting products in fixed and temporary showrooms. Much of this activity is taken for granted by prospective buyers, but for those involved in running businesses these preparations assume a very immediate and vital quality. Further, while much vendor activity is in pursuit of prospect investments, it is in the area of vendor preparations that we find vendors faced with a multitude of shifting options and dilemmas, for it is here that they put their money down. It is here that they gamble, in anticipation of customer receptivity.

We're part of _____ . They bought us out. We ran into trouble with our buying, and we needed capital, and they wanted to expand, so it was a mutual thing. We had a pretty good chain (about 100 stores), strong in the market. But we bought wrong, so we lost our capital. They knew we needed it, so they made us an offer, bought us out [men's clothing].

In the business world, every day is a risk and every customer, every potential customer, is the reduction of that risk if it is a potential sale or money coming in. It serves to work against the overall risk you are taking being in business. And that's something you experience as you're working with the customer. The degree of certainty that they are going to make a purchase in your store. That is something that you feel as you're relating to them, and something you're not really sure of, until you are actually ringing up that sale. And even then, it's always possible that the person may wish to return the merchandise [women's clothing].

It matters little whether one is discussing stockholders or independent owners, or is considering large or small business expeditions, businesses represent ongoing sets of gambles. Typically, people seem much more aware of the successful ventures than the failures. And, unless they have watched their investments in the marketplace over a period of time, they may not appreciate the vulnerability of business enterprises.[28]

I think we all realize deep down inside that it is a gamble, and there are a lot of things you have to pull together if it's going to work. But I don't think you really see it as a gamble, because you have the confidence in yourself that you can pull it together. And it's not like you only have one roll of the dice. You'll have problems along the way, but if you can work them out, you'll make it [giftware].

Of the stores that started in this area six years ago, we're the only ones left. The neighbors keep changing [appliances].

Notes

1. Attending to the interpersonal aspects of buyer-seller encounters, the companion volume, *Making Sales* (Prus, 1989), follows this sequence along. This book examines the ways in which vendors go about presenting products, generating trust, dealing with resistance and difficult customers, developing customer loyalty, and sustaining enthusiasm within the competitive context of the business community.

2. Although Kotler (1972), Levy (1978), and Fine (1981) have suggested that aspects of marketing theory could be adapted to promotions in other settings, our interest is in marketing and sales relative to the more general understanding of group life (relationships). Approached in this manner, marketing and sales represent but one of many realms of group life. As such, marketing and sales activity is most appropriately subject to, and the object of, sociological theory.

3. While we will be addressing the matter of "worth" in other parts of the book, readers are referred to Simmel (1978) for the statement that most clearly questions the matter of value being contingent on supply and demand.

4. The emphasis on activities contrasts significantly with Borden's (1964) conceptualization of market mix. Thus while material central to Borden's "4 P's" (product, price, promotion, and place-distribution) will be given much attention; of primary importance are the ways in which people work out marketing activities with others (ergo, the "P's" of people and process).

5. This is consistent with Merton's (1957) broader notion of system interdependence, but practicing functionalists generally do not consider the ways in which people actually work out their activities with one another.

As a result of these interdependencies, certain ways of doing particular marketing activities may be facilitated (or inconvenienced) relative to other ways of doing the same activities. This sense of interrelatedness is also expressed by Borden (1964) who contends that each aspect of one's market mix affects the other aspects of one's marketing program.

6. Insofar as the boundaries of the disciplines within the social sciences are relatively arbitrary, I would argue that the more consequential demarcation is between those who assume an interpretive approach to the study of human behavior and those who do not. This statement clearly assumes an interpretive frame and builds on the lived experiences of the participants (vendors in this case) as the primary data or reality for the study of human behavior. Although they did not anticipate what was later to be called naturalistic inquiry (Chicago style interactionism), much of the conceptual ground work for this interpretive approach may be traced back to the works of Wilhelm Dilthey, (1833-1911;

see Ermarth, 1978) and Georg Simmel, (1858-1918; see Simmel, 1900, 1918, 1950; Levine, 1971; Frisby, 1989).

7. It is ironic that while most social psychologists in both sociology and psychology ardently reject the concept of *needs* as developed by Maslow (1954) and others of that genre, this scheme has become central to many discussions of marketing motivation.

8. The interactive aspects of sales have not been entirely neglected among those in marketing. Thus, although not as fully developed as is the present project, the (more recent) works of Bonoma and Zaltman (1978), Levy (1978), and the Reingen and Woodside (1981) collection of articles directly address this topic, as does Anderson (1983) and Swan (1986).

9. One could level similar charges at most social scientists. One may ask to what extent their lived experiences in human groups are accurately reflected in their (largely positivist) academic depictions of human behavior. Academics in marketing as well as those in the social sciences more generally have heavily imported conceptual frames and methodological practices from the physical and natural sciences. This they have done without much regard for the centrality of human experiences (ongoing interpretations and interaction) for their alleged subject matter (the study of human behavior). In other words, one might argue that they have given little recognition to the differences between the production of human behavior and the physical qualities of other objects of our experience. This position is developed further in Prus (1987). The issue raised here is not a new one, and can be traced back to Dilthey (Ermarth, 1978) and Mead (1934). It is most cogently addressed in Blumer (1969).

10. Those interested in cross-cultural material on marketing are referred to economic anthropology. While minimally concerned with the actual processes by which exchanges occur (compared to the functions of exchanges for life within the groups studied), readers may find the collections of Bohannan and Dalton (1962), Brookfield (1969), and Smith (1978) valuable.

11. This point is addressed somewhat by Zakuta (1970).

12. This may have been encouraged by the exchange theorists (e.g., Homans, 1958; Blau, 1964) who in attempting to apply an economic model to social exchanges (relationships), provide very simplistic and misleading images of economic exchanges! The components of exchange need to be explained as social phenomena. There are fundamental elements of (social) exchange that exchange theory neglects. Particularly significant are the perspectival, emergent, and negotiable nature of meanings; reflective planning, variable strategies, impression management (Goffman, 1959), and possible deception; the uncertainties of characterizing the future (e.g., an ever-shifting marketplace); and desires on the part of participants to maintain working relationships (on any number of bases).

13. Although the marketplace is an area of considerable significance for sociology, most of the publishers with whom I discussed this project have indicated that they did not perceive a market for this subject matter (citing the absence of sociology courses in the area) and did not want to become trail blazers.

14. Of the early theorists, it is Georg Simmel (1900, 1978) who most incisively addresses matters of the marketplace. Unfortunately, *The Philosophy of Money* was not published in English until 1978. Weber (1947) also considers matters pertaining to the marketplace, but at a much more general level. Ralph Turner (personal communication) expressed this position most clearly, saying that the neglect of business by sociologists might be expected since no one had yet laid out a theoretical scheme to show us how we might go about studying the marketplace.

15. Perhaps it is worth noting that these critics (Marxists, especially) evidence little familiarity with marketplace exchanges in any society. This appears to hold no less true for those (Marxists) who modishly label themselves political economists. As well, most of these critics of trading patterns in capitalist society seem to disattend to (or are ignorant of) the (external and internal, as well as informal) levels of trade characterizing communist states.

16. In addition to my own efforts, this review reflects the contributions of a great many scholars who have discussed the project with me.

17. As the material develops, readers will also recognize my indebtedness to Simmel (1950), Garfinkel (1967), Schutz (1971), and those (too numerous to mention) who epitomize the ethnographic tradition of the Chicago school (see Prus, 1987). This project reflects an interpretive or phenomenological interactionist orientation.

18. As we take much of our own reality for granted (Schutz, 1971), the most compelling evidence for multiple realities and its relevance for people's activity may come from cross-cultural research. Weston LaBarre (1947) aptly illustrates that the meanings of gestures and emotions are *not* universal, while others, such as Malinowski (1987), Mead (1950), and MacAndrew and Edgerton (1969) provide powerful evidence suggesting that all our behaviors are culturally situated.

19. For a more comprehensive statement on generic social processes and their implications for theory and research, see Prus (1987).

20. This material is a reworked version of a paper presented at the American Marketing Association meetings (Prus, 1983).

21. Insofar as vendors are also buyers (see Chapter 2 on becoming owners, and Chapter 4), these notions also find support in this immediate study.

22. As some might realize, this statement denotes the base of a study on buyer behavior in its preliminary stages at the time of writing.

23. The term *involvement theory* was casually coined by my colleague Frank Fasick, but seems entirely appropriate.

24. As noted in earlier studies (Prus and Sharper, 1977; Prus, 1978; Prus and Irini, 1988), the career contingency model builds on Becker's (1963) work generally. The concepts of *seekership, recruitment,* and *closure* indicate our indebtedness to Klapp (1969), Lofland and Stark (1965), and Lemert (1972), respectively.

25. Two other modes of involvement might also be noted. In some cases people find involvements imposed on them, as when an engineer specifies the supplier and the product a purchasing agent is to buy. Inadvertent involvements denote unwitting or unintended events, as when a shopper mistakenly grabs a new or less preferred brand of canned goods in a rush to the checkout counter.

26. Matza (1964) uses the term *drift* to refer to situations in which persons experience decreased levels of responsibilities from their usual obligations.

27. The matter of people's positions in particular organizations is considerably complicated, not only as a result of the different positions people have held in one organization over time, but also as a consequence of occupying different positions in different organizations over time, and the relative lack of (internal) comparability noted in positions such as managers, assistant managers, representatives, and clerks for instance. A concerted effort was made to contact managers (and owners), but it should not be assumed that information from those higher up in the organization is necessarily more valid, more thorough, or more insightful than that of other staff people, simply because they hold a higher position in the organization. Those in higher positions can indeed provide valuable

and unique information, but people's experiences with, and observations of, the front lines are no less valuable in arriving at a more complete understanding of the marketing and sales process. Likewise, it should not be assumed that those operating as salespeople have little insight into other aspects of marketing (e.g., ordering, pricing, managing). Many have worked in a plurality of companies and have held positions entailing more responsibility than the title of *salesperson* suggests.

28. The two stores referenced in the following quotes had the misfortune of going under (as did a few other businesses in the sample) during the time of research.

Chapter 2
SETTING UP BUSINESS

The merchant is the middleman and you get caught up in a lot of different concerns because you have to deal with so many different people. You have to deal with your customers and your suppliers, all your different suppliers. You also have to deal with the government people, both the federal and the state [provincial], you have a lawyer and accountant, you are dealing with advertising people, and you are also dealing with the mall management. . . . You have to be concerned with many aspects of business, the buying, the accounting, shipping, the inventory, and all these things that demand your time and attention. And in the process, you try to reduce your risks in all the cases, because any one of these areas could be very troublesome for you [women's clothing].

Regardless of whether businesses concentrate on selling groceries, clothing, jewelry, or computer systems, or whether they are involved in manufacture, distribution or retail sales, all businesses are involved in "marketing products" and, as such, experience somewhat parallel pro cesses in promoting their products. Although some of the structures to be discussed are more appropriate to particular product areas and certain vendors within, certain legal and financial advantages may accrue to certain styles and sizes of businesses. Hence, some consideration of these variations is essential for a more adequate understanding of marketing and sales activity in general. The structuring of business denotes a first level of preparation for customer encounters.

In discussing the structuring of businesses, it is important to distinguish marketing activities from the functionaries engaged in marketing activities. Small businesses may be less complex organizationally, but it should not be assumed that small-businesspeople do not experience "real business." In fact, to the extent that small-businesspeople are involved in all the activities marketing entails, they may be more aware of the scope of marketing activity than are people working exclusively in large enterprises. As "specialists," the latter may be more informed about specific aspects of business, but they typically do not experience as many aspects of marketing as directly as the small-businessperson does. It should also be noted that all contexts do not afford equal opportunities to learn about all aspects of marketing. For instance, people involved in both manufacturing and retailing tend to be aware of more facets of business than are those who only retail. Similarly, people switching from one business or industry to another have greater opportunities to become aware of parallel (generic) occurrences than do those remaining in one setting.

Like other human products, businesses are dependent on social affirmation for their existence. Vendors may actively promote definitions of their activities as businesses, but in order for those businesses to survive, they have to be recognized (and acted toward) as such by other people. Should others not do so, the initiators are likely to lose resources, time, and interest in pursuing these endeavors. While any economic exchange can be seen as a business transaction, the term *business* becomes more applicable as individuals or groups acquire identities as traders. Everyone can be seen to engage in some trade, but as persons or groups are seen to engage in trade more frequently and over longer periods of time, they are more apt to be considered businesses in that community.

Examining the ways in which businesses may be set up, this chapter has three central themes. First, attention is given to proprietorships (including partnerships) and corporations, the two major forms by which persons may establish businesses. This is followed by a discussion of the major modes of housing marketing operations (e.g., single versus multiple outlets, malls, and franchises). Finally, the chapter discusses the routes by which people become owners of businesses and some of the dilemmas they face as entrepreneurs.

Establishing Businesses

The two basic ways of establishing businesses in western society involve proprietorships and corporations. As the following discussion indicates, each offers certain advantages and disadvantages.

PROPRIETORSHIPS

A proprietorship is a business considered financially inseparable from the person who owns it. Profits and losses from this enterprise are calculated against the owner's personal income (and income tax), and the owner is considered personally responsible for any debts and liabilities the business incurs. As with other businesses, the community may require licenses (and taxes) for proprietorships. There is typically no requirement that any business be profitable,[1] but in the case of personal businesses, losses in this area may be offset against other income proprietors have. A proprietorship is considered to end with the death of the owner,[2] but otherwise it can be closed at the discretion of the proprietor and/or can be extended (diversified) in other product areas as the proprietor sees fit.

Partnerships

General partnerships are proprietorships involving two or more parties. Although partners may develop contracts between themselves, no special registration is generally required beyond that necessary for proprietorships. Each partner's share of the income is filed with his personal income tax, but each person (as in the case of the proprietorship) is considered legally responsible for all debts and liabilities the partnership incurs (regardless of who was directly responsible).[3]

When one or more parties are willing to finance a partnership, but do not want to be involved in its daily operation (i.e., silent partners), they may apply for a limited partnership (be registered as such with the appropriate agency). These investors achieve limited liability (limited to the extent of their investment and any collateral they may have guaranteed against loans). In these respects, the silent partner status more closely approximates that of the shareholder in the corporation.

CORPORATIONS

The term *corporation* (also *limited, incorporated*) is often associated with size, but it is clearly not size that distinguishes corporations from proprietorships (and partnerships). The corporation is considered a legal entity capable of making binding decisions and assuming all liabilities associated with it, in its own name. Each corporation is registered with the government and is given a charter to operate.[4]

Incorporation is not difficult to achieve. In most cases, fees are likely to be less than a few thousand dollars even when a lawyer is employed. Although a slate of officers must be listed, one-man or one-woman corporations (he or she does it all) are permitted in some areas. Since corporations need starting capital, initial investors typically purchase shares, and in the process (theoretically) determine proportionate control. Corporations are typically taxed differently than are proprietorships, but a clearer, general advantage of incorporation is that of limiting the personal liability of the investors. Thus, while shareholders may gain unlimited profits, their liabilities are limited to the amount of their investments. Likewise, the officers are considered employees and as such are not directly liable for the debts and liabilities a corporation incurs.[5]

If a person is going into business, one of the things that they should do is incorporate. It reduces the liability of the people who invest in the company and you can also serve as a creditor to the company yourself. That way you can collect interest on any money you have in the company. Otherwise, should you have a partnership, it means that the company is liable for any debts that either or both of you may incur [women's clothing].

When you incorporate, it separates the business from the owner or owners. It takes on an identity of its own. You may be the only stockholder, but you become basically an employee of the company and its debts and liabilities are separate from your own. You're limited to your investments or your loans. In a proprietorship, it's all tied up together. . . . It's (corporation) a package deal in a manner of speaking, and if you want to sell, it's easier because of that. It's distinct from you. . . . Taxwise, it's a mixed bag, especially for the smaller business, where you might be better off in a proprietorship. If it's a partnership, you should incorporate at the outset. You can still be equal shareholders if you want, but it's a lot neater that way [shoes].

In contrast to proprietorships, which operate more informally, each corporation develops a set of bylaws governing the formal administration of the corporation (administering company stock, meetings, control duties, and the like). While owners (stock holders) may be synonymous with directors (and managers, staff) in smaller operations, larger, widely held corporations place effective control of the daily operations of the corporation in the hands of the directors and staff.

Housing Marketing Operations

In this section, attention is given to some of the ways in which businesses may house or physically set up their marketing operations. Of particular relevance here are single versus multiple outlets, multiple fronts, umbrellas, malls, and franchises.

SINGLE VERSUS MULTIPLE OUTLETS

One of the options facing vendors involves the decision of whether to operate as single or multiple (chain) outlets. In either case, vendors may do business by mail, through salespeople in the field, or from showrooms. Some multiple outlets are regionally based, while others assume national and/or international dimensions. The best-known chains operate in the retail sector, but chainlike operations can be found in any area of trade.[6]

Insofar as they provide greater opportunities for synchronized marketing (and management) programs, single outlets may be seen as advantaged over chains. There are some relative limitations, however. Thus chains enable vendors to access a greater portion of the potential market, balance losing operations against successful ones, and achieve various economies of scale, particularly as this pertains to volume purchases of particular products, services, and other supplies.[7] Were one able to achieve the same volume of sales in single locations, the advantage would be to the independent. However, chains operate on the assumptions of increased sales (and exposure) as a consequence of multiple, localized outlets and the resultant lowered relative costs for many aspects of marketing (e.g., volume buying of stock and all support materials, centralized promotions and advertising) associated with these (presumably) higher volume facilities. The extracts that follow depict these advantages and some others.

> With a chain, even with only three stores, like what we've got now, there are a number of advantages. Say you want to try something out, you can do it in one store first, to see how it goes, and if it bombs, your losses are spread out over three stores. . . . Also, you can get better prices from some of the manufacturers or suppliers because you can start to buy in larger volumes. Another thing is that if the one store is not doing so well, the others can help to carry you through, the slower times in the one store. Some locations will do better than others, but if you're just starting out in a new area, the others can carry you over what is normally a

more difficult time. . . . Something else, if you have more than one store in the same advertising area, the same ad in a newspaper can do double the work for you, or you can advertise twice as much with the same relative budgets. . . . If your stores are close enough together, and someone wants a specific item, or more of a certain item than what you would normally carry in a single store, you can often arrange to have the item brought over from the other location in a relatively short time. So you can add to your total sales that way too [giftware].

The advantage of the chain is that you have other retail outlets to sustain your level, keep you open. You might have budget problems in one store, but the others can help to keep you floating. If you're an independent, you've got to make it happen in that one store. With the chain, you also capitalize on national advertising, and on visitors coming into the city. They've bought from you in another store, in another town. They trust the name. They can buy it here, and if there is some problem, they can take it home and get it exchanged in another store. . . . From the employee's viewpoint, you also have better health programs, things of this nature, in a chain. An independent has to put out a lot of money if he wants to maintain his staff at that level [men's clothing].

A chain, you can work on volume, where with an individual store, you have to watch more carefully. Like you might get an item that won't sell in one location, but will sell in another branch of the same store, where with an individual store, it has to all happen in the one place. . . . And you can get a better price, because you are ordering in volume. And you'll get better service with larger orders. If anyone has to wait for an order, it will be the little man, not the big store who has ordered 10,000 or 100,000 of some item [women's clothing].

Somewhat offsetting the aforementioned advantages of chain operations are what might be termed the diseconomies of scale. Thus not only are mistakes multiplied in chain settings, but chains also face more complex problems of decision making, communication, and coordination, and variations in the clientele and the competition in each location. Thus although technology (e.g., telephones, computers) has greatly facilitated communication between functionaries, people working in chain operations more readily tend to experience bureaucratitis.

Head office has no idea of what is happening in this store. It is so frustrating sometimes, because they just don't understand our situation. They will make a general policy for all their stores. . . . They will introduce a policy with some stores in mind, that may be totally unworkable here, or costs much more to implement than what it's designed to save. Things like that. . . . You get all these memos from head office, and a lot of the times, you just end up laughing at them, because you just can't do what they're telling you to do. . . . Our store actually has very little to do with how we organize things. Like right now, we're reorganizing all the departments, their locations, the ways they're set up. It's getting to be the busiest time of the year, and head office decides to reorganize the whole store. It can get really frustrating working in a chain that way [discount department store].

With the chain, you have more financial stability. You've got all these branches, so you know that there's money behind you, and there's bargaining power in dealing with the supplier. But if you're making money, you're not making it for yourself, you're making it for the company. If you have items that are not moving, you can return it to the central warehouse. But you're more constrained by the company. Your advertising, your image, your hours, your staff, your expenditures, your products, you're limited by that. There are things I would like to carry in this shop, but I can't. You can't be as creative when you're managing for a chain. There are things that might work in this shop that wouldn't work in their other branches, but they figure if they have them here, they have to have them all over, and these things might not go over well in other shops, in other areas [cosmetics].

MULTIPLE FRONTS

A somewhat related marketing format involves the use of multiple trade names in the same product areas. By using a number of trade names or by creating additional businesses (e.g., new corporations) in the same product area, a company may give the impression of greater buyer choice. Although the different trade names may signify different qualities of products, different styles and the like, they can also be used with identical products to appeal to different audiences, provide buyers with a greater sense of choice, minimize the effects of comparison (price) shopping, and comply with mall management policies designed to prevent overt duplication in their marketplaces.[8]

[a sister chain] has a wider variety than we do, and they're also a little higher priced on most times, but pretty close overall. And we'll carry some of the identical lines, although we'll price them a bit differently, just so that shoppers think they can shop around [women's clothing].

It may seem funny in a way that we have this other chain, because we're already a discount store. But we'd been losing a lot of business to the deep discounters, so we've gotten into that too. . . . These stores are stripped down. Everything's in a pile, and the customers root through things more. Things are dumped in bins, that sort of thing. Less like a department store, less orderly. We're more of a department store. We carry a wider range of products on a regular basis. . . . There, it's more of a grab bag, seconds and what not, whatever their buyers can get. We do some of that for our "sales," but there, that's pretty well routine. But the prices there are better, if you can find what you want [discount department store].

We tried to get more stores (but with only one trade name) into (mall A) and (mall B) more than once. They're large malls and get good traffic. Their policies though, and most other malls' too, is to avoid having two or more stores with the same name in the mall. They want to keep the mall more varied, more interesting for the shoppers [giftware].

There are risks to these ventures. Multiple trade name operations typically lose some of the economies of scale that accrue to larger, more focused operations and the multiple fronts may effectively compete with one another for the same audience in the same locale. This duplication may be partially offset by shared buying,[9] as well as the recognition that the volume discounts beyond a certain level are relatively minimal. Additionally, should the multiple outlets result in greater product interest and a greater likelihood of a consumer expenditure within the larger unit, the costs of more extensive duplication may be nullified. As with chains more generally, the lessened success of one front may be offset by the success of another. Multiple fronts, thus, represent a way of hedging bets in the marketplace.

When chains are involved in multiple fronts, each chain front within the larger organization would have its own identity, image, and style. These chain fronts may cater to different audiences, but need not. They may appear to be in direct competition to many shoppers (and may be seen as such by some staff people as well). Even when catering to the same audience, some variation in product line, price, and management style is likely, although uniqueness may be largely defined by front material (e.g., name, location, displays).

Generally, our competition was owned by (our own parent company). . . . Over half the stores in this mall were owned by _____ . All small stores, but when the truck pulled up, he'd have something for everybody in the mall, pretty well. Centralized distributing, more economical. I didn't see myself as competing with these places all that much, but we were encouraged to do that. And some of the seminars you would attend, they would give you a snow job to that effect. I didn't like that, because you knew damn well that the competition really wasn't there. They're independent companies, but we've had to move things from our stores, to these other outlets. . . . We had some overlap with the other stores, so in each store, each different chain in the company, say in shirts, or pants, our top lines might overlap with their starting lines, things like that. Otherwise, it was the department stores that were our largest competition [mixed clothing].

(A) and (B) are the only two jewelry stores in this mall, not counting the department stores. Very few people know it, but (B) is owned by (A), so either way, we get you! Very different looking stores, but the staff work much the same way in both places [jewelry].

Although the general public may be most aware of multiple fronts in the retail sector, the use of multiple trade names is by no means so limited.

(Y) is another name for (X) products. That way they can get dealers for both in the same area without them feeling the competition so directly. That's pretty common, overall [appliances].

The overlap of companies and trade names is especially evident at the trade shows. Sometimes they will be featured in the same booth, but other times, as you are given business cards and other literature, some of the connections become evident. You also find some of the same people working at two or more booths and in talking with them, the interconnections become apparent [notes].

UMBRELLAS

The term *umbrella* is used herein to denote the practice of multiple companies sharing the same marketing front. A number of vendors may collectively establish a common marketing format or one vendor may invite others to lease his space and sell their products under his identity. In addition to the credibility that tends to be associated with larger operations, the vendors involved typically benefit from one-stop shopping convenience and may experience savings on staff, advertising, and other facilities. Arrangements can vary greatly, but each vendor is generally responsible for stocking certain product areas.

In this [part of the] store, you were the person in charge of the department. So you were involved in all the ordering, the stocking, much more of it because you were the only person there from your company. So the only person there who was really above you was the manager for the whole store. But that was true of all the leased departments. They were pretty well separate operations in that sense. So you learned more about the products, how to service them if there were problems [discount department store].

Customer payment in umbrella operations may be localized by department or combined through inventory tracks (e.g., code colors/numbers) and payment centers.

Because each vendor's investments are proportionately smaller, umbrellas lend themselves to chainlike arrangements.

(M) and (N) are both like that. The different departments, like shoes, clothing, jewelry, they'll be run by other companies. Each has some of their own departments too. At (M) you pay in each department, and at (N) you pay as you leave, but otherwise, the same kind of setup [department store].

They rent the space, they pay so much per square foot. (A) has the sports shop, (B) has shoes, (C) is men's wear, (D)'s the paint department. I don't know who has the pharmacy. The camera shop is someone's else. Most of the others are our own. It's like you've got a little plaza inside. . . . Most people are not aware of it, because they pretty well pay for everything under the same label, with our own tag. No one would really notice, unless you worked in the system [discount department store].

MALLS

In contrast to umbrella operations, malls involve vendors identified (by name) as independent of one another.[10] Beyond one-stop shopping convenience, malls also offer a wider range of stores and may include both multiple front and umbrella stores in their roster.[11] While mall managers are concerned with filling their showrooms, they wish to achieve a climate conducive to sales. Thus preference is given to the more successful chains (especially larger stores and anchors).[12]

The malls prefer the chains. They're more established, they draw the customers more, and they will pay the rent. They'll be here a year from now, ten years, that kind of thing [men's clothing].

You'll notice that the same chains, the nationals, are in pretty well every mall. Sometimes you have problems remembering what city you're in. The malls are so much alike. Well, the malls want that. They want the larger chains, and the good anchors. . . . Your anchors will make or break a mall. They're the real drawing cards, the biggies. So they get better concessions. They have a lot more clout. But they've also sunk more into the mall too [manufacture—cosmetics].

However, the emphasis is on promoting the entire mall as a place of business.

As part of our condition in being in the mall, we are required to do some advertising. Their reasoning is that as each merchant advertises more, and brings in more people in to see their products, the other stores will benefit from the spillover business their advertising brings in. . . . Mostly the malls want long-term clients, companies who've established themselves over the years, across the country [giftware].

You promote the mall, the whole mall as an interesting, exciting, fun place to shop. You have an overall advertising budget, and then you go to all the businesses and get them to promote the mall by cooperative advertising in the newspapers, radio, t.v.; advertise your "sidewalk sales," "Boxing Day specials," all those sorts of things [mall].

Offering a wider range of service and facilities than isolated merchants can readily attain on their own, one finds that mall rents, leases, and rules tend to be more constraining than those facing vendors locating in most other settings.

In a mall, a lot of things are more standardized. You have to be open this many hours. You can't carry this or that. Your displays can't extend further into the aisles than this. Your sidewalk sales are going to be on these days. . . . Your year is all planned out with mall events. You have to spend so much in advertising. All these things. Not that much flexibility [mixed clothing].

If a mall is doing well, it can be very demanding! Long-term leases, very selective in who it admits if it expands, lots and lots of rules. But if it's slipping, like _____ , where I was last, well it's a lot more relaxed. They have a high turnover, so they do what they can to keep the ones they've got. But they didn't have a good anchor and they didn't get the traffic. Maybe at one time, but you're getting more and more newer and larger malls [giftware].

When multiple malls are owned by the same company, they may require that vendors wishing to enter their chain of malls do so in all available locations. In this way, they tend to standardize their malls, but more importantly, from their perspective, strengthen the weaker malls by using the more successful ones as leverage for stocking the weaker malls with more attractive (and profitable) vendors.

We didn't want to be in that mall, but we really had no choice. It was a package deal. If you want to be in this one, you have to go into the other one. We figured, overall, we'd benefit more from being here, and try to break even in the other one [women's clothing].

FRANCHISES

Involving multiple levels of ownership, franchises are more complex than many other businesses. Franchises resemble chains in that they entail multiple outlets, feature similar products, and fall under centralized control. They differ from other chains in that while some outlets may be owned by the company, other outlets are separately financed by the franchisees. Arrangements differ across franchises, but the franchisee typically buys the rights to operate an outlet and in turn obtains a more or less ready-made (turnkey) business to operate. The contract usually entails an ongoing royalty fee, and may specify that all purchases of equipment and supplies be made through the franchising company. The agreement also generally requires that the franchisee operate the business in a manner deemed satisfactory (e.g., quality control, profits) by the franchisor.

> We try to do all that we can to insure that the guy is successful, but we want to maintain a profitable operation, so if someone's not doing enough business, we will cancel his franchise and offer it to someone else who can do more with the territory. . . . With us, the territories are leased out to the dealer, so we would cancel his lease if he's not doing enough business [fitness center].

Productwise, franchises seem virtually unbounded, as evidenced by drug stores, hardware stores, variety stores, dance studios, auto repair businesses, fast food operations, motels, auto rentals, income tax services, real estate, financial consultants, cleaning products and services, building supplies, modeling, shoes, and clothing operations.[13] Featuring this wide range of products, franchises have extensive appeal to those who would like to own their own businesses. They also offer a sense of immediacy which a do it yourselfer is unlikely to achieve. In a very short period of time, interested persons can find themselves in a complete business setup. They may also find themselves advantaged in other aspects of doing business as well.

> As a franchise, we try to be distinctive, and the idea is that as a result, the whole is greater than the parts. It makes you seem more prominent in the public eye. So if you're doing your job, and they're doing their jobs in the other communities, it may look as though we're doing a lot more business than we actually are. And that's precisely what we want to happen, to get a higher profile. It impresses people, and if we can do that, we're likely to get more business. . . . Most people, I think, feel more comfortable listing with a

national company. They feel that if it's bigger, it's better. They feel that a larger company, with a larger image, will do a better job. . . . In other cases, where they've been happy with your service, they'll contact you again, or tell others about you. We encourage that, but I think that more and more people are going to national companies and I think that that is why the franchise system has been so successful. The smaller companies just can't offer the training or the benefits of the larger organization. . . . For someone starting out new, one has to get the name, the recognition, the system, the back-up assistance the franchise system offers. It's very difficult for an independent to open up an office and be very successful these days. It can happen, and it will happen, but the odds are against you. There are enough uncertainties in real estate without that [real estate]!

Our dealers, franchisees, get a good product. But we also give them an image, a name that's going to open doors for them. We have training programs and sale aids, and advertising. But most important, I think, we're a company that's willing to help its agents, work with them along the way [manufacture—appliances].

There are a lot of side-benefits with a franchise system, like better rates on office supplies, credit card charges, insurance, things of that type. . . . So with us, there's that on top of the centralized buying of stock, the advertising, that type of thing [hardware].

From the franchisee's perspective, a franchise represents a pretested opportunity to make it, to achieve financial success and independence. For those willing to make the necessary investments, the franchise typically promises a comprehensive system. Completeness of operation will vary somewhat across franchises, but programs may include such things as assistance obtaining financing; locating, building, and furnishing the outlet; training owners and staff; complete stock selection and pricing programs; recruiting strategies (including advertising campaigns); sales promotions; and even programs designed to generate customers' loyalty and staff enthusiasm. Standardized accounting, inspection, and quality control programs may also be implemented. Independents are apt to have more difficulty becoming established than those buying into franchises, but they are also less restricted. In fact, the more complete (detailed) the franchise operation, the less discretion the franchisee has in any aspect of marketing. All businesses are subject to government regulations, but independents can expand or sell, as they wish. While overall rates of success tend to be higher for those involved in franchises (versus independents), the franchisee is financially locked into a system that, depending on the contract, may not have many degrees of freedom.[14]

A big advantage of franchises is that they provide access to management skills. But your ownership is less clear with a franchise. If it's bought out by someone else, you don't really know the direction your business is going to take [appliances].

I have friends in other operations. One is _____ , where they are charging more for their supplies than you could get for yourself on the (open) market. So you have to work harder to make a profit there. In that situation, it is more like you are an employee of the company. Here, you see, I am quite my own boss. I can carry the lines I want to carry and how much, and rearrange my store the way I want to [variety].

I was in this _____ franchise for nearly two years and I lost about $50,000 dollars in that operation. It seemed like a good thing when I started, but then you realize that there are a lot of problems with it. . . . I also found that with the franchise there were controlled costs and so you had to pay so much to the head office, but there were a lot of hidden costs that you had to pick up yourself. If you had unhappy customers, if you had problems collecting, if there were printing errors. The company still charges you, but you have to try and collect that from the customers and if they are unhappy, they may not want to pay you. I also found that I ended up doing a lot of the art work, which I hadn't realized initially. . . . What's sort of interesting about the whole thing is that I had the most successful operation in this part of the country and I still wasn't making money! I was the one who was the speaker when they were recruiting other people and I was sort of the one that everybody looked up to [promotions—magazine].

From the franchisor's perspective, the franchise offers an opportunity to establish the company on a more widespread basis; achieve the economies of scale associated with a larger company; obtain profit from initial franchisee investments, operating royalty fees, and the sales of equipment and supplies to the franchisees. Most of the advantages of the chain operation can be incorporated within the franchise system with a smaller franchisor investment. Further, once willing investors are found, franchisor control may be no less than that achieved by the head office of the company-owned chain. Those investing in franchises have considerably more to lose than do dismissed managers (in other businesses) if their franchise is revoked.

With a franchise, you've got something invested, but so has the franchisee. His money is out front. And if he's not doing this or that right, you've got that lever. He's got to shape up [fitness center]!

If the franchise is legitimate and the planning is on a long-term basis, then the franchisor is as apt to be as concerned about who acquires the franchise as is the prospect about what he is purchasing. A successful franchise can increase greatly in value for both parties.

We want someone who's hardworking, and it would be better if they already had an established business. Then they can add our line to their present business. That way, their immediate overhead is less. Also, for us to let them have a franchise, it should be in a related, but not competing merchandise. . . . We'll also provide training and support materials to try and make their operation as competitive as possible. Actually, we see our distributors as partners. I know it sounds corny, but they are like family to you. They become like family to you because you end up working so closely with them [manufacture—appliances].

We would go into a town and get a listing of the real estate brokers, see who's who in the community, and then plan to seek out the more successful people, the ones who look like they're going to be successful in the future. If it's a small operation and they're planning to stay small, they're not candidates for our company. And very large ones, sometimes are not good prospects, either, because they may figure that they don't need us. So you analyze the potential of the people in the community. And, as a general rule, we contacted everybody, but we did research on who was getting the biggest piece of the pie, who was doing the sales in the area. And we'd also do an advertising breakdown by contacting local papers, find out who was spending the most on advertising. Then we'd get an estimate on the staff they were using and find out more or less what their commission splits were. Then we could assess what their bottom line was, whether they were in fact successful. In a public eye, they might look good, but they might be losing a lot of money. So we wanted to get those facts for ourselves, and in talking with the people (owners), you could hold an intelligent conversation with them. And you could get them to level with you more that way. Someone might tell you that they're doing fantastic, and that they don't need you, and so you might say, "Well, I know you've been doing a lot of sales in the area, but is your profit where you want it to be?" So you couldn't be misled as much, and you could steer the conversation around a little better. . . . We would then encourage them to attend an information seminar. Now some people shy away from the presentation, but once they could see what was being offered, they would get a better idea of why we were so successful. . . . And there's always that fear that "If I don't buy as a broker, then my next door neighbor might buy." Because our system, if used properly, is powerful! And there is that basic fear, always, of the competition in real estate. And that would enhance the fear. . . .

In the franchise agreement, a trading area is stipulated. You want a certain penetration in the market, but if you overallocate the territories, the system gets too weak. . . . It's also balanced out by the agencies willing to join a franchise system, as well as those you would want to join in a given area [real estate].

Some franchises have been sought out by people impressed with their products, but franchisors also recruit through the media, agents in the field, and through trade shows. Franchises may entail larger investments than most other purchases (goods), but are sold in much the same way. As the following extracts indicate, franchisors may seek two target groups, novices and converts (those with established businesses in particular product areas).

There are a number of trade shows specifically devoted to franchise and other business ventures. These shows are more widely publicized on the media than are most other trade shows, but the setup is very much the same. For many prospects, the investment signifies a way of life as well as a major investment (e.g., $20,000–$200,000) [notes].

My job was to contact a lot of real estate brokers, a lot of agencies and see if they would be interested in joining our franchise. Because for an independent broker to compete with a national group, in the public's eyes, is very difficult. They just don't have the resources. So, it's a different kind of selling. Selling residential, it's basically a one-shot deal. They [home buyers] need something; they make their investment, and you might keep in touch with Christmas cards, phone calls, things of that sort and then, maybe two, three, four years down the line, they contact you for a resale, but it can all be completed in two or three days or a week. But with the franchise sales, talking with franchise brokers, it would be maybe five initial interviews, before a presentation would be made showing them exactly what we have to offer and then another number of interviews thereafter, before the actual contract would be signed to join with us. So it's a long process, making the sale. Also, you run across a lot of rejection, and you'll keep going with some, where their situations might change. . . . There's great resistance in some cases, where people have been in business a certain number of years and have a certain credibility to their name. They believe that their name is very important in that community. It's taken them many years to establish that. And we do a telephone survey in that area, to see who people would list their property with if they were selling. Now, sometimes people are surprised to see that their name was not mentioned more than it was. He may think he's doing big things, and he may have built his business up a fair bit, but he's not as well known as he thinks he is. So you get the resistance of identification. It's a prime factor, because you do get people who think they're selling out to a common name. . . . It's an emotional thing, losing their name, that's how they feel. So you might get great resistance on identification.

Another resistance is that they're going to be controlled by someone else. People have been independent, running their own show, and now they have to start filling out reports to a central office. So now they're starting to get worried about becoming an employee rather than an employer. Now, we use the reports to improve their business, give them more feedback on their business, show them their sources, their expenses, and give them comparisons, all of which is very, very helpful. . . . It can give an agency new life. It's easy to get in a rut. Some could do well on their own, but they have to be sensitive to change, and a lot of people are resistant to change. . . . So you get people who are concerned about the changes that joining a franchise would mean. They're being asked to use new systems, and they may be concerned about doing things that they don't really understand. And they may be putting more money into advertising than they were before. To some it seems so much, and they can get very, very nervous. You'll get some people who know it's the right decision, but they get so nervous, they can't make the decision to join. They can see the trends, and the advantages, but they won't make the commitment. And if they're still doing well, and they have that pride of identification, they just may be unable to make the decision. And many times, they'll go through many sleepless nights. They know it's the correct decision, but there's that resistance to change. . . . You would also look for new people in the business, people just opening up their own agencies, because it is difficult to start out on your own. It takes a year or two to establish your name, whereas with the franchise, it's instant, and as soon as they open the door, they know that they've got a known name. So it can save them a lot that way [real estate].

I got involved in a company selling motivational programs, we were selling a program designed to give people more self-confidence. . . . It was a franchise operation, and we would be selling a kit, a tape recorder, and a bunch of tapes on motivational subjects, self-improvement, with a number of different levels you could get into. . . . The people purchased a membership, and through these, you were able to attend these sessions. And you were able to come out to as many as you wanted at the level you purchased at. It was a lifetime membership sort of thing, and you could go as much as you wanted at the level you had invested in. . . . It's just like _____ does, and some of the people from this organization ended up doing these tours, giving motivational speeches. . . . It's just fascinating! They blow your mind when you go there, "Go sell the world!" Unfortunately, it's easier said than done [mixed sales].

Becoming Owners

In rounding out this discussion of setting up businesses, it seems instructive to spend some time considering the problematics and processes of ownership. It should be noted that this discussion of ownership is directed toward smaller, closely held businesses (or toward those larger businesses that at earlier times had these sorts of origins).[15] In addition to those interviewed as owners at the time of research, we were fortunate to encounter a number of other people who had been owners of businesses at other points in their careers. The experiences of these entrepreneurs are especially valuable in depicting not only managerial concerns and activities, but also for shedding further light on other aspects of marketing. Of immediate relevance are the ways in which people acquire businesses; their concerns with financing; and the tendency of these businesses to become central features in their lives.

ACQUIRING BUSINESSES

While every instance of ownership is somewhat different from the next, one can delineate three routings to involvement: recruitment, seekership, and closure. These often occur in combination, but the significance of each can vary dramatically. A fourth element reflects people's abilities to overcome their reservations concerning the risks business ownership entails. While not operating as a base of involvement, drift acts as a qualifier for taking the sorts of risks businesses involve.

Recruitment

When others facilitate people's involvements in activities, the concept of recruitment becomes significant in accounting for these involvements. While some businesses will be given to family members, family and friends may also provide other kinds of encouragement and suggestions, sometimes offering to help get persons started in their own businesses.

Growing up in the business, you learn it from the inside. You've also got someone to look out for you, introduce you around. It's a big advantage [manufacture—clothing]!

With the crafts, it's not unusual to see other members of the family getting involved. It's usually the wife to get involved first, and then the husband or the children get dragged into it. It works the other way too, but it often becomes a family thing [crafts].

My father helped me get set up. He had the financial backing I needed. He liked the idea. . . . Without that, it would have been really tough to get going [manufacture—industrial].

Others, such as those promoting franchises, may also foster people's business involvements.

Each year, one finds a number of "franchise" or "opportunity shows" in most major trading centers. These are organized in a manner similar to trade shows, but cater to the general public. The exhibitors at these shows recruit prospects for franchise distributorships (and other investments). . . . Many of these same and similar groups also advertise in the "business opportunities" sections of newspapers and magazines [notes].

Seekership
Albeit often with some encouragement from others, people may also find that they have developed strong interests in particular products and/or have become fascinated with the prospects certain ventures represent as the means of achieving other desired ends. In both respects, people may seek out opportunities to pursue these interests.

I was in accounting for years, and I decided it was time for a change. Then I went to work for this one card company just as a favor to a friend, and then I decided to go into retail myself, so it was a new thing for me. Basically, I was attracted by the idea of working more with people, because in accounting, you really don't have all that much to do with people. Besides, I thought it would be a real challenge, and I sort of like that [giftware].

I'm my own boss. I work harder than I did before, but I can do what I want. I always wanted to have my own business. I always thought that if you were in business for yourself, you would make more money, and with that extra money you would have extra freedom, but I also found out that it's not so easy to make the extra money. And sometimes, you have all the extra headaches and not the extra money [furniture].

Those starting new businesses have more options in reference to products, location, routines and the like. However, their choices are clearly limited by their abilities to achieve the financial base particular businesses entail and their willingness to risk their resources. Of the newcomers, those who have worked in related fields or with businesses similar to those in which they have now become involved seem considerably advantaged over the other new owners. Not only may they be able to emulate and improve upon routines with which they may be intimately familiar, but they also are more apt to be aware of suppliers, customers, and the marketplace exchanges characterizing those products.

> There's a fair bit of concern about agents leaving the company and setting up their own business. They essentially use the company as a training ground, a way of getting known, too. Then they go and set up their own operation. Basically the same thing, a few little differences here and there. . . . See, if they went to another area, it wouldn't really be a problem, but what they're doing is setting up as direct competition and then taking some of the accounts they've been working with, with them. So the company they're leaving loses in a number of ways. . . . It can happen in any business, though. My uncle, who has a garage in a small town, the same thing happened to him. His number-one mechanic decided to set up his own shop, the same town of course. Only now, he's well known there because of my uncle. If he had set up when he first came, it would have been really tough for him, but once you're known, it's easier. That's a big reason they open up in the same area [promotions—agency].

> Before becoming a distributor, I had been with _____ . That was really valuable in getting to know the products and the business. Essentially, what you do in that situation is you learn at their expense. You learn the way that business is done and the contact people. From that you have a pretty good idea of what you might be able to do [wholesale—giftware].

> We've only been in business for about three years, but I was working with _____ so I know a lot of the accounts, the contacts, from before. Our buying contacts were fairly extensive, too, and the lines we carry reflect that [wholesale—office equipment].

Closure

In some cases, people become owners when they envision owning one's business as the only feasible means (closure) of dealing with the lack of opportunities they encountered in the marketplace.[16]

> I went into my own business for a number of reasons. First, there had developed a conflict within the company I was working for. It had gotten large and more bureaucratic. . . . I could have gone into manufacture, but that requires a lot of capital, and it's a risky business, manufacturing. So I felt that the best thing that I could do at the time was to go into retail. . . . It was

convenient. I had been doing a lot of traveling with the company and I was getting tired of the traveling [appliances].

At the time I was out of work, so I was interested in different possibilities that might arise. I had no real intention of going into sales work. I had been in business with my brother and he had had experience in sales and although that partnership didn't work out especially well, it did provide me with some knowledge of the retail sales area [women's clothing].

Overcoming Reservations

Not all who seriously contemplate establishing their own businesses do so. Since business can be a costly and risky endeavor, a sense of freedom from one's usual obligations (drift) is exceedingly important in reference to taking the big step. Freedom from financial obligations can be enhanced by accumulating enough money to live on while the business develops, but supportive spouses and/or a lack of dependents also tend to define the situation as one in which business investments are less threatening. Conversely, people defining themselves as having greater obligations to others and maintaining existing levels of self comfort are less likely to entertain the gamble that ownership entails.

If I had it to do all over again, I would start younger. But if you're getting into something new, you need some sort of knowledge. You should see some potential for the product and have the capital behind you, because you don't want to have to worry too much about the bills. You can't worry about meals and keeping a roof over your family. You pretty well have to put aside enough money that you and the family could live on for a year. That is just so important! Otherwise, there is just too much pressure and when you're getting into a new business, you can't be worrying about where to find money for food and a roof over your head during the first year. You just can't operate that way. . . . Also, you need some sort of enthusiasm from your family, your wife. That is an important part of it too [manufacture—industrial].

Most people in business would like their own store, company, whatever. But most don't have the money and, like me, they're too chicken to risk what they do have. . . . And, if you move up in the organization and the pay starts to get pretty good, then there's even more incentive to stay with the company you're with [men's clothing].

A favorable appraisal of the marketplace represents another element promoting drift. Thus, regardless of whether one does market research,

looks for niches in the market on a more casual way, or merely antici-
pates adequate levels of business, expectations of success serve to
diminish reservations.

Some hedge their bets by starting businesses on a part-time basis.
While the business may represent something of an overload for the
owner, it minimizes the financial risk a more complete involvement
entails.

I used to work on the engraving and the molds [first business] like crazy to pay for
the losses in the plastics [second business]. This went on for about two years. I had
two people working for me, and meanwhile, I'd be working nights and Saturdays
and Sundays on the engraving end to make the money to make expenses. It was
tough for the first five years [manufacture—giftware]!

In the beginning, sales weren't what we had hoped for, so I kept my full-time job.
My wife worked the store during the day, and I went in on weekends, and made
the deliveries after work. . . . And business is never steady, so sometimes it would
be quite hectic. And then you think, "I should quit my job," but then it slows down
again, and you decide to say on longer. . . . I quit my regular job about two years
after we got into the store. . . . You never have a regular income, and in the
beginning, it was especially frustrating. Before, I would get a paycheck once a
week, and I knew how to plan out my money. You knew how much would be
coming in. But in business, you never know how much you have. You invest so
much money into it, and if business is bad, you lose money for a month or two,
and you have to take money out to live. And you don't know how much money
you will have coming in the next month. So you never know how much money
you have [furniture].

I've run across a number of people who started in craft operations on a part-time
basis and who later became involved in full-time businesses. Some have become
full-time craft exhibitors, but some basically have become full-time manufacturers
supplying to wholesalers and/or retailers, and still others have become mainly
wholesalers selling to crafters and retailers. This reflects the diverse contacts and
opportunities people (myself included) have in this setting [notes].

For those involved in businesses, financing remains a major concern.
In addition to accessing the funds (investments, loans, sales) necessary
to meeting the costs of doing business, owners may be unable to derive
incomes from their businesses for several years.

We were locked in, but we managed to do it. We watched what we were doing and
didn't bleed our business. And my wife worked, part of the good answer of this

business. My brother's wife worked, that was the other part. And we were able to survive and continue to go and, of course, the agency still helped us, but the agency businesses also helped us to get on our feet, by pumping in those extra dollars so that you don't bleed the business. So that is basically how we ended up where we are today. . . . It's still a never-ending battle because you are still never happy at this point [wholesale—giftware].

You're under pressure all the time, especially in the beginning. And with the bank, when you need the money the most, you have trouble getting it. When you don't need it, they ask you if you want any more. Like at that time our line of credit was pretty low, and if I went a few dollars over, the guy is on the phone, telling me that I had exceeded by line of credit, better bring in some money. . . . You have enough trouble as it is, trying to make ends meet, and then a bank manager bugging you about something like that, that's all you need. And now, they ask you if you need money [manufacture—industrial]!

People's experiences with recruitment, seekership, closure, and reservations should not be seen as constants. These elements are subject to definition and change, and they are interrelated. Thus, for instance, people selling franchises may in the process of recruiting targets, cultivate desires on the part of the targets to "seek their own" businesses; define ownership as the only way the targets may achieve happiness, independence, and success; and indicate how easy and risk-free the venture is to the targets. Likewise, family members, friends and other acquaintances may not only encourage involvements, but in providing assessments of these individuals and their situations can influence the sense of seekership, closure, and reservations their associates experience.

OWNING AS CENTRAL ACTIVITY

Although anyone could become more heavily involved in business activity than anticipated, this seems especially likely for owner-managers. They realize that their financial well-being will be affected by the success of their business ventures, but the impact of their business on their social lives is more surprising.

I enjoy the camaraderie that exists between the other retailers, say at the sales club, because there are people there that you feel that you have something in common with. Unfortunately, we've found that being in business for yourself, it has almost alienated ourselves from the circle of friends that we had before. A large part of it is that when you start out, you are almost consumed by the petty, and not so petty, day-to-day concerns of doing business. It's very hard to carry on even a casual relationship with people who have regular jobs and have a separate social life. Now, maybe it's that we're not relaxed enough, but we find that it's always on our minds [appliances].

In the store business, I was going seven days and seven nights a week, every week. I don't think I had a holiday for three or four years at a stretch. . . . There's so much to it, and it's exciting! We had every major chain in opposition to us, and it was one of the satisfactions to know that you can start a small business and keep it running. And there were a number of chains that tried to move into this area and eventually gave up on it. We held up against all odds seemingly, because we were the ones that remained in business and they were the ones that kept dropping out. . . . At the time, it didn't seem like it was difficult. I only realized the work load when it caught up with me [grocery].

This centralizing tendency is in part a function of the many tasks marketing entails in its more complete sense.

When you're in business for yourself, there are so many things you have to do. You have to work with your accountant, and hiring and selling, and ordering, and just so many different aspects that you have to be on top of. Another thing, of course, is that you just can't stay at the same level. Either you are moving ahead or you are moving behind. . . . You can't find a level you feel comfortable with and just maintain it on that level. There are too many things that are changing around which make that extremely difficult [furniture]!

If you're an owner, you have to work 18 hours a day, if you want to make it go. You can't work eight hours a day and take long lunches with the buyers and things of that nature. Your business is going to go down! If you want to make a success of it, you have to stay there and you have to work at it. It really boils down to that. And that's one of the big differences between owning a business and just kind of managing it. . . . When you're managing, you've got the people above you to keep happy, to get approval of your plans from. As an owner, you're freer from that, but you're more dependent on your customers. . . . It also means, though, if something goes wrong, you've got nobody else to blame. You're following your own plans, and if something comes up, it's you who has to deal with it [manufacture—industrial].

Even when people are able to hire others for assistance, the problem of delegating activities is compounded by a recognition that the owners' concerns may not be shared by their staff.

When you're working for another company and allocating responsibilities that is one thing. But when it's your own money that's involved, you have this strong tendency to be looking over their shoulder to see that they're doing everything right, which is wrong. Because, if you have faith in that person, you shouldn't be doing that. The problem, though, is that you didn't know how much confidence to have in someone else, and you can run into problems if you don't watch someone carefully enough. . . . When I worked for _____ , it was different. You were more in control of the people you were dealing with. . . . Here, it's more like you are at the mercy of the people you are dealing with. It didn't matter so much when you were working for someone else that they didn't like that company. It never entered your mind that their sales could drop off and you might be let go because of that. That was somebody else's problem. But now, we know that if someone comes in and walks out again, we know that we have lost a sale. So that's money right out of your own pockets. And it's very hard to generate that sort of loyalty in employees. We've tried different things, including profit incentives plans, but nothing has really worked out well [appliances].

As an owner, you really get all the problems you don't have as an employee. As an employee, when your day is over, you pack up your things and go home. When you're the owner, you live the situation much more. . . . You're more concerned about public relations with your clientele, for instance. Your employees aren't that concerned about maintaining a clientele. As an owner, it's something that strikes you as very, very central. You don't want to see people going away unhappy or going away when you think they won't be coming back [manufacture—industrial].

In Perspective

This chapter has examined a number of features central to understanding the organization of businesses and marketing structures. It began by outlining the differences between proprietorships and corporations. Next, attention was given to the housing of trading entities, as indicated by independents, chains, multiple fronts, umbrellas, malls, and franchises. As products may be sold within any number of marketing formats, an awareness of these marketing options is valuable in arriving at a more comprehensive understanding of marketing activity. Additional insight into the business was generated by a consideration of aspects of ownership. By exploring the processes by which people become owners, their concerns with financing, and the centralizing nature of business in their lives, one gains perspective on the situations of those involved in the marketplace as owners, managers, and salespeople. Despite the range of topics covered in this chapter, it should be noted that the portrayal of both marketing formats and ownership involvement patterns, by virtue of the larger project, have been rather cursory in nature. Each of these topics merits much fuller study along the lines suggested herein.

While the implications of many of the preceding features of the marketplace will become evident as the subsequent chapters unfold, Chapter 2 (along with Chapter 3, following) provides a frame in which to locate other aspects of marketplace behavior. Together they set the basic stages on which the dramas of the marketplace take place. Business denotes a dollars and cents enterprise, but it is best seen in the context of human relations and social process. Marketing consists of layers upon layers of socially constructed activities. The chapters following indicate just how germane this theme is for understanding the marketplace and all those who participate therein.

NOTES

1. Governments may nonetheless be concerned with operations they define as tax dodges.

2. As with other personal belongings, the physical features of proprietorships may also be willed to others. Should the new owner decide to take charge, the business becomes a new proprietorship as far as the government is concerned. The clientele base, the *modus operandi,* and the reputation of the entity, however, may be largely unchanged when the physical structures change possession.

3. In partnerships, the death of one partner requires a recasting (often awkward) of the business (e.g., develop a new partnership, move to a proprietorship).

4. Governments (including socialist and communist regimes, as well) may be seen as corporations (and monopolies) with wide-sweeping charters.

5. This is not to say that executives are not subject to the law. However, corporate responsibility is difficult to assess, and executives seem to fare better in court than other law breakers (Sutherland, 1949; Clinard and Yeager, 1980).

6. Although this is most noticeable among companies who have multiple office locations (e.g., regional, local), businesses employing multiple agents in the field assume some properties of chains, as they increase exposure of goods to more people than would prospect visits to single outlets.

7. Albeit at the sacrifice of some individuality, those involved in single outlets may engage in collective buying practices (e.g., establishing buying groups) to obtain greater savings in those realms.

8. Some instances of multiple fronts arise as a consequence of mergers and acquisitions. When a company acquires another company featuring similar products, it may elect to maintain the original name because of the market it is seen to command and/or it wishes to maintain the other company as a separate entity (e.g., a company with a "name" is easier to sell at a later date). Regardless of routings or rationale, however, the maintenance of multiple fronts denotes an important marketing option.

9. In addition to the better prices attainable by purchasing larger quantities of the same goods, vendors (including those using multiple fronts) may also seek discounts or rebates commensurate with the total dollar volume of purchases of items from the same supplier.

10. Contemporary shopping malls, as we know them, are variants of farmers' markets, trade fairs and the like. In contrast to many of these other trading centers, however, these shopping malls have fixed locations and are characterized by greater continuity (daily) of business.

11. It should be appreciated that other material pertinent to malls as marketplaces is interspersed throughout the chapters following. For a first sociological foray in the urban shopping mall, see Jacobs (1984).

12. The term *anchor* (or *major*) is often used to refer to the bigger stores (particularly larger department stores; sometimes larger grocery stores) in a mall, with malls being assessed relative to the power of these anchors to draw desirable customers into the shopping center.

13. See Sklar (1973, 1977) for a sociological statement on franchisee-franchisor relations in the dry cleaning and fast food businesses. Although not discussed in this book, party plans (see Peven, 1968; Prus and Frisby, 1989) may also be included under the broader family of franchise-type operations.

14. People managing their own businesses seem apt to make more mistakes than those involved in franchises. In established franchises, especially, the more common mistakes one makes in setting up and managing the business are supposedly eliminated. Likewise, all projections on estimating overhead, stock, advertising, and the like should be more accurate as a result of the experiences of the organizers. Presumably, also, any unique or perplexing problems the franchisee encounters in marketing would be solved through assistance with the organizers. It should also be noted, however, that persons investing in franchises are generally required to make much greater investments in these ventures than are those operating as independents in comparable businesses. Ergo, a stronger financial base is frequently established. This, in itself, may significantly affect people's overall success.

15. Although stockholders in larger corporations are also owners, most are far removed from the daily routines of those businesses. The question of how people invest in particular stock remains, however, and the processes may well parallel the routings by which people enter their own businesses. For a series of brief, but valuable, accounts of the (often humble and fortuitous) origins and histories of major companies across a variety of product areas, see Moskovitz et al. (1980).

16. A similar observation is made by Collins et al. (1964) in a psychologically oriented study of entrepreneurs.

Chapter 3
DOING MANAGEMENT

People are the most difficult part of the business. They're not like machines, they can talk back. But you can't do without them [manufacture—giftware].

In the preceding chapter, attention was given to the ways in which marketing operations are set up at a general level. While not fully defining the work role of managers in marketing contexts, this chapter considers topics central to the management process. Thus, as a means of providing a more comprehensive understanding of marketing programs, consideration is given to managerial duties and dilemmas, hiring concerns, the applicants with whom managers are expected to work, sales instruction, modes of determining payment, and concerns with generating performance.

Duties and Dilemmas

Although the owner-managers discussed in the preceding chapter may have greater investments in a business, and greater anxieties about its overall well-being, management activity is rather generic. This is not to suggest that all managers have similar levels of commitments to their companies or that their duties are identical. Indeed, over time the same managers are apt to be variously committed to their companies, experience different levels of responsibility, and face ever-shifting sets of tasks. People may occupy certain offices, but their duties are best seen in the context of a dynamic marketplace and the ongoing life of the organizations in which they find themselves. Likewise, people may approach organizations with varying levels of commitment, but their ongoing sense of dedication can fluctuate greatly as they experience external and internal (organizational) exchanges and assess themselves relative to these exchanges.

The following statement outlines the basic sorts of activities for which marketing managers find themselves responsible. These concerns are not uniformly prominent across businesses, but all may be major concerns at any point in a business's existence. It should also be appreciated that while the management of marketing activity need not be so different from supervision in other settings, our primary concern is with depicting managing activity as this pertains to marketing and sales. Thus, while many of these same themes are pertinent to managing in other areas (e.g., product design and manufacture), all the material in the following chapters is relevant to management activity. Varying immensely with regards to marketing, managerial tasks may include any and all of the following:

- developing marketing plans: This would include ongoing assessments and adjustments of policies and practices pertaining to the activities and preferences of the buyers (and distributors, if appropriate); the competition; and one's own organization
- satisfying upper management (where appropriate), and working within the range of politics and resources at hand
- arranging for staffing relative to hiring new workers, training, paying, coordinating, and motivating staff; and dismissing those thought unsatisfactory
- obtaining and pricing goods, including the selection of goods and/or supplies and decisions pertinent to competitive pricing
- attending to customer relations, particularly as this involves trou blesome customers and the development of loyal patrons
- representing the company to the broader community, as this pertains to government officials, and attaining good-will and positive images

Ironically, those studying management and organizational behavior (OB) have given little consideration to the ways in which people actually do management activities. Much attention has been given to organizational flow charts, personalities, attitudes, background characteristics, and mathematical modeling in the management, organizational behavior, and formal organizations literature.[1] And advice on how to manage has been most generously given. Unfortunately, these scholars have almost completely ignored the study of the ways in which managers do management work.[2]

From the literature that most directly focuses on managerial activities as a process (Davis, 1959; Dalton, 1959; Sayles, 1964; Mintzberg, 1973; Kotter, 1982),[3] it appears that management activities are much more mundane, organizationally disjointed, and short-run than many might assume. However desirable long-term planning may seem, it is beset by all sorts of uncertainties and complexities. Short-term managerial functioning in most cases reflects the present pressures (and quirks) of head office, the problems subordinates are seen to have dealing with the tasks at hand, and all the others (e.g., customers, suppliers, officials) who sporadically and unevenly impinge on them. Further, as managers often find themselves facing simultaneous (multiple) demands, many matters are handled on an expediency-urgency basis rather than with full and careful attention.

While their authority may be formally limited, managers may be held responsible for all that occurs in the territory under their control. As a result, they readily become caught up in the ongoing problems of maintaining a smooth running operation. When managers are involved in activities such as doing saleswork, arranging display, doing inventory, ordering goods, and the like, this tends to further promote short-term functioning (versus extensive planning and assessment), coordination, and negotiation.

> If you're managing a business, your job is to see that whatever needs to be done, gets done! . . . Part of it is deciding what needs to be done, and there, unfortunately, you run very short term, very immediate, because you've got all these deadlines and all these little problems that occupy your day [promotions—agency].

> In management, they say delegate responsibility. That's what you're supposed to do, delegate tasks so that you have more time for planning. But it doesn't work that way. On many things, by the time you explain the situation to someone and then follow it up, you are better off to do it yourself. On some things, you can delegate, but on other things, it defeats the purpose. . . . Every day, when I come in, there will be problems I didn't expect. Customers, staff, suppliers, another department, head office. Every letter, every phone call, everyone who wants to see the manager, that can be a time consumer for you [manufacture—industrial].

The actual duties of a manager will vary considerably with the organization of the company and the ways in which the others define their roles relative to the manager in question.[4] The amount of planning management entails in large part reflects the newness and the internal specialization of the business involved. Thus most planning is typically found in the early stages of a business's existence, and reflects the decisions of those with more authority.[5]

> Starting a new business, you've got to work out your program, financing, suppliers, find your staff, get your inventory together, get your advertising going, get your catalogues together. It's very different from stepping into management where everything is pretty well set up. You have to do everything they would do, and get these other things going as well. . . . Afterwards, it's just like the other, but as an owner and a manager, you've got much more latitude in what you can plan to do [manufacture—industrial].

> In the beginning, you have to plan, decide what you're going to do, major decisions. Then you have to live with these plans. And unfortunately, afterwards, you get so caught up in the day-to-day things, you don't really get a chance to go back and look at your overall procedures, until someone like you comes along. . . . You think about this or that, try to solve these problems as they come along, but nothing systematic. And you always have these other things coming up. You get tunnel vision, not really looking at the whole thing as much as you should to be effective [manufacture—giftware].

Since it primarily involves people work, management activities are more common across situations than might first seem.[6]

> I don't think there is actually any difference between managing a department store [had managed several] and a variety store like this. It's again a matter of getting the right staff, educating, training them, and making sure that your store is clean. That you're giving them service, and that you've got the place clean because people don't like shopping in a dirty store. And the more variety you have, the more selection you have, the more customers you'll attract. But again, inventory is one of the criteria you work with. You have certain stock allowances and you have to watch your inventories when you're ordering. If you go over that, you can have problems. You've got your money tied up in inventory and it's not going into the bank to pay my bills. . . . At _____ , each department is run like a separate little store, and you would be responsible for the sales, the stock, and you had to pay the interest on the stock from your money coming in. The interest was charged to your department, which is exactly the same thing we have here. I've got an investment, and I've got to make a profit on that [variety].

Doing franchise sales, you can find out a lot about business that the average businessman doesn't know. As you travel around, and talk to all the different brokers, you're learning things that these people wouldn't be discussing with the people down the street, the competition in some cases. And they're more likely to open up and share their problems with you. And you find that the problems are pretty well the same all over. . . . But what a lot of them don't realize is that a lot of them have been there before. You have all these different stages, and depending on how many people you've got, you've got certain kinds of problems. So you've always got problems, and you go from one crisis to another. It's a continual flow of crises! It made me much more aware that the problems I had with my own company, everyone was facing the same problems, but I though it was just me [real estate].

Much management work is emergent and problematic in nature, but people managing in more established companies also have the routines and experiences of others in that company on which to contextualize their experiences and develop lines of action.

Every day's the same, but every day's different. The names and the faces change, but the situations are always the same. In September, we have the new car announcements. Then comes November, and we're starting to run out of the prior year's models. Then in January, we're having last minute sales on the last year's models and we're all trying to get out of them. Then in April, you have to stop ordering that particular year's model, so you decide what your orders will be for the rest of the year by the end of April. In May, you start getting the following year's orders together. Then you have to plan out the rest of the year in terms of the stock you have, and then it's September again and it just goes around like that. . . . Also, you get the same questions from your staff, and the same problems with the customers. The customers are different, and the models of cars are different, but the situations are the same [auto].

You know the seasons, when things are going to move better. You know when you have to order things, when the trade shows are going to take place, when to start getting ready for them. So there's a pattern there, overall. You've got that to work with. It's just that within that, you've got to make all these other adjustments [wholesale—giftware]

CAUGHT BETWEEN

The position of each manager will vary somewhat, but managers are apt to find themselves caught in a series of cross-pressures reflecting the others to whom they are accountable. Thus, in addition to the input of any upper management or owners, one finds a plurality of others making demands on the manager. These may include managers in interconnected departments, suppliers wishing to sell goods and/or receive payments for goods sold, staff, prospective and current customers, government agencies, and union representatives. While managers tend to readily become absorbed in running the day-to-day operations of the company, any of the aforementioned parties can dramatically interfere with the tasks at hand. It is unlikely that all parties would be involved in any dispute at one time, but managers face the dilemma of serving a number of task masters at the same time.

In management, you're caught between. You've got the salesmen biting and gnashing at one cheek, and the upper management biting and gnashing at the other. So that's part of it. You've always got someone you have to answer to. Always! . . . As a sales manager, your job is trying to get your salesmen motivated, more so than answering to management, much more. Because if my guys are no good, I'm out the door! If my guys are good, I don't get too much shit [manufacture—industrial].

The further away you are from head office, the easier it is for them to forget about you. But, you're more under the control of your field supervisor if you're further away from head office. So you lose both ways. Less opportunities for advancement, and then you're more under the control of your supervisor. You're more subject to whims of your supervisor that way. And if you don't like your supervisor, then it's more of a problem. . . . To the supervisor, the managers are like the regular staff are to the managers. So whatever he or she can do to hold your salaries down, the better they look to the company. . . . A major problem for a store manager is to enforce policies that you don't agree with and the staff don't agree with [mixed clothing].

Hiring Staff

Although not necessarily a first task facing managers, hiring decisions reflect an area of considerable importance. Those doing the hiring do not know (despite interviews, tests, and so on) just how well applicants will fare, but turnovers can be costly in time, training, and productivity. Some employees may view a sales/marketing position as "merely a job," a way to make money, but those doing the hiring tend to view prospects as both sources of assistance and investments. Each employee thus represents a gamble, not only in reference to his or her pay offs relative to company costs, but also in reference to the other people the company could have hired in lieu of the present employee (prospect).

> When you're hiring a new person, in a sense you're taking on a partner, even though you're not giving them stock in the company [manufacture—industrial].

> In hiring new people, you want to get the one that's going to do you the most good. You invest in each person, compared to someone else you could have hired, so if you make a mistake, it's going to cost you the difference between what that person does for you and what the other one would have done for you [mixed clothing].

Overall, four concerns emerge as central in hiring salespeople. These are (1) social skills, (2) reliability and dedication, (3) technical skills, and (4) experience. There is some overlap among these elements, but each denotes a number of dimensions that may affect hiring decisions. It should be noted, however, that regardless of concerns and modes of assessment, a great many hiring decisions reflect compromises.

SOCIAL SKILLS

Social skills emerge as a prime requisite in most contact sales situations. Generally speaking, social skills assume the following dimensions: having a socially acceptable appearance, being able to establish and maintain working relationships with customers, and being able to fit in with the other staff (and management). Although individual managers may stress some of these qualities over others, they represent fairly fundamental concerns.

Appearances

Two main themes emerge in discussions of appearances: acceptability of applicant appearances to the business' clientele and consistency of applicant appearances with the images the business wishes to project. The two may be synonymous, but those doing the hiring may be much more concerned with one than the other.

> I would look at their appearance. If they look sloppy, you don't want that. If they're well-groomed, that's a big asset. And how they present themselves to you, how they express themselves. And you look for a real go-getter, usually. . . . You want a responsible, motivated person. . . . Some of the applicants, you want to tell them, "Look, if you washed your hair or cleaned your fingernails, you would be making

a much better impression." But some people, they just don't seem to understand that these things are important [shoes].

Here, appearance is very important. We try to convey a pleasant, feminine, businesswoman image. So, like when the braless look was in, for instance, we didn't have that. It was not in keeping with our basic image. . . . We also encourage our people to wear our items. They needn't be the latest, but we do encourage them to dress in the store's fashions. . . . I try to have a range of people, different ages, so that most customers will be able to feel comfortable if that's something of concern to them. . . . I look for a girl who has a certain look, our look. I don't know exactly how to describe it, but someone who looks sensible for the type of merchandise we sell, in terms of their dress style, their hair, makeup, posture, where they would convey a desirable image for us, for the merchandise we sell [women's clothing].

Establishing Working Relationships

Somewhat related to matters of appearance is the concern of whether applicants will be able to develop working relationships with customers. Given the limited time spans sales situations generally entail, it is thought important that salespeople be willing and able to approach prospects and quickly establish rapport with them.

You want someone who's not afraid to talk to customers. I've seen people hired who wanted to just go and ring the sales in, because they're too afraid to go and talk to people. You've got to have a rapport with customers. You have to! And you have to go to them, you can't stand behind the counter, waiting for them to come to you, because they won't have the time. Forget it! You have to be aggressive, but you can't be pushy. You've got to keep your eye on the customer, and when you see that they could use some help, go for it! . . . You've got to look well-dressed, too, in any retail business. That means a lot. A person who doesn't take care of themselves is probably not going to care how they take care of you either. . . . You'd want someone who's bright, and has knowledge, but then you're going to get that by being around [jewelry].

I want someone who's pleasant, has good eye contact, puts the customer at ease, someone who's honest. And the customer's got to trust you. You're selling an item valued at several hundred dollars, and you've got to be able to establish that relationship with the customer. You can teach anyone how to run the cash register, the prices, and all in a week, but you need someone who enjoys working with the public, and someone who wants to get out there and hustle his butt. It's soft sales, not a hard sell, but you still have to hustle [appliances]!

In addition to their abilities to relate comfortably and confidently toward their clients, managers may also be concerned about applicants' abilities to project credibility and sincerity.

I look for someone who has a good overall appearance, someone who is not going to try and bullshit the customers. If you don't know something, tell them you don't know, that you will find out for them, and then follow up on that. If you don't, you are going to lose credibility with the people, something that you must never do. That's an important thing to me, credibility with the customers [manufacture—industrial].

We want someone who's nicely dressed, neat looking, not necessarily fashionable. Pleasant looking, someone with an air of confidence. . . . You want someone who is going to get along with people. When you interview them, you have to sort of pull things from them, see how they react to them. Can they talk to people easily? And that's a basic thing, because you're always talking with strangers. Can they get along with them? And they have to be willing to do menial chores, dusting and all, because in the end, we all do that. Someone who's generally pleasant, someone that you can get along with. . . . It's nicer to have females around. If she's a good looking chick, she can draw the guys into the store. But they have to be able to sell too. They have to have that selling ability. And a lot of the girls are better at selling than the boys are, women, men, whatever. . . . Some of the men's shops have a thing about not letting the women sell suits, but that's crazy! Because here, we've had the girls outsell the guys on suits. And if she says that it looks good on the guy, it can really help! But I tell them to be honest with the customers, "Don't tell them it looks good on them if it doesn't, because if he gets home and they're telling him how poorly it fits, well, you might make the sale, but he probably won't be back" [men's clothing].

Fitting In

While most of the emphasis on one's social skills is directed toward concerns with client relationship, some managers also indicated rather clear concerns about the abilities of newcomers to fit into existing routines and the staff community.

I find that in hiring a young man in my type of business, in one sense it is good, and one sense it isn't. I know that everybody says, "Hey look, I want an opportunity. I am a young man, I don't have sales experience, but I will learn, I am ambitious." Well, what if the young fellow is overly ambitious, and damages account relationships, damages other situations in the company with other salespeople by trying to do things, trying to outshine other people to make him look like the fair-haired boy, because he wants to be number 1? I can't say that I am going to hire him. That is what I am afraid of. . . . Then the problem of a young fellow not being totally responsible for keeping everything in good shape for selling purposes. Samples in good shape, bag in good shape, clean, and your most important thing, your catalogue, that is your Bible! If that isn't in good shape, cleaned up, changed around from time to time, pages fixed up, you are in trouble! . . .

So with the young fellow, you have to sit on him. Even though he will hustle you business, you have to watch him. He may try to overload the account, oversell. Give the retailer too much merchandise because he really wants to look good. Comes the next year, he is in trouble because he has sold so much into the previous year that its backed up on him, he can't get it out. So the next thing you know, merchandise starts coming back, and then he starts fighting with the customer over credit, "No, I don't want to take it back." "But when you sold it to me, you said you would look after it." "Oh yeah, next trip." Next trip, next trip, and next trip, and next trip. It never comes out and then the bad relationship, which falls back on the company. And that is bad! These are some of the problems I run into with young people. . . . I am not saying that a middle-aged person can't give me the same problems. But I have experienced this more with young people. I would rather have a fellow 30-35, not 25, not 22. I know it is being unfair in some respects, unless this young man really has something special about him [wholesaler—giftware].

It's like a team. You don't want to spend your time bickering among yourselves, not if you can help it anyway. So that's something we take into account, "Can they work with the people here? Is it someone I can work with?" If they seem agreeable, and are willing to learn, and help out, then I'm less likely to be concerned with other things, like experience, say [manufacture—industrial].

RELIABILITY AND DEDICATION

Although social skills are given considerable prominence (and may be easier to gauge initially), a concern no less basic centers around the general dependability of the applicants considered. Thus employers want salespeople who are capable, responsible, self-reliant, and trustworthy.

It's not the education that makes a good salesperson, it's you, your responsibility, punctuality, friendliness. You have to be outgoing, willing to approach people, able to talk to people. . . . I want someone very alert, pleasant, friendly with the customers, someone who's efficient, who can do things quickly when it needs to be done. Also, someone who's reliable. That's very important too. You also want a person who doesn't need to be pushed, someone who's self-starting [stationery].

You can't find out much in an interview, because everyone is going to try to be very good in the interview. You've got to get a general feeling of the guy. Does he seem like someone that you can work with? Does he seem like he has the desire? Does he have empathy? Honesty, tenacity, and empathy, that's what it boils down to. That's a big thing in sales. . . . I want a guy who's basically honest, or he's going to screw the company. And tenacity, you want someone who's not afraid to call on someone the second time, the third time, the tenth time, whatever it takes [manufacture—industrial]!

TECHNICAL SKILLS

The emphasis on technical skills varies much more than the other concerns employers have in hiring salespeople. One area in which this is evidenced is in reference to advanced education. Some companies will tap into training programs (e.g., real estate, travel, graphics, engineering, science) offered by others as a means of minimizing company training, but technical preparation may also be a very important aspect of the training programs of companies unable or unwilling to locate and pay trained people to do sales work. Thus, while some companies require university degrees as a matter of upgrading their program (and image) in general, others feel that they can provide the required technical training in short periods of time and/or indicate little concern about formal education.[7]

Some companies are hiring B.Sc.s, while other companies are looking for promising people and train them. The companies will lock you up for a couple weeks of classes, a crash course. They go back to square one and teach you pretty well everything a doctor would go through. They teach you much more than you really need. When you walk in to see a doctor, he doesn't want to go into a long history of that drug. What he wants to know is what the drug can do, how it works, what group does it fit in as far as generics, what side-effects does it have. If he wants to know anything more, he would probably ask for a pamphlet on it, which has all the jargon on it. . . . They also had a sales course for us, basically along the lines of the _____ course, just different titles, different words. They give you all facets of the sales pitch, whatever you want to call it. It helps in a lot of ways, gives you a much better idea of what's involved [manufacture—pharmaceutical].

I've got a salesman with a grade-seven or -eight education. His orders are never spelled properly, written properly, but he makes top money every year. . . . He doesn't have to be especially clever, but he has to remember how to deal with objections, how situations worked out in the past, to try something similar in this situation [auto].

When technical training is given by outside agencies, one typically finds some redefinition of actual job skills relative to technical skills.

The real estate course gives them the technical skills, but it doesn't help in selling at all. They don't give the people any courses in selling, so when they come out, if they haven't had that before, you've got to teach them that or let them pick that up on their own [real estate].

When we hire new staff, we hire new people with training in interior design, but basically we are hiring people to be salespeople. That is one of the transitions they have to make when they come to work for us, to realize though they are using their skills in assisting the consumers, helping them create the certain kind of look, but basically they are salespeople! . . . The average consumer today is not prepared to pay for interior design as an art, they just don't see the value as such. And when new people come here, I tell them that we are a retail sales outlet and that all our interior design people are especially knowledgeable, qualified, professional salespeople. And I emphasize that to them, that we provide service, that the service is essentially a free one that comes with the merchandise that we are selling. And if they are not prepared to sell, then I really don't have a place for them. . . . One of the problems with the courses on interior design is that they don't teach communication skills to the students. They are mostly all bad in that regard, some are a little better than others. Also, after the program, the graduates are not going to be out actually designing furniture and such. They are going to be working largely in retail establishments and to some extent in commercial settings, but basically in a business context. You want people who know how to react to people and who know what people are saying. You have to learn to be sensitive to other people and be able to pick up meanings from more than what they say. And that is something I think that is neglected in the university setting and the community college setting, because they are largely impersonal, austere settings [furniture].

PRIOR EXPERIENCE

When considering job applicants, it is important to distinguish novices from those with experience. Although generally preferred, experienced salespeople may be inaccessible for managers with tight budget limitations.

A problem is that if you could get someone who is dynamic, who has a lot of product knowledge, they're usually out of your price range. They can do better working somewhere else. Capable people are more expensive [women's clothing].

It's pretty well minimum wage, but we were budgeted to about 7% of sales for our salaries, so you would try to keep within those hours. So if you had a big week, you had certain hours that you could put towards another week, but time was measured in terms of dollars. If you were paying people more, you couldn't have them there for as long. So if you had two people and one you were paying a dollar more an hour, and they could do the same job, you would be better to get the lower-priced person for that time, because you could show greater efficiency on your books. . . . In a high-volume store, you're more willing to hire a cheaper younger person, someone to do more clerking, help people find their sizes, and ring up the sales, basically. Then, with the same budget, you could hire more people, take care of more customers. It's not quite that simple. There is some salesmanship in the high-volume store too. But in the lower-volume store, you need the better salespeople, someone able to sell them two or three things, to make your money. . . . We wanted people with experience, people who could sell more, but generally we ended up with younger people, because we couldn't get experienced people with the money we were hiring at. So we would get a lot of people working with us, getting experience and training, and then they would move on to another store where they would be getting more money. That was the continual story. . . . Your more expensive places, they would generally have better sales staff, because they are willing to pay them more [mixed clothing].

In discussing experience, it should not be assumed that novices are inexperienced in sales. If one considers applicants' lives at any point in time, it becomes apparent that a considerable amount of "anticipatory socialization" (Merton, 1957) may have taken place. Thus, in addition to children playing store, one finds numerous points at which people may be involved in selling prior to sales applications. For instance, youngsters may become involved in selling raffle tickets, chocolate bars, cookies, and other items to raise funds for their schools, organizations, charities, or their own pursuits.[8] Other experiences with sales reflect contacts with close friends and family members involved in saleswork.[9] Even when these people's interests are minimal, some awareness of sales routines is apt to emerge.

In some ways, even more important than people's experiences is some indication of their seriousness in pursuing careers in sales. Experienced workers are likely to be more adept at doing sales work, but they are also more likely to have accepted as appropriate the label of *salesperson*.

I prefer seasoned people. You have more of an idea of what to expect, fewer surprises, problems. They've been around, they know how to talk to people, they're more comfortable meeting strangers. It takes a while for a lot of the new people to get over that. . . . And the experienced people may have some existing contacts in the field if they've been in a similar product before, so that's good. Then too, you want someone who's in it as a career, prepared to take it more seriously, planning long term, who's accepted the idea [manufacture—industrial].

What you want is career people. Someone who's serious about selling. None of this, "Well, maybe I want to be this or that." All this overlapping stuff. You want someone who wants to make a career of selling. . . . The bottom line is, "Do you want to sell, or do you want to mess around" [mixed sales]?

Having outlined a set of concerns managers commonly express in hiring new salespeople, it seems advisable to consider the applicants they encounter. We will subsequently return to matters of determining payment and generating performance, but it is valuable to give some attention to those with whom managers may be expected to work.

The Applicants

When discussing prospective salespeople, it is important to note that a great many people have mixed attitudes toward sales work. Sales work is recognized as a legitimate means of earning money, but it is an activity held in low esteem by many. Thus reservations as well as attractions to saleswork are pertinent to understanding involvements. As indicated in Chapter 1, there are three main ways by which people become involved in situations. First, people may seek out situations they define as desirable. Second, they may envision particular involvements as means of solving existing problems (i.e., closure). And third, they may be recruited into situations by others. These elements may occur in any variety of combinations, but involvements are qualified by a fourth element, drift. This refers to people's sense of freedom from their usual obligations (including concerns with respectability). While these elements may be discussed in any order, it seems instructive to outline some reservations people may have about saleswork before discussing the routes of involvement.

RESERVATIONS

From discussions with vendors and observations of the general public, it appears that many people are reluctant to pursue careers in sales.

The origins of these reservations are unclear, but in addition to their own shopping experiences, people are likely to acquire orientations toward saleswork through their observations of, and interactions with, parents, friends, spouses, and others. Everyone's perspectives may be seen as shifting over time, but people generally seem to recognize that their resources are more limited than their desires (therefore it is to their advantage to be choosy) and merchants plan to make money on their dealings (ergo, buyer-vendor interests are not identical). Most purchases may be considered acceptable by those making them. But negative definitions from others and purchases defined as disappointing introduce elements of skepticism and negativism which may be generalized to subsequent situations. Likewise, experiences that buyers define as having been manipulative or pushy are apt to promote distancing from, and distrust of, salespeople in subsequent encounters. People generalize unevenly, but any perception of salespeople as (potentially) deceptive, manipulative, and aggressive may contribute to people's reluctance to enter sales work as a way of life.

I don't know where salesman became such a dirty word, but you look at the courses people are offering and they will use just about every other word than salesman. . . . I just don't see it, because you can have all the geniuses in the world inventing products and all the skilled manufacturing going on, but if you don't have a salesman moving that item, everything else ceases to be. I don't know if we are actually teaching people to look down on sales on a blackboard or just teaching us that attitude in more casual ways. But I know that there are very few salespeople who would want their children to go into sales and even probably fewer people overall who would be proud of their children if they were successful in the world of sales. They would rather have them doctors, lawyers, and teachers, and university professors, and such. And in sales, you can be very successful, living a good life-style and doing an interesting job, and yet they are looked down on. When you think about sales, it's so basic in terms of all areas of life and it just seems true for all different societies and throughout history [furniture].

Before being with this company, I saw selling as a slightly unprofessional job, a job as opposed to a profession. At one time, I would have thought of selling as trying to con somebody out of their money, or trying to convince them, etc. Now I don't look at it that way at all, because I understand what selling is, in my job. To me, it's looking after an individual's needs. . . . Showing them how they can get what they want. If they want to pay off their mortgage, if that's something they need, want, I show them how. I guess that's what selling is [investments].

Another element that may contribute to people's reluctance to become involved in sales work is its outreaching nature. Insofar as sales work may entail a great deal of public relations work, often with relative strangers, it may seen unnatural to people who define themselves as shy or reluctant to interact with strangers.

> When I first started into insurance, I had a lot of reservations. I thought, "My contacts, my friends, and family, there's not enough there, I'll go broke!" And then you wonder if you can approach people enough [insurance].

> If you would have told me five years ago that I would be doing sales, I wouldn't have believed you! I never thought I could do sales. My image of a salesman was that you had to be aggressive and so pushy. I just couldn't imagine doing it. . . . I still don't think I could do door-to-door, vacuum sales, something like that [publisher—books].

As the following discussions indicate, reservations appear to decrease when applicants attribute greater prestige to the company being considered; anticipate salary rather than commission; plan to work on a part-time and/or temporary basis only; define these positions as ones entailing greater technical skills or expertise; perceive these positions as entailing service, rather than sales; define company products as being "better quality"; perceive sales work to be more prestigious than other available options; define the clientele as more prestigious; and expect the clientele to seek them out rather than vice versa.

ATTRACTIONS (SEEKERSHIP)

Not all the images associated with sales work are negative. Thus, in addition to representing a means of making money, sales work may be seen as a relatively clean, and physically nondemanding activity, and as work that affords interaction with other people. Applicants may also define particular products, practitioners, or the clientele as especially interesting, denoting attractions to particular realms of sales activity.

> I got into sales because of the money. I had been in publishing, doing editorial work, and I just saw that the better money was in sales. What I like about sales work is that if you work hard at it, it can pay off much more for you than the other can. Also, when you're selling, it is a face-to-face relationship that you have with the people and so you learn more about them and about their situation than you would otherwise [promotions—magazine].

I thought it might be interesting to be in sales, and then when I saw this ad, for
computers, I thought I might give it a try. And up-and-coming field and all. . . . I
didn't want to do paperwork in an office, and for sure I didn't want to get stuck in
a factory. I like people, talking with them. And the money's good, better than in an
office somewhere [manufacture—computers].

Another attraction to sales for many is that they can work on a
part-time (or temporary) basis. This may represent a payroll advantage
to some businesses, but it also offers people who cannot and/or do not
want to assume extensive obligations as a means of earning money. As
many of these employees eventually do become full-time workers,
part-time (or short-term) arrangements may offset some of the initial
reservations these people have about doing saleswork.

I started in sales when I was 15, a part-time job. I had good bosses. They instructed
me on what to do and the right ways of doing things. So whatever I learned from
them, I learned well. And I've stuck with it. It's been good, for me. Interesting! A
fairly good career for me, put it that way. . . . I didn't have any goal in mind when
I started. It was a job, a way to make a little money. It didn't require that much
education, and it was easy for me. As long as you can talk, and well, I like to talk.
That'll help a lot. . . . I imagine I'll be doing it for a few years. At least I've no other
plans right now [cosmetics].

For a lot of people, sales is something to do right now. It's a clean job, not like at
a factory. You are dressed more nicely. The money's not good. Not like a factory.
If I wanted to make a lot of money, I would go to a factory. You'll make double
the money. You maybe suffer more in factory work, but the money is so much
better, and with the factory job, you don't spend as much money on clothes, shoes,
cosmetics. Your appearance is not important in the factory [shoes].

Some people specifically seek out sales positions after their high
school, college, or university careers. In other cases, however, sales
work is a second career, reflecting disenchantment with earlier pursuits.

I don't think that anyone really leaves school and says, "Here's my career. I'm
going into real estate." It's usually been some other profession and then there's
been a change in some point in their life-style. . . . It's a secondary thing. No one
really directs their life to go into that sort of thing. You'll get former teachers, people
from other retail businesses, people from management. . . . I had been in mortgag-
ing, which is related to real estate, and I had met a lot of people who were directly
in real estate, and I could see the potential of real estate. I could see that after one
made the initial investment in time and money, that one could get better returns.

And I wasn't feeling fulfilled where I was, so for me personally, it was a gamble, but a rather enjoyable one as it worked out. I had been reanalyzing my position and thought the change would be good for me [real estate].

When I went into sales, I was looking for something different to do. I had a university degree, but completely unrelated to sales. . . . I wasn't ready at that time to go back to university for more training, so I decided that something like this would be a learning experience, so I thought I would give it a try. . . . I had experience in music, but I had no experience in selling. But I liked music, and when the opportunity came for this job, I was delighted, because it was something I always wanted to do, to show organs, pianos [music].

NEEDING JOBS (CLOSURE)

Although sales represents only one of a number of work areas, many people account for their involvement in sales largely as a matter of needing a job (i.e., closure). Even in these cases, however, reservations and attractions remain significant.

I had a teaching degree, but I couldn't get a job. I had communication skills, and I thought I would be good in dealing with people, so I thought sales might be a good line to get into. I wasn't sure that I had the ability to sell. I knew that some people considered salesmen pushy and unprofessional, but I knew that is not the case. . . . And it was a very reputable company. . . . I had decided to change, that I would do sales rather than teach [manufacture—office equipment].

I needed a part-time job, well, any job actually. I went around looking in all the malls, and I kept asking and asking, and finally, after two months, I got a job at this other mall in a clothing store. And that was how it started. . . . I had no family or friends in sales. Nothing at all, so I pretty well had to go looking on my own. . . . I thought it would be interesting to do, meeting people and all. And I do enjoy it [women's clothing].

RECRUITMENT

Should businesses not have adequate access to desirable applicants, they may recruit prospects in a variety of ways. The major modes are those of media advertisements, employment agencies, employee contacts, and "staff stealing." Also noteworthy are those involvements seen as inadvertent by those assuming sales roles.

Media Advertisements

One of the easiest ways of accessing prospects is to advertise in the classified sections of newspapers, trade magazines, and the like.

We advertise in the gift magazines for agents. And we'll put notices on the bulletin boards at the trade shows. There, though, in both places, you'll be getting the people already in sales. I don't think people not in the gift lines would know about these. But in our case, we'd like someone who has an existing territory, contacts with the merchants [manufacture—giftware].

Employment Agencies

Another source of contacts for sales work are the public employment agencies and the private personnel offices.

The employment agencies get a lot of people coming through. You don't have to hire the people they send you, but you might as well have them working for you. Just tell them what you want [manufacture—industrial].

I started part time, my dad got me a job in a department store. . . . From there, I just kind of kept going with sales. And, of course, with the employment office, you get slotted very quickly, and to try to get out of that slot is something! So gradually, I kept on with sales [mixed sales].

Employee Contacts

Family members and acquaintances working in particular businesses may also recruit for those businesses. Not only may they provide inside tracks to company openings, but they may also give acquaintances a better sense of the realities of the workplace.

Often, you don't have to advertise. These guys have friends or people they know and they pass the word around. We don't just hire anybody they suggest, but if they look good, look like they'll fit in and do the job, we'll give them a try [mixed clothing].

A lot of the people we recruit are from our clientele. They may have a better understanding of what it's all about. However, if I recruit a number of people, and I'm good at recruiting, and I have some obvious organizational skills, it'll be to my benefit if I'm hoping to be selected as a manager. And then if I do become a manager, those people that I've recruited can belong to my division, and then I earn a percentage of their action. So that way, if you're an aggressive person and you want to go into management, it's to your advantage to recruit from the first day you're here. . . . Even if you're not in management, you still take an active role in recruiting. And you are paid if you recruit someone.... We're paid $___ for getting someone to come in for testing and $___ if they're hired.... I would look for someone who has a fair amount of discipline, who can manage their time properly. Obviously they need social skills, good listening is imperative! ... The majority of the people here were clients. We've pretty well all come from a client base.... When you get into this, you're into a very private part of a person's life, sometimes more private than sex, and you begin to develop a very close relationship and they begin to talk to you about things like their jobs, and whether or not they're unhappy or whatever, so it's kind of a natural thing to recruit from the client base. Those people have a little bit of understanding of what you do, and some of them are very excited and motivated into changing [investments].

Staff Stealing

Should suitable applicants not be otherwise available, or should employers have specific objectives in mind, they may head hunt or attempt to lure employees from other businesses.

They hustle you, tell you all the advantages of working with their agency. It's marvelous for your ego.... The real estate agencies will welcome you with open arms. It costs them virtually nothing to employ you, other than desk space and a bit of advertising money. And the advertising money is not lost, because it assumes that you've obtained a listing that needs advertising. And it's on the premise that all property eventually sells. So it's an investment, even if you're a rotten salesperson [real estate].

Ray is now with _____ . It's another computer company. He said that he became acquainted with a rep from this second company and this rep later offered Ray a better position with his company. Both Ray and his new boss made reference to "stealing" Ray away from the first company.... I've found this is a fairly common way of recruiting established salespeople, through the friendship networks of one's existing staff. These friendship networks often include competitors met while making calls, in clubs, and at conferences and trade shows [notes].

Inadvertent Involvements

Not unlike some of the owners who became involved in business as a result of other activities, a number of people in sales have taken rather indirect routes. Albeit denoting recruitment activities on the part of the employer, some sales positions have come about inadvertently from the salesperson's viewpoint.

I started out in engineering and ended up much more in sales than I expected. It's just been developing that way, increasing more it seems every year.... It's a high technology area, so it's a big help if you can speak the same language as the buyers. At first, I was at the trade shows to demonstrate, to consult, but now I'm spending more and more time in sales. Almost all my time, actually [manufacture—industrial].

My training had been in graphics. . . . When I started working for the paper, I never thought it would be related with sales at all, but I just enjoyed the creative aspects of the layouts and all and eventually it ended up with me in sales. Over time, the sales aspect became more evident [promotions—newspaper].

Sales Instruction

Reflecting managerial and employee concerns and experiences, attention now turns to the training of salespeople. This education assumes two, often interrelated, forms: formal and on the job training. What follows is a brief depiction of each.

FORMAL TRAINING PROGRAMS

The formal training programs offered by businesses vary greatly both in extensiveness and emphasis. Typically, it is the larger companies (and especially those dealing in more technical-complex product areas) that have more extensive training programs. Larger companies seem concerned with providing standardized instruction, while those dealing with more complex products (e.g., insurance, computers, chemicals) intend that adequate technical competence be attained by their salespeople. In most cases, however, even when explicit training is provided in sales techniques, this is often embedded within material pertaining to product knowledge, company history, organizational structure, career opportunities, billing systems, refund policies, and the like.

We have a two-day program teaching them how to do a little selling, how to approach people, do a little suggestive selling, and how to run the cash register and all. . . . Then, if they move up in the company, we'll have more of these two- or three-day sessions, more on management instruction, that sort of thing. . . . Actual selling, though, I don't know how much they really learn about that. We do emphasize suggestive selling and especially the public relations, customer service aspect of it, though, and we do have training films and video tapes so they can watch themselves and others doing sales. So some techniques . . . We try to get the people to stay away from the, "Can I help you?" approach, but I think a lot fall back into that [department store].

In addition to, or in lieu of, in house training packages, some companies enroll their staff in courses being offered by others.

I found the sales courses really helpful, especially the one that _____put out, a three-day course. A very intensive course just on how to communicate better with your customers and it really works! Instead of wasting a lot of their time and your time, you can be more effective, faster [promotions—newspaper].

A lot of companies will enroll people in these sales courses. Spend a few days in extensive training, and they then try to apply this to their own situation. It's a fair bit of money, but they figure that now they know how to sell. And they didn't have to be bothered training these people themselves or they didn't think they could do as good a job [manufacture—industrial].

Suppliers may also provide training for those involved in promoting their products.

The different manufacturers will sometimes invite you and your staff down for a product knowledge day, so we'll sometimes send some of our people off to that. . . . But you'll have problems getting everyone together for these things, because someone has to watch the shop [luggage].

The schools the (cosmetics) companies have are useful. They give you new ideas on how to show their products, give you some samples, demonstrations, things like that [department store].

Without endeavoring to assess formal training programs, two practical shortcomings become readily apparent. These involve the perceived relevance of the program on the part of the salespeople and their abilities to apply what they've learned to the situations they encounter.

From my course in sales, I learned the "how to" aspects of sales, but what I found the hardest part, and what you have to learn on the job, by doing it, is the relationships! Nobody actually tells you how it is. Nobody does that [wholesale—giftware]!

I don't think salesmanship courses help you that much, because you have to look at it this way. Each time you are making a call, you are facing a new situation. You have to approach this situation carefully, openly. You have to adapt. There is always something different about the people, or about the products, and you have to approach people differently. You can't just go approaching everybody the same way. You have to try and figure the people out, try to understand what is going on in this situation. No two people are the same. . . . So it's an ongoing adjustment, and you have to know when to be a philosopher and when to bullshit with the people, and when to sit around and have a drink with them. And you have to be able to size up the prospective clients. You have to try and keep the advantage over him, not overpowering the person. You have to be able to read the situation [manufacture—industrial].

Manuals, Brochures, et al.

In addition to verbal communication, businesses may also use written material as instruction devices. These commonly assume the forms of manuals, brochures, and newsletters.

Serving as instruction books, manuals may be used to complement training programs or in lieu of these. Manuals may be used to outline company history, policies, and organization; give product knowledge and information about the competition; provide information about customers and styles of prospecting; elaborate on selling techniques and means of dealing with common objections; and suggest tips for maintaining enthusiasm. Manuals assume a variety of formats, and as with the material contained, seem limited only by the desires and imagination of the designers. As with other training programs, manuals tend to be more common among the larger companies and those dealing with more complex products.

As part of your training, they give you this book to read, about this thick [half an inch], and they want you to remember it all. You're tested on it, a little test, not really that difficult. . . . It [manual] deals with the company, its policies and organization, and the qualities they want in people in sales and management. . . . There's tips on how to sell, deal with customers. It's very complete! But I don't know who remembers it all. And even if you do remember what's in it, do you put it into practice [discount department store]?

We don't have any manuals now. We used to have manuals, but we found that they weren't all that helpful [manufacture—industrial].

Brochures (also fact sheets, catalogues) provided by suppliers represent another basis of product information.

You get all these brochures from the manufacturers, describing their products. They contain a lot of information, some of them, but they're not exciting reading. So often you learn about the products as you're going over these brochures with the customer when they've asked you some questions. They might be useful there [department store].

In addition to providing news about company operations, staff situations, and the like, newsletters and other circulars may also be used to provide product information and sales tips.

In a bigger firm, you get these newsletters. Ours comes out once a month. They have information on what the company's doing, news of expansions, openings, things like that. You also get cartoons, tips on how to sell things, who got promoted. Sort of a gossip sheet too [shoes].

LEARNING ON THE JOB

As with formal instruction, on-the-job learning involves both product knowledge and sales techniques. In addition to learning from managers, co-workers, and suppliers, salespeople also acquire product information and sales techniques from competitors and customers.

Acquiring Product Knowledge

Denoting information pertaining to product origins, compositions, applications, and limitations, product knowledge not only represents a means of providing better service, it also generates confidence (and effectiveness) on the part of the salespeople involved.

After I knew more about the instruments and felt that I could handle them better, I began feeling much more confident in approaching the customers. I've never had any difficulty talking to people, this sort of thing, but it was a matter of, "Do I know enough to tell these people?" And on top of it all, you also have the competition coming in and asking you questions, as if they were a customer. And they can tell if you don't know what you're talking about quite easily. And you'll get people coming in who may have one of the models at home or maybe shopped around quite a bit, and they may know quite a bit more than you. It can get somewhat embarrassing when you start to realize that they may know more than you about the items in the store [music].

You have to know your equipment, what it can do, and also the competition. They're (customers) putting out a lot of money and they want to know. . . . There, you have your product information, books, manuals, but a lot of it you learn as you go along, as you're on the job showing your systems, going to trade shows [manufacture—computers].

Acquiring Sales Techniques

For most salespeople, even in larger businesses, learning to sell occurs primarily on the job, often with a minimum of explicit instruction.

When someone comes in, usually the first thing you get them to do is to help out straightening things in the store, getting your racks back in order after the customers had been through them. But basically with the new staff, it was sink or swim. You're thrown into it, and you're expected to take it from there. The cashiers had to be trained on the cash register. . . . We had some staff meetings where sales techniques were discussed, where I would be talking about how to sell, things to watch for, how to approach a customer, little stories about things that happened to you, how not to insult the customer, but nothing systematic. . . . Your training was better in the small stores, because you would be more aware of your staff, what they were doing. So you would have more of a chance to show them things, talk to them about sales and all. In the larger store, you sort of lose track of the people easier, so since we had no training program to speak of, you would be in a better position if you started out in a small store. . . . The same thing with managing, you would be better to start in a small store, where you have a chance to learn things, more basic things and then go on to the larger store [mixed clothing].

We had a training program where you are given some self-training sales materials, demonstrations on how to show the machines, how they work, and then some in-group training on sales techniques, in salesmanship. The formal training was stronger than the field training. We had very little field training. For the first day in the field, you went along with someone more experienced, but it's a very tough business. They don't give you any allowances for any sort of weaknesses. You go, and you make it, and that's it. . . . You learn to sell in the field, by your mistakes. You learn on your own. . . . That's because the people who train you formally are very good, but then you're with people from all over the country. Then you have the people at these various branches and they do not have the time, or they do not have the training, to properly train you. . . . In part, the managers are people who have become good salesmen, not necessarily good trainers. That's their reward for doing well in sales. . . . The problem was that the manager also had his own territory too, so he had a problem in time that way. Then too, some of the people had their own method of selling which may or may not have been in accordance with what the company was trying to get the new people to learn, so they might not talk about personal styles there. But it's a very personal thing, and what works for someone may not work for you [manufacture—office equipment].

On-the-job training seems facilitated most when the new people are located within apprenticeship situations. This may be by design or may reflect emergent relationships, but it offers newcomers more complete understandings of the situation.

Usually with the new salesperson, I try to make sure that they are organized, that they have some kind of routine. You don't want them running all over the place. You help them plan their time, so that they can make more efficient use of their calls that they are making. . . . With a new salesperson, I try to discuss their calls as these are happening, and I want to know what happened, "How did they go?" If you're losing sales, "What went wrong?" A lot of times, salespeople will come back to you and say, "The client wasn't interested," or "They didn't like the color," or they will come to you and say, "The last two were not good prospects." You try to get them over that. You ask them, "Why is that? Why aren't they interested?" . . . "They didn't like the color? What is the objection? Would they have bought it if it had a white handle on it instead of a red handle?" . . . "Were they worried about the size? Did you try to see what we could do with fitting it in?" . . . You can't assume that because someone says they aren't interested, or that they don't like something about what you have got, that you couldn't make that sale." That's something you try to get new people used to [manufacture—appliances].

If someone takes a liking to you, someone in the department where you're working, it makes it easier, I think. Like this one supervisor, she helped me out a lot, especially when I made mistakes. Also, she would explain things to me, help me, show me easier ways of doing things, pointing out things you ought to do to keep the department looking good [department store].

LEARNING FROM OUTSIDERS

In addition to learning from those involved with the company on either a formal or informal basis, a significant amount of learning to do sales work is derived from contact with outsiders. Thus, in addition to the knowledge that one may have acquired from previous sales work, one may also learn from other vendors, including the competition.

You get it both ways, actually more than that, at the craft shows. You get some exhibitors, competitors who try to avoid you. Others, though, they'll come around, try to find out how you do things. Some will tell you how they do things, give you tips on suppliers, things like that. So you get quite a mix that way. Usually, though, the more different your product, the more willing you are to discuss things with the other crafters [crafts].

I find I learn a lot from the other vendors at the trade shows. Their products may be different, but a lot of the problems are the same, so the trade shows are good that way, too [manufacture—industrial].

Although often considered "uninformed," customers should not be overlooked as a source of instruction.

Often the buyers [customers] will tell you about features of the product you might not have thought of yourself. They'll maybe look at things a little differently, or maybe have other uses for your products that you never thought of. So with the next one, you can tell them about all these features. . . . You also learn about the problems they're having with things, see where you might be able to improve your products. So they're good that way [manufacture—industrial].

You learn their objections, so that's something you can work on when the next ones come in. The ones that come in before, they're practice for the ones that come in later [mixed clothing].

Determining Payment

Another task facing management is that of determining payment for sales work. The following discussion indicates not only the range of options managers face in determining payment, but also the ways in which salespeople view these options. In this sense, straight salary and straight commission represent little more than starting points.

SALARY

Insofar as a regular salary entails less risk than does commission sales and is more predictable, most salespeople favor the consistency of regular paychecks.

I've worked on commission, straight commission, and it can be tough! Especially when you're first starting out. With a salary, it may not be as much, but it's regular. That's what people like about it [mixed sales].

Salaried salespeople also tend to see themselves as less aggressive and more team oriented than their counterparts on commission.

A difference between us and some of the other men's shops is that most of the shops pay salary plus commission, where we just get salary. I think it makes a difference.

They're probably more aggressive in their sales. Also you're in more competition among the staff there, because of the commission. Here we can work more as a team, helping one another out, without people getting concerned about money and hurt feelings [men's clothing].

We run our sales on a salary basis. I don't like commission because then I think you tend to oversell too much. You're not providing enough service with the sales. It seems good at the time, because you're making your money on the commission, but that may be the first and last thing you will sell that person. They will remember you and you will be someone they will shy away from dealing with later on [manufacture—industrial].

When sales take longer to develop, salary becomes a more feasible option.

In our business, it may take six months or a year or two to develop an order. If you're on commission, you can't handle it. There is just too much pressure, so we just don't deal with people on a commission basis. The way that I look at it, too, is that if you are a sales representative, you're there for that company's [buyer] benefit. Your job is to give them the product that best fits their situation [manufacture—industrial].

When paid by salary, those in commercial and industrial settings usually fare better than their retail counterparts. Salaries in retail sales work typically do not compare favorably with union factory work. The following extracts provide other indications of salary levels in retail work.

Managing in a store, in a lot of stores, does not pay well. It's okay for a married woman who is having some money come in from her husband, where her job is the extra. But if it's a man, trying to support a family, he would be a lot better off working in a factory as a laborer. The men's shops and the women's shops, they're much the same that way. Salespeople don't get paid well. The manager makes a little more than the other staff, but not that much, a few bucks a day for all the headaches. The job is good for high school girls, for a young woman living at home, for a married woman with another income coming in, people like that. But if you have a lot of expenses or you want to support a family, it's going to be tight, really tight. . . . It's a good work experience, but if you're trying to support yourself, like I am, well, you'll just be making it. I'm not starving, mind you, but I really have to watch my buying. So when I see people buying some of the items in our store, I just wonder, "Where do they get the money from?" It just amazes me! . . . You get a lot of customers who come in and say, "Boy you've got a lot of nice things, here. You must buy a lot of things here!" But you don't. You don't have the money!

A lot of nice things come in the store, and you unpack them, "Oh, that's nice!",
and you put them on the shelf, and walk away. And that's the way it's got to be,
given my financial situation. Even with your discount, you can only get so much.
Now if you're living at home, where it doesn't cost you much for room and board,
that's different. You can buy a lot more. You've got a lot of surplus money.
Otherwise, you can work in a store and not shop in stores much. You don't have
that luxury. Long-distance phone calls, fancy dinners, entertaining, that has to go
by the wayside. I have some priorities, say wanting to look nice, not especially
fashionable. So that, and the basics, that's pretty well it. You can see a lot of nice
things, but that's as far as they go [shoes].

If money's important, you can usually make more money in the factory, but it
depends on what factory work you get. . . . It depends if you were comparing it
with a top paying factory job or what. A top paying factory job would be much
better than almost any retail job you could get, even if you've been working there
for a few years. You would have to move up pretty high in the organization to have
any hope of making that much. Now if you compare retail work with the mini-
mum-wage type of factory, then you're much better off in retail. The work is much
easier, it's much cleaner, it's socially more advantaged, and you're not doing shift
work, like in the factory, working nights, and it's a crummy job all around. It's
more prestigious for a female to work in a store. It's a nice clean way of making
money. It's respectable, acceptable, like being a secretary [discount department
store].

COMMISSION SALES

The following discussion outlines aspects of commission work as this
pertains to percentages and volumes; distributive justice; uncertainty,
risk, and hard feelings; and independence. Subsequently, attention will
be given to a variety of salary-commission compromises.

Percentages and Volumes

Since the percentages that those on commission receive for sales can
vary considerably, unit costs and volumes of sales are critical in determining one's take-home pay.

You can make better money on commission, although what you get paid on
commission can vary quite a bit with your product. It might vary from ½% to 35%.
Or if you're selling goods for yourself, there is really no limit to the sort of
commission one might make on a particular item. But usually, if you are working
for a company, then it's some place between ½% to 35% and more likely
10%-15%. . . . You can also draw against wages with a lot of companies, but usually

your better commissions come when your draw against wages isn't there, or when it's less [manufacture—appliances].

The big money is in industrial sales. It doesn't take any more effort to sell 500 units than to sell 50, but your payoff is a lot greater, so that's where the real advantage is, in industrial sales. . . . Selling to a factory, your commission percentage is less, but you make it up on the volume [manufacture—industrial].

Distributive Justice

Compared to salaried positions, commission sales are seen by many as approximating "distributive justice" (Homans, 1958), wherein one's outcomes are in proportion to one's efforts.

Until I got into car sales, I never liked commission sales. I never thought it was for me. But I found myself sort of getting lazy towards the end (of my last job), and part of it was that I wasn't rewarded for working hard. . . . My biggest regret was that I didn't get into it [auto sales] sooner. It's a very lucrative business, there's a lot of money in it, but you have to work very hard at it. But it's one of those businesses, where the harder you work, the more you get paid, because it's on commission. So it's worthwhile that way. . . . A good car salesman doesn't want advancement. If you go into management, you're not on a commission basis anymore, and a good salesman will make more than management. So any good salesman will want to stay where he is, in sales. . . . It's the money that motivates most salesmen, and the money is on the floor! You can't get away from it [auto].

The best part about sales is that if you're good, you make a lot. You can make more than the boss! But then, if you're making too much money, they would like to redesign your job at that point. What they would like to do is to take you off commission, and put you on salary. Maybe give you a new job title, sell the salesman on a title, become a sales manager, stable income, a bonus. When it gets to that point, you might be better to get another job [manufacture—industrial].

Uncertainty, Risk, and Hard Feelings

Should returns not be commensurate with effort or expectations, those on commission are likely to experience additional pressure.

My main reservation was with commission. I had been on salary before, and that was a main change, from a salaried employee position. And one's thinking has to change, because selling is more emotional than doing office work. In selling you have to adapt to the other person far more than you would in management. In management, they have to do more adapting to you. . . . And with commission, it's more of a gamble! And that's one reason that a lot of people, with a lot of potential for selling, do not go into selling. You get used to the security that a lot of people want or feel that they cannot get out of that. . . . With commission, it's either feast or famine, where you're making a lot of money or you're making none [real estate]!

I find July and August bad months. Also, the middle of December to end of January pretty well, that's a bad time. Nobody's interested before Christmas. They're sort of spaced out, because the holidays are coming, and then after Christmas, they're feeling a little sluggish. And they're both important times to the family man, because he takes his holidays in July, August, and he's got the expenses of the holidays to get back, not necessarily gone over his head or anything, but he wants to have a holiday like everyone else. And then at Christmas, you like to have as good a Christmas as everyone else. . . . And during the rest of the year, the money you make is the money you make. . . . If you're doing fantastic for six months, you're going to be living to that level. Then, if sales go down in the next six months, can you cut back to that level? And you don't know from month to month what your income will be. That is the frustrating aspect of it. The positive aspect is that you can make more money on commission. The negative is that's it's tougher on the whole family. And if you're down, you can't sell too well. If you're down, you can't deal with people effectively. . . . It's supposed to be the great motivator, because you're only limited to the amount of effort you put into your sales. . . . However, if you're out there humming and hustling, and nothing comes through, it can be very negative [manufacture—industrial].

The uncertainty of commission sales seems especially devastating on new salespeople. While veteran salespeople can draw upon a previously developed clientele and may have accumulated resources and confidence, newcomers are typically not so advantaged.

It scares you at first, though, because if you've never been in commission work, you feel that there is no security there. And there isn't, because you can have a bad time! I've seen myself go for a couple or three weeks and not sell a thing. And it gets you down. You wonder what you're doing wrong. And the way I look at it is that if you don't sell the guy, he's gone out the door, the salesman has done something wrong. Somebody else will sell him. And unfortunately, you don't sell everyone. . . . You can go through a dry period, and that's what scares you! If a newcomer in the car business happens to hit that dry period when he's starting, it can be very, very hard on him. It can be very discouraging for someone new in the business, and then they start to think that there is no money to be made and they leave [auto].

There's a very high turnover in real estate sales. . . . It takes six months before you can expect to start making money, reasonable money. There's going to be a period there of frustration, and through lack of knowledge or confidence, you're going to blow deals. And there's the competition there. . . . So you have to be self-disciplined, self-motivated, and a lot of people fail in the first six months [real estate].

Hard feelings. People on straight salary may be very concerned about who gets credit for the sale, vis-à-vis performance ratings, but even smaller commissions can be major sources of resentment.

With a 3% commission [plus salary] you'll get $15 for $500 in sales, but it adds up over the week, and you take it seriously! You can see the commissions adding up over the day. You take it pretty seriously! People can get right ornery sometimes over it. It can go towards covering your meals for the week, your bus fares, things like that, so it's good that way. You do get to rely on it, so you watch your totals, because that's where your commission comes from [shoes].

If it gets busy, you can get some commission-stealing there, too. Say you get a customer going on a suit, and while they're looking at it thinking about it, you start with someone else. Then, if someone else comes along, another salesman, he might just finish up that first sale for you, complete your sale, and he gets the commission for it. . . . That's bad if someone steals a sale on you [men's clothing].

Commission is less of an issue when the salespeople are busy, but slow times and indecisive shoppers represent particular trouble spots as salespeople worry about others "grabsting" their sales.[10]

Sometimes, you'll have someone who says they'll "be back" and maybe asks you to hold something for her until she makes up her mind. Well, there, that's your customer and you don't want anyone else ringing up that sale! That's the commission that you've worked on. It can be a problem sometimes, especially with this one part-time girl. I've had to approach her about it, "Look, I'm the one who's putting in the work, and I'm not getting the credit." I told her, "If I'm waiting on someone else or someone else is waiting on someone else, back off! Don't interfere with other people's sales. I'm on commission!" It can get very aggravating that way, but if you don't speak up, they will take advantage of you. That's where I don't like commission, but it gives you incentive. If you don't work, you don't get paid [women's clothing.

Split deals can be a problem, where a customer is essentially sold on the car by one person and then comes back and another salesman writes up the order, because the first man is not in or the customer hasn't mentioned that he was talking to the first person. . . . Some salespeople will work in sort of a partnership, where if they're working in shifts, they will look after one another's sales. If I'm not in when you return, ask for _____ . He'll take care of you. . . . But this is something you have to work out beforehand, and then follow up on your arrangements. But it can be good if you can work things out with a buddy like this, but that's not always possible, and then you can get into situations where you have some hard feelings among the salesmen [auto].

Equalizing outcomes. Recognizing the sorts of dilemmas just discussed, some managers implement forms of turn taking in attempts to achieve more equalized distributions of commission.[11]

When it's really busy, the commission is not a problem, because there's plenty to go around. But if it gets slow, you have to be more careful. There, you might take turns with the customers, or if one is really ahead of the other, where there's two on duty, you might back off and give the other person a chance to catch up. Maybe take a break, but back off. Give the other person a chance to catch up. . . . That is another place the manager has the advantage, because she can get you doing a lot of other things than selling when it gets slow. They can get more of the sales for themselves. There are some managers who have reputations for doing that! They are famous for doing that, for eliminating the sale staff from selling when things are slow, getting more commission for themselves [shoes].

It differs from place to place. In this other place, we worked on what we called the "up system," where salespeople had their business cards, and when a customer came in, the salesman whose card was on top would get him and then his card would go to the back and the next customer would go to the man whose card had been second in the pile. . . . Here we work on the "honor system," where everyone tries to take no more than their fair share. It seems to work better than the up system. First, if on the up system the salesman goes to the can [washroom] or to the service area, everyone is running around looking for him, and "Who's up?, Who's up?" and the customer is standing around waiting, possibly feeling embarrassed because the whole group is running around looking for this one man. And sometimes, you get a run of people, so you can come up much more quickly than you thought, so you don't feel relaxed the same way as with the honor system [auto].

Should the selling take place in the field, managers may strive for equity by dividing the market into territories that seem more even in their potential:[12] They may also allow people to trade territories in order to achieve mixes they find more consistent with their personal preferences and life-styles.

Some territories are better than others. You do better in some places and you like the way some places are laid out better, where it's more convenient to get around, so you will prefer some places over others. . . . There's some trading going on, and

there's some people are in a better position to get what they want. But you can't
keep switching reps around, so those kinds of things affect your territories [publisher—books].

Everyone has a given geographical area, so when you start, you are assigned a
territory. So you work at that, trying to build it up. Now, when someone leaves, the
people who are there already, they can request this territory, a territory that they
think is better than the one that they have now [manufacture—office equipment].

When newcomers are involved, one way of nullifying some of the
pressure of commission sales is to provide them with some existing
accounts.

We work with lists. And if you are a new person coming in, they give you a list of
people to service. . . . Everyone has a list, and you call on those that you have on
your list. Say someone else has _____ (on his list), well, I can't walk in on
them. . . . But when you're given a list, you call on those people, introducing
yourself as the person servicing that list. Find out how things are going. . . . And
from your list, if you see that you've got _____ and they've been doing
$100,000 in advertising with your station a year, you can pretty well figure out
how much commission you're going to be making from that one company on your
list [promotions—radio].

When someone new starts in a territory, you turn over the listing of the regular
customers, the previous customers, and tell them to stay with these people and see
how many new customers they can get [manufacture—industrial].

Independence

As salespeople work more extensively on straight commission, they
achieve a sense of independence that is more akin to that attained by
the entrepreneurs discussed in Chapter 2. For many practical purposes,
those selling on a straight commission basis may be seen as being in
business for themselves.

When you're on straight commission, it's like you've got your own business in a
lot of ways. You have to pay all your expenses, keep all your bills for tax purposes,
things like that, all your travel expenses. . . . Also, you budget your time. Work
your own hours. And you can pick and choose the places you want to hit, at least
in some lines [promotions—signs].

I operate on a straight commission, 10% for retail sales, and 5% to 7% for
wholesalers. Since the retailers generally don't deal on as large a scale as a

wholesaler, if you get a wholesaler, you try to keep them happy. . . . I wouldn't be in this business if it wasn't to make money, and the wholesalers are your more profitable customers, so you do try to keep them happy. . . . Out of my commission I pay for all my own expenses, my car, my office, plane fares, motel rooms, meals, all my own expenses. That is how it is when you're an agent. . . . I prefer to work for myself. I find I can have a better living that way, I would rather be in business for myself [manufacture—giftware].

COMPROMISES

In order to attract prospects by offering salaries and still generate sales incentives by offering commission, companies may develop a variety of compromise arrangements. Particularly noteworthy in this sense are draws against commission; salary plus commission; spiffs; bonuses; and side benefits.

Draws Against Commission

Draws against commission provide salary structures for people on commission. Normally denoting amounts less than average commission, draws can be very important tools in attracting new people and maintaining their continuity through what typically are slow starts. When draws against commission programs include veteran salespeople as well, it provides a budgetary hedge against seasonal slow times and personal slumps.

For the first few months, you're on salary. They give you a draw against your commission. If you don't earn that much, you still get paid, and if you're over, the excess goes into an account for you. But if you're not making your own way, there's going to come a point where they're going to want to let you go [insurance].

I prefer to work on commission. I sell well. I like commission, especially if you can draw against commission, because then if you have a bad week or month, it's not like you're out of it [appliances].

Salary Plus Commission

Companies with salary plus commission arrangements typically use the salary to provide security to those who want something coming in on a regular basis and the commission as an incentive to promote sales. Compared to straight commission, the risk (to the employee) is reduced, but generally so are the potential earnings.

We get our basic salary and then we get 3% commission on our sales. . . . If you really want to hustle, you can make more, but if you want to make a lot more than the others, you would really have to push, because with a 3% sales commission you would have to sell a lot more [department store].

Here, it's salary and commission. What I like about the salary is that it keeps you going between issues. And then the commission, that is basically your extra. We are paid commission on the basis of the number of pages we obtain, so basically we're trying to sell space [promotions—magazine].

Spiffs

Denoting another variant of commission, spiffs (also PMs—push money, premium money), refer to the practice of paying salespeople extra for selling particular items. Payment may be on a flat rate (e.g., $5 per unit) or a percentage of the item cost. These premiums may be used with any other form of payment, but are employed as special inducements for staff to sell older, slower moving, overstocked, or higher-profit merchandise.[13]

We have spiffs, especially around Christmas. Say we have some watches. They might be older watches, or we might have gotten a deal on them, we got them on "Sale" from the manufacturer. Then we might put a spiff on them, where the employees could make, say 5%, on all their sales of these watches [jewelry].

The first thing you do, when you're hired someone is take them into the storage area and introduce them to the spiff section, "If you want to make money, you just go through here and learn every shoe that's in this section. It's [money] not in the new shoe section!" That's the first thing you do. Then you show them the regular stock, explain how the inventories run. . . . And [from] there, basically, if you think you're any good, you try to build a little you out of the new salesperson   Some of the spiffs will get you an automatic set fee, say $2. On the others, you get a percentage, say 10%-20%, but the manager [also] makes more or less on the spiffs in the end, depending on how successful he's been at the end of the year getting spiffs sold in his store. . . . In that way, you're almost in business for yourself. . . . And between managers, you buy and sell spiffs between us. You'll have certain areas that are really good for certain kinds of shoes, especially if the people are getting a good deal on them [shoes].

Other spiffs originate with suppliers who, in an attempt to gain an edge on the competition, offer financial incentives to salespeople pushing their lines.

Say we want to get more action on a given product or line, we often put spiffs on
them for the store's employees. . . . It's different from knocking off a couple of
dollars for a "sale," at the retail level, because the employees have an incentive to
push your line. That's something we'll do for the employees, the stores too
[manufacture—hardware].

They (suppliers) will also have spiffs. For each mattress you sell, you might get
$5, and while it is good for the mattress company, the staff can make money at it
too. But it's really bad for the consumer, because no matter what mattress might
really be the one they need, the one they [salespeople] are going to feature for you
will be the one with the additional incentive [furniture].

Bonuses

Combined with other means of payment, bonuses may be used to
promote long-term planning, team work, and loyalty. Usually, bonuses
are paid on overall sales totals (or profits) generally a seasonal or yearly
basis. They may be defined on individual as well as team sales totals,
but tend to be implemented at management levels more frequently than
at staff levels.

Most of our managers are on salary plus bonus arrangement. . . . It depends on how
much profit your store makes, not necessarily how much business you do, depending on your overhead. Your rent, your electricity, your heat, your staff. That can
vary in every city. And this all affects the bottom line, and before there's any profit
sharing, everything is taken off. . . . Profit sharing is a bonus that's paid once a year,
at the end of the year, based on the profit of the store over the whole year [hobby].

Pharmaceutical companies are mostly on salary and bonus. The bonus can be paid
individually or on a group basis. There, the whole division's sales would be the
determining factor. You're working as a team in terms of the bonus. . . . There can
be pressure too, if your territory isn't doing as well as you think it should. Usually
the guys are pretty good, understanding, unless they think you're slacking. Then
you'll hear about it. Management doesn't have to tell you. The guys will tell you
to pull up your socks. And you don't want to let the guys down, and you don't want
to let yourself down, so there's pressure there [manufacture—pharmaceutical].

Side Benefits

In addition to salaries, commissions, and the like, salespeople may
receive other forms of payment. While some benefits such as merchandise discounts promote staff shopping, these other perks may make the
position more attractive overall.[14]

We gave the employee 30% [discount on purchases], more on some things than others. Up to 50%, especially on new goods that we wanted people to wear in the store, to promote that way [mixed clothing].

The demonstrators are considered an income benefit. They have to declare that on their income tax. I allocate the cars, and the way that I do it is that the better salespeople get the better cars. So if someone wants a better car, they have to sell more, so there's some incentive there. . . . . If you see a salesman with a really fancy car from this place, you know that he's doing really well in sales. It may be different in other places, but that is how we do things here [auto].

Generating Performance

Effectively, everything managers do, including planning, monitoring, delegating, negotiating, hiring, training, and developing payment programs, can affect performance. Although this chapter only scratches the surface with regards to coaching and defining performance, these topics merit some early attention.

COACHING

Regardless of the salary arrangements, managers face the task of encouraging dedication in the face of the ongoing obstacles and disappointments their staff encounter in dealing with customers, co-workers, or their home lives.

The sales manager's job is to motivate his staff, to maintain their enthusiasm. He has to sell them on selling their products. He can't make them feel good, and he can't make them sell, but he can sell people on selling! The staff will all have their highs and lows, and there are times when you feel you can't get any lower than doing sales. . . . He has to be able to pick up on the salesman's problems, help him work his way out of slumps, his problems. He has to figure out what motivates that salesman. Is it a house, a home, more recognition from the boss or his fellow salesmen when he makes a sale? Is it that he wants more say in the way you're doing sales? Maybe he doesn't like his territory, maybe you could solve some of the problems by giving him a new territory. It's selling! It's the sales manager selling his men on selling. You've got to find out what will put the spark, the energy, the drive back in his sales approach [manufacture—industrial].

Your sales staff are most important, because without a good sales staff, you've got nothing. Your money comes in from your sales staff selling something. If they don't sell, you can't pay your bills, your salaries. . . . A manager must be able to get along with his staff. He's got to treat his staff like gold. And he's got to feel that they are almost superior to him. Not quite, but he's got to realize that without them, he can't exist. . . . He's got to be able to keep them up. And he's got to know the business inside out, the likes and dislikes of the people, so he orders the right products. He's got to know what sort of money he can accept on a certain deal, and still give the salesman a fair commission. And above all, the salesman has got to be able to trust him, that they're getting a fair shake from the manager [auto].

Viewed in this manner, managers may be likened unto coaches and counselors. And in addition to resolving the problems salespeople may have as individuals, the manager is also faced with the task of maintaining smooth working relations among the staff as a group.

You also want a staff who will get along with one another. If there's disputes, that's not good for anyone, and it'll spill over into the way the customers get treated. So it's not good there either. So you have to watch how you dole out the jobs, and you can't be petty, because there's a lot of little things that never work out evenly, and you have to be understanding with one another. That's another reason I don't like commission, because there, you get people being more petty. We have to watch that you balance out the customers, so that one person isn't always making better commission than the others [shoes].

You'll have people at work, and they might be good workers, but they're constantly upset about things. You just can't satisfy them, they just have a bad disposition on life. If they didn't get their break first, they'll be upset about that. They would immediately think that there's favoritism there. Or, if a few people on cash get to go on the floor, and they're not one of them, they'll get upset about that. They just have this whole attitude that they're being picked on. These are difficult people, because they cause trouble for other people. They gripe and gripe, and they get other people going, dissatisfied. So they can make managing tough [department store].

DEFINING PERFORMANCE

Sales totals provide only one indication of performance. However, since they represent the quickest and easiest method of assessing performance, they often assume considerable significance in ratings of both salespeople and their managers.

Financially, if your totals are up, you're having a really good day in sales. That's what the company considers a great day. They really don't care what you feel like [men's clothing].

The bottom line is, "How much did you sell?" And, if you sell more than the next guy, head office is going to think you're the better salesman. They don't really know what you do all day, so that's how they gauge things [manufacture—industrial].

They figure volume of sales relative to your overall costs, and if you have a better ratio than some other managers, then you're more likely to get the bigger store when it becomes available. That's a big thing in moving up. Can you kick the sales ratio up from where it was [giftware]?

As might be anticipated, companies paying salespeople on a commission basis are most attuned to individual sales figures.

We keep close track of our sales, absolutely! How many deals we made as a group, what they were, what each individual's sales were, for months at a time, and each day of the year, so we can compare how we're doing from last year at this time, who sold what, that sort of thing [auto].

In any line of sales, the very bottom line is whether or not you're selling. Everything you do for a client, the servicing, the little extras that you do, like if they're having a grand opening, actually going out and helping them with that. All those little things in the end help increase their confidence in you, help to make you get along better with them and in the end they will continue to buy. And that's what management looks at. You've got a budget (target) and you've got to hit that. If you're not hitting that budget, they're going to want to know why. If you're selling well, then you're doing your job. . . . Second to that is attitude. If you try to be up, try to be positive. If you don't bitch or complain, which is so unproductive, they will also see that [promotions—radio].

In some settings, little record is kept of personal sales totals, but concerns with sales totals are by no means limited to those in commission settings.

They keep track of our sales, so you can see how much you've been selling last week or over the past few months, things like that, and how well the other people are doing on their sales, and what the store's goals are in sales for the next little while or in the future. . . . The store wants us to sell so that your wages work out to 10% of your sales at least [department store].

As long as the overall sales meet company expectations, little attention may be given to how the salespeople or managers are spending their time. Should performance become problematic on either an individual or team basis, however, those involved may be asked to provide more information on their style of operation.

Most companies say, "We don't want quantity, we want quality calls." In other words, "Don't play the numbers game, where you're listing all these calls and not making sales." But management doesn't know what the guys are up to out there. If the guy's only making two calls a day, they start saying, "What the hell's the guy doing out there? He's not working. He can't be working!" But if you've got a lot of quantity, but you're not making enough sales when they've averaged it out, they'll tell you, "We want quality, not quantity." And the problem is that they can't really tell what you're doing. And some salesmen do a lot of paperwork, so it looks good that way. Others are not interested in doing paperwork, "Get someone else to do the paperwork. I'm in sales! . . ." Paperwork is a wonderful thing, management can justify their existence with paperwork! Most salesmen do not like paperwork, other than writing up the bill. . . . If they want a more extensive report, you know you are going to get a lot of bullshit. Like the salesman is not going to write, "Tuesday, I didn't feel like going out, so I didn't," or "Wednesday, I had a terrible day, so I went and had a couple of beers." The salesman is never going to write that, so most of these reports are not worth much. . . . And the manager might have the idea he could use some of this information, and maybe he does for a couple of weeks, but then he forgets about it, but the reports still keep coming in. . . . They give you all this paperwork, and part of it is that they don't know whether they want quantity or quality, or how to determine how well you're doing except through sales totals. . . . Probably the best thing they can do is to accept the idea that the guys are there working, and to try to build them up to that [manufacture—industrial].

Basically it all boils down to bottom-line cash register totals, what the cash register says. . . . If you're doing a good job, then your staff is happy. You don't have a big turnover in your staff, you have the same staff from month to month and year to year. Their sales represent whether they're happy or sad. . . . When the head office people walk into my store, they can see the attitude of the store. The attitude of the store is generally reflected in sales at the store. If the manager has a poor attitude then he's passing that on to his staff and if they have a bad attitude, then people coming in can feel that right off. The consumer's going to know that and they're going to back off. So it's just a chain reaction that's either a good reaction or a poor reaction and I think it shows in your sales.

They call me every month, maybe three times during the month. They'll say, "How's the month doing?" They'll come in and ask, or they'll call and ask, just quickly to find that out. And if I'll say, "I'm down a little bit," they'll say, "Well, is there a problem? Can we help you? Do you know why you're down?" If I say, "Yes, this is why I'm down," then they'll say, "Well, what do you want us to do about it?" They expect me to have done something about that already if I know why I'm down. If I don't know why I'm down, and there doesn't seem to be a general reason, they may say, "Well, don't worry about it because [branch]'s down, and [branch]'s down, and [branch]'s down, and everybody's down. It's just the way it is right now, so don't worry about it." They're very good that way. If I was drastically down constantly and really taking a nosedive and showing month to month to month, then they would want an accounting. They would want an answer [jewelry].

Moving Up

In many sales settings, most opportunities for advancement come with departures and/or expansions. At those times anyone judged to be doing a competent job becomes a candidate for upward mobility.

I went to work part time. The manager was doing a lousy job, and he got fired. So the full-time girl went to management and I went to full time, assistant manager. . . . Then after I was there about six months, they gave me a store to manage. . . . In our company, they're not so concerned about whether or not you've been to college, or by seniority, or how old you are, things like that. If you've done a bang up job in a low-volume store, done a good job, they will move you up, and they don't ask whether you've got a high school diploma or a college degree [shoes].

It slowed down a little, but before that they grew about tenfold, big expansion. And if you were a regular full-time worker, and you were any good, you could move up very quickly. Just a tremendous opportunity for promotion [mixed clothing].

Many of the same qualities attributed to "good salespeople" were indicated as desirable in "good managers." Overall, however, more emphasis was placed on the prospective manager's organizational skills and sense of dedication to the company.

In a manager, I would like someone like myself. I just do the work until it's done. Very conscientious, dedicated, capable. Keep careful track of the stock, watching your budget. You also want someone who's honest. Someone personable, and who can manage staff [women's clothing].

I like to get people from within, because you can recognize the people with smarts a little easier that way. I don't have to have people with degrees, or an intellectual, but someone who has smarts and can handle the situation. . . . Another problem for a new manager is that of being accepted by the men. You have to prove yourself to the salesmen, that you can do the job. Not just someone who can handle the books and give quotas and the like, but someone who has shown that he can do the job he is trying to get other people to do now [auto].

Despite the prestige (mystique) associated with management, not all who are eligible for management are willing to make the move.

Some are willing to go into management and some would rather remain in the field, selling. And we've had people come into management who haven't spent enough time recruiting [new agents]. They're spending too much time in the field, selling. We've had to let them go as managers. But some of them, they like to concentrate on door-to-door sales. Forget about management, building up territories that way [in-home—household].

Another problem with sales is all the transfers you can get, especially with some of the larger companies. . . . With sales, there's always the possibility of being on the move, all the time. If you take a position with a company, say you get a promotion, or they make you sales manager, it's quite likely it could be at the other end of the country. . . . Some moves just wouldn't be feasible financially. They might give you a few thousand more to be a manager, but when you figure the cost of living in some places, you're going to have to spend another year's salary on a house [manufacture—industrial].

In Perspective

This chapter has focused on a number of elements critical to under-standing management in sales settings. Thus attention was given to the sorts of duties for which managers may be responsible, and to those on whom they depend in meeting their obligations. We find managers caught between upper management who want results and the day-to-day situations managers encounter. To better contextualize the work world of the manager, materials dealing with hiring concerns (i.e., social skills, reliability, technical skills, and experience) were followed by a consideration of the ways in which people become involved in sales-work (reservations, attractions, closure, and recruitment). Next, we focused on sales instruction, noting both the formal and the on-the-job learning experiences of salespeople. This was followed by a discussion of the modes of determining payment for saleswork. While particular attention was given to straight commission and straight salary, other combinations were considered, as was the practice of spiffing products. Finally, concerns with performance as this reflects teamwork, assessment, and mobility within sales settings were briefly introduced.

In reviewing this chapter, it is most important to recognize that there is much more to management than this statement has been able to cover. Thus, for instance, the strategies of influence and resistance on the part of managers or those with whom they interact merit much more research as do the dilemmas and uncertainties management entails. Likewise, the dynamic features of coaching, assessment, and mobility deserve much closer attention than they have received both herein and in the literature more generally. Clearly, these are interactional matters worthy of extensive study on their own. Nevertheless, this discussion of management provides an important backdrop to the chapters following.

Much like the unseen stage director, managers may play central roles in casting and shaping the settings in which the drama of the marketplace unfolds. At the same time, however, and mindful of managers' dependencies on all those with whom they have contact (head office, suppliers, staff, customers, and others), this chapter represents little more than a starting point for appreciating the range and dynamics of management activity. Every single chapter following affords us opportunities to gain further insight into the processes and problematics of management in the marketplace.[15]

Notes

1. See Mintzberg (1973) for an excellent (and still relevant) review of this literature.

2. It should not be surprising to see that little attention has also been given to those who are managed (i.e., to the experience of being managed or working with management) or to the interactive aspects of worker-manager relationships. Thus we know little about how instructions from management are interpreted and implemented, how workers assess their own performances, how they indicate that they are doing "good jobs," how they avoid work, or how they "manage the managers."

3. This view of management as a process is also reflected in the conceptual statements of Bittner (1965), and Dingwall and Strong (1985). Viewing management as "ongoing practical accomplishment" versus rule-guided behavior, these scholars provide a formidable challenge to the more traditional, management literature. Further, as Schutz (1943) so cogently indicates, rationality is a much more elusive and multifaceted element than many academics seem to appreciate. Rationality is of minimal value in explaining organizational behavior. As with other aspects of management, rationality is best viewed in problematic, processual, and interactive terms.

4. In addition to internally performed tasks, companies may contract (farm out) any numbers of tasks to outside businesses. The amount of outside help can vary considerably over time, but it also means that a manager's duties can be radically altered in a very short period of time. Thus even one-person businesses may be arranged so that a great deal of work is farmed out with a single person coordinating these services in a manner not very dissimilar to that of managers in large businesses.

5. Otherwise, the major times of planning revolve around anticipated/experienced crises and are problem-solving in orientation. Noteworthy too, are managerial efforts intended to justify, rationalize, or otherwise provide impressions of performance, planning, and organizational coherence. Although considerable planning may go into these

statements, it is important to distinguish actual operating routines from organizational statements about operational routines.

6. While focusing on other contexts, this point evidences itself in Drucker's (1964) "concept of corporation," and in discussions of how managers use their time (Davis, 1959; Sayles, 1964; Mintzberg, 1973; Kotter, 1982).

7. Skepticism concerning the worth of college degrees in sales settings is not a recent phenomenon. Donovan (1929) describes vendors' post-World War I experiences with college girls as generally unfavorable, indicating that managers saw these salespeople as too "high hat" and impatient in their relations with others.

8. Additionally, any persuasive skills people develop in other settings (family, friendship, recreational, work) may prepare them for sales encounters.

9. Family businesses afford one of the most powerful learning situations for members of the family. While the amount of learning is a function of participation, these settings are especially valuable in providing persons with a more comprehensive and intimate view of business than they may be able to otherwise achieve.

10. See French (1958) for another account of salespeople "grabsting," "gonophing," and otherwise "stealing" one another's trade.

11. French (1958) provides another discussion of turn taking in a commission setting.

12. Since territories also represent means of organizing the sales staff for greater overall efficiency and conveniences of various sorts, these concerns may interfere with individual equity in the assignment of territories.

13. This may include stock purchased as "special" deals from suppliers attempting to clear their inventories. It is generally more profitable for vendors to put spiffs on merchandise than to put these on "sale" later. Although the term *spiff* need not be applied, similar practices have been in use for some time (Donovan, 1929). French (1958) also discusses spiffs.

14. Other incentives and elements affecting vendor enthusiasm are discussed in Chapter 9 of *Making Sales* (Prus, 1989).

15. Attending to matters such as presenting products, generating trust, pursuing and obtaining commitments, holding "sales," dealing with troublesome customers, developing loyalty, and maintaining enthusiasm, the activities examined in *Making Sales* (Prus, 1989) are also central to a fuller appreciation of management as a social process.

Chapter 4
PURCHASING PRODUCTS

The biggest fear of the buyers is that of making a mistake. They have a pretty good job, and they know there is probably someone else in their organization who would like to have that job, and there might be someone else in that organization who is close to the boss. So if they make a mistake, that could create problems for them. So that's one of the reasons they are cautious. They don't want to make mistakes [manufacture—industrial].

How do people in businesses purchase products to be used for resale, manufacture, or as supplies? What products and/or supplier concerns do they have? How do buyers try to avoid making mistakes? What roles do suppliers play in the process? What sorts of buyer-supplier relationships emerge in these contexts? Focusing on questions of this nature, Chapter 4 sheds light on the interests of those buying products for businesses as well as those selling products to businesses.

Buyers (also purchasers, procurers) want "good products" at "good prices," but buying is far from a static or simple dollars and cents exchange. It involves a great deal of reflective planning on the part of buyers, and is strikingly qualified by the activities of the suppliers. Further, although more company emphasis is generally placed on selling than buying, what and how one buys can greatly affect not only one's eventual profits, but a great deal of one's overall marketing program. For instance, buying practices may affect subsequent company image, merchandising styles, pricing, staff enthusiasm, sales presentations, and customer relations.

Meeting in an interactive context, buyers and sellers face the task of negotiating their interests in a competitive and shifting setting. While attending primarily to buying activity, this chapter affords an opportunity further to consider supplier perspectives as they enter into these situations. What and how suppliers sell will likewise affect their supply programs (e.g., purchasing, lines carried, inventory, pricing, anticipations of repeat patronage, and growth).

Recognizing that their partners in trade can influence the well-being of their own business, one finds both buyers and suppliers endeavoring to assess one another for compatibility. The general public is most sensitive to buyer bewarisms, but suppliers are also concerned about the integrity of their customers. Bigger (volume) buyers can more readily threaten the supplier operation, but any buyer can create problems (and costs) disproportionate to his worth.[1] Further, while suppliers can attempt to minimize risks by running more extensive (and expensive) credit checks, refusing credit to less known accounts, and the like, every business transaction engenders some risk. In what follows, we will examine some of the concerns and reservations buyers and suppliers have in doing business with one another.

Buying as Activity

Buying decisions are focused on two main themes, restocking existing lines and ordering new lines. Although these activities differ in many respects, they are much more interrelated than may first seem. Consequently, the ordering of new and existing lines will be discussed together, indicating differences as these seem more consequential. Buyers may have more reservations in dealing with new, untested products, but new products may also promise more stock turns (turnover) than some existing lines. The onus is not on the new products alone. Each product, new or familiar, has to perform (sell well) in order to verify the purchasing decision as a wise one.

Generally speaking, buying tends to be considered a more glamorous activity than is selling. This seems a function of possessing an item (money) that is more readily negotiable in the marketplace than other items. Having something that "everybody wants" seems to accord more prestige to people than those having something whose value is more ambiguous and for which the desire is less generally certain.[2]

It varies with the company and the rep involved, but they all want your business. You can get a lot of freebees in purchasing. . . . It's like they're courting you in a way. Some people say they don't care for these things, the free lunches and all, gifts. And I don't either, if it's going to put pressure on me to buy something we shouldn't or wouldn't get. But it depends on how it's done too, because it is a means of getting your attention like all advertising, and some you don't mind. . . . And sometimes, it's a matter of a company being grateful for you having done business with them. So if it's something not too big, why not [manufacture—industrial]?

In dealing with the chains, we do wine and dine them, we really do. We don't do it to the extent that some companies do, but we do give them smaller gifts, and we do wine and dine them. It's a kind of a public relations aspect of the business [manufacture—giftware].

More glamour may be associated with the buyer than supplier roles, but people whose business and/or jobs depend on good buying decisions are very sensitive to the uncertainties, risks, and dilemmas that buying entails.[3] Buyers may be courted and their rudeness is more apt to be tolerated, but they are expected to perform.

Buying trips are quite wearying. The suppliers are quite nice to you, but they're there to sell you, to hustle you. They want to move their products and when you come along, you're it! So that's on your mind, trying to sort out what they're telling you and what the product is actually like for your store. You've got to think about your own lines, and the other suppliers too, what they've got, the price, the quality, what you've got to spend right now, all things to think about. . . . Sometimes you make bad buys. It's inevitable, I think. You can try to have it planned, but you still have to make quick adjustments, decisions. So you've got all that going on. It's tiring, really it is [mixed clothing].

We buy both ways. We deal with the reps, either with them coming to you or going to the trade shows, or you go directly to the factory. The shows are kind of interesting, especially at first, but it's work. After, you see it almost exclusively in work terms. You want to check everything out, compare prices, concentrate on the lines, the deals, and all. You're there to do a job and that's it . . . We'll do a lot of price comparisons, and the suppliers do too. They want to know what the others are selling particular lines for [manufacture—shoes].

LEARNING THE ROPES

While buyers may attempt to make good buys, they are apt to find that their relative success in doing so is a matter of learning the marketplace and how to deal with the other players.[4] For many participants, much of the groundwork has been done by their predecessors or associates, and their task is a matter of filling new accounts as these can be developed. For those lacking preexisting routines and/or apprenticeship periods, the ongoing challenge of the marketplace becomes especially demanding.[5] Not only do new buyers face the problem of not knowing who to contact, but they may also be unfamiliar with the routings (e.g., trade shows, industry magazines, personal contacts) with which to do so. Further, and no less importantly, newcomers have to learn what practices are conventional in that arena and become sensitive to the sorts of arrangements competitors are negotiating with their suppliers, as well as any existing ownership interconnections between relevant buyers and suppliers. Thus, in addition to dealing with market uncertainties and the problems of predicting good products, newcomers are also faced with the prospects of sorting out prospective partners in trade and learning more effective ways of doing business in that context.

> With buying, you go through the fashion magazines, trying to get some idea ahead of time what you might like, because when you go to the manufacturers, they try to sell you whatever they have. If you listen to them, it's all beautiful, in fashion, and it will all sell like hotcakes. But you've only got X number of dollars, and you've got to get things that fit into your store's image. The best buy reflects what you need and what will sell, where you get the best value for your dollar. So you look around, shop around. You have to know the market! And that takes a little time and experience, but it's really very important, so basic to buying! You also have to know the people you're dealing with, who you can trust, who is likely to substitute or delay on orders, who will process your orders and who will make you wait until their other customers are taken care of, where you get what, if anything is left over. And everybody has their good lines [items] out, and they're all complimentary. They all want your money, and they'll find many ways of doing that. . . . Most buyers are owners, and then your buyers in big department stores are buying, and you don't want the same identical items in your stop, so that's a problem too. And you have to know the styles, the body styles different manufacturers make, and the quality. A new buyer is at a large disadvantage!
>
> First of all, nothing is exclusive. If something is exclusive and a high price, somebody will copy it, if it's good. If it's no good, no one will copy it. If someone had something great, someone else would get one or go to a show window, and sketch it and copy it. Then they would go and make it up in masse. Then another person decides that he can make up the same item in a cheaper line, maybe not as good quality, but cheaper. So first thing you know, it's circulating around, and that lovely little number that there was not too many of, has become a mass-produced item. And then it becomes so popular in the cheaper lines, that it loses its appeal. . . . There are kings in the industry, manufacturers that are well known for producing your better, more exclusive lines. Items for the beautiful people, the jet set, whatever you want to call them, or the people who are in the know, a name that really means something. They buy labels. These names mean something at that

level. And if another manufacturer wants to make an impression on a buyer, he might say, "Look, I've just copied this from so and so. This is his running number. A little different class, but it looks almost the same. He's got it at $300 and I've got it at $125 retail." So that's quite a difference. Perks up the buyer's ears. . . . They also use the method, "I've sold this to _____ ." They take a very prosperous, prestigious store, and say how the buyer loved the line and bought so many pieces. Now maybe when I leave, they may say to the next couple of buyers who come in, "Look what the last buyer bought from me." So they will play one against the other. Or they may use someone that they figure that I have a lot of respect for in the industry, and they'll say, "Look what so and so bought." But they may have bought that line, not to feature it, but to have some in the event that someone still wants it, so that can be misleading too. But even if you're not a person who impresses easily, you would still be interested, "Oh, is that so?" You give it some thought, "The guy may know something." . . . They feel you out, trying to see how you think, who you have a lot of respect for, things like that. Now sometimes they'll guess wrong and they may select the wrong buyers, people you don't respect. Then you can turn the tables on them, "Do they always but the right things?" "How do they know?" "I hear that they've had some real problems with some of their lines." Then you back them up! You have to keep up your guard, every time you step into a buying situation, because even when you're on your guard, you can be taken. You can come out having spent several thousand like this [snap], and you don't know what you spent it on. . . . It can also be a little confusing with all the different numbers, keeping them in mind, across a number of manu-facturers [women's clothing].

A distributor will often carry lines for a number of different companies. Usually, though you're just interested in certain things they carry, maybe only one item. You know that they're taking a margin on the goods. How much, you don't know for sure. If it's something you don't use that much, fine, pay them their price. If it's something you use a lot of, where it becomes a significant cost to you, then you would like to go direct. Find out who the manufacturer is, where he's located, see if you can deal with him direct. Sometimes, it can really pay off. It can save you a lot of money, because the distributor has marked something up, maybe 300%. . . . Often, it's not worth it. Either the manufacturer won't sell on your volumes, thinks it's too small, or they have quantity discounts that make the distributor's price look very good, especially with the service you're getting. And if his margin is pretty fair, it's not worth the trouble of having the distributor getting unhappy with you. So over time, you learn what a good price is and what to buy from this and that distributor [manufacture—industrial].

Learning the ropes is an ongoing process. Not only are buyers apt to find themselves dealing with new suppliers over time, but they are also likely to experience changes in the products, the personnel, and the strategies of those with whom they do business.

> I try to offer a fair bit of diversity in my products, have a number of different lines, and deal with a number of different companies. You also don't know what the companies will be doing in the future, so it is advisable to work with a number of manufacturing companies. It gives you more options in the future. If the company is more flexible, credit, inventory, then I'm more likely to deal with them [furniture].

> You can't rely on only one supplier, at least you don't want to be in that situation. There are some things that you might only be able to get from one supplier. There is no place else to get it, so there you watch your stock and let them know if you are getting low and put this aside for you, but you are really better to have some options in your suppliers [manufacture—giftware].

Suppliers face somewhat parallel problems in identifying viable buyers with whom to do business. While some businesses are well established in the public eye and/or in particular product areas, most others have relatively obscure identities at best. Sales representatives in the field gain some perspective on accounts by calling on businesses directly or by reviewing community business publications and the like. Other information may also be gathered through research, credit checks, and through mutual contacts, but in many encounters, such as those taking place at trade shows or those initiated by the buyer, suppliers are faced with the problem of credentialling prospective customers.

> You want to know who you're dealing with. It's good for developing a relationship with the person, but if you know more about their business, you also know where your products can fit in better, how much you should move. Are they up and coming? How do they pay their bills [manufacture—clothing]?

> One of the concerns we have is how much are they going to push our products compared to the other lines they carry. If the volume is good, fine. If not, there's not much advantage to dealing with them [manufacture—giftware].

Not unlike those to whom they sell, suppliers value loyalty on the part of their customers. While the lack of loyalty can create immense problems when a larger buyer is involved, suppliers tend to lose interest in accounts thought less likely to repeat.

The guy who just went by, he's not the kind of customer I want to deal with. He's always looking for the best price and if it's .0003¢ a unit cheaper elsewhere, then he's going to buy there. He doesn't seem to realize the value of being with one company. Or that if the price is reasonable, and that there are other things that are important, he is basically better off. He will dump you the first time he gets a little better price. People like that, I don't like dealing with [manufacture—industrial].

From the manufacturer's view, credit is a major concern, but another thing is "Can you get a working relationship with the retailer?" Are they going to level with you or say one thing and do the opposite? Are they going to work with you or try to use you? Are they going to upset the balance of your distribution? Those are the main problems. . . . You try to get a good working relationship with your retailers. But that is something that is extremely difficult to do with the big people, the big chains, because you're never going to be sure what they will do next. They're always playing their own games. And you might give them a good price, but in the ad it's listed for less than it's supposed to be, so then they come back to you, "Oh gee, we've got a problem here. Can you give us a little break on the price?" That type of thing. . . . The manufacturer is more vulnerable on those large accounts. But it's the old cooperative thing. You want to get a good working relationship, one that benefits both parties over the long run [manufacture—appliances].

IT'S A GAMBLE

Despite attempts to make purchasing more "professional" (via business schools, associations), buying remains a gamble.[6] Not only does buying entail strategies and gaming, trust and cooperation, and deception and competition, but buying activity takes place within a setting of shifting uncertainties and reflects dependencies on others outside the immediate transaction. Buyers may deal shrewdly with suppliers, but no one knows for sure just what market value purchases will actually hold at later points in time.[7]

It's hard to tell. There are things you figure will move for sure, and a lot of times you're right. But you can get a lot of surprises, too. Things that looked too gaudy, or impractical, or expensive, turns out they sell. And other things, nice things, good quality, you end up putting them on "sale" to try to get rid of them [giftware].

There's a certain excitement to buying. You know which ones you like, but you also try to guess what's going to move best, so you kind of waver between that and all the choices you could make. Hope you've picked out the good movers [mixed clothing].

When you're buying shoes, you have an idea of what's going on in Europe, and then you've got an idea of what's going on in your stores, and basically, you're thinking for your customers. You're doing all the questioning for them. Can I sell this? How much can I get for it? You look at the price differences, and you're trying to weigh the difference between the styles and the price and the quality, the look, and you've got to come up with a mix in that. And you make your decision half a year before it hits the store. . . . And you don't want to get a whole line wrong. If you hit a whole line wrong, you are in lots of trouble [shoes]!!

In ordering goods, buyers are not only predicting that others will wish to continue (or start) consuming the item, but further that they will do so with certain frequencies (not consuming too little) and within certain time frames (i.e., within shelf and fashion product lives, with sufficient stock turns to be profitable to carry). They are also predicting that sufficient numbers of consumers will be able to afford the goods and will elect to buy their products rather than those of their competitors.

We order on experience, and we try to hold our inventory down. So we work basically short term. The manufacturer would like to work long term, but he can't because his business would get so badly fouled up. He has to go short term. Otherwise, he would have merchandise, orders that he'd be throwing out. But they vacillate between carrying more inventory and less. They want you to order six months ahead of time, if you want something special in any volume. But we've found that they can't always deliver on that because of some foul-up. And with the chaotic state of the economy, up and down, up and down, it is hard for anyone to predict what is going to be moving and how much. Also, they have to be careful with people stockpiling inventories, because then they think they have to gear up for production and then, later, find that nothing is moving. . . .

When you talk to the manufacturers, they don't really know what to tell you about predicting lines, or overall sales for that matter. The economy is chaotic, and these environmental conditions can dramatically affect your overall business. You have these uncontrollables, the legal aspects, bank rates, imports, and cultural changes. And these are the things that have the manufacturers shaking their heads. You talk to them, and they tell you that they just don't know which way to go [appliances].

In many cases, you have to order six months in advance. So you're actually projecting what your sales will be. And, so long as your business is more or less consistent, you feel a little more confident. But given that we've just expanded, it's getting a little more dicey for us because we're not sure just how much we can actually move. You don't want to sit with a lot of stock, and yet at the same time, you want to have the merchandise in when the people are around to buy it. But predicting the market is always a problem, something you can never guess accurately, no matter how smart you are, or how well you know your business, and how well things are working out for you. It's largely a matter of being lucky. It can really be tricky and there is no formula that can assure you of success. Right now, I know a number of people who are expecting a really good summer and they are sitting with thousands of dollars worth of inventory in storage. Other people, I have found, are cutting their inventory down and when you go there to buy things, they have such a limited supply [furniture].

With the large brand names, you never know what's going to happen with price wars on the brand names. Say you intend to sell _____ running shoes for $26.95, and then [A] will put them on for $19.95 and the [B] will put them on for $19.95, and then you find that you have to do the same. You have to take the dollars off to sell the product. You'll probably sell them all, but you've got that stock around before you can sell it. You could probably sell it for $26.95, eventually, but you've only got so much time to turn so many units [shoes].

Purchasers may attempt to buy rationally, but as Schutz (1943) and Garfinkel (1967) note, rationality is not only subject to a variety of interpretations, but more importantly is something to be worked out as situations unfold. Using Garfinkel's (1967: 263-268) formulation as a base,[8] we find that buyers could be considered to act in accordance with most conventional notions of rationality. Thus, although not uniform in their practices, buyers generally may be seen to act rationally in reference to (1) categorizing and comparing products; (2) searching for the best-fitting goods; (3) building on past experiences in their selections of products; (4) weighing and assessing alternatives, and considering the consequences (e.g., long term, short run) of particular selections; (5) planning for a range of future contingencies; (6) exhibiting concerns for the timing of purchases relative to other events; (7) attempting to predict future outcomes (e.g., market demands); (8) trying to make reasonable decisions and/or assessing selections relative to the standards of referent others (e.g., company policies, those to whom one is accountable) (9) exercising conscious choices in reference to purchasing decisions; (10) being able to explain their choices; (11) using principles of logic (means-ends deductions) in arriving at product decisions; (12) seeking clarification and understanding of products and/or vendor capabilities; (13) noting differences between ideal and existing states of the products encountered, and striving towards that ideal; and (14) being agreeable to having their purchasing decisions subject to critical evaluation.

Buyers can relate to these notions of rationality, and they are encouraged to do so by those in marketing (and purchasing). However, self- and other directed encouragements to "buy rationally" are of limited value. Not only may people arrive at very different purchasing decisions when operating from particular combinations of the preceding notions of rationality, but the "best buys" can be known only after the fact (by virtue of customer purchasing commitments). In the interim, buyers must make decisions, acting "as if" they know what the future will hold. Thus, when one inquires into the operationalizations of these notions in the marketplace, some striking contrasts emerge. Buyers can weigh and compare products, plan for the future, employ backups, and the like, but much ambiguity exists.[9] Given these uncertainties, one finds that much like gamblers at the race track (Scott, 1968; Lesieur, 1977), buyers frequently attempt to beat the odds by hedging their bets.

HEDGING BETS

In recognition of the risks entailed in shifting market interests, many buyers adapt strategies they hope will provide them with some protection from the uncertainty of the marketplace. The most common of these are (1) seeking consensus from others, (2) concentrating on the basics, (3) purchasing established lines, (4) sampling the market with smaller orders, and (5) diversifying one's lines. Also noteworthy is the strategy of (6) cultivating relationships with suppliers.

Seeking Consensus

Realizing that their personal preferences need not coincide with those of their customers, buyers tend to be concerned with the generalizability of their viewpoints. Like gamblers betting on future outcomes, buyers often seek information from others and/or find themselves more susceptible to definitions from others than they had anticipated.[10] In addition to reading trade publications and/or noting trends in their daily observations, it is not unusual to find buyers consulting with others.

> The trick is to stay a step ahead, and know which way to step when you are buying. You hope that you have stepped the right way. So with me, I am always reading up on the business trends and talking with the people, trying to get some idea just where it is going before I make my purchases. . . . I find that just watching myself, and other people in some other businesses, that you have to be careful how personalized your buying is. If you have someone who becomes more set in their

ways, then they may be closing off part of the market. I've found it is even useful to take another person along when I'm buying, just to have another opinion [women's clothing].

With new equipment, I might go to another company that's using it. . . . That way, I can see the equipment, how it works, ask the people about the maintenance involved. Then I get a good idea of how I could handle it on a day-to-day basis. . . . And what's the record on the equipment, in terms of breakdowns, from the actual owner. And ask them why did they pick that particular piece of equipment. Go through that. That way you can narrow it down to what you want pretty fast. . . . You would only talk to four companies, say, half a dozen at the most, the companies you think are the most reliable. . . . When you're working with them on a more or less continuous base, you start to see how their judgments work out. . . . Or when you talk to them, you get a feeling about them. If they seem like they're always trying to impress somebody, I have a tendency not to trust them. If they're fairly straight forward, doing their job, I think they're a bit more honest. . . .

I try to play on other people's expertise, ask questions of people in the plant. Or I'll call up companies that I know that have bought similar stuff. In a company as large as ours, I'm not unique in what I'm doing, I could call up a sister division or call up a company in similar manufacturing and ask them, "Who did you go with? How has that worked out?" Try as many different avenues as I can. . . . There are a lot of industrial magazines that are available to companies, that are basically no-charge to companies, the advertisers pay for them. I don't use them all that much. . . . I trust word of mouth more than anything else, because they've dealt with it, gone through it. . . . I would try to contact as many people as possible, not just go on one person's opinion. It's a little risky with just one person. You might only find one person, in which case you have to, but there, if there is only one person, you might contact some companies making similar products and ask them about theirs and ask them to compare with the one you were planning to buy and you can learn that way. . . . Each situation dictates a little bit different. Working in a larger company, I have the flexibility, the luxury of calling other companies and spending the time researching. As a result, hopefully, the company is getting a better decision. Whereas in a smaller company, it's a little riskier. They don't have the luxury, so they run the risk of making poorer decisions. . . . Likewise, people contact me, "I hear you've used such and such." [manufacture—industrial]

Concerns with performance, in the midst of uncertainty, make buyers more sensitive to all sources of information pertaining to their purchases. One may speak of more knowledgeable buyers and it is not uncommon to encounter buyers who know much more about the products to be purchased than some vendors do. However, even though buyers may have confidence in their abilities, they are still amenable to

vendor suggestions. They may not know how much trust to place in a
particular vendor's suggestions, but recognize the vendors' opportunities to be aware of other aspects of the marketplace than that generated
by their own experience.

> To some extent, you have to trust the judgment of the salesman in terms of what
> is a good mover, but if he's given you some bum steers, you're not going to put
> much faith in him in the future. But you also try to judge by what has been moving
> for you in the past. You will get people, though, who will try to unload a lot of
> garbage on you, and sometimes, you go for it, although probably more so when
> you're first starting. . . . But you are dependent on the honesty and integrity of the
> salesman [appliances].

> In ordering, I'll talk with the salesman, get his advice, but you also have to think
> of the general area you're serving, what sells best for you. Do we sell more fancy
> things, plain? Is the new line something that agrees with the area, our customers,
> and then we go from there. . . . You also have to take the price range into
> consideration, what prices you think you can move the merchandise for [jewelry].

> When we got an account with _____ , it was a big help with the other chain
> accounts, you could name drop. If they saw we were dealing with _____ .
> "Well, not too bad. Let's take a look at what you've got." That might have been
> one of the reasons that we really got started [manufacture—giftware].

Concentrating on the Basics

By concentrating more on more conventional styles (products), buyers may gain a greater sense of security in their purchases. While
anticipating some loss of sales among the more fashion conscious, these
buyers strive for a clientele they perceive as more predictable.

> Our image as a chain is middle of the road, and that way, you don't carry the high
> fashions. If you carry the high fashions, you've got to have the high turnover. We
> carry middle of the road. If the ties get narrow, we'll carry some, but keep a more
> moderate width as our basic stock. And the same with our lapels, they don't go
> way out or way in. We move them around, with the fashions, but never to the
> high-fashion extremes. So we'll carry some trendy things, but mostly we'll go with
> the more basic lines. And so we'll have some things for the younger men, but we'll
> also have things for the older gentlemen. And the things we sell will stay in longer
> [men's clothing].

We do some different things, but mostly, it's a variation of something that's been going well. That way, it's not so much of a gamble. It's still the basic item, just in another form that might appeal to the shoppers [manufacture—giftware].

Purchasing Established Lines

Another means of hedging bets is to buy from those with proven track records. Thus one finds buyers preferring to purchase name brands, and/or brands they have found satisfactory in the past. Although name brands are generally more costly, vendors using this strategy anticipate that their customers will have greater faith in these products and will be willing to pay more for them (i.e., also go with the winners).

People have more confidence in it, so that helps. It's the advertising they've done, their size, but it pays off for you. . . . Another thing is the displays some suppliers provide. If it's a more attractive display, it'll help you sell those products [department store].

The retailer has to be concerned primarily with quality, getting goods that would be acceptable by the consumer, because he's the person that's got to buy it. If it's not acceptable to the consumer, there's no point stocking it in the first place. . . . We always like to stick with a product that we know has public acceptance. And you always try new products. There's dozens and dozens that come out every week. And you've got to try the new products too. Give the consumer some variety. But the staples are still the products you stock, and you deal with the suppliers of long-standing reputations [grocery].

Testing the Ice

Should lines (or specific products) be less established, buyers may also attempt to play it safe by initially placing smaller orders. This strategy assumes an ability to obtain quick delivery from suppliers, for low stock levels may entail some loss of sales. Smaller orders generally result in higher unit costs, but are especially commonplace with new lines.[11]

If it's selling, you reorder, but if it's something new, you would get a smaller amount to test it out [department store].

I don't buy much at the gift shows. Some people buy twice a year. I don't know how they can afford it. They're spending a lot of money at one session. Buying merchandise in August for Christmas, trying to guess what they're going to need four months later, and if they guess poorly, they're out of luck. Or they're stuck with a lot of crud. And how can they afford it, at the price of money today? To me, it just doesn't make sense. . . . I go to a show to see what's new. If I see a new product, I'll buy a small quantity of it. If I get good response on it, I'll go back and buy again. I look at what a lot of people get stuck with, and what they have to get rid of at clearouts, and I hear them say, "Boy, did I get stung on that one!" and I try to avoid that. So I take a small amount, try it first, and then if it moves well, go back and get more. If it's moved the second time, go back and get more this time [giftware].

With a new line, you're more hesitant. You don't know if it will sell as well. It's good to offer variety, but you don't know, so you order smaller amounts if you can. See how it moves, and you'll be watching it more carefully [jewelry].

With a new line, one you've never had before, you don't want to lay in a hundred thousand dollars of inventory, if you don't know what is going to happen, but you do want something. Even we, as distributors, it might sound as though I am contradicting myself a little bit as to what I was saying about the retailer, but even myself, I won't load in the stock until I know the movement. But the difference between myself and the retailer, I am willing to try it, where getting the retailer to try it, you have to convince them more. If I think the item is good, then I will say, "Fine, let's start with so many samples." Then I can supply my salesmen, my showroom, and the gift show. Once we get that rolling, everybody has everything in hand, then we start selling. I say to the potential supplier, "Give me at least four to eight weeks, which would give my people enough time to bring back an answer, and we will cover one or two gift shows. That will give me some feedback, so I can judge my quantity I want to place with you." Once I know what these people think of it, then I will back it up with X number of dollars in stock. But you see, that still is a partial answer for inventory. . . .

In an established line you don't have to do that. In an established line, you already know what your spring is going to be. For spring you have to get ready to order in October of the previous year. You go to your supplier and you set up your levels for spring. After that is done, you run through your spring, then you start your Christmas orders. . . . You go through all your items in March so that they will arrive by August. In other words, by March 1, we already have information just what it was going to be at Christmas of this year. There could be a few items that we don't, but okay, we will put them into the gift show and we will show them there. And our second time [a later show] around, if they are there we will show them again, and say, "This is another item you may have forgotten about. Do you want to book it? It looks good. What to give it a try? We'll add it to your order." That is an established line. That covers the two, a new line and an established line. . . . A new line, that would be where your biggest gamble would be. And it's a bigger gamble for me than it is for the retailer [wholesale—giftware].

Diversifying Lines

Diversification represents another means of hedging market risk. While depth in lines may be sacrificed, greater diversification in lines is presumed to increase the likelihood of selling something. While denoting additional potential liabilities (e.g., extra expenditures, reduced space, pressure from more suppliers), diversity seems to add interest to one's entire selection when dealing with regular as well as new customers.

> If you have a more extensive line of equipment, you can make more sales with the same amount of calls. If you make the same number of calls, you're selling a higher dollar volume. That's why we've been adding a few new lines, to take advantage of that [manufacture—appliances].

> If there is a new line, something different, and sort of attractive overall, I will grab it. I may not get that many of a particular item, and I will get it in the more popular sizes, but it is something that gives more visibility to your other items in your store. It is something new and exciting for your customers to look at it, and even if it doesn't sell very well, it can be valuable to you in that regard [women's clothing].

> Candy's pretty basic for us, so we'll stay with it, but we're continually giving them variety. Different kinds of flavors, candy, gum, trinkets. The kids like the change. Then there are some, like the licorice you're buying, that we have to have. Even there, though, you can still give them some variety [variety].

Cultivating Relationships

Another means by which buyers sometimes hedge their bets is by seeking good working relationships with particular suppliers. Consistent with Bigus's (1972) study of milkmen, and Prus and Irini's (1988) account of bars, we normally think in terms of vendors cultivating relationships with buyers. However, as Adler and Adler (1983) aptly note in their depiction of drug dealing, buyers may also strive to maintain these relationships. Many buyers seem unconcerned with this tactic, but others indicate that it is a valuable means of reducing risk.

In some cases, suppliers are viewed as "insurance," and although buyers may do proportionately little business with them, they view these contacts as having long-run utility. Thus business (or other contacts) directed toward these vendors may be thought to pay off should these vendors later get hot lines, should major suppliers be unable to meet buyer requirements, or should buyers wish to make major suppliers more competitive in some way.

There are real advantages to dealing with several suppliers, even if you're not doing much business with some of them. You find out what each one is doing, and you never know who is going to get what. Plus, if you have some problem or other with one supplier, you have that to fall back on. You've already laid the groundwork [mixed clothing].

In other instances, buyers may explicitly attempt to develop strong relationships with major suppliers. This too is often defined in long-term results. And while these buyers may concentrate their buying with particular suppliers in an effort to show loyalty, it is typically with the anticipation that this will result in an inside track on the competition (e.g., price, service concessions).

Overall, we deal with about four to five companies, but we try to keep it down. The trend is to have less, but to carry more important ones. Also, that way you can develop a closer working relationship with the individual manufacturers. The manufacturer likes to know where they stand with you. If you've got a lot of lines in a smaller outlet, they don't know where they stand with you. And if you can concentrate on a few suppliers, concentrate on the basics, you increase your bargaining power. . . . Even if you're working completely as an independent, you can develop stronger relations with a supplier if you deal more consistently with a smaller number of suppliers. The manufacturers are looking for loyalty too. More things come your way because you're a little more loyal. They're looking for people that will work with them [appliances].

If you deal with certain suppliers more, they do get to know you better and they will cut some corners for you. Like with _____ , we give them a fairly steady stream of orders and they do make concessions to us that somebody new or less loyal wouldn't likely get. . . . And they're more open with you too. They're more open with us, steer us away from the deadbeats, say [giftware].

Although not always defined in reference to cultivating relationships, much of the following discussion depicts elements promoting continuity of buyer-supplier relationships. In purchasing products, buyers are making commitments that typically extend beyond the products being considered. As a result, buyers tend to become caught between buying products and entering relationships with suppliers. Hence, the relationships these purchases entail represent especially noteworthy aspects of buying activities.

Partners in Trade

There is a tendency to envision suppliers and buyers as opposing entities, each endeavoring to pursue their own interests at the expense of the other. While this view has some validity, it very much needs to be tempered by the recognition that buyers and suppliers are partners in trade. Their economic well-being and interests are much more closely intertwined than might seem on the surface. If buyers and suppliers expected to deal with one another on a very autonomous, one time only basis, one would expect to find more rip and run transactions.[12] In most cases, however, stability is valued by both parties.[13]

Since repeat customers represent the backbone of most successful businesses, buyer loyalty is central to the notion of intersecting interests as experienced by suppliers. Although repeat purchases may be made under many different conditions (e.g., convenience, lack of alternatives, perceptions of superior quality, and so on), the repeat business is critical for most suppliers. Regular customers are valuable not only with regards to direct repeat purchases, but also relative to tendencies of trusting customers to broaden their base of purchasing over time, and generating referrals.[14]

Buyers sometimes intend to deal with vendors on a discrete one-time only basis, but insofar as they wish to establish a stable business, they will be looking ahead to subsequent purchases (consistent with the expectations they are establishing with their customers). Viewed in this manner, buyers are not only purchasing products, they are becoming involved in relationships with the suppliers featuring these products. Regular suppliers add elements of predictability to the buyers' operations. They allow buyers to achieve greater consistency relative to their clientele. In conjunction with the other elements directly affecting their choices, buyers want to know that suppliers can and will deliver orders as indicated, so that anticipated sales may materialize. Since delays, poor quality merchandise, and inadequate service can play havoc with the buyer's overall marketing operations, these are taken as seriously as any concerns the suppliers may have.

As the following material suggests, matters pertaining to relevancy, quality, service, price, volume, financing, and private brands assume considerable prominence in buyer-supplier encounters.

RELEVANT PRODUCTS

Given the seemingly unlimited products one could obtain from suppliers, notions of relevancy serve as a major filter to subsequent buyer-supplier contact. As might be expected, suppliers tend to indicate (and innovate) more relevancies than buyers are willing to acknowledge. From the buyer's perspective, relevancy is generally defined by perceived goodness of fit of the merchandise being considered with their overall marketing plans (preexisting and/or emerging). Since the addition of new lines can affect the overall image a vendor projects, concern with product compatibility (and store image) is especially noteworthy in adding new lines.

> You look at the goods in terms of what would sell well in your store, and then, if you find a number of things in their booths that would sell well, I look around to see if it would be worth my while to open an account with them. If I would only be spending a couple hundred there, what am I wasting my effort for? Two hundred means four hundred in gross sales. Do I have to go through all of that for four hundred in sales, and go through another supplier, have another salesman pounding on my door, and he's pushing the hell out of you to carry this and carry that. I don't need that. . . . And it's interesting, once you pick a theme or standard for your store, you will find that the suppliers that fill that theme well are suppliers who will continually do that in the future. They think the same way you do. They have other clients similar to yourself, retailers who have a similar type of client to you, in other cities. So when they do their buying, they're buying for me, when they go to the manufacturers. So I know when I go to the gift show, or go down to their showroom, I know that so and so is going to have 20 or 30 or 40 new products that will fit in with my business. So why should I have all the hassle of getting two new items from this other guy? And I don't need the hassle of people coming in, telling me how the rest of their lines would fit in my store. They get the idea that they've got to sell you everything they've got in their whole line. So with your occasional suppliers, there might just be a few things I want, and I also want to keep the relationship in perspective, with them as an occasional supplier [giftware].

> If you carry poor lines of merchandise, what it can do is threaten your whole store. And even though people may be able to afford the higher-priced, better quality merchandise, they tend to buy the lower lines, simply because it is more economical. So the poorer quality lines may be good on volume, but they may not be good for the sales of your merchandise in the store more generally, and what you want is to get all your merchandise moving [women's clothing].

Hot Lines

Despite the general applicability of several suppliers' merchandise, it may be anticipated that some products (or suppliers), and especially newer items, will be more popular than others. These hot lines not only heighten buyer perceptions of relevancy, but also serve to define the relative prominence of each party in the buyer-seller relationship.

With a new line, you want to know, "How fast can I sell it? How long will it take me to deal with it and prospective buyers?" The turnover time is money. . . . You want it to turnover, get repeat orders. And it has to fit in with my other lines or else I wouldn't be able to sell it in the same types of stores [wholesale—giftware].

When a man has a line that is really selling, he gets very independent. When you go to buy the line, he may not want to sell it to you. He may be already selling to a few stores in the same area, and he can't really sell to everyone. Then he can be very independent. "No, I can't sell to you," for which you should really give him credit, although he may already be selling to too many [retailers]. Or as soon as you're in the door, he may ask, "How much are you spending today?" before you look at the line. If you're going to spend a lot, he'll let you look at the line. It might be that straightforward. As this one man does it, "Good morning. Have a seat. How much are you going to spend today? I hope that you are here with a large budget." And then if he doesn't think you're prepared to spend enough at the time, he'll tell you that he doesn't think he has time to consider the smaller orders right now. He's too busy. And part of it might be whether you see him before or after you've seen some other suppliers. Or you might hem and haw with him, and maybe work something out where you buy less than what he wants. Nobody really likes him, but you go there as long as his line is doing great. . . . Now suddenly this man has had his line go down. He didn't make some changes that he should have, where his line is just not as competitive as before, he's lost a lot that way. Now when you go to see the same man, he has time for you. The same man is calling you on the phone, very complimentary, and how he's been looking over his line and has decided to give you a chance to purchase this and that you wanted from before. Now when you go in, he gives you the full treatment, buys you lunch, everything to get you to buy. Now he'll call me up, and sometimes I'll get a line to do him a favor, or I'll tell him that last time I got a line from him to do him a favor and it hasn't been moving well, so I can't get anything from him now, but that I'll be by to check things out next time I'm out buying. Something like that, because if his line goes up again, you want to keep on good terms with them. They'll remember that you were giving him some business when it was slow for him. Now if you figure that it's a losing line altogether, you might be more abrupt. Otherwise, even if your not buying from someone, you might still drop by and say hello. Maybe nothing about business at all, but keeping in touch, because if they then get a line that hits, well, you're in a better position to get in on that [women's clothing].

They're [merchants] also looking for new lines, they have their regular customers and they get tired of seeing the same merchandise over and over. And if they're happy with the product, and you come out with a similar type of package, but some difference, something new, the merchants will generally go for it. The customer will buy something a little different, something new, exciting. And that makes the merchant happy, the producer happy, and the salesman happy. You have to constantly come out with new products even though the old product is great. It's going to die sooner or later [manufacture—giftware].

Exclusiveness represents another dimension on which buyers tend to define lines as hotter, more worthy of possession (and protection!).

[A], [B], and [C] all have good lines, and we carry some of their products. But a lot of people have them. With [C], though, we're the only ones carrying them. They're all good, but [C] is worth more because no one else around here has them. So if they want their designs, they have to get them here. So they're a really good line for us, that way [mixed clothing].

We've been cutting back on some of the lines, some of them are just too general, like _____ . They've flooded the market, everyone's got their lines, and we just found that we no longer have the profit margin or the exclusiveness we wanted. So we're trying to clear out the balance of our stock in that area [wholesale—giftware].

We have become especially concerned with more exclusive lines in the past few years and some of the companies will come to us and ask us if they can take parts of their lines to other retailers in the area. Sometimes there is no problem. Other times, you just tell them, "Sure, you can, but only if you don't want to deal with us any more." I don't try to dictate to the marketplace, I don't think that is really my right. But what I can do is dictate to the store and what goes on in here. I'm not threatening, but simply stating that if that lines goes in the other store, then they are going to have to prepare not to do business with us. So it's their decision. I'm not going to force or threaten them, just tell them how the situation will work out [furniture].

Winning Numbers and "Dogs"

Suppliers may test and evaluate products on their own and/or do market research. However, as the earlier material on testing the ice suggests, it is the willingness of the buyers and their customers to put their money down which ultimately defines products as winning numbers or "dogs," and which subsequently affects the overall success of any given supplier.

Buying is critical for the survival of the business and if it doesn't move, then you're in a lot of trouble. This is where fashion buying becomes especially risky, because what people say they want and what they end up buying are two different things. So one of the big questions you ask yourself, when you are looking at new merchandise and new lines is the question, "Will it move?" It is also tricky, because what may be popular one week, where your racks get cleaned out of a particular line of merchandise, may not be a good item to reorder for the next week. You just don't know where the customers are going to concentrate their buying [women's clothing].

In every business, there are your winners and your dogs. Now when they come out, you hope you've got a winner. But you don't really determine that, although you can try through your research and your advertising. You hope that at least you're in the running, not losing too much on any line or model. And you can promote it hard, but if people are not buying it that much, then you've got a dog and you better spend your money promoting other things. . . . That's one thing that discourages you from coming out with many different things. You can spend a lot of money in research and development, and if it's seen as too different, you'll likely take a beating. On the other hand though, you can come out with something that the market research boys weren't so keen on and it can really do well. A new and different product can really hit it big. The timing when you bring it out, is a big thing, too [manufacture—industrial].

QUALITY, SERVICE, AND PRICE

The existence of alternatives allows buyers to assess suppliers on the basis of quality, service, and price. While price is most readily defined, it should not be assumed that price is more important than quality and service. It is much more accurate to see these elements as contributing to the buyer's total assessment of the products involved. All buyers are in somewhat different circumstances, and even those in similar situations may attribute different significances to each of these elements.

Quality

Since buyers typically have minimal acceptable levels of quality (versus useless), buyer conceptions of standards cannot be considered less consequential than price. While assessments of quality may reflect personal experiences, reports from customers and staff, comparisons with competing products, and supplier definitions, buyer perceptions of quality need not correspond with one another or with those of the suppliers. In this regard, quality is significantly defined relative to the concerns (tasks, preferences) at hand.

Quality depends on what you want to do with something. We'll often have several levels of merchandise, often two or more levels from the same supplier. . . . We want to be able to offer something for the people who need something who can't or don't want to go up to that level. So we look for a minimum acceptable quality, but not really a brand I would recommend to anyone if they asked me [discount department store].

"You only get what you pay for" is easily said, but you may not want to pay for the quality. You may not need all that quality. . . . It's true in the fact that the more you pay, conceivably the better the quality you get. But you may not need all that quality, you may find a lesser model is adequate for your purposes. . . . For many things, I want to know how durable it is. Is it easily understood? Something that any bozo could use [manufacture—industrial]?

Further, since products to be purchased are generally contextualized with the broader relationships buyers have with suppliers, definitions of quality tend to be considerably more holistic than direct product comparisons would suggest.

Quality is most important. If the product doesn't stand up, you are going to get a lot of people coming back with returns. If you don't have the quality, it's better not to carry it. . . . Quality control is important, because it reflects back on you, and on the name brand. Also, if you've got good quality control on the production line, it can really cut down on service costs. By the time you send the service people out, and if they haven't got the part, have to run back, or get it on order, go back again, and the paperwork, it can take all the profit out of the sale. So it has to be right when it goes in. So you're better to invest a little more at the factory [manufacture—appliances].

In dealing with suppliers, basically you want a good quality item. If they don't have that, as far as we're concerned, there's no point dealing with them, regardless of what their price is, because it'll back up on you along the line. If they have good quality, you may stock some of their merchandise, depending on what your other suppliers offer and how fashionable their line is relative to your customers. Then you start to think in terms of accessibility, delivery, and price. Also, would they be willing to deal with you in the quantities that you want? You would also be concerned about credit lines. Will they give you credit? What sort of quality control do they have? That's important. The samples may look good, but what does the routine merchandise look like? What sort of stock do they have on hand? Can you get extra merchandise as you need it, because if you can, then that's worth something too. It cuts down on the bungles you make overall, especially with something new, that you have very little idea of what might prove popular. . . . How are they with returned merchandise, if there's some problem with it [giftware].

As the preceding quotes suggest, service is an important aspect of buyers' overall notions of quality.

Service

Definitions of good service can vary greatly across product areas, but suppliers who (relative to their competition) offer greater product availability and product protection tend to be preferred. As buyer profits reflect availability of products at the times their customers wish to make purchases, buyers are concerned about the abilities of their suppliers to deliver goods at the most opportune times. Thus consistently well-stocked suppliers and those able to process orders more expediently are given preference.

A good supplier is someone who can get the merchandise to you when you want it, quickly. With imports, you want someone who has all the necessary customs slips and they process it from there. Also, people who pack their merchandise so that when you get it you don't have to worry about things being broken or damaged in transit all that much. Also, a lot of times, suppliers don't have the merchandise you want to order, either. They just don't have enough stock to give you what your customers want [wholesale—jewelry].

With our suppliers, one of the things we are most concerned about is shipment time. You don't want to have to wait for your stock. Especially if you have back orders, because you are going to get cancellations and when they cancel, you lose the business [manufacture—industrial].

Although each item introduces unique inventory concerns (e.g., production time, shelf life, fashion, and so on), adequate buyer stock can readily become an area of mutual concern.[15]

We're depending on the repeats. That's why when we get orders, say after a gift show, we want to get them out quickly, because if it's not on the shelf, then we're going to get the repeat orders. It's of no value to have the orders sitting on the shipper's desk. Then there's a possibility of a few repeats before the next show [manufacture—giftware].

If you go to the manufacturers, you can build your own shoe. You can go to them and select the parts, and the styles, so you can get a shoe which is exclusive to your own store. . . . Then you get a shoe, which if people like, they can't go elsewhere and find the identical shoe, and you can get a little better margin (markup), that way than if they could find the same shoe at another store, where their comparison shopping would be most effective. Most of the large department stores will do that. They can deal in that kind of volume. . . . With the factories, you have to allow them some lead time to get the items out. It will depend, for example, whether you're buying a very basic line, but even there, you may have to allow a couple of months or more between when you place your order and when you can expect the shipment to arrive [shoes].

Policies tend to vary across product areas, but vendors offering more extensive product protection (returns, replacements, repairs) are likely to be perceived as superior to others. These practices may add to the overall costs of the product to the eventual consumer, but they are generally defined as desirable practices on the part of the buyers who can now order and sell with greater confidence.

Some of the companies wouldn't go on a guaranteed sales basis with a smaller business, but if you're larger and better known for promoting a certain type of product, they may very well do that for you. They figure that their product is going to go well in your shop and so they'll do that if it means meeting or beating the competition, the other suppliers you might be dealing with [giftware].

We want to be identified with quality products, and we only want to deal with suppliers that we can have confidence in their products, in our relationship with them. We want a company that has a good service organization, one that works close with their marketing organization [appliances].

Regardless of whether one considers products or service, quality remains an elusive element at the time of purchase. Definitions of quality reflect the images purchasers have relative to their expectations. Testing and prior experiences may generate greater levels of confidence in some purchases, but quality will be known with certainty only in the future as purchases perform (or do not) as anticipated and other people confirm (or disconfirm) these as having been accurate definitions by their reactions to these items (e.g., by making purchases, subsequent complaints).

Price
Perceptions of quality can dramatically affect purchasing decisions, but price represents a readily defined comparison point. Since a reduc-

tion in costs can result in more competitive resale prices and/or greater profits, lower prices can also affect definitions of suppliers as desirable partners in trade. The ideal combination of best quality, best service, and best price is often not available. Therefore, direct price definitions are generally weighed against other aspects of buying.[16]

> We found the people at _____ very pleasant to deal with, and their prices were outstanding, but we found their quality control was rather poor. About 25% of the merchandise we found unsalable. So then, you're either into a lot of returns, which isn't convenient given the distance, so we just stopped dealing with them. Their prices were very good, even with the built-in cost of poor quality control, but we just felt it wasn't worth the hassle of sorting through all the materials, looking for flaws. We would rather pay more and get merchandise you have more confidence in [crafts].

> Some of the distributors are pretty good, and since they buy in a larger volume, they can get you prices that are fairly comparable with what you would get from a manufacturer on small orders. But some really mark up the materials before you get them. I've seen markups of 600% and more at the wholesale level. If you double that before you sell it, your customers may be paying 1200% of the original cost. And those wholesalers would likely do more if they could. But usually, it's not that much, but it does happen, especially if there's no competition in the area, they will take what the market will bear. . . . But it's also self-defeating in a way, too. Once you realize that they're taking a big markup, you start to look for other ways of getting the same product. You figure that they have to make a buck, just like everyone else, but let's keep it in reason. There were certain groups we used to give a lot of business to, before, but then we realized what they were doing, so we started looking elsewhere. Now, we only deal with some of these companies when we're stuck for something. . . . You have to gauge your market too. "What will people pay? Can they get the same thing from someone else?" Now, we don't worry about smaller differences, you can often overcome that in your selling technique or your service, but you want to be in the ballpark if it's an identical item. Otherwise, your customers are going to move away, just like you and your suppliers [manufacture industrial].

Buyers are not only very uneven in their definitions of acceptable price ranges, but also in the extent to which they allow their purchasing decisions to be predicated by what others would define as very minor cost differences.

> You'll get buyers from two different kinds of stores and one will think that something is pretty reasonable, while another will say, "Holy mackerel, is that ever high!" It's because their price ranges are totally different. Say someone in jewelry

and someone in a department store. . . . You'll find that the jewelry people will go into the more expensive stuff, and they would display it in a more attractive way. In some other stores the same things will not sell, unless they've got them very well-displayed [manufacture—giftware].

Your buyers differ quite a bit in how much emphasis they put on prices compared to service, say. Some are really chintzy, and if it's a nickel cheaper here or there, that's where they'll buy. No sense of loyalty really, not much stock in service, just more on price [manufacture—industrial].

Not unlike concerns with relevancy, quality, service, and the like, definitions of acceptable or desirable prices reflect buyer perceptions of their customers' expectations.

_____ has some very attractive merchandise, but their margin as wholesalers is excessive and if we were to double their price, it would very likely take us out of our customers' price range [jewelry].

We don't worry about the people above us in class, what they're ordering in shoes. We'll be on a larger volume. But the guys below us, if they go out and get something made up that looks like the same damn thing we've got and he's underpricing you, that's what we've got to worry about. So basically, it's on your cheaper ends that you're worrying about, not the more expensive ones [shoes].

When you're buying to specifications, for a company, you can get the manufacturers to give you bids on these. . . . So you'll talk with the different suppliers, see their samples. Then you'll make your preliminary selections, get quotes on those. So you've come up with price ranges that meet the criteria, then it's "Which one do you want?" . . . Where here, I buy things for resale. I buy them for their salability, what will run with the trends people are buying in [giftware].

Special prices. Recognizing that better prices and special incentives can influence buyer decisions, one also finds suppliers offering "specials." These reduced prices may reflect "slow movers" and "old stock," but may also denote "introductory offers," "seasonal merchandise," and supplier attempts to increase their cash flows.

They should be on the lookout for "specials." That is something you can sell for $10, that you can buy for $2.50, but you know it is going to sell if you do something to help it. At least they are helping their slowest times by doing something, so they carry a bit of inventory and the cost of it is negligible. Because you are bringing it in at $2.50 cost which is still going to be a $10 retail and the normal cost in a $10 retail is $5.00. So you are making a 75% markup, instead of 50 [wholesale—giftware].

One of the things you have in dealing with manufacturers are their end of season clearances. Here you might have an item you might have purchased from them for $25 before the season started, and charged $50. Now, you are able to purchase that item from them at $12.50 or half price. Using the normal markup, the new price would be $25. Now what you can do is put that on "special," and the customer thinks they're getting an exceptional deal because it is now half price. So that is something that will happen, and your actual markup hasn't changed [women's clothing].

It is not uncommon to find some suppliers at almost all trade shows offering "show specials." These displays not only tend to draw more attention to the exhibitor's booth, but these time-limited bargains may also generate a sense of urgency [to order now] on the part of prospective buyers [notes].

Special incentives. Not all supplier deals involve better item prices. Suppliers may also offer bonuses or prizes for each unit and/or volume levels buyers purchase/move. These offers are generally available to all buyers and/or employees selling a certain line.

The manufacturers give trips and such, especially in the television industry. They've been going on for years, and I would have thought they would have gone by the boards by now, but the retailers seem to like them and the manufacturers seem to think it's good for business, so they've kept them. . . . But you have to watch it because you can build a lot of inventory that way. You can overextend yourself that way. . . . From the manufacturer's point of view, you have to watch that you don't overload your retailers with your merchandise on these competitions. We've done that, and the next couple of months after the trip, you're sitting around while they're trying to clear out the stock they bought for the competition or trip. So you have to watch that end of it too [manufacture—appliances].

The mattress companies are notorious for all these trips they offer to the merchants. Sell so many mattresses and win a trip here or there. The way I look at it is, if you want to take a trip, you take a trip, but don't take it because you have stockpiled so many mattresses and now you have to unload them [furniture].

The buyer-supplier relationship also lends itself to a variety of more clandestine deals. It should not be assumed, however, that these practices are always initiated by suppliers wanting to sell goods. Either party may make proposals to the other.[17]

There are all kinds of deals that might go on between the buyer and the manufacturer, especially if the supplier really wanted to sell to this person or wanted to keep them as an outlet. All sorts of kickbacks, extras, reductions, things of that nature.... It depends on the items being sold to some extent, but a lot of things could be worked out to keep people happy. You do have these things going on, sort of a set of understandings that buyers and suppliers will work out over time. Sometimes it benefits the company, sometimes it benefits that individual buyer [manufacture—shoes].

The conventions can lead to some private deals, kickbacks, and also good times, women and all, for the buyer. But then, if there's a big price difference, he has to justify that. That's the thing that limits friendship deals [manufacture—industrial].

ACCEPTABLE VOLUMES

Another element affecting purchasing decisions are definitions of acceptable volumes on the part of prospective traders. Depending upon their capacities, individual suppliers and buyers may have quite different notions of suitable order sizes for business transactions. Regardless of whether suppliers define volumes in dollar purchase totals or in units purchased, desired orders (versus too big or too small) represent one basis on which prospective buyers are screened (and excluded from purchases). While typically providing better prices with higher volumes, price reductions are not strictly matters of manufacturing economy. It means that less time and/or money is being spent per unit in all aspects of processing (e.g., packaging, delivery, bookkeeping). Thus, in addition to the manufacturing process itself, the related overhead costs represent additional bases on which manufacturers could provide better prices on volume orders and/or be more reluctant to consider small orders.

The bigger you are, the better prices you get from these wholesalers, until you go into your own warehousing and buying direct. That's when the big savings start.... We started buying direct as much as possible, very early in our career. There's always a supplier if you go after him that will sell direct, even when they're not supposed to. We usually had some warehouse space, in the basement or near the stores, anything convenient. Then we could handle the large carload or tractor trailer lots. But it's a matter of contacts, and we kept quite active in supermarket institutes and we were quite active in meeting suppliers. And, once they knew that you would be moving their goods in volume, you didn't have to run after them, they started coming to you.... Then with the volume buying, the growing, the more stores you've got, the better your acceptance by the suppliers.... Volume buying benefits you all around, not just in the staples, but in all the accessories you need in running the store [grocery].

Volume buying is a powerful thing. It's not only a matter of laying out less money on a given order, but if you get a better unit price, either you can charge less and get more sales or if you charge the same amount, say the suggested retail price, you're making a better margin. More on your profits [giftware].

While vendors might like to hedge their bets by ordering smaller quantities of goods at a time or ordering goods from a larger number of suppliers, other contingencies such as production time lags, minimum orders, and better volume prices tend to discourage these practices.

If you order several different lines from the same manufacturer, it's much easier to get the total volume of your order up, and that way you get a better price on the merchandise overall. So with this one company, I can easily get an order for $10,000 almost any time, where with the other one, we just deal with them on the one line, so it's a little more difficult to get a good total [wholesale—jewelry].

Many of the manufacturers will offer you benefits, like prepaid freight if your order totals so much. Now the dollar value of the freight can be quite significant! It can save you several hundred dollars. And you need every saving you can get to make you competitive with the chains! So if you're in a situation like that, it can be very worth your while to add a few extra items to your order to make their quota to pick up that kind of saving. You could see it as an inducement, but they've got the freight costs built in, based on what it costs them for the paperwork, and the processing of the order [appliances].

Buyer Bigness

Supplier concerns with volume are not limited to small orders. Exceptionally large orders can also create dilemmas for suppliers. While suppliers like to make big sales, many express reservations about dealing with unusually large orders from a single source. In addition to the complexities that dealing with large entities may entail, many suppliers are also concerned with their subsequent dependency (loyalty and control) on that source for further orders. Beyond seeking alternative suppliers, buyers dealing in higher volumes are also more likely to consider it economically viable to manufacture and/or directly import these goods themselves. From the big volume buyers' perspective, the make or import options are more apt to represent genuine alternatives.

Generally speaking, bigger buyer business is desired and sought for the total purchase dollar involved and its growth potential, but the relationship may engender significant risk. While bigger buyers are apt to receive (and sometimes assume) better service, larger discounts, and the like on a more routine basis, we find that not unlike the hooker who has become heavily dependent on her "sugar daddy" (Prus and Irini, 1988: 69-74), or the bookmaker who takes larger bets than he can actually cover (Prus and Sharper, 1977: 142-147), suppliers' involvements with proportionately large buyers can significantly affect their futures.

We do have our priority customers, people who order a lot of merchandise. We try to take care of them first. With some of them, if we don't do everything right, send the order right away, we have a good chance of losing the business and nobody wants to lose a big account. So the larger accounts, you have to cater to them all the time. It's not fair. You know it's not fair, but you have to do it to stay in business. And they take liberties in paying. If they're late, they know you're not going to say too much to them [wholesale—jewelry].

Dealing with the chains, there is very little loyalty. If they come across something else they like, a little different style, a better price, that is it. They are going to the next company. . . . And what happens is that you have to get all geared up for the large buyers, so if they drop you, you can be in really big trouble unless you've managed to pick up someone else along the way to offset that. . . . That's why it's a gamble, and that's why you always need to be digging up new business. And where a bigger account is concerned, you may have to generate a lot of new accounts to try to get around that [manufacture—giftware].

The larger companies have more bargaining power. Because they're buying in such larger quantities, they may get dollars off the individual item over what someone else pays. Then if you have the same markup, their price is less or if they go with the suggested retail price, they can make more on each item sold. So a dollar or two off each garment, that can really add up. So the larger chains really have an advantage there. . . . The manufacturer's problem there, of course, is that if they begin catering to the larger chains, they become increasingly dependent on that one chain. . . . And you can't lock these companies in on a long term. You're only good as long as they need you. When they don't need you, when they can find someone else who will do it better or cheaper, they'll go to them. So you may be making a larger dollar today, but tomorrow, they may decide to pull out. Then they make bigger demands on you, and since you don't have other customers who could pick up the difference, you're in a corner. They can really squeeze you. They virtually own you, and there go your profits, or they may bankrupt you that way.

So a lot of manufacturers are hesitant about taking on a larger department store. They prefer the smaller businesses. The large chain sounds great, but it's not. You're much better to have a lot of small accounts. It's more reliable. They're not going to order 10,000 and so you just don't find yourself in the same situation [women's clothing].

Deep Discounting

Buyers engaged in deep discounting can also create problems for suppliers. A more dramatic discount makes items more accessible to the suppliers' end-customers, but it tends to saturate the market in that area. As more people buy an item at the discounted price, fewer prospects are left, and all may be more reluctant to buy that item at the regular price. Deep discounting can also give suppliers a very misleading impression of future market potential (suppliers might increase stock only to discover a vanishing market). Further, other buyers may become upset with suppliers for dealing with big discounters. They may not only have lost business as a result, but may also find themselves stuck with merchandise difficult to move at their regular margins. Suppliers are not empowered legally to determine prices of their products once they have been sold to others. However, they can effectively avoid doing business with companies they see as disruptive to their enterprises.

Dealing with the deep discounters is tempting. They get such large volumes that it's a real good chance to unload some of your goods [manufacture—giftware].

The deep discounters, like [A] or [B], can create problems for you. They do operate on high volumes and lower margins. And that's fine, but your other dealers are not in a position to compete with them on price. Then they want more off to be competitive with the deep discounters. It is tempting [to deal with the deep discounters], but we're very wary because of the other [manufacture—appliances].

FINANCING CONCERNS

Although an agreement to purchase may appear to conclude the transaction, this only marks the beginning of many business relationships. The buyer provides an arena in which to market the supplier's products and whether or not credit is provided, their mutual fate to some extent depends on the subsequent sales of that product by the buyer. If the goods obtained do not move adequately, further orders are unlikely. When credit is extended, their interdependency is further intensified.

As a traveling salesman, you're not only depending on the merchants for your sales, but you're also depending on them to sell your products. You can't come back and sell them more if, when you go back, they still have the same products there. You have to convince them that these products are great, fantastic, that they're going to sell. And if they don't sell those products, you have to figure out why they're not selling. You have to help them display them right, suggest that the products be put in a different area, set up a display for them. Do all the work for them. Unpack the merchandise, put up a nice display stand, move some things over here, move this other merchandise over, but do it nice and neat. Maybe put some things around the cash register, encourage a few sales. . . . You can't tell what actually happens with the merchandise when you leave the store. The merchant may decide that he didn't like the way you set up the display and change it around. Or he may decide to move your merchandise to the back of the store, or another salesman may come in and move it around to better suit his products. It happens all the time. If he can convince them that his line is better, you come back and you can't find your stock, and you tell him, "No wonder it's not selling. Look, you've got this stuff hidden over here." And then, while you're there, you've got to try to make it worthwhile, so you've got to try to sell him the new part of the line. "We've also added this to the line, it's going great!" "How can you tell me it's going great, when I haven't sold what you sold me before?" "Well, you had it hidden, just take a few of them." Help pay for my gas, right [wholesale—giftware].

The retailers do run on your money. They would like to pay you after it sells. And there, you have to keep after them to collect because you have to have your cash flow coming in too. In my situation, I order from the manufacturer and I pay him at the time I take possession of the goods and so it's often several months before I actually see my money coming back to me. . . . It's the big orders really that make it worthwhile, and also people who can sell your products, because even if you get a big order and they can't sell it, and they can't pay their bills, that's no good. So you're very dependent on their ability to sell it after you get the order from them [wholesale—giftware].

As noted earlier, suppliers commonly extend some form of credit to their buyers. However, even if they themselves have periods of credit from their suppliers, they have invested time and labor costs and other overhead in their products before realizing a return. To reduce risk, suppliers will often run credit checks on new customers and/or require cash, ship C.O.D., and the like. These practices may offend new customers and may result in some business loss (should customers be able to arrange lines of credit elsewhere). Thus their actual implementation reflects company policies and desires for growth.[18]

In the beginning we used to take everything we could get. We used to get burned more often. But even now, we get burned because of bankruptcies. Some fairly respectable company all of a sudden goes bankrupt. What can you do [manufacture—giftware]?

Clearly, not all financing problems are related to new accounts. As a result, all accounts are subject to some monitoring and decisions must be made on whether or not to carry accounts that have become delinquent in their payments. The situation becomes especially sensitive when these accounts are seen as good prospects for the future.

If people aren't paying their bills, we charge them interest after a while, but then you get some who don't want to pay interest and it's especially a problem with some of the large companies because they just don't worry about it. We do have an account with the collection agency, but then you lose a fair bit of money. Something else you take into consideration there is whether the people are likely to be placing more orders with you. So if they're your more steady customers or your bigger customers, then you're not so likely to make an issue over them being slow paying their bills [wholesale—jewelry].

Collecting can be a problem sometimes because the accountant doesn't see things the way the salesman does. All they basically know is that the account is overdue, so they're not very sensitive to the people. They just want to know, "Why is this account overdue?" [manufacture—industrial]

With the increasing interest rates, you have to chase people more now than you used to. It really keeps you going, trying to keep your accounts updated. Also, you have to push for your payments, or you don't get them. You have to call people up when those 30 days are over. And you get this line, it's in the mail, or the invoice hasn't been received yet, send me another one. So they can postpone or delay in that way. . . . Some companies, long-term payment is part of their contract with you. It's 45 days or 90 days and they just work it that way. But with the high interest rates, that is how business is being run more and more. . . . I have all the people calling me, and I do the same with them. Give them the runaround for a while, because you have got all that money moving around. Then somebody calls you, and they say, "We need a couple more days or weeks," so you work something out there, because you have to do business there too. You have to be diplomatic about how you are dealing with them, because you realize that everybody's business has its ups and downs, so you try to work something out. But you know that the other companies try to postpone payments if they can, and we do the same thing here. Then they get on the phone to you and you know they're needing their money, and you send it out to them. It works that way. We only actually had to go through a collection agency twice in the 18 years we have been doing business, so overall it has not been too bad for us [manufacture—industrial].

PRIVATE BRANDS

Another element that speaks to trading relations, especially to the fragility of buyer-supplier relationships, is that pertaining to private brands (versus supplier name brands). Private brands refer to goods that, while produced by a particular manufacturer, bear no identification of that supplier (i.e., these goods carry someone else's brand or are no-names). The end result is that private brands are effectively controlled by the distributor.[19] While realizing that these other brands may engender some quality-based resistance from their customers, this practice may allow buyers to gain a larger share of their customers' business by providing a less costly alternative to the name brand. Not only may usual (or greater) margins be obtained through resale of these private brands,[20] but insofar as the buyers' own brands become better established in the marketplace, buyers become increasingly independent of any particular suppliers.

> With the house brands, you have more control. You have "sales" when you want them, rather than when the supplier wants it, where everyone is offering the same product, the same brand on "sale" at the same time. . . . But you have to promote your own brand if you go that route. That can be tough to establish. Very costly! It can take a lot of money to build your own brand [department store].

As suppliers generally wish to establish a selective demand for their products, they are typically reluctant to promote the sales of these other brands. And, so long as they have an exclusive and/or are unable to meet existing demands, they are unlikely to entertain private branding. However, when a number of suppliers find themselves in a competitive context for a less certain market, they become especially vulnerable to private brand proposals. For suppliers so approached, private brand options represent a set of dilemmas with which to deal. On the plus side, suppliers anticipate that while selling comparable items for less than for their own name brands, they will generate some gains by making greater use of their existing facilities; and if they were not to do so, their competitors might be so tempted, gaining a relative advantage over them in the process. In this later regard, they would face even greater competition from the combination of the competitor's name brand and the private brand the competitor is supplying. Cast against these relative gains are a set of fears that one's own name brand (given equal quality private brands) could lose its marketplace identity and selling power; the additional advertising needed to offset price differentials between the supplier's name brands and private brands may increase further the costs of the supplier's own brand; and should buyers find that they could get better prices elsewhere, they have less incentive to deal further with particular suppliers in the future.

If a company doesn't have strong media promotions or effective displays and packaging, then their credibility is a problem. . . . We give them some credibility just by carrying it, but otherwise we'd likely be just as well off with our [store] brand [grocery].

You worry about that. If [X] or [Y] has you put their labels on your garments, well, that sort of kills your label . . . That business is not as valuable to you in the long run. Next time, they can go to whoever they want, and you have nothing over them, except whatever track record you've established with them. And some buyers don't seem that concerned, or they're switching around, so not as much loyalty as you'd hope [manufacture—clothing].

Despite the seemingly clear advantages of private brands, they have not become as dominant as some buyers might like. Thus a major element promoting continuity of the name brands among businesses able to develop private labels are the preferences of their customers.

We do have our own brands, but we wouldn't do as well if we didn't carry the name brands. We make a lot of sales because people want these name brands. If you didn't have them, you would be out of luck in many cases [shoes].

They [customers] want the name brands. It's the image it has. The label is worth something apart from what they're buying. People are buying the labels, the images they associate with it [department store].

_____ is a well-known brand. Our products sell themselves. The name is known, trusted, respected, and we advertise a lot. That's what we can offer the retailers [manufacture—appliances].

Dropping Suppliers

While trading relationships may be severed by either party, buyer decisions to drop suppliers reflect concerns similar to those they express in ordering goods. However, notions of relevance, quality, service, price, and the like, are defined within the shifting interests of individual buyers and suppliers. Thus the search for partners in trade may be best seen as an ongoing process.

We've stopped dealing with some suppliers because we've changed our lines or they've changed their lines. They may have been good to deal with, but they're no longer relevant. . . . Usually, you will stop at their booth at the show, but often just for small talk, maybe see what they're into now [giftware].

We've had to drop a number of suppliers. Sometimes their merchandise isn't moving or, in some cases, the items are not standing up to the usual wear and tear that are required of them. Or you will get some that are very slow in shipping or they are not very careful in their packing and so you have more problems with returns and just delays that way [wholesale—jewelry].

Some of the equipment we will be selling the people will last them for years and so you may not see them for quite a while. And also, it's becoming more common for companies when they want equipment, to ask for triplicate bids. So they will approach three companies and they want to know what price the item is, and what the quality is, and they want to know what the reliability is of the company that they are dealing with. But they will buy from you, even if you don't have the best price, if they think you have the better quality, or if they think you are more reliable in the services you are giving them. . . . Something else that they will do is they will order from suppliers even when they are not happy with them. That's something that I would encourage them to do myself, just to keep the channels open, because you never know in this business when you might have to deal with these people. And even if they are not your favorite suppliers, you might still try to do a little business with them, just to keep that relationship with them. So if you have a number of identical items, then you might seek out bids. Then your agents will come and get these products and test them out, and go back and ask your customers what they know about them and what their preferences are. . . . If you like the company, you're more likely to deal with them. If you like the salesman, you'll be more likely to deal with that person, but there again, you would want to know that the company will back up the salesman. . . . But again, service is a very important part of it. If you have a reputation of giving good service, that is going to overcome price differences that can be quite substantial [manufacture—industrial].

Similarly, it seems that loyalty is intensified as buyers:[21] (1) rely more exclusively and more extensively on a particular supplier's goods,[22] (2) acquire reputations for carrying that supplier's goods, (3) organize their marketing routines around specific suppliers' products, and (4) develop more congenial personal relations with suppliers.[23] To the extent buyer-supplier relationships are buttressed by definitions of these relationships as denoting effective partners in trade, loyalty is further enhanced. While these buyer dependencies are particularly evident in franchises wherein the entire (supply and) marketing program may be contractually defined, it is also apparent that these are elements making it more difficult for all buyers to shift suppliers whenever they might like.

In Perspective

Cutting across issues of commitment, rationality, risk-taking, and relationships, this chapter addresses a number of issues central to ongoing group life. In the first instance, buyers making commitments are betting on the future. Some buyers will purchase only goods for which they have standing orders, but for the most part the rightness of buyer commitments is dependent on prospective customers' selections at later points in time. It is these end customers who ultimately define the winning numbers and the dogs.

From all appearances, buyers intend to purchase rationally. However, as Schutz (1943) and Garfinkel (1967) posit, rationality is something to be worked out. In attempting to deal with the unpredictability of demand, buyers commonly hedge their bets. To this end, one finds buyers seeking consensus, concentrating on the basics, going with winners, testing the ice, diversifying their lines, and cultivating relationships. However, this gaming is best seen within the context of ongoing buyer-supplier relations.

Were buyers to anticipate one-time only purchases, their decisions would more completely reflect the immediate situation at hand. However, to the extent that purchasing activity signifies emergent (and continuing) relationships, these relationships (anticipated and experienced) become important elements affecting commitments. Caught between their anticipations of customer preferences and concerns with viable supplier relationships, buyers often find themselves shifting between products and suppliers as a primary focus in purchasing decisions. While interdependencies emerge most readily when stable relations are desired by both parties, any commitment (and the expectations resulting thereof) tends to facilitate long-term (and mutual) versus highly situated risk taking. Not only are suppliers apt to prepare for and encourage repeat patronage in the future, but should products catch on, the buyer's customers promote these associations through the expectations these customers create.[24] As buyers become known as dealers of particular products, they (as Lemert, 1951, 1967, would suggest) are more likely to find their relationships with suppliers stabilizing.

Buying activity on the part of businesspeople suggests many parallels with purchasing activity by consumers. These comparisons would seem especially prominent when consumers explicitly anticipate seeking approval from others for the purchases they make (e.g., gifts for friends, items hoped to enhance one's popularity or standing in a group), and consumers envision themselves as dependent on the goodwill of the retailers with whom they deal (e.g., follow-up service, warranties). Under these conditions, one would expect consumers to be torn between products and those from whom they purchase these products. Concerned with the (purchase) approval of others, consumers may question the viability of their own tastes, and standards. To this end, they are apt to find themselves guessing at what others would like, taking others along, and hedging their bets in the process. Insofar as they are concerned with maintaining working relationships with particular retailers, these (other) customers are apt to find themselves defining products within the context of those relationships.

Notes

1. James Henslin (1968), in his discussion of "Trust and the Cab Driver," develops a parallel theme as he portrays cabbie assessments of the appearances, circumstances, and actions of prospective patrons relative to trustworthy fares.

2. As the discussion later indicates, vendors with hotter (including more prestigious) lines may be able to reverse the tendency, at least so long as their buyers maintain these definitions.

3. It is generally easier to judge (not necessarily accurately) buyers in direct resale settings ("Did it sell, or didn't it?") than in the manufacturing sector (denoting more intervening processes).

4. These experiences readily coincide with Glick's (1957) study of buyers and sellers in the futures market. Similar observations are made by Hayano (1982) in his discussion of gambling in poker games frequented by a more or less regular set of participants. In

each of these settings, as in gambling and gaming more generally (e.g., handicapping, systems), losses may be seen as lessons for the future.

5. Some buyers have degrees in business, but much buying activity can be learned only through practice and/or apprenticeship. People may learn some principles of buying in academic programs, but as Strauss (1964) suggests, the main function of these credentials may be to provide prestige and occupational entry for those thusly professionalized.

6. For another indication of gambling in the marketplace, see Glick (1957). While speaking to a rather different setting (futures trading), this study is strikingly similar.

7. Even when one purchases on the basis of existing orders from one's customers, some risk is involved. Orders may be canceled or products returned at some later date.

8. Readers should realize that these statements on rationality are abbreviated and recontextualized versions of Garfinkel's analysis.

9. Buying is simplified when purchasers are requested to buy according to specifications, but these people tend to experience some ambiguities relative to the larger dimensions of their positions (e.g., saving money, ensuring delivery, obtaining viable warranties). To the extent others (e.g., engineers) define quality, timing, cost limits, and so on, much responsibility for the purchase lies with those generating these orders. Even though these decision makers need not cover their bets themselves (i.e., company costs), they still gamble. See Strauss (1964) for an elaboration of interdepartmental purchasing arrangements and conflicts.

10. Glick (1957) and Adler (1981) make similar observations in their analyses of stock market exchanges. Their research suggests that investors and fund managers also follow like-others and/or those thought to be well informed. Additionally, as Glick (1957: 193-248) notes, these discussions with and observations of others may serve a number of important functions. In addition to exchanging and evaluating information about the viability of particular transactions through these contacts, buyers may diminish reservations about risk taking, and console one another over losses; thus, facilitating planning as well as promoting optimism in a setting characterized by much uncertainty.

11. Testing the ice is a marketing strategy clearly not limited to buyers. Thus, one step closer to the eventual consumers, the buyers' territories represent crucial testing arenas for the suppliers' products. Serving as "gatekeepers" (Katz and Lazarsfeld, 1955), buyers provide indications of the feasibility of supplier products by their comments, buying decisions, and subsequent feedback. Not only do suppliers learn that products may not move equally well in certain areas or through certain buyers' organizations, they also get feedback (sometimes product returns) on the viability of their products in the marketplace. If suppliers are to plan more astutely, make product adjustments or improvements, or add new lines, information from the buyers can be invaluable.

12. Kriesberg's (1956) discussion of the general reluctance of regular steel suppliers to raise prices during a period of widespread shortage is particularly relevant here. Even though buyers would have paid considerably more for their steel, gray marketing (gouging) was largely confined to those who saw themselves in the marketplace on a more marginal (especially transitory) basis. The others were concerned with maintaining good buyer relations.

13. Further evidence of concerns with maintaining working relationships may be noted in Macaulay's (1963) discussion of the informal (versus legal) settlement of disputes on the part of both buyers and suppliers.

14. We ordinarily think of referrals as occurring mainly among consumers, but they are by no means so limited. It is not uncommon, for instance, to find purchasing agents

contacting other companies (including competitors, in some cases) to inquire into their experiences with particular products/suppliers.

15. This is one reason suppliers frequently discourage their salespeople from overloading their customers. Not only may these customers (feeling stung) be more reluctant to deal with suppliers who have suggested excessively large orders, but the suppliers involved attain a misleading sense of the popularity of these items (resulting in a costly surplus inventory).

16. Although bids are not considered in the present discussion of buying, it should be recognized that bids accepted on price alone assume constancy of other elements. Otherwise, the main effect of seeking bids is to provide another mode of comparison shopping.

17. For an account of aggressive buying practices, see Andrew's (1950) discussion of A&P.

18. Albeit somewhat risky, the extension of credit represents an important means of generating action. See Bigus's (1972) material on milkmen and their customers, Prus and Sharper's (1977) discussion of bookmakers, and Adler and Adler's (1983) statement on drug dealers, for other examples.

19. Haring (1935: 66-80) provides an early and valuable account of private branding. He indicates that this practice was well established by 1930.

20. Since they may have a choice of suppliers, and are not requesting price cuts on name brands, these buyers are in a position to obtain very competitive prices on these items.

21. Generally speaking, the development of enduring buyer-supplier relations seems consistent with Lemert's (1951, 1972) notion of "secondary deviation." Lemert posits that as persons are identified as "deviants," come to identify themselves as such, and adjust their lives to this definition of self, they will find it increasingly difficult to disinvolve themselves from those endeavors.

22. Suppliers may also attempt to build customer loyalty into their purchases by developing tie-in sales. In some cases, discounts or credits based on present orders may be given on future orders (inducements to reorder). In other instances, suppliers may be in a position to develop uniquely fitting components to reduce common availability of parts and supplies. Weigand (1980) uses the term *buying in* to refer to this latter (monopolistic) phenomenon, providing illustrations with cameras, razors, radios, public utilities, air-traffic control systems, and franchises.

23. For other materials pertaining to loyalty, see Chapters 3 ("Generating Trust"), 7 ("Developing Loyalty"), and 8 ("Holding Sales") in *Making Sales* (Prus, 1989). Discussions of milkmen's (Bigus, 1972) and bar staff's (Prus and Irini, 1988: 144-60; and 192-204) relations with their customers offer additional illustrations of loyalty-promoting behavior. As is evident in all of these works, many of the actual strategies employed reflect on-the-job socialization rather than managerial policy and instruction.

24. The role of supplier advertising should not be overlooked as an element promoting customer interest in particular brands. It is to the vendor's advantage to carry commonly requested brands. Sofer (1965: 185-185) indicates that merchants in Britain experience similar pressures to carry advertised brands.

Chapter 5
SETTING PRICES

It's hard to know where to set your prices, because on some things you don't make much, but that's all the market will bear for that item. Where with other things, you can charge more, and they will still do well. So you have to balance things out that way. Some things you carry, even though it doesn't pay off all that well for you. And there, a little business may be better than none, not having it. Although, there are times when these can cost you more than they're worth, just to carry them around, or if they interfere with your sales of other things. . . . There are some things that just do not pay off for you, in terms of your efforts. We could sell them, but they're maybe smaller things and people do not realize what they cost us to produce, timewise [crafts].

What are objects worth? How is value defined in the marketplace? How are prices set? When and how are prices adjusted? Is there a best price? What role does competition play in the pricing process?

It is toward questions of this sort that this chapter is directed, as it considers the price-setting activities of vendors in reference to profit concerns, the anticipated behavior of buyers, and the dynamics of the marketplace.[1] In one of the few sociological discussions of money, value, and price, Georg Simmel (1900: 81) postulates that "the value of an object becomes objectified by exchanging it for another object." Recognizing that "the worth of an object is a socially attributed quality" Simmel lays a theoretical cornerstone for this chapter.[2]

Pricing as Social Activity

Whereas scholars in the fields of marketing and economics tend to assume abstract rational-economic models of price setting,[3] we find

173

vendors pitching prices to imagined and typically rather nebulous audiences.[4] Despite the confidence with which prices are sometimes stipulated, price setting assumes a tentative and reactive quality. In practice, vendors not only indicate general concerns with developing loyalty within shifting competitive contexts, but also find themselves adjusting to buyer assessments of their prices. Consequently, attention will be given to the ways in which prices are symbolic products that emerge and are transformed in group contexts.

The term *joint activity* (Blumer, 1969) refers to the process by which people work out activities with others. It involves both a lateral-situated element and a temporal-processual dimension. While people approach situations with previously developed understandings, each encounter is problematic. Each sequence of interaction has to be worked out by the participants involved.

> Even in the case of preestablished and repetitive joint action, each instance of such joint action has to be formed anew. The participants still have to build up their lines of action and fit them to one another through the dual process of designation and interpretation [p. 18]. . . . The participants involved in the formation of the new joint action always bring to that formation the world of objects, the sets of meanings, and the schemes of interpretation that they already possess. Thus, the new form of joint action always emerges out of and is connected with a context of previous joint action [p. 20]. . . . One cannot understand the new form without incorporating knowledge of this continuity into one's analysis of the new form. Joint activity not only represents a horizontal linkage, so to speak, of the activities of the participants, but also a vertical linkage with previous joint action [Blumer, 1969: 20].

Viewing marketing in processual terms, it becomes apparent that joint activity on the part of the vendor not only begins prior to actual encounters (previous experiences, preparations, anticipations, price designations), but that it also extends beyond these encounters (re-assessments, readjustments) to subsequent encounters with the same and/or other people. Accordingly, attention will be given to the ways in which symbols (prices in this case) emerge and are transformed in group contexts.[5]

PRICING AS NAMING ACTIVITY

Drawing heavily on the experiences of vendors, one finds that pricing not only denotes marketplace strategy, but a negotiation context as well.

Thus, not unlike other situations involving actor choices, such as police officers' decisions to make arrests (e.g., Bittner, 1967; Black and Reiss, 1970; Rubinstein, 1973) and persons affixing labels to others (Prus, 1975a, 1975b, 1982), price setting emerges as a reflective (discretionary) and negotiable phenomenon. Subject to choice and strategy, pricing becomes an element in the vendor's "presentation of self" (Goffman, 1959) and a way of dealing with the ambiguities (Lyman and Scott, 1970) of the marketplace. Price proposals are also dependent on others in the community for confirmation of their "reality" (Berger and Luckmann, 1966). As price symbolizes a form of exchange (sacrifice) requested of the prospective buyer, and is subject to interpretation, negotiation, and competition, price setting is best seen as an ongoing social construction.

The socially constructed nature of price setting may become more apparent by introducing a model originally developed to explain how people acquire identities and reputations. While the subsequent discussion will make largely only implicit reference to this model, the processes outlined are basic to the analysis of price setting as activity. In discussing the process by which people become known as certain kinds of people (i.e., become symbols, are labeled), Prus (1975a) delineates four processes central to the formation of social identities: typing; designating; assessing; and resisting.[6] *Typing* refers to the process by which one person (agent) arrives at a private definition of another (target). Not all typings are made known to the target and/or others, and although agents may occasionally blurt out their private typings, they are seen to make decisions as to whether or not to make these typings known to others. *Designating* refers to agents providing indications (verbal and/or behavioral) of a somewhat public nature, suggesting that targets are particular types of people. As others (including targets) learn of these designations, they tend to *assess* these for their appropriateness relative to their knowledge and views of the target. Where target references are seen as inappropriate (too soft, too harsh, inaccurate), interested persons then decide whether to *resist* target designations or to let these go unchallenged.

Applying this model to pricing situations, the process is as follows. First, vendors may arrive at private definitions of product prices, reflecting their estimations of product popularity, desired profit margins, and such. Then, based on their anticipation of price-product receptivity by buyers, they announce prices (which may be, but need not be

identical to their private estimates; i.e., some discretion may be involved). The buyers assess the designated prices relative to their perceptions of product worth. Buyers may accept those prices as reasonable; challenge designated prices (possibly refusing to buy); and/or may
succumb to stipulated prices because of perceived limited options.
While acceptance of stipulated prices serves to objectify these (i.e., the
label fits), rejection may lead the vendors to reconsider their designated
prices, with the possibility of subsequent adjustments. The model is also
applicable to group pricing decisions (e.g., partnerships, committees).
This means that prior to announcement, price designations may have
already been subject to internal negotiation (designation, assessment,
resistance) on the part of the vending entity.[7]

It should also be apparent that price resistances are not uniform across
audiences, and prices may be adjusted upwards as well as downwards
as a consequence of the resistances designators encounter in their
pricing activities. Pricing reflects both the perspectives of the vendors involved (e.g., pricing practices of particular industries or product areas, preestablished company policies, managerial concerns for
growth), and the anticipated (and actual) responses of their prospects.
Using this model as a conceptual point, the processual aspects of pricing
will become much more evident. Some product prices will be much
more stable than others, but insofar as prices are dependent on acceptance by the buyer, continuity is problematic.

Price and Profit: Some General Considerations

When discussing the setting of prices, one notes that profit is not a
simple function of markup (margin). Profit would seem to increase with
price increases, but this equation neglects the dynamics of the marketplace. Thus, although vendors are highly concerned with profits, they
also come to realize that pricing assumes a variety of other dimensions.
Pricing may be used as a tool in attempts to determine profits and
otherwise structure markets, but it also takes its shape from the marketplace. Summarizing a number of themes from conventional marketing
approaches to pricing, Lynn (1967) notes that vendors may price products in attempts to achieve (1) maximum company profits, (2) specific
levels of profits, (3) satisfactory levels of profits, (4) increased unit
volumes of sales, (5) increased cash flows, (6) price parity with com-

petitors, (7) certain company images, and (8) greater market stability. Pricing practices may also reflect vendor attempts to (9) develop new markets, (10) maintain customer patronage, and (11) eliminate competitors. Presumably any number of these objectives may be pursued on a simultaneous and/or sequential basis, but it should be appreciated that each objective is in itself quite ambiguous. Additionally, and ultimately more importantly, the realization of any objective requires ongoing cooperation on the part of those able to affect the outcomes vendors experience.

In the following discussions, attention will be given to more situated vendor tactics, dilemmas, and adjustments; but even at a general level it is instructive to consider price setting in dynamic terms. While the attainment of any one objective is likely to conflict at some point with the achievement of others, pricing decisions are made within shifting contexts. This promotes sporadic, if not perpetual, reassessments of specific pricing decisions and practices. Pricing both affects and is affected by a multiplicity of other marketplace activities. Consider briefly the problematic significance of increased volumes of sales. With volume increases, it is possible for prices to remain the same and for profits to increase considerably. However, if buyer interests were to diminish sharply, as might result from present contentment, shifting preferences, or an awareness of new options, vendors anticipating profits on increases in volumes may subsequently find that their investments (and "profits") are effectively located in dead stock.

I think everyone in business has had that experience. Actually, it happens a lot. Just not always so dramatically. You'll get something that starts to take off on you. And you, of course, start producing more. You pretty well have to, because that's where your orders are coming in and you can't afford to start turning down too many orders. Now, you might do really well on that item, but you might end up taking a real beating on it too. . . . Whether you can survive or not depends on what you've got to balance it out with. If things are slow and then you get a hot item, you pretty well have to go for it. But if you go over on your stock too much, you can have a real problem on your hands. Real bad news [manufacture—giftware]!

Expansion is one of the real dangers in business. A lot of companies have been badly hurt that way. If you expand at the right time, fine. But, it's a real risk. You don't know when it's going to fall back on you. Business is fickle, you know [manufacture—appliances].

Similarly, vendors attempting to skim the market (reaping high profits on early sales or achieving early recovery of initial costs) may discover that they have outpriced the market. By the time price reductions are instituted (by choice or pressure to minimize losses), these vendors may find that prospects have lost interest in their products, have become suspicious of their price reductions, or have found competitors who, in the interim, have produced viable copies of, or alternatives to, these products.

Regardless of company objectives, the price-profit relationship is much more uncertain than many might suppose. Although new products may bring pricing dilemmas most sharply into focus (Dean, 1974), decisions to continue existing lines are also contingent on price-profit-product assessments. Even vendors (jointly or individually) in positions virtually to monopolize markets face pricing dilemmas (Scherer, 1970: 85-110; Phillips, 1977). Higher margins, for example, can generate short-run profits, but they also invite both direct competition and the development of alternatives. In contrast, lower margins may result in lower short-term profits, but they have the effect of deterring entry into those markets by prospective competitors.

While the preceding paragraphs have outlined some abstract objectives and theoretically important implications of pricing policies, an analysis limited to goals and functions misses much of the action characterizing the marketplace. In the following pages, we move toward a preliminary description and analysis of the pricing orientations and strategies developed and pursued by vendors in the real world situations of the marketplace. To this end, attention is given to some of the considerations, sensitivities, and strategies vendors take into account as they do price-setting activity.

INITIAL PRICING STRATEGIES

Building on past experiences and traditions in the field, vendors tend to rely on certain rules of thumb in initially contemplating product prices. In Schutz's (1971) terms, these "recipes" reflect the vendors' "stocks of knowledge." Operating in the context of inevitable uncertainty (no one knows for sure which products will sell, much less at what particular prices), these rules of thumb or pricing recipes generate a sense of stability within marketing programs. They represent predictions of customer activity and denote guidelines by which products may be purchased for direct resale, integrated into manufacturing and processing routines in anticipation of sales, presented in the media, and so forth. Pricing is thus both a way of dealing with the ambiguity of the marketplace and a realm of uncertainty in itself.

Taking Margins

The term *margin* or *markup* refers most basically to the difference between the cost price and the price for which products are being sold. There are many ways of arriving at margins, but end-of-year profits are dependent on all sales and expenditures; and operating budgets are based on projected sales and expenditures. Thus, regardless of the manner of ascertaining markups, one is gambling on both sales and overhead.

> With your margins, you try to predict how much you need to make to stay in business. You have all your expenses, mall rents, staff, all your overhead. And when you're ordering your products, you take that into account. How much can you sell this for? Can you make a profit on it in the end? That's where you make it or you don't. But it's all these things. So on something it might seem like a big margin, but it has to cover all these things. The bad buys, the flops, your price reductions, everything [shoes].

In what follows, two general pricing recipes vendors may employ are outlined. These reflect standardized and opportunistic orientations to pricing. Although some vendors may pursue these strategies with considerable rigor, they generally represent starting points rather than definitive price policies. Moreover, the same vendor may use one such strategy for some products or in some situations, and another in other circumstances.

Standardized margins. Standardized margins reflect (cost + profit) formulas vendors may use to routinize their pricing decisions. While some merchants may calculate selling prices as multiples or percentages of the purchase price (e.g., double the cost price, or a take a 100% margin),[8] others may calculate margins by adding a profit percentage to all costs incurred. In the first instance, the margin can vary greatly (e.g., 5% to 1000%), but vendors cover all their overhead with that margin. In the latter case, all overhead is calculated before the profit margin is added on. Regardless of the procedure, the eventual prices (or profits) need not be different.

I was talking with a rep for a manufacturing company and we were talking about markups, and he says, "We only mark up 7%." And I said, "Isn't that kind of low?" and he says, "No, that's kind of high, actually. What do you mark up?" I said, "We mark up 100%." Of course, the next thing, he's calling me a thief. And when he talks about his 7% markup, what he means is that after they cost something out, say the cost of the goods are a dollar, they add so much on for advertising, overhead, and then they add so much on for profit, and then they sell it on a wholesale level for say $1.75. But when I buy that item for $1.75, and sell it for $3.50, I have to take all those things off of that $3.50, and then if there's something left, that's my profit on it. . . . What a lot of people don't understand is that we're assuming all those costs from our selling price, where their selling price is costs plus profit. As long as they make a certain run, they're guaranteed that profit. Now, if they go beyond that run, they either discount for volume or they will be making even more on their profits [giftware].

It should also be appreciated that businesses using standardized margins may use different margins for different products they carry. These differences may reflect turnovers of stock, but they may also denote attempts to be competitive in different product areas.

The markup on groceries, cigarettes, is quite low compared to other things, like greeting cards, for instance. But it reflects your turnover on these items. With break and milk, your turnover is going to be better than once a week, so you'll get a great number of turns on that merchandise, cigarettes too. Same with the lottery tickets. If it's a weekly draw, you'll get 52 turns a year [variety].

Our markup is about the same as the other retail businesses, and even with the 50% [2×; wholesale is 50% of retail price] markup, what you find is that by the time you have subtracted all your expenses, it doesn't leave very much for you in the way of profit. Our markup is such that it is the same on all the items. And, if I get an extremely good buy on a particular item, then the margin will just be the same as any other, so I will pass that along to the consumer. A lot of people don't do it that way, but that is what we have used as our policy [furniture].

Standardized margins facilitate pricing decisions (especially impor-
tant in larger companies), but they also affect buying practices. When margins are preset, those buying goods for the company are effectively (pre)pricing those goods at that point in time. For example, if the policy is to double the wholesale price, buyers may ultimately base their

decision on whether or not to order a relevant $5 item on whether or not they think the item would move in their outlets at $10 (or $9.95). The item may not be tagged until much later, but initial pricing can be largely synonymous with ordering goods.

Standardized margins may also be encouraged by merchants' suppliers. For instance, suppliers may provide merchants with list prices (e.g., manufacturer's suggested retail price), or otherwise alert vendors to existing margins in the trade. As a result of fair trade legislation, it is illegal for suppliers to force vendors to charge fixed amounts for goods they purchase for resale. However, suppliers can (and often do) suggest selling prices. To the extent these are followed, they would encourage standardized prices. Merchants reselling products may charge prices at variance from the suggested prices, but suggested prices represent benchmarks of objectivity that merchants may use in establishing their own prices.

> A lot of manufacturers give you a suggested retail price. It's good. It gives you an idea of what the other people might be charging, and you can show it to your customers, give them an idea of that too. Then, if you give them a little off, they're more likely to appreciate that, because they have an idea of where the ceiling is, say where the (suggested retail) price is marked on it. . . . I've noticed lately that a number of the manufacturers tell you that the suggested retail price is not what you're required to charge, and that if you charge a lower price, that won't affect their dealing with you. But they don't like you to charge much less, because it knocks the bottom out for everyone, and then the retailers gripe about not being able to handle that product anymore, that the overhead is shot [appliances].

> The manufacturers have suggested prices on most of their merchandise. Sometimes they may essentially demand that you hold that price because other merchants may be complaining, but it really is a suggested retail price and anything beyond that is supposedly illegal [women's clothing].

> In the card industry, the prices are set by the manufacturers and it is basically the same across the country. . . . The manufacturers suggest a retail price, and we pretty well go along with that, a keystone price. Basically, you double the wholesale price, so you will take a 100% markup, although I've noticed some will take a longer margin, and we, ourselves, will do that on some things [giftware].

As the following indicates, suggested prices may have more impact than legally intended. Vendors may resent those who undercut accepted margins and may complain to the suppliers involved, in some cases threatening to discontinue dealings with suppliers who do not ensure fair margins. Vendors doing more business with particular suppliers (who are hence more dependent on these particular buyers) would seem more able to dissuade suppliers from dealing with those they consider to be deviants.[9]

> If you're undercutting the other stores too much, the suppliers are not going to like that. . . . Did you read about [another department store] in the paper the other day? That one got a little messy. (a major supplier) put it in writing, in a more threatening way. Basically, they said, "Hold our prices up or we're not going to supply you any more." They didn't want them to use their lines as a loss leader. . . . The suppliers can do a lot of other things that are less direct if they don't like the way you're pricing. Hints, back orders, short shipments, wrong shipments, to where you either get the hint or more or less give up on frustration. They don't like doing that, and they don't want to lose the business. But they don't want to lose their other customers either, and the one that's undercutting is the biggest threat [department store].

> The markup on retail is usually 100%, but the manufacturer sets the price, sometimes 120%, 140%. . . . Now, one of the problems we have had has been with the competition, where other stores carrying the same lines have been selling for the suggested retail price, and we have been using maybe a 90% markup, something like that. Some have gone to the manufacturer and threatened to discontinue carrying their lines if they couldn't get us to use the same markup, the suggested markup. It might only be a matter of two or three dollars, and you think, "Free enterprise. You should be able to set your own prices!" but they might complain, and the manufacturer might threaten to discontinue doing business with us. And on certain lines, we can't afford that, because they are our bread-and-butter lines, and they would just refuse to sell to us [women's clothing].

Opportunistic pricing. Opportunistic pricing refers to the practice of pricing items according to anticipated buyer tolerances of price and value.[10] In contrast to those more firmly relying on standardized markups (e.g., all items in general categories are marked up by a preset amount), more individualized variations are implemented at the outset. This practice may define the central pricing style for some vendors, but insofar as vendors anticipate profits from sales, this tactic is typically employed in conjunction with some minimal markup.

Mark it up! Mark it up! Rah, Rah, Rah! I used to take markups to the hilt. I'd mark things up as high as I could. If something came into me at $5, I'd often start it off at $11.95, see how it would move. If it didn't move there, maybe knock it down to $10.95, or even $9.95, but that was it. My markups were responsible for most of the store's profits. Anything that I could mark up, I would. I would put things in for $3 and sell for $12. I would. People would buy them at that, so what the hell! And if I charged $6 for it, they probably wouldn't have bought it. They would think it was inferior merchandise. But charge $12 for it and they buy it, "Good deal!" [giftware].

We have an idea of what we need on our margins, but we do experiment too. Basically, we try to find that niche where people don't think it's too expensive on the one hand or too cheap on the other. You can lose a lot of sales either way. And try to price it out relative to our other lines. If you don't, your sales on other lines can be hurt too. So if we get something that looks really good for the price, we will take a longer margin. We try to maintain an overall quality-cost perspective for our customers. So we take longer margins on some things, shorter on others. . . . On some things, of course, you're happy to clear them out, even if you only get a little money back. Then you can use that display space for something that'll move a little better [mixed clothing].

Considering themselves partners in trade, suppliers may also assist vendors with opportunistic pricing by indicating items lending themselves to increased margins.

50% (resale is 2×) is the giftware markup normally, but some articles are fine articles and there are stores marking it up 75%. Some stores will mark up an article covering their cost of shipment which will be over and above the suggested retail price. Whatever their freight it, they charge it on their cost and then double up. It depends, you can play with the price as I suggested, but you are doing it legally, but I can't come in and say, "This is what that price must be sold at.". . . . I know it and I won't play with it. But, if I have a clear-out of merchandise in my warehouse and I have an item that sells for $3, that price is five years old suggested retail. Today, that same three-dollar retail should be at least six, seven, eight dollars, maybe even ten would be better. I won't hesitate to say to my retailer, "Look, I can help you make a few extra dollars." I will show him the particular product and, say the price retail is $3, "It costs you $1.50." And he will say that is a fantastic price. And he will recognize the product as a good product. He can move a lot of it at that price. But then I say, "As much as you are going to move it at $3 and make $1.50, why not take it in a good quantity, maybe a hundred dozen, and promote 50% of it at a higher retail. In other words, sell as much as you can at today's retail price. Then, you could put it on "sale," regular $10, on "sale" for $5,

and still make one heck of a profit. You point this out to him. You have done
your job on that. He sees the potential, he will thank you up and down because
he may not think about it [wholesale—giftware].

There may be a tendency to equate opportunistic pricing with prof-
iteering. But in addition to any concerns vendors may have in developing customer loyalty, this view overlooks the possible large firmly
standardized margins merchant may use, the risks particular items
represent relative to other lines, and customer skepticism in reference
to "good buys."

PRICE AND VALUE AS SYMBOLIC

From the perspectives of both buyers and vendors, pricing has a very
practical (limiting) quality; objects exchanged affect people's abilities
to enter other transactions and to pursue other interests. Further, while
one can argue for correctness of price once a sale has been made
(validated), price is only one symbolic element denoting worth. Price
suggests value, but so do all the other elements buyers associate with
the particular items under consideration (e.g., store decor, reputation,
vendor styles, brand names, anticipated enjoyment, pride of ownership,
and so on). Thus, in addition to price, vendors can try to shape the
valuing of the goods by the ways in which they present products, relate
to the prospects, and so forth. In every case, however, the vendor's
efforts are dependent on the interpretations of prospective buyers.
Vendors may attempt to take prospects' perspectives into account, but
in addition to the problematic accuracy of their role-taking endeavors
and their inabilities to set the stage exactly as intended, they also face
an ongoing, shifting diversity of perspectives, interpretations, and interactions on the part of the prospects encountered. As prospects may
have quite different estimations of both object value and the significance of the involved monetary sacrifice, vendors may routinely anticipate variability in buyers' reactions to their pricing decisions.

You can't sell some things very well at a 100% markup. The customers think
that it's too cheap, that there must be something wrong with them. Some
things, you mark up 150, 200% and then the customers seem to think that
they're getting a good bargain, then. It's funny, but I've seen that happen with
some of my things and some of the other people with similar lines have had
similar experiences [jewelry].

There is something to be said that the price determines the value put on the goods. You can see that with our name brands and our own labels. The quality is just as good, and we stand behind it just as much, and the styling can be identical, except for the label. It might even be made by the very same company for us, using the very same materials, techniques and all, but it costs less. And generally, people think, "Why are they selling this for less? It can't be as good." And the same thing happens when you put things on "sale." They generally don't think in terms of a loss leader. They want to know, "What's wrong with this that it costs less than that?" [mixed clothing].

It's funny, with cosmetics, the people seem to think that if the product costs more, it is going to be better. It's going to look better on them [department store].

Buyers objectify the asking price by assuming the (financial) sacrifice necessary to obtain the item (Simmel, 1900: 81), but higher prices may be seen to suggest greater worth, better quality, and the like. Whereas prospective customers may resent the sacrifices required to obtain objects, they may also distrust items whose value seems beneath its price.

We bought some slacks from _____ . A very good buy! Very good quality. Their prices on most things are really good, as a matter of fact. Made in this country, too. But they aren't moving at our regular markup. Some did, but we were getting a lot of skepticism too. Eventually we bumped up the price, 2.5 (250% markup), which is a big margin for us. Most things we'll go 1, 1.2, less too. But they're moving much better now! . . . We will still make more if we sell a _____ or_____ brand, but only because they are a very exclusive brand. The dollar difference is greater on each pair even with a smaller markup [men's clothing].

In considering the price-value relationship, analysts would want to distinguish vendor-perceived worth from buyer-perceived worth. Price is one aspect by which prospects may assess value ("You only get what you pay for!"), but other concerns (symbols), such as perceived utility, familiarity, uniqueness, comfort, esteem, and the recognized alternatives available, may effectively distort the price-value relationship. However, prices provide standards against which the wisdom of people's purchases may be assessed through past experiences and over time by buyers as well as others.[11]

These themes strike at the heart of the rational-economic model. Vendors expect to receive prices for their products in some proportion to what they have paid for them, the costs they incur in processing them, promoting them, and the like. Further, as an ongoing practical accomplishment, marketing requires that vendors settle on a series of decisions (e.g., products carried, prices asked and accepted). Given concerns with financial survival, vendors are interested in predicting and maximizing the outcomes afforded them by differing lines of action. To the extent their offerings correspond with the time-situated interests of prospective buyers, their rules of thumb stand to be confirmed. But as Schutz (1971) suggests, the realm of action takes marketers into an intersubjective world in which reality is not theirs alone to determine. To presume otherwise is to invoke psychological reductionist and/or absolutist reasoning rather than *socio-logical* reasoning. It is in this sense that the rational-economic model is inadequate. It does not allow for vendor dependency on buyers who are characterized by multiple perspectives, shifting interpretations, and ongoing interactions. Likewise, it overlooks vendor dependencies on their suppliers (and the relationships vendors develop with these partners in trade). Simply expressed, it does not acknowledge the fundamentally cooperative and symbolic nature of exchange. In this regard, Simmel (1900) indicates a particularly profound appreciation of the significance of group life for exchange.

> By being exchanged, each object acquires a practical realization and means of its value through other objects [p. 78]. . . . The value of an object acquires such visibility and tangibility as it possesses through the fact that one object is offered for another [p. 79]. . . . The value of an object becomes objectified by exchanging it for another object [p. 81]. . . . Exchange is a sociological phenomenon sui generis, an original form and function of social life. It is in no way a logical consequence of those qualitative and quantitative aspects of things that are called utility and scarcity which acquire their significance for the process of valuation only when an exchange is proposed. . . . The difficulty of acquisition, the sacrifice offered in exchange, is the unique constitutive element of value [p. 100].

From this perspective, price setting can be seen as a multistage process in which vendors set initial prices in anticipation of specific subsequent reactions by buyers. However, pricing is much more than the implementation of preexisting recipes; it denotes an activity ultimately dependent upon others for confirmation of its rightness. So long as these others seem willing to accept the vendors' pricing definitions (as indicated by their purchases), the operational rules of thumb remain intact and achieve further verification as the right ways to proceed. Should others not accept the prices vendors propose, vendors face the task of realigning their prices or finding other ways to dispose of the products in question.

Market Adjustments

Regardless of their (standardized or opportunistic) origins, the weakness of firm margins is that the business world is a dynamic arena. Like tacticians in other settings, vendors can endeavor to put tradition (via preset margins) to work and/or try to make shrewd guesses regarding optimal prices on the basis of past experiences, but ultimately they do not know what will sell and at what price. Since businesses are dependent upon stock turns (turnovers of goods) for their very existence, anything seen to interfere with that process becomes a source of trouble. Price is sometimes directly isolated as the probable cause of the lack of sales and may be subject to change as a result. However, of the various components of vendors' marketing programs, prices are also generally the easiest (and least disruptive) changes to implement. Consequently, price adjustments may be used as quick fixes to offset any number of shortcomings signified by the lack of sales.

Pricing is a means by which vendors may strive to increase their odds of winning the gambles their overall investments entail, but it is also a ready tool as vendors endeavor to offset other elements thought to affect adversely the sales of particular items. Hence, while vendors may periodically readjust their margins to offset shifting market conditions, concerns with viable stock turns result in more day-to-day price adjustments than might first seem likely. This holds true even in larger companies (in which most adjustments are more cumbersome). The following discussions of comparison pricing, promotional pricing, and internal consistency, attest to the significance of ongoing market adjustments for price-setting activities.

COMPARISON PRICING

Since few businesses have monopolies on particular items, one of the most significant forms of market adjustment involves defining prices relative to one's competitors. Vendors may attempt to justify higher prices on the basis of reputation, quality, service, and the like, but the ability of shoppers to comparison shop creates a sensitivity on the part of vendors to locate their goods in an attractively competitive package, part of which is defined by the price.[12]

If people have been shopping around, they have more knowledge about the product they're looking for. . . . Our store policy is to match any other store if it is exactly the same product. We'd rather have them buy the item from here than from somewhere else [women's clothing].

If they tell us that they can get something cheaper elsewhere, we just say, "Sorry, this is our basic price." But we might later lower the price if it seems to be a problem, if we're getting a fair bit of that on an item. . . . We've had people do that with our own branches too. Maybe the group at _____ has this or that on for a price lower than us, but they may have had to do that there because of the competition they're facing in that immediate area [discount department store].

Thus even businesses that use firmly established margins and disapprove of dickering with individual buyers may find themselves making unanticipated price discounts on a general and/or individual basis when the loss of sales to competitors seems likely. Since business lost to a competitor may be business lost in both the short and the long run (multiple purchases, repeat customers), many businesses routinely shop the competition for the express purpose of reassessing their own prices. As the following extract indicates, the competition has a way of playing havoc with standardized margins.[13]

You want to know what your competition is charging for similar, especially identical, items because the people do comparison shop. So whenever we get a chance, we'll try to check things out, see what just arrived, what they're charging for things, because you have to be prepared to deal with that. That's what you're up against too, not just the customers. So we've taken things off our displays, and we've lowered our prices on things, because you figure, "Even if you're not making as well on an item as you wanted, it's better to make something on it than to lose out altogether." That's where it's good to have exclusives on things, so if you buy better, you can get around that somewhat [mixed clothing].

The problem of pricing becomes especially apparent when competitors put identical items on sale and not only threaten acceptable margins, but also threaten to dramatically shift patterns of buyer demand.

If they're not doing well, one of the competitors may put something that you're selling on at a lower price. And, it might be something that's selling very well for you at the regular price, so that's frustrating. Or sometimes they'll put things on "sale" too early in the season. Sometimes they'll put their entire inventory on "sale." That's not good for you, because with all the "sale" signs all you get then is the stragglers, and your more loyal customers [women's clothing].

Your markup is about 25% (on the selling price) on the average, but it varies with your lines. Also, you could make that, but you'll have other people in the community dragging you down. Often it's people who are hurting for money, in some financial straits, people going out of business. Or you'll get people who think, "Gosh if I lower prices, I'll sweep the market." And they usually end up going under because it's just not profitable. . . . You'll find with the major department stores, their markups are higher than ours, but they have to have that, because their overhead is greater. Their gross margin on selling price would be about 30% [appliances].

PROMOTIONAL PRICING

Promotional pricing refers to the practice of featuring discounted merchandise in attempts to increase one's total sales. It matters little, whether one is discussing dollar and cents reductions, percentages off, coupon discounts, and the like, or whether vendors put items on "sale," on special, or run discount operations; the basic elements of promotional pricing are very similar.[14]

When regular cost merchandise is used, vendors may assume shorter margins on the premise that they will increase volumes of sales on that merchandise and/or other merchandise because of the increased traffic flow. Some other losses of margin may be nullified by better volume prices from suppliers and other economies of scale (such as shipping and processing).

Merchants may also feature regular stock that has become troublesome (e.g., slow movers, broken lines, damaged goods, seasonal merchandise) as promotional items. Here again, the margin is reduced relative to cost price, but the objective is to salvage earlier investments, and if other sales result, the relative loss is lessened.

> If something isn't moving, you've got to get rid of it! You've got to replace it with something that'll pay your bills. You can't tie up your display space with deadbeat merchandise. You're paying X dollars per square foot per month rent, and if you keep this around and that around, pretty soon you have no place to put your hotter items. . . . Storage, what's the point? It gets expensive. It eats up your profits. So reduce the price, keep knocking it down till somebody wants it. Let them [customers] store it. And you can't wait too long either, because if you don't catch something that's not moving soon enough, you're going to have to let it go for a lot less. . . . That's another problem too. How long do you wait [department store]?

> It has to turn over. I get very nervous if something has been sitting around for a couple of months. Often I'll try moving it around, maybe you can get some takers that way. Put it where someone has to trip over it, almost. If that doesn't work, you pretty well have to drop the price. Stick it out if you've got a sidewalk sale coming up. You can't hold onto these things very long. You've got to get some return on it [giftware].

Other promotional merchandise denotes supplier specials (slow movers, end of lines, new products, seasonal goods, and so on). Suppliers who want increased action on their inventories (to cover expenses, maintain employment levels, grow) may offer first-line (and in-season) merchandise at dramatic discounts. Vendors may be able to acquire this merchandise at much greater than usual discounts and may be able to achieve usual (or greater) margins and still offer this merchandise at deep discounts. Most retailers' (seeming) loss leaders reflect these supplier specials.

Some promotional pricing, although probably much less than some customers suspect, reflects merchandise introduced with high initial margins with the explicit intention of repricing these items for more dramatic (larger reductions) "sales." This practice is discouraged by authorities concerned with fair trade, but merchants are more apt to feel closed into these practices as they try to achieve some profits from shoppers they define as more "sales"-oriented.[15]

> Another way of dealing with the pricing game is to use an inflated markup, so that you have provided a buffer against some of your other costs. Then,

even if the merchandise does go on "sale" again, what looks like half price isn't half price [mixed clothing].

You can double ticket. Bring something in with the regular price and the "sales" price on it. But we've moved away from that. We're more likely to say, manufacturer's suggested retail price is so much. Our "special" price is this. Save this much." . . . (deep discount) down the street does it a little differently, "Sells elsewhere for up to something. Get it here for this much less, while supplies last." They do that in their fliers all the time, and they have the same kind of signs in their stores. . . .
  But you see, there are two kinds of "sales." Stock on hand and special purchases for the "sales." If we only did stock on hand, it wouldn't be much of a "sale." So we bring in these buys from the suppliers. They're usually your big volume "sales." And there, we might do, "After 'Sales' price will be so much." And you might do that with any remaining stock. Or if it's a regular line, you go back to the regular price [discount department store].

In other instances, low-price introductions (promoting trial) may be used as part of an advertising campaign designed to create product use and preference.

It's something new on the market, and we want people to try it out. The lower price is one way of building product awareness. If they like it, then we can charge a regular price, like with our _____ and _____ flavors, which are selling very well for us now [manufacture—groceries].

Still another variant of promotional pricing involves using low-cost introductions when it is assumed that subsequent (tie-in) patronage will pay for the vendor's initial product investment.[16]

We don't make money on the initial installation. We actually take a loss at that point. We just assume that it's going to require parts and service, so there they pretty well have to come to us. We look at it as an investment that'll pay off for us over time. It's easier to sell that way, you don't get the same price objections as when you're asking them to lay all that money out at once [manufacture—industrial].

ACHIEVING INTERNAL CONSISTENCY

Should vendors carry more than one differentiable category of merchandise, each item may become a reference point for the others in terms of value and price. As comparisons seem most readily made between similar merchandise, vendors may find that they are not only asked to account for the pricing of two or more related items, but as a result they may also feel obliged to price more consistently with buyer perceptions than incurred costs.

Say we have three different unit levels in one line of major appliances, like washers, or microwaves. Okay, we're going to need a price spread, but that gets a little tricky. You would like so much between each unit, but your costs will be greater or less for any set of features. So you try to balance that out, plus show the customers some differences in design, size, whatever, so they can see more of a difference [manufacture—appliances].

This line actually cost more than this other one here, but we can't charge as much for it. It wouldn't move at all. The quality isn't quite as good. You could sell it by itself, but when you put the two together, you can see the difference. So we don't make as much on these, and we won't order many next time, but they give us a middle line [this store carries a lower line as well] as it were. They give the customer some choice, even though most will pay the extra for the others [the top line]. So they don't do us all that much good, but we think that they actually help sell the other lines, so they're of some value that way [jewelry].

SOME REVERBERATIONS

While price changes seem an inevitable feature of marketing, these changes can generate additional problems for vendors. Price changes affect other aspects of marketing, and however vital ongoing price adjustments may be to the financial well-being of the business, their significance does not cease at that point. Apart from necessitating internal adjustments, such as revised price lists, book work, staff familiarity, more cautious return policies, and the like, recognized price changes (increases and reductions) become additional elements subject to interpretation on the part of the prospects.

Raising Prices

Should vendors raise prices, they run a number of potential risks as a consequence of buyer reactions.[17] Noticed price increases break pre-established understandings and may engender both suspicion and hostility.[18] Vendors sometimes endeavor to offset price increases as Oxenfedt (1975: 28) notes, by increasing advertising (creating greater interest) or adding extra features. Likewise, vendors may try to justify higher prices on the basis of increased supplier costs, overhead, and such. Nevertheless, recognized increases are likely to create some resistance and costs.

We have to be careful about raising prices, because we are thought to be one of the lower lines. The people next to us, here, can raise the price of a skirt or dress $5 or $10 and their people [customers] don't seem to grumble so much. But we might have a three-piece item, and if we raise the price 50¢ or a dollar, we are going to get a lot of flak from our buyers. They are going to tell us how we are putting them behind the eight ball and that's the reason they are having trouble competing and such. But it is difficult to switch lines too. We have tried going up, but we get no support from our buyers in that respect. I imagine the other companies have the same kind of problem. They may not be happy where they are, but the buyers get used to you offering certain levels and certain price ranges. If you change, you're going to be getting away from your buyers and you are getting into another market and you pretty well have to start all over again [manufacture—clothing].

People are funny with prices. Some almost expect them to go up and they'll sometimes comment on how well you're holding the prices down on something. But you do get the others, the gripers. They're the ones who want to know why this went up and this went up, and why is this so expensive? You can explain it to some, but some just want to complain about how you're ripping them off. If they were in business themselves, they'd understand, but they're just taking it out on you. And you don't need that, someone yelling at you because this costs so much [groceries].

Though it may be somewhat ironic in light of the preceding, the (up)pricing of older stock in line with new stock price increases provides a further indication of the effects customers have on the pricing practices of vendors. Some vendors welcome price increases as a means of making a little more on existing stock. But even those who are reluctant to reprice existing stock in line with new cost increases (because of inconvenience and/or desires to sell the older stock first) may find that old prices become troublesome reference points.

If you don't reprice your old stock to the new levels, and there's no big difference between the two, you'll get more questions, arouse more suspicion from the customers. We tried doing that on a few different things, as our costs for the new ones went up. It just doesn't work. There's too many hassles! You don't mind giving them a break, but then you get a lot of griping. They just don't understand. So now, everything in the line goes up. No more fooling around. They don't appreciate what you tried to do for them anyway [crafts].

We went for a long time when we didn't increase the price on the old merchandise, but now, when we get a new price list, everything goes up. You have to, because that's what you have tó pay to replace it. And there are some things that if I figure the traffic can bear it, I'll raise the price right from the start, like if I know that I've got an exclusive on something, for this area. And then if a couple of months down the road, when I go to reorder, if the price goes up, I've got that margin [giftware].

Reducing Prices

Although buyers may welcome noticed price reductions, these changes may be fraught with more anxiety by vendors (and their suppliers) than are price increases. As Oxenfedt (1975: 27-28) observes, price reductions at the supplier level may reflect disappointing sales, increasing inventories, and sometimes desperate desires for cash flows. Supplier initiated reductions may promote some sales, but actual profit per item drops for vendors employing fixed percentage markups. Supplier discounts also may generate some hostility among vendors sitting with larger inventories in these same lines. Not only have they made costlier purchases from these same suppliers, but now face decreased profit margins.

Further, as the following discussions of "sales" imply, lowered prices may foster suspicion of quality and value along with a host of other marketing dilemmas.

When things go on "sale," people want to know, "Why? What's wrong with it? How come it's on 'sale?' " They tug and pull. Really scrutinize things! They don't trust you either. They're hard to relate to. Different from your other customers [department store].

As a manufacturer, you hate to see your things go on "sale." It sort of tells people that it's not worth so much anymore. And too, it gets people in the habit of waiting until the next "sale" before they buy their products again. . . . The retailers can kill your products that way. And then they gripe that they're not getting enough margin on your lines anymore, that they can't get enough for them. They want you then to reach into some magic area and get them the products for less now, even though everything else might be costing you more. That's why you hate to see a "sale" [manufacture—giftware].

Neutralizing Prices

So far, attention has been directed toward vendor concerns with best prices. This analysis would be shortchanged, however, were not some considerations given to the ways in which merchants may endeavor to offset the significance of prices for prospective buyers. While by no means exhaustive, the following discussions of contextual effects and exclusive branding attest to vendors' resourcefulness in nullifying the impact of price in the marketplace.[19]

CONTEXTUALIZING PRICES

Recognizing that some customers are apt to be influenced by the manner in which prices are presented (Goffman, 1959), merchants may endeavor to have items featured in ways that makes them appear more accessible and/or worthwhile. Thus vendors sometimes attempt to define products as "bargains" without significantly discounting these lines. Vendors may use a variety of tactics to this end, including reducing prices by an insignificant amount (e.g., from $5.00 to $4.98) from their usual margin; putting items together in sets (e.g., six for $1.49, instead of 25¢ each); using larger and/or brighter colored price tags; dumping merchandise in large bins to provide a greater sense of bulk savings; and providing other indications of conspicuous cheapness.[20]

If the customers sees something at the end of the aisle, they are more likely to buy it, think it's on "sale." Or if you set something on a table by itself, they are more likely to think it's on "special." Or you can use bigger signs. Or if they see volume, like a pile of cases of something, they'll think that it's on "sale." Like this one section, we'll have things from all different departments there, and it's rarely stuff on "sale," but it sells like hotcakes! We have the same stuff in the departments, at the same price, but it doesn't sell so well there [discount department store].

The effects of context are by no means limited to generating impressions of greater accessibility. Ergo, vendors may also use displays to signify greater value.

That's just it. The price is not the most important thing! What kind of background are you working with? What kind of shelving? What kind of lighting? These things can make a big difference. How are things arranged? Cluttered? Spaced out? All these things tell people that something is a good price or isn't. If you have a strong display, you can raise your price and it needn't hurt your sales [wholesale—jewelry].

These sorts of strategies indicate that while price is an important element in the sales of products, its significance can be shaped dramatically by the context in which prices appear.

EXCLUSIVE BRANDING

Another way in which pricing may be neutralized is by carrying exclusive (versus supplier) brands. When engaged in the resale of goods carrying their own labels, vendors may not only avoid some price comparisons on the part of both customers and competitors, but typically are able to purchase these items at lower prices than comparable name brands. Private brands usually become more available as a product is better known and widely used, but sales of private brands rely heavily on the savings these goods represent and/or the vendor's general level of credibility. Since this merchandise usually represents an overrun on the part of the manufacturer, it may be available at a considerably discounted price. Vendors using exclusive brands may charge prices comparable to those of name brands (thereby gaining a greater margin) or charge less and still achieve their usual margins.[21]

> The markup varies with the products. Brand names, we're a little more limited in what we can do with them because we are trying to undersell other department stores and any speciality stores in the area that might be carrying the exact same lines. Now if it's something with our own name on it, that we've imported or had specially manufactured for us, the markup can be much higher [discount department store].

> You can go for the private brand, and you may be able to get a good price for volume on an item that's exclusive to you, but the manufacturer may find that they're stocked up on a particular model and you may be able to get the manufacturer's national brand at a better price than what you can get on the private label. . . . They say, "You've got two approaches. We'll produce a special product just for you, but you take that product and give us your forecast six months ahead. The other route is to concentrate on our regular line, and if you can pick our pockets, go ahead." So if they get loaded up and

they have a discount on a particular product, we can say, "Fine, what will you do for us if we give you an order of 500?" [appliances].

In Perspective

Despite its depersonalized (dollars and cents) referents, price setting is a socially derived activity. Not only does pricing reflect the perspectives of the vendors involved (and their attempts to anticipate prospective buyers), but like other aspects of group life, pricing represents an ongoing and negotiable phenomenon dependent ultimately on others for objectification. As with labels attached to people (Prus, 1975a, 1975b, 1982), prices attached to objects are subject to definition, designatory discretion, assessment, challenge, and revision as interested parties jointly strive to determine reality.

Price setting facilitates commodity exchange by defining parameters, but it is also a product of emergent exchange. Operating in a business context, vendors intend to act rationally. To this end, they seek out pricing formulas (and other rules of thumb) designed to reduce the ambiguity they experience. Unfortunately or otherwise, they find themselves in situations involving considerable uncertainty. Not only may they be unsure about the intentions, plans, and resources of their presumed competitors, but they are also uncertain of the ways in which prospective buyers will interpret their prices. While endeavoring to stock products for which they perceive a market, they are faced with the task of determining the best prices in advance of buyer assessments. The wisdom of setting particular prices will not be known until real prospects make actual buying decisions. Vendors may experiment with price adjustments in attempts to promote greater levels of sales, and they will sometimes select (seemingly) winning prices, but the best price remains a very elusive target.

While pricing guidelines are themselves problematic in content and implementation, they represent important themes in organizing people's marketing programs. These rules of thumb not only represent attempts to reduce the risks marketing ventures inevitably assume, but also shape the ways in which vendors pursue other features of their marketing programs (e.g., decisions regarding products carried, promotional concepts). Further, these recipes generate elements of expediency and coordination in organizational settings. In larger organizations, pricing formulas foster head office control over buyers as well as managers and sales staff. And, as long as these standardizations are taken for granted, they also reduce the time individual pricing (and related) decisions entail in all settings.

At another level, pricing may be used to promote immediate purchasing decisions as well as to induce buyer loyalty. Thus, pricing strategies may be invoked in attempts to define value (higher price, higher value), connote savings (emphasize price reductions), facilitate customers decision making (provide sharper price ranges), and create closure (limited time only). Price-based loyalty seems especially vulnerable to competition, but price levels may be used to provide higher levels of purchasing predictability for vendors' clienteles (e.g., places to find snob appeal lines, square deals, bargain basement prices). Albeit on a more individualized basis, vendors may also attempt to consolidate themselves with particular customers by offering them special prices, volume discounts, and the like.

Noteworthy, too, is the interdependence of vendor pricing practices and the maintenance of viable working relationships with their suppliers. Even within the realms of fair trade legislation, these partners in trade may be instrumental in shaping vendors' product prices (as well as the products they carry).

Finally, the interrelatedness of pricing and other aspects of vendors' marketing programs should be appreciated. Thus pricing also emerges as a tool for managing mistakes and other unexpected setbacks. As the marketing feature generally most amenable to alteration, pricing represents a quick organizational fix. Price reductions may be implemented to unburden vendors of slowly moving merchandise (bad buys, tombstones) and damaged goods, as well as to offset a host of other marketing problems (e.g., seemingly ineffectual displays, advertising campaigns, or sales staff; localized competition; head office blunders). As the following chapters indicate, other facets of vendors' marketing programs may be implemented in attempts to offset pricing blunders and other price concerns.

Notes

1. Although vendors and buyers may individually bargain (dicker) on prices of items, this paper focuses more specifically on the formulation of standardized (list, asking) prices. Likewise, minimal attention is given herein to the problematics of custom pricing (on an order-per-order, or product-per-product basis).

2. Marx also discusses the relationship of money, value, and price, but Simmel's position is notably at variance from that of Marx. While Marx (1967) says that "the value of commodities has a purely social reality" (p. 47, Vol. 1) and "that values can only manifest themselves in the social relationships of commodity to commodity (pp. 47, 60, Vol. 1), he confounds this by arguing that the human labor required to transform products is the base of their value. Although rather convoluted, his analysis runs from the assumption that all things of value are products of human enterprise, to the (nonlogical) conclusion that value is defined by the enterprise necessary to produce (specific) items. Marx seems not only insensitive to the social nature of demand, marketing and sales activity, and risk taking, but he also fails to distinguish the valuings of objects by prospective owners (traders, consumers) from material, labor, and asking costs. Contrary to Marx's presumptions, business exchanges are not "objective matters of fact." Production does not, in itself, determine valuing, and consumption is far from automatic.

3. Edwards (1954) provides a fuller depiction of the literature and assumptions underlying the rational-economic model of decision making. Albeit from a different standpoint, he also provides a critique of this explanation of human behavior. See Anderson (1983) for a cogent insider assessment of mainstream marketing theory.

4. In Mead's (1934) terms, price-setting activity is very much an exercise in assessing, acting toward, and readjusting to one's notions of the "generalized other."

5. For a most valuable examination of the symbolic nature of price, supply, and demand, see Glick's (1957) analysis of futures trading. In striking contrast to economic assumptions, Glick found that although traders made frequent reference to supply and demand in explaining prices, the prices at which traders were buying and selling products largely defined (rather than reflected) the traders' notions of supply and demand.

6. For more complete statements on initial typing, designation, and the problematics of resistance, see Hewitt and Stokes (1975) and Prus (1975a, 1975b, 1982). Klapp's (1962, 1964, 1969, 1971) discussions of heroes, villains, fools, and other social types are also most relevant.

7. Likewise, agents, distributors, government agencies, and even competitors may play a role in defining the eventual prices attached to the objects consumers encounter by the feedback these other people provide in reference to the appropriateness of designated prices.

Although preceding the development of this model, Glick's (1957) research on price-related decision making in the futures market is very consistent with it.

8. Some vendors calculate margin by defining markup as a percentage of the selling price. A 50% margin in this circumstance would generate $5 on a $10 item, for instance; the end result with this 50% margin is the same as doubling the cost price (or taking a 100% margin in other vendors' terms).

9. Reflecting concerns with fair trade legislation, vendors are presently apt to be more subtle in the ways in which they discourage price cutting. Haring (1935) provides a most interesting statement on earlier supplier attempts to maintain acceptable margins.

10. Kriesberg (1956) provides a valuable account of pricing restraint on the part of suppliers during a steel shortage. Despite the willingness of buyers to meet higher prices, most regular suppliers shunned opportunistic pricing in favor of maintaining good buyer relations.

11. For an indication of some of the marketing literature on the price-quality relationship, see Shapiro (1968), Riesz (1978), Lambert (1981), and Wheatley et al. (1981).

12. Donovan (1929: 196) indicates that the practice of comparative pricing on the part of department stores was well established by that time.

13. This practice is sometimes reflected by the different prices individual branches of chains charge for the same item in different locations of the same city, for example.

14. For other materials on price-cutting promotions or specials, see Chapter 8 ("Holding Sales") in, *Making Sales* (Prus, 1989).

15. Lemert (1953) uses the term *closure* in describing the strikingly parallel experiences of consumers writing bad checks. These options are generally defined as undesirable by those involved, but represent a means of meeting pressing obligations.

16. As Weigand (1980) notes, by tying customers into operating patterns, committing customers to an inventory of parts and supplies, developing product-specific training programs, helping customers establish product specifications favorable to its own products, and providing uniquely integrated systems, vendors can generate repeat patronage beyond the original purchase.

17. Consistent with Kriesberg (1956), the data suggests that concerns with retaining loyal customers and remaining competitive discourage vendors from raising prices when they get hot items.

18. Should price increases be interpreted as trust violations, the resulting moral indignation may account for some of the hostility vendors experience from customers who notice price increases. See Emerson (1977) and Prus (1978) for other statements on troublesome relations and trust violations.

19. Readers should note that I have not herein attended to vendors' attempts to redefine the significance of prices in more direct interactive manners (e.g., via presentations, efforts to neutralize price resistances). Likewise, minimal attention has been directed toward dickering, haggling over prices, and other direct price-related negotiations. Chapters 4 ("Neutralizing Resistance"), 5 ("Obtaining Commitments"), and 8 ("Holding 'Sales' ") in *Making Sales* (Prus, 1989) provide materials pertinent to other aspects of pricing in the sales setting.

20. This term was suggested to me by Dorothy Counts. The effectiveness of bargain pricing may be further enhanced by providing other indicators of cost cutting merchandise (e.g., deep discount, warehouse, bare bones images). As with Veblen's (1953) notion of "conspicuous consumption," the clear implication is that "image sells."

21. Generic (no-name) brands follow a similar routine. Purchase costs may be reduced somewhat, but so is (no-name) credibility. Further, as with other brands, bad experiences with no-names tend to promote skepticism of other similarly labeled merchandise.

Chapter 6
USING THE MEDIA

You're not selling advertising! You're selling productivity, sales, contacts, icebreakers, ideas, services, introductions [promotions—agency].

How do vendors use the media in recruiting prospects for businesses?[1] What tasks to vendors ask of media promotions? What forms do these promotions assume? What dilemmas do vendors using media promotions face?

Media promotions refer to the sorts of nonpersonal sales efforts of business characterized by the print and electronic media. This term is preferred over *advertising*. While the concept of advertising directs our attention to one area of marketing activity, people thinking in these terms frequently overlook the advertising that personal encounters entail, miss the interrelatedness of media and other forms of selling, and neglect promotions that may not commonly be defined as advertising. Advertising agents may prefer to distinguish themselves from other salespeople, but the distinction is largely an artificial one and should be recognized as such by anyone wishing to understand marketing (and media sales) activity. This is not to deny the creative or technical skills (or their value) of those involved in advertising, but rather to emphasize that their central mission, like that of other salespeople is to generate sales.

Media promotions can assume a variety of formats, and can have a wide range of consequences. Regardless of format and directness, however, media programs are intended to facilitate sales. One may sell products exclusively through the media, but it seems most accurate to envision media promotions as supporting rather than replacing personal selling activities, and view all those involved in media selling as extensions of the staff of the business being promoted.

It's funny. The people selling advertising in the newspapers and radio, and all, they try to give you the impression that their media can do it all. But if it could, what are all these (media) companies doing with all their reps in the field? They're already plugging their own product in their own media, and in others, too, like a radio station advertising on television, but then they have all these salespeople. That's something that really struck me when I first started, and started to realize just how large their sales staffs were [promotions—agency].

When used in conjunction with field or showroom sales, media promotions can be instrumental not only in reference to such things as getting leads and increasing traffic flow, but also in terms of generating credibility for businesses, developing product mystique, and defining product worth. When used alone, media promotions may assume all the sales tasks entailed in making contact with customers to obtaining orders ("Send your order to." . . .).

Following a consideration of media recruitment objectives, attention turns to an examination of the major media variants and the dilemmas advertising decisions entail for those opting for this mode of market-place recruitment.

Recruiting Through the Media

Although primarily oriented toward first-time buyers, media promotions may also be used to develop loyalty, discourage disengagement, and foster reinvolvement of former patrons in product purchases.

PROMOTING INITIAL PRODUCT PURCHASES

While people may learn of and pursue vendors' products on their own as a consequence of seekership (self-defined attractions) or closure (felt obligations), vendors using the media to recruit customers may strive for customer contact, encourage seekership on the part of prospective customers, promote a sense of closure on the part of prospective buyers, and attempt to reduce customers' reservations concerning purchases. Media messages need not be conceptualized in these terms, nor need they be directed toward all of these tasks. Nevertheless, these are common elements promoters attempt to achieve in their use of the media as a sales tool.

Making Contact

People's involvements in situations (including product purchases) require or presume some awareness of their opportunities. This feature of differential (and shifting) opportunity contexts is often taken for granted in many situations, but as an explicit outreaching activity this element assumes central importance in media promotions. Thus a first (and probably the single most effective) media objective is that of generating awareness of vendors and their products on the part of potential customers.

> Advertising is "How many people are you going to talk to on my behalf?" [mixed sales].

> In sales, you're really in a people business. . . . Whatever you learn about people, with people, is going to be a decided plus, but basically, sales comes down to a very simple bottom line, communication. Communication between people in a meaningful way, that's what sales is all about. It doesn't matter what you're selling. . . . Marketing can be boiled down to something that says, "I've got it, you need it, let's make a deal." The missing link in that simple equation is communication. That's basically the business that I'm in, the business of advertising. It's setting up the communication between the buyer and the seller. . . .

> One of the things that you try very hard to get a merchant to understand and perhaps appreciate is that you're really doing a numbers game. You go out and you talk to so many hundred thousand people on behalf of the client. If you're talking to the right people and you should know that from your research, then you know that if you talk to them in a positive way, that you are going to make an impact and you just keep firing on the impact and then the consumer starts to respond. Believe it or not, it's very hard for a merchant who can put the newspaper ad up on the wall and stick pins in it, to change this kind of thinking around to understand that all he ever bought in the newspaper was impact [promotions—television].

Once contact has been made, the next step is that of encouraging people's involvements in product purchases. This is commonly attempted by developing product interest, creating closure, and minimizing buyer reservations.

Promoting Seekership

The term *seekership* (Lofland and Stark, 1965; Klapp, 1969; Prus and Irini, 1988) has been used to refer to a self-defined interest, attraction, or fascination people have regarding some situation. As self-reflective entities, people are not only able to develop likings and desires for particular objects, but they can also pursue these interests somewhat independently of others. It is also evident, however, that others can initiate, intensify, and discourage these interests (i.e., interest is negotiable). It is here that we consider vendor attempts to spur seekership activity on the part of prospective customers. Particularly noteworthy, here, is interest encouraged by qualification or selective identification of prospects, promoting explicit definitions of product relevancy, and making reference to people's side-involvements.

Qualifying prospects. Media promotions very much involve one-way messages, but it should not be assumed that promoters are unconcerned with prospect perspectives (vis-à-vis maximizing receptivity to the products being featured). Hence, people involved in media selling often attempt to qualify their audiences (i.e., define/uncover prospect interests). By specifically appealing to the identities (e.g., mothers, students, homeowners) of those attending to the media messages, promoters strive to invoke a general framework for action. These attempts at qualification are typically combined with efforts designed more explicitly to direct people's action toward specific products (and vendors). However, even at the more general level, promoters intend to encourage receptivity to particular purchases by drawing upon people's identities and the perspectives these imply.

Some promoters qualify customers by selectively advertising in media (e.g., certain magazines, directories, radio stations) patronized by particular audiences.

> A priority item is, "Who do you want to reach?" Once you know that, you start looking at the media. Do they want to reach women, teenagers, executives, sports enthusiasts, truckers, or what? That'll influence what magazines you go into, what sections of the newspaper you want your ads in, what types of radio stations you deal with [promotions—agency].

Promoters using more general media (e.g., community newspapers, family magazines) may attempt to qualify their audiences by requesting that their ads appear in certain contexts (e.g., sections of the newspaper, in conjunction with certain television programs, or timing of radio commercials); designating categories of people ("Attention . . . homeowners/women/teens") in their advertisements; prominently asking questions ("Have you ever . . . ?") designed to appeal to certain categories of people; and presenting their products in ways (e.g., expres-

sions, images) thought consistent with their target audience's preferences. While largely one-way communications, qualification in media
promotions need not end at this point. It can continue throughout the
message as information is given, questions are raised ("Does this ever
happen to you?"), and responses are suggested (e.g., "Pick the payment
plan best suited to you!").

> Sometimes you'll get products that appeal to a wide range of people, but other
> times, you're interested in a narrow band. There, you've got to try and get their
> attention, "Hey Ladies, I'm talking to you!" sort of thing. You can do that in a lot
> of ways, like spotting your ads in certain places in the newspaper or on the radio,
> or featuring people they could identify with in those ads. Something they can relate
> to [promotions—agency].

Establishing relevance. Beyond the identity work qualification entails, media users often attempt to define product relevancy by shaping
the social worlds prospects experience. This represents an explicit
attempt to build on existing notions of prospect interest. Advertisers
may be able to generate product interest in the process of making
contact, or doing qualification work, but some more specific focusing
is likely. To this end, promoters may foster selective definitions of
companies, products, user situations, aspirations, and the like.

> With the ads they run in the paper, you want to tell them enough information to
> make it attractive enough to call in. And it might be the mortgage, or the backyard,
> or the view, whatever. You've got to find something about that house that's going
> to attract the buyer, and you've got to know in advance, what kind of buyer you
> want to attract. Every house has a buyer, and you've got to assess the property in
> terms of that. . . . If you're trying to sell a classier house, you want a classier ad. If
> you're trying to sell something on the price, make sure that that's apparent. . . .
> You've got to tell people enough to arouse their interest, but there are other things
> that you want to leave out. So it might be a rotten house in a rotten area, but it's
> very clean, so say it. Start your ad with a "clean house" [real estate].

Viewed in this manner, vendors become *cultural entrepreneurs.*[2] In
addition to creating specific company/product awareness, advertisers
may further educate prospects in reference to

(1) existing problems and impending solutions represented by the
      products (company) featured;
(2) the desirability/value of products;

(3) general and unique features of products;

(4) accessibility of products; and

(5) modes of using products.

To the extent prospects acknowledge this information, media promotions may not only facilitate field and showroom selling, but they can also directly create sales.

While much consideration may be given to product applications (e.g., "Does this ever happen to you?" "Tired of . . . ?" "Here's a handy little item!" "Have you tried new, improved . . . ?"), attempts are often made to embellish further the claims being made. This is the pizzazz or intrigue of media promotions. This is what makes walking great fun, flying provocatively romantic, and driving downright exciting! Everything is made more meaningful, more dynamic! Products burst into color, action becomes adventure, purchasers become stars.

> There are so many ways of getting attention. It's a matter of which theme do you want to go with? One way, and we do this a lot, is to make something exciting. You put it in exciting places, with exciting people, the latest whatever, music, dancing, travel, whatever. Or get a lot of "Oohs" and "Aahs" worked in. With this exciting whatever, you become a somebody, type thing. . . . Then there's the problem-solver approach. You help them get rid of the nasty, whatever it is. Or with this wonderful product, you don't even have to worry about getting rid of this, because with this, you'll never have this problem in the first place. . . . You can go with durability, or safety, or convenience. Lots of different themes. And people have been successful with all of them. But you have to get their attention and hold it long enough to give your product a chance. Because it has to compete with all the other ads that the other agencies are running [promotions—agency].

Side involvements. In addition to product descriptions, applications, and other significances, the media also represent means of enticing customers through special offers. Building in relevance by attending to other interests buyers may hold, these promotions include such things as contests, draws, free samples of goods and services, package enclosures, mail-in redemptions, reusable containers, trading stamps, coupons, and direct price reductions (sales!).[3]

> Contests, draws, all these things are drawing cards. They spark interest. Get attention for the products or company you're trying to promote. You need something to slow people down long enough to see what you're promoting. Like in a

grocery store, for instance, you have thousands of items. You do what you can to stop the customers at your products [promotions—agency].

We've had a lot of promotions, "Two for one!" "Buy one of these and get one of these free!" "Buy one of these and get a third off a box of chocolates!" "Win a trip, a car . . ." Things like that. Anything to draw the people, and they do! People really go for it. Same with the instant prizes they could win with a purchase. It really draws the people in, these promotions. But the competition does the same thing, so you have to, too. You want to get your share of the business too [candy].

Creating Closure

In lieu of, or in conjunction with, attempts to generate seekership on the part of their prospects, vendors may also use the media to invoke definitions of obligation, urgency, and limited options.[4] By stressing target concerns, such as those pertaining to personal and family safety, prestige, efficiency, or the wisdom of frugality, promoters often emphasize the necessity for action. Focusing people's attention on certain outcomes, advertisers can dramatically increase prospect sensitivity to products. Once prospects have been alerted to problems, it is proposed that these problems can be successfully resolved only by obtaining the designated products. Closure (in problem and solution!), thus emerges as a negotiable, definitional quality on which advertisers can build in promoting sales. By encouraging prospect to "Act now! Before it's too late!" or to "Take advantage of this time-limited offer!" media promotions may emphasize the urgency of action, as may special incentives for "being first" or "acting in time" (to take advantage of discounts and other advantages that will vanish later).

It depends somewhat on your client, but a lot of people, small businesses especially, when they run an ad, they want immediate action. That's one reason they run so many "specials" ads. And that's how you do their ads, "Hurry! Buy now! Before it's too late!" [promotions—newspaper]

You want to get them to act. Not just say, "Yeah, that's a good idea. I'll have to do that some day." You want them to run out and get some, or pick up the phone, now. That's where you get the hard sell in the media. A lot of dramatizations. People dying, houses burning, auto wrecks. Probably there's less scare tactics than there were years ago, but you still get it. Sometimes it's made more humorous, or they might use cartoon characters to make it less offensive. . . . If it's something like deodorant, then you can't do with that what you can with insurance or tires or fire alarms, but you can show people being embarrassed when they've had to sweat it

out someplace. But it's the same kind of message. "Get it before it happens to you"
[promotions—agency].

Reducing Reservations

As part of their overall recruitment programs, promoters may also use
the media to neutralize concerns customers may have about impending
investments. Insofar as buyers are skeptical of those with whom they
do business, credibility becomes particularly central as buyers attempt
to ascertain the quality of the items they are considering. Albeit generally of secondary importance to quality (i.e., some minimal quality is a
requisite to most purchases), another set of concerns revolves around
the expenditures particular purchases entail. There is no guarantee that
media messages will be interpreted as promoters intend, but the production of credibility and the minimization of costs are two important
elements to which promoters may attend in the neutralization of customers' reservations.

Generating credibility. While promoters may foster involvement by
encouraging seekership and closure on the part of prospective buyers,
the success of media promotions is also dependent on the levels of
credibility these promotions establish relative to their audiences. Prospects seldom define advertisers' objectives as synonymous with their
own, but all messages seem more relevant when the source is considered
more trustworthy. To some extent, credibility may be established by
noting the size, popularity, and longevity of a company ("If we're this
large, do this much business, and have been around this long, we must
know what we're doing!"). However, much more is involved.

One may ask to what extent media promotions provide "profile"
or enable vendors to achieve "identity" in the marketplace. Generally
speaking, media selling seems more effective when the objects (vendors
or products) promoted are recognized as more significant, vital elements in the prospect's frames of reference. Advertising thus may
generate a mystique by distinguishing featured objects from other
aspects of group life. Advertisers (and products) are highlighted,
featured as special! These objects become "signified," identities are
projected.

> Advertising creates an aura. The advertiser convinces the consumer that you are
> the best person to go to. . . . They're your front man! It's kind of a recommenda-
> tion. . . . The unfortunate part of it is that as a new person going into business,
> you're more dependent on advertising than an established business. But, unfortu-

nately, the costs of advertising being what they are, you can't get the kind of advertising you really need [appliances].

There are a lot of ways of building up your credibility. You can use studies, with graphs and charts, do demos, testimonials, or combine these in some way. It depends, too, what you've got to work with from the company. If they've done these studies. . . . With the testimonials, your celebrities are good there, because they're interesting, already liked by a lot of people. So they've got some credibility already. But if you can find some likable guy, an "average Joe" type, or Josie, that the people will take a liking to, you may be better off because people figure that celebrities are doing it for the money more than the product, not so natural, even though they've got good interest. . . . Even a cartoon character can be effective if the people like them, find them interesting. The bottom line is getting someone believable to say something good about your product [promotions— agency].

Although "evidence" may be provided somewhat independently of identity promotions, it seems most effective when combined with intensive identity campaigns. Promoters may provide demonstrations, testimonials, warranties and guarantees, or make other claims about quality and performance, efficiency, training, specialization, customer satisfaction concerns, and the like, in an attempt to establish higher levels of buyer confidence. Any evidence is subject to different interpretations by audiences, but these sorts of credentialling practices serve to promote a sense of reliability for both the company and its products. Defining products as denoting reasonable, sensible, or desirable choices within the realms of common wisdom and good taste, activities of this type serve to "objectify" (Schutz, 1971) people's decisions to purchase particular products (or brands). These messages may reaffirm the wisdom of people having dealt with that particular company in the past, but are generally thought most critical in reference to new prospects.

Your advertising is most important with the new people, the ones who haven't dealt with you before. You have to give them some reason to deal with you, spark some interest. Give them some confidence that they should spend their money with you. It's good for your existing customers, too, to help keep you in mind, but it's the new people that you're really aiming for there [promotions—agency].

How else are they going to know that you exist? You need that exposure. You can cover some people in person, but even there, it's nice if they already know something about you. It gives you more credibility, "Oh yeah, I've heard of you." [manufacture—industrial].

Unless the company name and the specific product being promoted are largely synonymous, vendors using media sales have to make decisions about the relative prominence of corporate versus product identities. The dilemma is this: While the company would seem to benefit in the long run from being more prominently featured, company-oriented ads tend to obscure particular products. The promotion of particular products is apt to increase sales of those products, but the company is less well-known for future reference. And, unless a company has a "new" and "unique" product, product-oriented advertising may generate an interest in the more generic product. Thus the company's own sales may increase as a result of the promotion, but so too may those of the competition. Product trade names help to generate stronger product identities, but tend to obscure company prominence. Finally, company-oriented promotions suggest a more encompassing longevity than that implied by the particular products they carry.

> With corporate advertising, you are basically promoting a name. And for a lot of companies, it is refreshing to themselves to see their name associated with a product in a magazine. It protects the trademark and it also jazzes up the company image. If it is a new product you want to introduce, then you might want to focus more on the product than the corporation [promotions—magazine].

> Some people will do what we call an image campaign. There, what you do—and you don't have to have a particular product in mind—is remind people that you're still in business. You're still around. . . . You find that a certain percentage of your population in any city changes over a year. People are moving, transferred. So that percentage of the new people wouldn't know that you're around. And another percentage of the population might have known that you were there, but this way you let them know that you're still there. Now if you're off the air for three or four years, that percentage multiplies. So this image campaign, even when you don't have anything in particular to sell will let people know that you are still around and let a lot of people know that you're around period, because they've never heard of you before [promotions—radio].

Minimizing costs. Since monies invested in particular purchases may affect people's abilities to obtain other items, media messages often attempt to nullify people's reservations regarding impending expenditures.

In their most obvious forms, media messages strive to promote purchases on the basis of alleged price savings. Regardless of the medium (e.g., radio, newspaper, signs), the messages are much the same

Reduced by ____ %!

Save $ ____ !

Sale price only $ ____ !

Guaranteed lowest prices!

These messages are typically combined with a sense of closure (an obligation or pressure to act now).

Limited time only! Hurry in for best selection!

Today's Special!

Clearance Special! While they last!

At this price, you can't afford not to buy! Sale ends Saturday evening at nine.

The variants on neutralizing expenditures seem limited only by vendors' imaginations (and fair trade legislation). Thus, in addition to claimed price reductions, vendors may also use the media to define regular prices in less imposing terms.

You want to get their attention, but you also want to show them how easy it is to own a new car. It's only so much a month, "Own this beautiful car for only $275 a month." That might be your main heading, "Only $275 a month!" You push that [auto].

You can break it down in different ways. In our ads, we'll often present it in weekly or monthly payments. "You can own this lovely unit for only so much a month. No down payment required, and no interest for six months." [furniture].

PROMOTING REPEAT PATRONAGE AND DETERRING DISINVOLVEMENT

While most media selling seems directed at new prospects as opposed to existing patrons, its impact on existing customers should not be neglected. And, insofar as these people have an existing base of familiarity, they seem especially likely to notice these promotions. Thus these efforts may establish a prominence with which present customers may identify, as well as provide reaffirmations that they are dealing with viable businesses.

Most companies want their ads to bring people into the store or try out their products. After that, they think their products will do it all, or their service, whatever. Most don't realize that advertising can be much more than that. Your existing customers like to see it too. It tells them that they're buying at a popular place, the right things. That kind of thing [promotions—agency].

This function of the media was only mentioned occasionally, but vendors sometimes use the media to *generate loyalty*. This seems most likely to occur when vendors define the product as consistent with user perspectives ("It's for those who . . ."); identify the user as a "user" ("If you've already been using . . ."); emphasize the costs of switching to other products versus existing commitments ("Don't go out and get a whole new . . ."); indicate techniques for use and/or new applications ("We'll show you some new ways to use _____ easier, and more effectively"); and foster patron relationships ("If you have any problems with our _____ , just let us know. Our customer service number is . . . .").

Even in the literature we send to new people, we emphasize our service, our interest in working with them over time, that we want to develop long-term working relationships. We want to show them that we can help them, but we want to get the other message across too [manufacture—industrial].

Although the themes depicted are far from uniform across advertisers, one could also make the case that much corporate advertising (discussed earlier) is intended to foster long-term patronage. As the following quote suggests, however, this objective tends to be blended with concerns with attracting new prospects.

[Let's] divide the marketplace, for simplicity purposes and for practical purposes, into two different sections. I call one the "now" market. The now market, very simply, is a market that is ready to buy, it has developed a need and then it's a dogfight as to who is going to fill a need. The other market is the "future" market, and that's a much more difficult market to get to because if you think about the business of merchandising and you take a look for a moment at why does a consumer go to store A rather than store B or why does a consumer have stores A, B, C, D, E on their shopping list and not G and Z . . . They want the product to perform up to standard, up to their expectations, but I think probably more than anything else, they want the good advice of someone they can trust. And they want the knowledge that if anything goes wrong with that product, that they will be protected by the seller. . . . Now when a person decides to buy a new car, it is probably a safe bet that they will go through a mental shopping list and they will say, "Where would I look for a car? I would look for a car here, there, somewhere." . . . Basically they know something about them, and that something they know about them is, in the main, positive. So they're prepared to go and discuss an investment, because no matter what you buy as a consumer, it's an investment of your net dollars in some goods or services and it's terribly important that that investment is right. It's just like investing in the stock market, in a manner of speaking. If you don't know about someone, why would they be on your shopping list? Even if you know their name but their whole process of doing business is very grey with you, why would they be on your shopping list? Chances are they won't be. It's a little bit late, when a market develops, to try and turn this person as a customer for your business. It's very late, because there's probably only one way you're going to do it, if you're going to do it, and that's buy him. Buy him through price. And that's very expensive because you've got your advertising on the one hand, which is expensive, and you've got to offer an attractive price, which means you're cutting your gross margin, and that's very expensive. So where are you going to make profit? It's very difficult, isn't it? Now, if a person is not in the market to buy a pair of shoes, the chances of them doing any research or reading ads of people who sell shoes and finding out something about them is very, very remote. The same thing with a suit. There's only so much time you give to that kind of reading and you will go to those things that have an interest to you at that particular time, if it's advertised. The rest of them won't be seen, and that's fact. That is not speculation. That is basically fact. It's very unusual for a person to go scanning the ads for information on something they don't have any need for, and yet you have to get to them and you have to develop a rapport with them before their need develops. . . . You have to go to a medium which is intrusive enough to demand attention and then insert into that kind of media your message for the period of time so that they will start to become acquainted with you and what you do and so on. . . .

If when the person is ready to buy, if you've done your job well in advertising, then you've got a chance of being on their shopping list, and that's how you move customers from store A to store B. If they weren't comfortable in store A, they wouldn't be there, so you've got to make it attractive, which a move over to your store would be, and you've got to do it before they get into the market in those cases. So that's the job that television can do very well. It works fine in the now market, but really it does its job best in the future market [promotions—television].

RECLAIMING PATRONAGE

Another relatively neglected media objective pertains to the use of the media to reinvolve former patrons in product purchases. Like existing customers, these people may be considered targets for more general appeal promotions, but they tend to be largely taken for granted.

Media messages which capitalize on changes in the situations of the buyers and/or the suppliers may foster reassessments of their former relationships, but salvaging efforts also seem more apt to be successful when earlier relationships end on a more congenial basis.

We do mailings, in which we tell our [charge] card people that we haven't heard from them for some time. Basically, we tell them that we hope that all is well with them, and ask whether we've done anything that's bothering them. Have we offended them in any way? We don't like losing accounts, and if we've done something wrong, we want to know about it. Maybe we can make it right in their case. Maybe we can try to prevent that from occurring in the future, or cut down on it [department store].

It doesn't happen all that much, but you do get some who try to get their former customers to come back. Usually, it's, "We've added this . . . ," "We've improved this and this." They'd like to get back some that they've lost. The question is whether they're [former customers] going to be willing to give you a second chance. If they feel stung, it could be tough with the second-timers [promotions—agency].

Media Formats

In what follows, a brief outline of the features of various media will be presented, indicating their relative significance to advertisers. Seven media categories are delineated: newspapers and magazines, radio and television, direct mail, catalogues, directories, signs, and specialty advertising. Each of these media categories will be discussed separately. However, some overlap is inevitable.

NEWSPAPERS AND MAGAZINES

Beyond drawing people into showrooms and developing preferences for particular products and brands,[5] newspaper and magazine advertising can also be used to provide leads for field sales staff, and encourage prospects to order directly by mail or by phone. Both newspapers and magazines allow advertisers to use a wide range of printed material (e.g., extensive text, logos, diagrams, photos, prices, coupons, testimonials, and product descriptions), and in addition to black and white effects, ads can be further dramatized by color.

One of the features people will request is that their ads be run on certain pages. There is a premium [e.g., 15-30%] for you having your ad listed in a particular section and page as well as right- or left-hand preference position in the paper. So that is one of the things that will affect the costs of advertising. The frequency of advertising also counts as well. The more frequently you advertise, you are more likely to fall into a different rate category, and that will affect how much each ad costs you. And this is the full advantage of actually planning your advertising in advance, because you can work towards a better rate. You might save as much as half of your advertising costs that way. So if you know how much you are going to spend, then you get billed at the better rate than at the higher rate. . . . Color is another advantage to the ad. The larger ad also gets more attention, but color gives you more impact than the black and white. Color also has more retention. And a half page of color will have more impact than a full page of black and white. And sometimes it may be less expensive to buy a half page of color than a full page of black and white. So it depends where you want to go with your money and you may have enough left over to do another ad later [promotions—newspaper].

We also include response cards in our magazines, so if people are interested in products that they have, it is very easy for them to send the cards back to us and these will be processed. It makes it easier for them [suppliers] to get in touch with the readers later on. And if you know that someone is interested in your product, it sure makes your sales call a lot easier later [promotions—magazine].

Of the two media, newspapers (dailies especially) offer greater immediacy than do magazines. Magazines feature the same basic range of messages, and generally offer higher quality advertisement reproductions, but typically require a longer lead time (e.g., weeks or months versus one or two days).

In discussing the print media, it is essential to distinguish between local and national (and multinational) distributors, as well as those geared to general versus specific audiences. Newspapers tend to have more local and general appeal than do magazines, but the range of circulation is a concern regardless of whether one is discussing newspapers or magazines.

What happens with a lot of the papers is that when they increase their circulation, they also increase their advertising costs in their paper. Now this is good for some of the companies, so they really don't mind that extra circulation. So for some, it isn't economically viable to advertise in the same paper any more. So there, the smaller companies will be looking to the smaller newspapers, those that have a readership more limited to their own areas. So when the newspaper expands like that, what it does effectively is to create a new market for smaller, more localized newspapers, because these smaller businesses simply can't afford the high costs of advertising and it doesn't bring in the returns for them either. So if you have a bigger paper, it will do fine with the big companies, and it might be able to draw more big companies into it to advertise, but it will be losing some of its earlier accounts [promotions—newspaper].

_____ is a local magazine. That's one of our advantages. It gets more attention in the industrial sector because it's a magazine rather than a newspaper, and it's local, so it's good for a lot of businesses that way [promotions—magazine].

While many magazines also appeal to the public at large, magazine consumers tend to be more widely dispersed. In widely circulated, general appeal magazines, only vendors distributing on a national basis may consider it feasible to advertise therein. However, widely distributed specialty magazines may hold considerable appeal for those whose product interest is defined by specific audiences. Although by no means so limited (e.g., consider recreational magazines), this seems especially true of trade (i.e., industrial, commercial) magazines.

Magazines like ours are different than newspapers, because when you put an ad in a specialized magazine like this, you aren't going to get consumers calling on you. You're going to get the stores calling you and they're the people the suppliers want to deal with [promotions—magazine].

At most trade shows, one finds one or more magazines oriented specifically towards the products featured therein. These magazines are generally of high-gloss quality and are often sent out free of charge to those involved in purchasing those sorts of products. In particular, I have been struck by the number of nationally distributed industrial magazines in existence and of the flair and color with which industrial products [including ball bearings, nuts and bolts] are presented to prospective buyers [notes].

Recognizing differential interests in audiences on the part of advertisers and that they also compete with one another as well as with other media, newspapers and magazines frequently provide readership files. In addition to estimates of circulation, data are often provided on distribution and composition of the readership. This material may be used to help advertisers (vendors or their agents) select the media most appropriate for them, but it is often presented as evidence for the wisdom of using that particular outlet.

When they ask about the competition, what I emphasize the most is our readership. I think that is the most important aspect of it. Basically, we strive for an upper echelon of buyers, so we try to feature high-quality items and the magazines will be sent to good credit people, and also a lot of the larger accounts will be receiving our magazine as well. So it's very good in terms of readership. Something else that we will stress is the excellent quality of our editorial content, and that their ads will be interspersed with that, making them much more effective [promotions—magazine].

The newspaper and radio people, the salespeople from TV, they have all these figures and charts telling you who's reading or listening to your ads. It's part of their sales pitch, to get you to go with them, their style of advertising over the others [mixed clothing].

In actuality, readership (or other audience ratings) is a rather elusive concept. It does not, for instance, tell how thoroughly (if at all) people attend to the printed media. Nor does it indicate how selectively (e.g., sections, features) they do so. This is not to deny the general value of advertising in printed media, only to note that readership may generate misleading images of "effective exposure."

There are so many statistics on readership and who is reading. . . . There are just volumes on people's reading habits. You can get all sorts of surveys from institutes, so you can use that to back up the power of your advertising in the newspaper. . . . Then if you want to know who read the paper last week, or how many women are reading newspapers and such, you can get those sorts of breakdowns from the computer. What it can do is identify your market for you and help you get a better market . . . For a lot of those smaller accounts, you don't use it. It's too sophisticated for them. They wouldn't really be interested in that. But with the larger accounts, it would be something for them. They're very impressed with that and they rely on that very extensively [promotions—newspaper].

There are two ways of auditing papers. One is how many copies you send for distribution and that is what some of the papers will do. But then you will go and see them all stacked up in the apartment building and you realize that is not their actual circulation. The other way is your actual paying customers [promotions—newspapers].

The problem of effective exposure is further compounded in that advertisements are located within a mosaic of other advertisements. This means that advertisements that may be eye-catching by themselves, can easily be lost in the midst of others.

Making contact is a problem, because, say, in newspaper advertising, you're one of many and as they're going through that paper, they're not looking for your ad! You need something that's going to grab them, get their attention. If your client has money unlimited, it's a lot easier, go to a full page, color, big campaigns. Otherwise, you have got to get your ad to stand out, to stop the reader as they are going through the pages. . . . And then too, you don't know what else is going to be run with your ad. So you might do a negative [background reverse] layout only to find that nearly every other ad they put in that section of the paper had the same idea. So it's like that. You want something that's going to have impact! Something they're going to notice, remember, hopefully. But if they don't notice it first, then everything else doesn't matter [promotions—agency].

To offset these "losses," newspapers and magazine salespeople typically encourage vendors to repeat ads, run larger ads, and add color. They may also provide statistics on retention rates to establish their point. However, they seldom mention that 60%+ of their media may consist of advertisements; nor are they likely to indicate the proportionate percentage of one's advertisement relative to the whole medium in which that ad is located.

It might also be noted that newspaper advertising generally has a shorter life than that of magazines. This is especially true of newspapers, which may outdate themselves on a daily basis. However, printed material may be clipped and saved. Thus, in contrast to the more fleeting radio and television media, it can be "studied" at length by interested parties.

Most of our advertising will be done in the newspaper. What I like about the newspaper is that it provides that visual retention that you simply can't get on the radio or on television. Home decoration does need that visual retention. And in our newspaper copy, we try to target the type of people that would be interested in our store. So we try to be very precise, very consistent, very careful with our advertising copy so that it does convey to the reader the overall image of our store [furniture].

When you place an ad in the newspaper, you get a lot of exposure in the community, but that ad is usually in the garbage can in a few days. Where if you place it in a magazine, our magazine, it's kept as resource material. So the ad in the magazine is not only here the first week, but also a year from now, when the person is looking through the magazine for a special article or item. So that's a point in our favor [promotions—magazine].

RADIO AND TELEVISION

The audio-visual media provide some interesting contrasts with the print media just discussed. It may be valuable, however, to first delineate some aspects of radio and television which affect their relative value (and usage) as advertising media.

Featuring both audio and visual effects, television captures the sounds and conversations of radio, but adds the advantage of moving images. A "show and tell" medium, television, can generate more precise images than its audio counterpart. Television is also especially effective in illustrating settings, procedures, and applications of the featured products.[6] Both can dramatize and both can convey images, but television can sensually do so more completely.[7] However, as it is less reliant on audio effects than is radio, television generally requires higher levels of visual participation. Radio can be more readily combined with other activities (e.g.., driving, work), and radios are more accessible to audiences in a wider variety of settings than are television receivers.

> Television is a visual medium, by and large. So to be effective, you have to concentrate on the visual and work the audio material in around that. You write to the images you're giving them on the screen. . . . Each image is like a message, so you can do a lot that way, the "one picture, thousand words" thing. It's not that simple, but if you don't provide strong visual images, you might as well advertise on the radio [promotions—agency].

> With radio, you have a choice of doing your own reading or have someone read the material for you from the station. We like to do our own tapes. You get more variety that way, more control over how the script is read [promotions—agency].

Like newspapers and magazines, radio and television stations sell advertisements on the basis of (estimated) audience exposure.

> If someone has a product that they want people to know about, and hopefully there is a demand for that product, they need a vehicle they can use to let people know about that product. That becomes my business. To help them sell it, to create as much traffic as possible. People become aware of the product and they can then go to my client who is selling it. . . . And in radio we're selling air time. That's the vehicle. . . . When you're trying to push a product, you're telling people what it will do, what money they might save, the different reasons for buying a product. . . . You can create demand for a product. A manufacturer, say, can create a demand for his product where customers will go to the store and ask the retailer to start

carrying a particular line. You're selling them an audience. Radio, TV, newspaper. Newspaper, it's the readership. TV, it's audience; and radio, it's audience. And that's what you're selling them. It's nothing concrete that they can touch, but it is there. You're reaching people, and because you're reaching people, they can reach people. You're selling them audience figures. You're selling them a vehicle [promotions—radio].

When you're talking about the various medias, you've got to get a common denominator in order to get a comparison. Now there is no common denominator that will totally do the job, but you can start with a cost per thousand. Now by using the measuring services that are available, and we can argue those pro or con, but . . . by using that measure, you can come to a cost of what your advertising is costing you per thousand people delivered. . . . Delivered is the key word! There's a difference between circulation and delivery. Circulation is not delivery. Circulation is availability. Delivery is when you actually deliver the message. Somebody reads it. Somebody watches it. Somebody listens to it. Circulation and delivery are not the same thing. . . . To be very carefully noted, because that is one of the great fallacies and one of the great pitfalls in media selection is that people start to look at circulation. . . . I wouldn't sell anybody on that. What's a main concern to the advertiser is how many people do I deliver to when the ad is on the air, because that's what you pay for. Now that only tells part of the question because then you have to examine the media in terms of how does print function? How does radio function? How does television function? Direct mail? Billboards? You've got to look at them and say, what do they do? Then you say, what job do I need done, and what are my priorities [promotions—television]?

While readership for the print media may vary greatly by issue, audio/visual audiences can vary dramatically by times within a single day. Like the print media, audio-visual ads are also located within competitive contexts, and just as people may be concerned about where their ads appear in print media, so is there jockeying for position within the audio/visual media.

The morning is prime time because most people wake up to clock radios. You've got them! And in their cars, driving to work, they're listening to the radio. And a lot of businesses, and we run promotions to try to create this, will have their radios on during the day. . . . You can pick your timing. If you are, for example, in the restaurant business, most people will make a decision of two hours of actually going to that place and eating. . . . You can get them, put it in the back of their heads with your restaurant, within those two hours [promotions—radio].

[Prime time is] 6 to 11. That's how it's dictated. That's a bit of a misnomer because prime time is where you find your audience. In other words, you look at your target and you may find your target at 3 o'clock in the afternoon, so that's prime time for you. You may find your target in the morning. That's prime time for you. Prime time is any time that efficiently delivers an audience which you can use [promotions—television].

However short-lived the print media are, the audio-visual media are even more fleeting. People may record programs, but seldom would they be expected to intentionally do this with ads. Radio and television ads, for instance, frequently run 10-30 seconds and those not tuned to their receivers have no chance for exposure other than through repetition on the same or other stations.

We sell a fleeting moment. Our inventory doesn't exist until it is manufactured and it lasts for 30 seconds and it's off into infinity. You can't touch it. You can't hold it. You can't feel it. You can't put it on a shelf. So it's very understandable that a merchant would say, "When I'm on there for 30 seconds, does that really work?" We get that all the time and it's something that you have to work with [promotions—television].

That's why you get saturation advertising. One advertiser will buy up a lot of time in a short time span. That's why you see these ads on every station for a week or two, or more. Then they drop it off, work on a retention factor. The frequency is way down then, but people remember the ads because they were blitzed with them before [promotions—agency].

Frequency, you have to hit the people X number of times to make an impression. And if your budget will not allow you to do that, then you really should be looking elsewhere. With radio and television, you have to keep on hitting them. With that, it's very important to be in prime time and you very rarely, unless you happen to be [major corporation] and you're buying a million dollars TV time here and there. Unless you've got a huge, huge budget, you can't buy enough prime time. . . . With radio, and with the same amount of money, and with radio we have prime time as well. You're going to be able to reach that [higher] frequency, and it is going to have results. But if you're only running one commercial per day for a week, and you expect people to come flocking into your store, then you are misleading yourself. And any salesman that would sell you that is misleading you. I wouldn't deal with him [promotions—radio].

As with newspapers and magazines, it is valuable to distinguish local and national levels of electronic media. Both radio and television may be used by nationwide vendors, but local stations are apt to be preferred by others. Likewise, one can also achieve some audience selectivity by stations and/or programs (e.g., country, pop, classic, business). However, since the electronic media are more generally oriented to the consuming public, they offer limited advantage to most vendors selling to industry, trade, and other select audiences.

> If you have a shoe store, clothing, cars, something like that, it's probably good for you to advertise on the radio or on television or in the local papers. You're going for the mass market. There's not much point us doing that. How many companies in any city need our products? Most of that would be wasted for us. We need to be much more selective [manufacture—industrial].

The lead time for radio ads is especially short-term, as ads may be read at the next opening. Showing more, television generally requires more preparation time and is a slower medium for advertisers to access.

> With radio, if something goes wrong with that commercial, we can change that in, say, half an hour. We can create an image by use of voices, music, creativity, where people listen and laugh because they think it's funny, that sort of thing. You can be very creative with radio, depending on what you want to do [promotions—radio].

> We can go on with very little lead time, if we have an opening. But it's more of an "on the spot" shot. But it can be effective, depending on what you want, like the cases I was just telling you about. Then too, it depends on what your client feels comfortable with, and if you want a more elaborate commercial, that is going to take longer [promotions—television].

DIRECT MAIL

Direct mail refers to mailings via the postal service or other deliveries.[8] As with other media promotions already discussed, materials delivered directly to prospects may be used as sales devices in themselves (e.g., mail this coupon in with $39.95 and receive . . .") or as tools with which to support other marketing formats (e.g., fliers announcing "sales," new products, store openings).

> We do a lot of mailing, mass mailing, because we find we can reach a lot more people than we can through direct calling and sending salesmen into the field because that gets expensive. And that is just getting there, the person hasn't produced yet. And, if you're flying them [salespeople] around, or they're driving

down to another part of the country, then that's really costing you [manufacture—industrial].

We do a fair bit of direct mailing, especially on the "sales." . . . We've developed our list based on people who have bought here before, so you have to figure that they're better than average prospects. It's hard to tell exactly what it's worth, because we do advertise in the newspaper as well, but we do have a lot of repeat customers [men's clothing].

Direct mail relies very heavily on printed materials, but it is even more flexible than newspaper advertising. In addition to including printed material of all sizes and shapes, these deliveries may also include samples, gifts, and other attention getters. Further, in contrast to the more diffuse, general messaging of newspaper and magazines or radio and television, direct mail can be as limited and precise as one's specification of recipients. And while these items typically compete with other mail, they seem more likely to be noticed than are advertisements in many other media. Much direct mail may be dismissed as junk mail, but the material is retainable and tends not to become as readily dated as newspaper advertising, for instance.

Businesses using direct mail may use lists (developed in-house, selected from directories, or purchased from others) as a means of selecting targets or they may define specific regions of cities as denoting more likely prospects for their mail programs. And unless advertisers have reason to believe that their listings are fairly comprehensive or wish to be more selective, more sweeping deliveries may be advantageous in providing new inquiries and leads. Further, advertisers using lists may find that these are not as complete, accurate, up-to-date, and devoid of duplications as might first seem (or as described by agents selling lists).

Accuracy is a problem with lists. If they're not updated frequently, you're going to waste a fair bit of your mailing budget [manufacture—industrial].

You can buy lists. Usually, you would only get them if you think you can reach a new set of buyers. The problem, though, with a lot of the lists is that there may be a lot of duplications or maybe they've got a lot of outdated names or addresses, and that's going to cost you. But it is a faster way of getting prospects, reaching more potential buyers [manufacture—industrial].

Direct delivery programs may involve single mailings, multiple mailings, or packages of advertising. Insofar as repetition tends to promote familiarity, some direct marketers use multiple mailings to the same targets. Regardless of whether these mailings contain the same or different promotional materials, they increase the likelihood of attention and serve to establish stronger definitions of credibility than do single mailings.

> What I like about the multiple mailings is that you build up an image with your customers over time. You get more recognition that way. It costs money, but I think you need that [promotions—agency].

Direct mail packages represent a form of cost sharing among two or more businesses seeking compatible prospects. Packages are more difficult to coordinate, and require involved parties advertise at the same time and generally within particular limits (e.g., size, number of enclosures). However, while the competition is intensified as any given message may "get lost in the package," costs may be reduced somewhat in the process and larger packages may receive more initial attention.

Advertisers using the mail need not worry about finding people in at particular times, but these seem most effective when used to help establish credibility and otherwise facilitate telephone and/or personal calls.

> If you do a mail program, you should follow up on it by phone as soon as possible, before it ends up there [wastebasket]! Sometimes, people are interested in what you've got, but they don't act on it, themselves. That's why I think a strong phone program is so important [manufacture—industrial].

CATALOGUES

Although they are often distributed by direct mail programs, and can be viewed as larger, longer-term versions of fliers, catalogues reflect some noteworthy features and problems of their own design. Representing a resource for future reference, the life span of catalogues tends to be greater than other printed materials. Catalogues also provide shopping convenience and, where product information is more attractive and extensive, the items featured may sell themselves. Larger catalogues are seen generally as more useful, but they entail greater investments for the advertisers. Also, considerable planning may be involved to ensure that the goods featured are available for sale and that the goods available are featured.[9] Thus more extensive uncertainties of stock and/or possible alterations of lines render unit catalogues inconvenient.[10]

> I wanted to get into a catalogue, but it's a tremendous expense! And to coordinate the project is something else, because you've got to have all your merchandise picked out well in advance, and get guarantees on your shipments. And you've got to guarantee them that you're going to take so much of this stuff. So you would have to have the capital for the inventory. Then you've got to go and get the artwork all done, and the printing and the distribution [giftware].

> This is our third attempt at catalogues. Our first catalogue was a brochure, a one-page foldout. We only had about 10 or so items, and that was about four or five years after we were in business. And then our product lines started to expand, so we came out with another one. Then about five years ago, we came out with our first full-color catalogue. Quite an expensive item. Quite an investment [manufacture—giftware]!

Businesses may use catalogues as substitutes for showrooms and/or agents, but their role as supporting media should not be overlooked.

> The catalogue is a tool to refer to, for reordering, if the salesman doesn't come by in time [wholesale—industrial].

> There are a large number of mail-order services (manufacturers, distributors) operating that way, where they have put out a catalogue and they really do not have a display area. . . . Also, If you go to some of these manufacturers and suppliers, you might be quite surprised at the poor upkeep of the buildings, the doors and all, the general conditions of the building inside and out. And the people you're dealing with, they're sometimes embarrassed that you see them there. . . . If they're using catalogues or sales representatives, you might be surprised to find out just how much difference exists between how the catalogue looks, compared to the place they're actually doing business from. . . . But in a way, they're wise to do that. That way, they can keep their overhead down and put more money into marketing [giftware].

DIRECTORY ADVERTISING

Telephone and trade directories represent another advertising medium. Businesses may be listed under one or more categories as a matter of directory policy, but vendors may also use part of their marketing budgets to obtain more category listings and/or more prominent ads than those routinely granted by the compiling agency. Not unlike the other media discussed earlier, directory agencies tend to promote competition. The implication is that those who do not advertise extensively are apt to get lost in obscurity as prospects search out particular categories of businesses.

It's to their advantage. If you have a bigger ad, people are going to notice it sooner. You look more prominent too, a going concern. You're more likely the one they're going to call. . . . You also have more room to give them more information, more reasons to buy from you, more reasons to call you than someone who just lists a name and an address [promotions—directory].

The advantage of the trade directory is that you're advertising on a national basis. You get greater exposure than, say, from the (telephone) yellow pages, because it's more national. . . . That's where the buyers are going to look. . . . If you have a local business, then it's not so valuable for you. [manufacture—industrial].

Generally speaking, directory advertising seems most valuable to those offering more specialized services and goods. Nevertheless, listings for well-known companies may be useful for maintaining profile, as well as helping prospects find locations of businesses, inquire about office hours and the like. In addition to monies obtained from advertisers, those compiling directories often generate additional revenue from directory-related materials. The advertisers and directory subscribers thus become targets for other promotions.[11]

SIGN ADVERTISING

Encompassing billboards, store-front signs, in-store point of purchase (P.O.P.) displays, and the like, sign advertising relies much more heavily on passing traffic than do the earlier mentioned advertising formats. Both print and electronic media may be used in sign advertising, and while signs may have mobile qualities (e.g., names on commercial vehicles), sign advertising generally has maximum value in high-traffic areas and for those companies whose prospective customers are greater in number and/or more geographically concentrated.

In the real estate industry, the basic assumption is that your sign is a 24-hour advertiser, and that's why if you have a real hot listing, you don't want a sign on it. You don't want to advertise the fact that you've got it. . . . If I had a good listing,

I would encourage them [home owners] not to put a sign on it for a few weeks. And then I was vague enough in my ads in the paper, that if I put it in, they (other buyers) wouldn't be likely to find it from that alone. . . . It depends where it is. If it's in a good traffic area, and it isn't necessarily in relation to that house, because if you get a call and you're able to pick up a client, then the least of your concern is whether he buys that house! If you've got a good prospect, then your concern is that he buys a house and that he buys it from you, through you. So there are several areas of loss if the people don't want a sign in a situation like that. . . . You also want signs on your houses in high-profile areas, because then when someone wants to sell their house, they're more likely to list with you [real estate].

Newspapers, they're one of our competitors, too, because they'll [businesses] want to know if for the same amount of money they're investing in a sign, if the newspaper ads wouldn't do more for them. And there, we stress the lasting quality of the sign. The sign may cost this much or that much compared to the newspaper, and the newspaper may help bring some people in from the other side of the town, but with our signs, you've got something that's going to last longer. It's not like the newspaper that they wrap up the fish or throw it out with the garbage. The sign's going to last, and it'll attract attention from the local people, the people passing by every day, so they're more likely to stop by and they're more likely going to be your repeat customers too. The people from across town, they might be good for some "sales" item, something like that, but there's a lot of stores between here and there, and if they see the signs, they may stop there. So we tell them, right on location, that's the best place to advertise. . . . You have to keep your store signs simple. Attractive, attention-getting, but not so cluttered that people have to park (their cars) to read it [promotions—signs].

Packaging denotes another form of "sign advertising." This may take the form of point-of-purchase display packaging as well as product containers. Since packages represent a medium on which to print messages, they can be used to advertise as well as provide protection for the goods featured. As with the media more generally, packaging may be used to attract attention, appeal to certain audiences, arouse interest, and the like.[12]

Packaging is more than giving something protection during shipping. You want that too, but with these things here, the package is designed to sell the products put in them. We design it for that, to enhance their worth [promotions—packaging].

How you package things makes a big difference to what people think things are worth. The package dresses your products up. Makes them look classier [manufacture—giftware].

SPECIALTY ADVERTISING

Specialty advertising refers to the practice of giving prospective and existing customers items on which company and/or product names are printed. It differs from the other print media in that the advertising is located on specific objects that recipients may retain for their entertainment and/or other purposes. Specialty advertising items are generally intended to provide greater longevity to advertising campaigns by incorporating messages into a form that has greater relevance and durability. Thus by placing company names, logos, and messages on items such as hats, playing cards, rulers, calendars, and so forth, advertisers may achieve repeated exposures by prospects. Some items such as matchbooks, balloons, and pens are more transient. Others, such as letter openers, paper weights, and glassware, may last for decades. If the product is found useful, it may gain the advertiser much goodwill as well as continued advertising as the recipients use and/or otherwise take notice of their possessions.

> The specialty items are nice to give. It's nice to be able to give something to someone. They last, they're useful. It's a very effective way of advertising [manufacture—industrial].

> You see lots of little stores putting their money into advertising in the newspapers, but unless it's a local newspaper, I don't think it can be worth their while. And they have a very small budget to work with. And with a small budget, I think you can show that specialty advertising can really work to your advertiser. With most companies, I will recommend a couple of levels of specialty advertising. You'll have some of the least expensive items that you'll use for the wider market, matchbooks, pens, small things. Then something more for those who are dealing with you more regularly, maybe a buck or two apiece. For the people who are dealing with you more extensively, something more expensive, perhaps $5 to $25. But you can set levels like that in most businesses, depending on what market you're dealing in. All your customers are valuable to you, but they're not equally valuable, so it's just a way of expressing your appreciation to them, relative to that. So with the better clients, you give them a little better item. Or you might have buttons at one level, and a better quality of pens at the next, something like that. When you approach the people, you try to get the people to understand the value of promotions. . . . But you have to watch it too, because you want to get items that are a good quality. If you give someone a poor quality pen, is that going to suggest that you have a poor quality company [promotions—agency]?

It is clear that not everyone who receives specialty advertising items will appreciate them.[13] It seems even more certain, however, that almost anything can be used as a promotional device, and vendors can influence how effective premiums are by the ways in which they use them. These items can be especially valuable when used as door openers, conversation pieces, and as a means of consolidating repeat patronage.

> Another reason for us to leave our gifts with people, whether they buy or not, is because each gift has our name on it, and that sitting there gives your name exposure. They see it, and when other people come over, neighbors, they see these little gadgets, "Where did you get that?" That's another reason we leave these little gadgets, to remind them that we were there [in-home—households].

> We've been using these premiums for a long time. They're great for stopping people [at trade shows]. Then it's "Here you are [handing someone a gift]. Are you familiar with _____?" It's a great lead! And you'll have people telling you they looked all over the show to find the place where you get these things. So they're good, and it makes selling a little more fun, a little easier [manufacture—industrial].

Media Promotion Dilemmas

The preceding materials on potential uses of media promotions and on the major variants of media used in promoting products provide valuable background material on advertisers' situations. It should be recognized, however, that there exists great uncertainty among advertisers as to (1) the tasks associated with the message to be conveyed, (2) the media best suited to particular promotions, (3) the resources to be allocated to media promotions, and (4) the effectiveness of advertising ventures. What follows is a brief consideration of the dilemmas media promotions may engender for users.

DEFINING EXPECTATIONS (TASKS AT HAND)

When discussing media promotions, it is valuable to ask about the concerns taken into account by people contemplating media sales programs. Individual advertisers are unlikely to consider all the following points in any given instance, or to give the elements they do consider consistent weightings even from one advertising program to another.

Likewise, the planning of advertising programs is subject to considerable uncertainty, agonizing, and negotiation, as those involved try to maximize results within budget limitations in an ever-shifting marketplace. With these qualifications in mind, however, the following list provides an overview of the sorts of concerns advertisers may have in developing messages for media sales programs.

Support: What tasks are messages expected to accomplish (e.g., profile, credibility, introduce product, and so on)?

Totality: How much of the sales function, from contact to completed sales is the message to accomplish?

Recruiting Objectives: Is the message intended to attract customers, intensify purchasing, encourage repeat patronage, reactivate (former) accounts?

Selectivity: To what extent is the message directed toward a specific (versus general) target population?

Emphasis: What is the central theme (image) to be promoted? What is the relative importance of company, product(s), features, problems, solutions, clientele?

Exposure: What is the estimated number of people who (theoretically) have an opportunity to experience the message (e.g., readership, viewing audiences, mailing lists)?

Saturation: To what extent will all members of the desired target population have an opportunity to become exposed to and/or familiar with the message?

Impact: To what extent is the message acknowledged by the target population? Does it achieve attention, profile, credibility, retention, purchasing activity?

Longevity: What is the duration of the message? Does the medium provide multiple exposures for targets over time (e.g., television, newspaper, specialty advertising; in order of general longevity)?

Consistency: Does the message contribute to an overall desired image or theme the company wishes to promote?

SELECTING MEDIA

Regardless of their concerns with the preceding objectives, the following elements appear to shape vendors' eventual selections of particular media for their promotional messages.

Relative cost: What financial outlay does any advertisement (campaign) entail? Includes set up and running costs. Effectiveness per unit may be calculated by exposure (an easy, but unreliable measure) and/or increased traffic flows, comparative sales totals for the quarter (year), and the like. Costs may also be shared/subsidized through joint advertising ventures (e.g., franchises/mall/suppliers).

Preparations entailed: What sorts of time spans, efforts, or skills are required for assembling and conducting particular media programs? How does this compare with the desire for immediate action?

Competitors' activities: Are vendors concerned with using media and/or media messages similar to those of their competitors?

Prestige: What definitions do vendors have of various medium/message styles as more prestigious, sophisticated, respectable?

Anticipated target receptivity: Will the intended targets find the promotions and media selected acceptable, worthwhile?

Familiarity: Have vendors had exposure to particular media as advertisers, targets, or through advertising agency contact?

In selecting media, vendors are faced with another set of marketing dilemmas. Not only may vendors contemplate the viability of one medium over another, but they may also be concerned about the relative trustworthiness of the various media representatives they encounter and the accuracy of the images (and hopes) they associate with this or that media campaign. Like buyers in other settings (see Chapter 4), those involved in media promotions are apt to find themselves hedging their bets (e.g., seeking consensus, diversifying, testing the ice) in this realm of investment.

SETTING BUDGETS

A third and related set of concerns focuses on monies to be spent on media promotions. Examining the matter of media spending, Wasson and McConaughy (1968: 372-374) note five basic methods of establishing advertising budgets.

- *Arbitrary sum allocations:* The company sets a specific amount aside for advertising.
- *Percentage of sales allocation:* The company establishes a percentage of sales (last year's usually; may also project on the basis of anticipated sales) to be used for advertising purposes.
- *Competition parity:* The company assesses the advertising campaigns of the competition and endeavors to match (or exceed this level of activity).
- *All that's available:* The company uses any available money for advertising (i.e., as much as they can afford).
- *Objective task advertising:* The company sets an objective and determines how much advertising needs to be done to achieve that goal (e.g., 20% increase in sales).

While any one of these themes may be most central in a company's decisions, it seems likely that most decisions will reflect some combination of the foregoing as vendors work toward budget consistency, proportionate expenditures, competitive policies, growth, and short-range and long-term objectives. It should be noted, however, that none of these modes of budgeting, either individually or in combination, resolves the issue of maximal optimization of resources. People may propose various formulas for success (e.g., 5% of one's sales be put into media promotions), but the dilemma ultimately remains with the vendors involved. It is they who take the gamble.

Setting an advertising budget can be difficult, especially when it is acknowledged that that same money could be used to improve the business in other ways (e.g., more stock, space, staff). Viewed thusly, media budgets compete with other ventures designed to increase business. But their long- and short-term benefits are generally not as readily apparent as are the effects of increased space or new equipment. For smaller companies especially, media promotions are more apt to clearly compete with other necessities.

We were spending around $5,000 a month on advertising, newspaper, and radio advertising. But I found that the advertising dollar generated just enough business to pay for the advertising costs. Now, eventually, the new customers that the advertising brings in will become regular customers, so it pays off that way, but initially, you're pretty well working for nothing. You spend a thousand on advertising, and then you recover that, so the money comes back to you there, but if you have to pay extra help for the extra business, that's something else you have to figure in your total volume. Or if you're trying to do more yourself, you may have to work an extra 20 hours a week, just to cover the extra business the advertising brings in, and you're not making any more money. . . . Then, when business turned down again, it was like business stopped, so we cut back on the advertising. We lost money a couple of months, so I decided to stop spending money on advertising. . . . I will advertise more again, when I expand again, when I can add some new lines and pay for the extra staff. Then if I can bring in enough business through advertising to pay for the extra staff, fine. Then I don't care [furniture].

Your advertising budget for your first several years should be more than later. Now, whether we can actually afford it, because of the rest of your overhead is something else. . . . The salaries, the rent, the heating, they add up too. . . . The large companies still need the advertising because of their high overhead, but they have already established themselves in the marketplace. We advertise to the best of our ability and the best of our budgets, but if we advertised more heavily, and were able to saturate the market more heavily, we would really reap the benefits. So to us, now, $25,000 seems like a lot of money to spend on advertising in one year [appliances].

Cooperative Advertising Programs

Another element that may affect media budgets is co-op advertising. Supplier-assisted promotions provide further indication of the extent to which suppliers and vendors are partners in trade. Assisted advertising may involve all the preceding forms of promotion, and reflects the assumption that whatever helps the vendor sell more of the supplier's product is beneficial to the supplier as well. Thus, while many suppliers will assist even the smallest vendors with point of purchase displays, catalogues, samples, and the like, vendors who do more business with particular suppliers are apt to find themselves more advantaged relative to their overall promotions. Thus in addition to (other) price discounts that normally accrue with larger volumes, vendors dealing in larger volumes of name brand products are also more likely to qualify for more extensive advertising support.

Dealers sometimes approach suppliers for assistance, but it is the suppliers who normally define the parameters of support. This joint advertising venture is generally with the provision that the supplier's name brand be prominently displayed, but it may result in a major (e.g., 40-70%) reduction in the cost of particular promotions for the vendor. Vendors may thus advertise more with the same outlay. Either way, the vendor is likely to benefit in increased traffic and/or the effectively decreased overhead.

Your catalogues and fliers are heavily co-oped. If you see the supplier's brand on it, it's probably co-oped. It'll often be as much as 70% [supplier supported] co-oped [department store].

You'll find that a lot of the major companies, and I'm thinking of the national and international companies, like _____ or _____ , any of the major appliance dealers, will help out an individual businessman or store with his advertising costs through co-op advertising. . . . That one company, he might give you 75% in co-op. So anything you do in advertising is subsidized by 75%, so you'd be kind of crazy to say, "Well, no, I don't particularly like that product. I'm going to go with this other guy here who isn't paying me anything, and I'm going to foot the bill myself." In advertising, you can easily go over $10,000 in a month on a promotion. So instead of that $10,000, if you could make it $2,500, you'd be silly not to push that particular product. . . .
    There are different types of co-op campaigns. Some will say, "Well, as long as you push our products, you can do whatever you want." And what you do then is give them [supplier] a confirmation of the product, the times that it ran, the company script. Sometimes they will get a little more picky, where they want this line mentioned, that kind of thing. You have to say that somewhere in the commercial. Another thing might be where they will pay half, but half of the commercial is submitted by them, with the dealer tags. So you might have some appliance manufacturer, and then, "Your _____ dealer in this area is . . ." That would be your dealer tag. And in the other half, the dealer can push whatever he wants as long as it refers to their products, but it can be what the dealer himself wants. So it depends on the company. Every company has a different co-op arrangement. . . . You don't know for sure, but I would assume that if it's a big radio campaign or a big ad in the paper, that someone is co-oping it. . . . It's often 50%, but it's based on your business with that company. Often it'll be based on 2%, 3% of your business. So if you're doing a lot of business with a particular supplier, you can build up quite a kitty. So that's part of it. You've got to buy enough stock from them to meet that advertising cost [promotions—radio].

As Haring (1935: 42-59) observed, "advertising allowances" were well established by that time. Also evident by then were many of the same problems presently associated with co-op advertising programs. Not only are some promotional media (e.g., newspaper, radio) easier to monitor than others (e.g., window displays, mail programs), but suppliers may also find that once they venture into these practices they are apt to encounter some buyers who significantly stretch the items covered by these programs. As well, once individual suppliers or industries begin these practices, it becomes increasingly difficult for these same suppliers to do business in other ways (i.e., failure to maintain co-op programs may be defined as trust violations by buyers accustomed to these arrangements). While some suppliers perceive this as a valuable avenue to encourage initial patronage and heavier stocking of their products by buyers, other suppliers have explicitly tried to avoid these sets of entanglements. Thus, despite the seeming advantages of shared promotional programs, some buyers, suppliers, and media people express reservations regarding their viability.

> A lot of the manufacturers will go for co-op advertising. And the newspaper people really like it. They all do, radio, TV, what have you, because it's more business for them. Like _____ is always pushing that when they call on you. But it's more trouble for you than getting, say 2-4% off on your supplies. The ads have to take this form. Their products, logos, have to be this large proportionately. Plus, you are maybe ordering this much more stock to cover that percentage, depending on how they work it out with you. And you have to send them copies and all, so it's more of a hassle. You do benefit from it, but I have really mixed feelings about the gains [appliances].

> Here, we haven't gotten into co-op advertising. We tell them, "Sorry, we're not into that." "Well, we may not be able to carry your lines, then." Or, "Gee, we won't be able to promote your lines as well as the others." And you may very well lose some customers over that. But you can't have it both ways, or you'll screw your reputation if you start making concessions for this one and not that one. You have to decide which way you want to go. Either you go co-op, or you don't. . . . We had co-op at _____ , and I saw all the problems with that. You have a lot more hassles with it, and then you don't really know where your advertising dollars are going. . . . We give pretty good discounts with volumes and any money we put into advertising, we know where it's going. With co-op, you really don't know, and your advertising is not very uniform [manufacture—clothing].

> Our financial concern, I suppose, is our own bottom line. I like to think that we are a little broader in our thinking and we're very concerned about whether it's worked out for the advertiser. Because an advertiser who's not successful is not a continuing advertiser. So they're very expensive for us, if a campaign is wrong. Co-op advertising can be very successful. Frankly, I sometimes question what it does for the individual merchant. It does a great deal for the manufacturer or the distributor, whatever the case may be, but I sometimes feel that the advertiser really should be

getting equal billing with the manufacturer. Indeed, we encourage that to happen and in many cases in the last five years, we've been able to attain that. . . . My argument is that it is not just to the merchant's benefit if we encourage the manufacturer to change his sights a little bit and give equal billing, because when he does that he raises the profile of the retailer to an extent that the retailer starts to stand out as somebody special because they're running with equal billing kind of thing. If we can attain that with co-op advertising, plus the suppliers running their own national advertising and their brand awareness and their brand education campaigns, then they can't help but win because they have raised their retailer up too. Their dealer is on a higher plane, a higher level. He's got a little more importance in the mind of the consumer, so I think they both win. It's interesting that you should ask that because there are some manufacturers in the last year or so who have indeed encouraged their retailers to take equal billing and they have begun, in those instances, to use some small, regional advertising agencies to create commercials which will reach this end [promotions—television].

Joint advertising programs may be implemented on other bases as well. Thus, in addition to the savings that can accrue to chains and franchises, other clusterings of business, such as malls or neighboring businesses may "gang up" their advertising to provide more and/or larger exposures, with the hopes of drawing larger crowds.

This is another area that it's better to be part of a franchise. We do more things, with better artwork, color, and all, and yet it needn't cost them [franchisees] more because we do it in such large volumes [franchise—appliances].

One of the advantages of being in a mall is that you get more advertising space or time for your dollars. You may not like all the promotions the mall runs, but you do get better rates overall. You're able to buy bigger chunks of newspaper space, or more spots on the radio, say [mall].

Malls differ, depending on the company that owns the mall. Some companies will, like _____ mall, promote itself. Everybody in the mall contributes a certain amount of money for advertising. And out of that you have one person who's responsible for buying the most effective media campaign, and that money is spread out over a year, contracts signed, and that is mall advertising. The idea being that if they can bring traffic into the mall, they're going to visit your store. . . . Then you get into other malls whereby the mall management takes X number of dollars out of your rent and allocates that for advertising. If it's a smaller mall where there isn't a lot of money, they might go co-op. Half-and-half for any of the merchants inside the mall who want to advertise that way. So there, after they've paid for their square footage and what they believe is their mall advertising, you're going back to them and you're saying, "Now the mall will go half-and-half on you on advertising." Which can cause problems. Sometimes they'll do both, where part of their budget is institutional, promoting the mall, and then if they have some left over, anybody who wants to go advertise on their own, they may have a kitty there that you can draw up for co-op ads. . . . Every mall is different, depending on who owns them and who's in charge of them [promotions—radio].

ASSESSING EFFECTIVENESS

Like other aspects of marketing, one cannot readily determine the effects of media promotions. Thus, shifting seasons, selections of goods available, staff skills, pricing, and efforts of the competition, along with other aspects of one's marketing program will color the effects of media promotions. One may speak of the relative effectiveness of particular ads under test conditions, but it is difficult to access accurately one part of a larger program in isolation from all the other images and experiences that prospects may have with a given company, its competitors, and any diversions.

It's hard to see the direct benefits regarding sales. Very, very rarely are you going to get someone who says, "I just heard your name on the radio and I'm calling you because of that." That has happened, but that's very rare. . . . But you might be sitting down with someone, and they'll say, "Oh, I happened to hear your ad on the radio." It makes you more credible. You're not a company they've never heard of, that their neighbor said you should talk to this person or whatever. It's just another way of reassuring the client that you really do exist [investments].

I don't know how you can really evaluate advertising programs. What if 30% of the people who heard the radio remember your ad? How much business do they get for you? And how do you separate that from everything else you do to try to make sales? Things are constantly changing, with the seasons and all. . . . I guess you can tell most with your "sales," whether you're busy or not, but even there, you're often doing that on the radio, the newspaper, and you've got your signs up. So who really knows? . . . Overall, it creates awareness, but how much is that worth? There are a lot of stores I know about, but how many do I shop at [giftware].

A related difficulty of assessing effectiveness reflects the different expectations vendors have for their advertising efforts. Even when the same media are used, vendors' objectives can vary considerably. For some, a message that results in greater familiarity with the company name or product may be considered successful. For others, success is defined by a sudden, dramatic increase in traffic flow or sales totals.

> You judge by your sales results. There's what you can call A advertising and B advertising, A being action which is where you count the dollars in the till, so to speak, and B being image advertising. Image advertising is very, very hard to assess [department store].

> The paper comes out about 3 o'clock, 3:30 in the afternoon here. If an ad is good, a good ad, we will have phone calls before 6 o'clock that night. "Are you open until 9 tonight? I saw you had such and such." Or first thing in the morning. Like 9 o'clock the next morning, the phone's ringing. "I saw your ad last night," or they come in with the ad in their hand. . . . I would never take any money away from newspaper advertising! I just believe in it wholeheartedly. I have seen enough feedback in my store and on the phone and people walking in the store, "Saw your ad. Where's the so-and-so that was in the paper?" You get many phone calls every week from the newspaper ad [jewelry].

Vendors may increase their likelihood of obtaining particular kinds of exposures by using certain media. But the message conveyed, the way it is presented, and the context in which it is presented in that media will also affect its general impact. We know that assessments are unlikely to be uniform across members of target audiences, but more specific predictions are more problematic. Those who wish to measure effectiveness by doing market research are apt to find this an expensive, time-consuming, and elusive endeavor.[14] There are all sorts of market surveys that vendors may use, but the costs of these may be prohibitive and/or impractical for all but the larger companies. And even in these cases, the general types of survey research strategies used are generally insensitive to the symbolic nature of communications. Messages do not have inherent meanings or uniform effects. While advertisers may intend to convey certain images in their messages or to achieve particular results, these are subject to a seemingly infinite set of ongoing and shifting interpretations on the part of those attending to their messages. Thus, for instance, not only may recipients attend to many other features of the message (e.g., peripheral artwork, color, background characters) than those intended as central by the advertisers, but even when they attend to the components of the message intended as most central, they may do so in ways quite at variance from that intended by the advertisers (e.g., humor may be interpreted as fact, or demonstrations may be seen as silly or pointless).

Although typically vague as to impact, those more involved in advertising, such as agents and advertisers, generally contend that advertising must be conducted on a fairly continuous basis if a company is to maintain profile in the marketplace.

In business, you have to keep up your advertising, or you will lose more of the market share. It's especially great for us when one of our companies gets involved in a major advertising battle, like with _____ and _____ right now. But you figure, for most companies, advertising should be a certain size of their operating budget. You can cut it somewhat, but if you do, I think you're going to be defeating yourself [promotions—agency].

For some, a couple hundred of dollars seems like a big investment in advertising. And, for some of them, they think that if they run one ad, it is good for a year! And with some people, I just tell them, "Look, if you're planning to run just one ad, don't even bother to run it, because it just isn't going to have any significant effect. You would be better to hang on to your money and put it into stock, or something." You run one ad and not much is going to happen. What is the point of it? And if you are new in town and you run one ad, there is just no point. No one is going to know you are around any more than before. You might get lucky and have a few people in your store because of the ad, but if you're new, you should be promoting yourself a lot. Although what may be happening is that people are just getting into business, so they may not have planned for the advertising aspect of it. So maybe they would like to take another look at their budget overall, because advertising is good money in terms of business. And, if you are doing $100,000 in business and just spending a couple hundred on advertising, you are probably not getting the most out of your business you could. . . . So one of my main tasks, actually, is to educate people on the value of advertising [promotions—newspaper].

If you're going to advertise, you've got to think long-term. Too many people run one ad and then expect their business to take off. That's not too likely. It takes time to establish yourself [promotions—magazine].

The radio works by frequency. A good commercial will be remembered if you hit the people somewhere between three and five times. So they can keep it in the back of their heads. And that costs money. So if someone only has $500, you'd probably be farther ahead to perhaps rent a sign for a month. It's not going to get as many people in the door as commercials would if they're done properly, but it will help. And at least you have been up-front with the people [vendors], and that's so important, the honesty. And it hopefully will work for them, so that they can get to the point where you can really do a job for them. And my feeling is that until you can do it well, you should be working at other areas [promotions—radio].

When discussing the impact of any promotion, one should also consider the different targets at which advertisements may be directed. Thus, while the consuming public may be aware of trade/company names of household goods, this sort of general awareness may be of little value to vendors featuring products for very specialized subsets of prospects. These latter vendors may benefit somewhat from general familiarity, but the value of becoming a household name has by no means the value to these merchants than it would to producers of more broadly consumed goods. Thus prominence in the marketplace is not synonymous with prominence in the general community. A very effective advertising campaign may go unnoticed by the general community. Another campaign may be much more evident to the general populace, but have little impact on the subpopulation for which it was intended.

The significance of media promotions is not limited to the direct company or product images presented to prospective buyers. It is also noteworthy for those associated with the company in other ways. By generating company profile, credibility, and product demand, advertising may promote confidence, enthusiasm, and loyalty on the part of employees. Each becomes somebody who's more significant in the community more generally. Promotions may make the business appear more attractive to prospective employees. Likewise, suppliers generally prefer to affiliate themselves with vital enterprises, and in addition to opening up new lines and products to these vendors, may provide them with better than usual service. Finally, vendors may acquire more esteem in the community more generally, thus finding additional opportunities and support (e.g., investors) over time.

In Perspective

Media promotions may be used to promote first time purchases, repeat patronage, and reinvolvements in purchases of particular products. Especially significant in these respects are the ways in which vendors may use the media to make contact, promote seekership, create closure, and reduce buyer reservations. It appears, however, that most media promotions are directed toward first-time or immediate users with existing customers more readily taken for granted.

Insofar as these promotions are most commonly represented in the form of newspapers and magazines, radio and television, direct mail, catalogues, directories, signs, and specialty advertising, some time was spent considering the features of each. In all cases, like the products they promote, these media are themselves subject to much sales activity. Thus, without disputing the claims of those representing particular media and outlets therein, it is apparent that the marketing of the media deserves considerable attention as a focus in itself. We have only begun to scratch the surface here, as is also the case with the purchasing of media promotion packages (e.g., selecting particular media, themes; hedging bets on various options), and the development of buyer-supplier (i.e., media source-agency-client) relationships in this realm of activity.

While often hailed as (magic) formulas for success, media promotions engender much ambiguity. Thus, some attention was given to the dilemmas advertisers experience in reference to the tasks associated with media messages, the eventual selections of media, media budget allocations, and assessments of media effectiveness. Viewed thusly, media promotions not only lose some of their mystique, but this discussion also draws into sharper relief the ongoing human enterprise and frustration underlying the planning, production, and implementation of media messages in the face of uncertain, diverse, and shifting audience interpretations. Other aspects of media promotions surface in the chapters following. Particularly instructive in this regard are materials depicting the interlinkages of media promotions with field and showroom sales endeavors.

Notes

1. Schudson (1984) also provides a sociological statement on advertising. This work features many tidbits of insight, but provides little conceptual depth regarding marketplace promotions. Although not directly focused on advertising, Klapp's (1964) portrayal of symbolic leaders and his (1969) analysis of the search for identity is much more conceptually valuable. In another vein, McKendrick et al. (1982) and Pope (1983) offer two insightful historical accounts of advertising. The McKendrick et al. statement on "the commercialization of eighteenth century England" is especially valuable in depicting early advertising practices as well as the overall impact of promotional activity on the industrial revolution. Pope provides some instructive material on the emergence and persistence of early advertising agencies and their arrangements with publishers and clients.

2. Here, I am much indebted to Howard Becker's (1963) account of the role that "moral entrepreneurs" play in the definition and regulation of *deviance*.

3. Sales are examined at greater length in Chapter 8 of *Making Sales* (Prus, 1989), but discounting in the form of dollar (and/or cents) savings, percentages off, coupons, or

extra merchandise for the regular price, also tends to define exchanges as more favorable to those "wise enough to take advantage of their opportunities."

4. Although the concept of needs is so vague and subject to highly diverse interpretations and assumptions that it is better avoided in analysis of human activity, the notion of closure used herein is often expressed in reference to perceived needs.

5. As McKendrick et al. (1982) indicate (particularly in reference to"George Packwood and the commercialization of shaving"), the art of puffing (advertising) in print was well established over two centuries ago.

6. Wrighter (1972) provides a most interesting and valuable depiction of the power (and illusiveness) of visual and verbal symbols in television advertisements.

7. There is no doubt that radio can invoke powerful images. However, these images are not as sensually articulated as those provided by television (i.e., radio projections are open to a greater range of interpretation).

8. See Hodgson (1974) and Fairlie (1979) for detailed discussions of direct mail practices.

9. Should vendors not meet this first condition, they are apt to encounter prospects disenchanted over the lack of availability of goods (or those suggested as substitutes).

10. Some vendors rely on replacement components for their catalogues, but this entails extra processing on the part of both promoters and recipients.

11. This practice is by no means limited to those assembling directories. For instance, many magazines will sell lists of their subscribers as will many credit card companies.

12. Products may also be packaged in multiples (e.g., six-packs) to generate additional sales as well as for shopping and clerking convenience.

13. Dempsey et al. (1980) indicate that about 20% of the industrial buyers they surveyed said that they did not accept "gifts" from salespeople. Apparently, academic experts had anticipated that the rates of refusal would have been much higher. Ironically, academics (e.g., sociologists, marketing professors) are themselves most receptive to the freebees (premiums) given by book publishers at conferences!

14. Jacobs (1979) provides a valuable account of fudging and slippage on the part of frontline market research workers. My own observations of market surveys suggest that Jacobs's statements tend to be generalizable across market research organizations.

Chapter 7
WORKING THE FIELD

At one time, we started thinking that we wouldn't need any salesmen, but we don't think that way any more! You need that personal contact [manufacture—giftware].

How do vendors in the field make contact with their prospects? How do they permeate organizational contexts? What pressures do agents in the field experience? How to they achieve consistency in these shifting occupational settings?

Field selling (also direct sales) refers to outreach programs in which vendors approach prospects at an interpersonal level in attempts to make sales. It is somewhat akin to media selling in that vendors direct messages to targets "out there," but it is more similar to showroom selling as a consequence of the direct interaction both entail. However, in contrast to those selling in showrooms (in which the prospects approach the vendors), agents in the field face the additional task of locating their prospects. Thus considerable anticipation, strategy, and frustration may precede contact with prospects in the field.

Media, field, and showroom selling may be combined in any number of ways for any given business, but the present chapter will concentrate on elements especially noteworthy in field selling. These include (1) prospecting, (2) screening prospects, (3) making calls, and (4) the problems of maintaining continuity. Thus, although variations among people involved in field sales will emerge, the primary focus is on the activity of reaching out for sales. Field selling includes both in-home (door-to-door) and account (promotional, wholesale, manufacture) sales, but as some of the following extracts suggest, sales started in the field may subsequently move to the showroom for further development.

Prospecting

Prospecting denotes attempts on the part of vendors to locate potential buyers.[1] In addition to desires for growth, vendors are concerned with finding new prospects for two other basic reasons. First, they want to be able to replace customers who cease to be active buyers and/or who have fallen into disfavor with the supplier. Second, some sales involve one-time (or long-lasting) products, generating the need to locate new prospects as a means of survival.

> My job is to find new customers. We have other people who are taking care of existing accounts, but my job is to go and find new accounts [manufacture—appliances].

> We don't get many people walking into the office. We mostly have to go to the people. You have to go out and find the clients. . . . There's a lot of ways to get contacts. You might go out to the new home divisions and introduce yourself, go to malls, and stores, read newspapers. Usually, what I try to do is find out something about the people, where they work, if they're married, what their wife's or husband's name is, if they have children, how old, as much as you can. Sometimes I'll send them letters in the mail, sort of introducing myself, telling them how I might be of service to them. Or sometimes, I'll just call them on the phone, ask them if they've ever had anyone explain insurance policies to them, if they know the difference between term and permanent insurance, the different sorts of programs available on the market these days. Things like that. If they know what an annuity is, and such, to try to get the ball rolling that way. . . . Your contacts, that's what makes it or breaks it for you! And that's why you want as much information as possible on the person. You have a better idea about how to approach them. If a woman is divorced, for example, and you don't know that before you call, and you ask about the coverage of the husband, you can blow it right off at the start. You want to know what you're up against [insurance].

In many businesses, the people completing the sales will have also done the original prospecting and will provide other services. In other operations, these sales functions may be much more clearly divided. Thus one person may obtain leads, another may provide supporting materials (missionary or detail sales), a third party may do presentations and/or close sales, another may write up the order, and still others may follow the sales along ensuring that the proper merchandise arrives, that a certain level of stock is maintained and so forth. It should not be

assumed that this division of labor is limited to, or necessarily characteristic of, large companies. Small operations may organize in this
manner; and large businesses, while more subject to divisions of labor,
may elect to keep these functions intact in order to provide greater
continuity of contact between the prospect and the company. Regardless
of who actually makes contact, prospecting is a vital element of field
selling. Concerns with presenting products, making sales, and the like,
will be discussed later, but of much more immediate concern is the task
of making contact with prospects in the field.

Prospecting may assume a great variety of forms. People working
with established businesses may be encouraged and/or instructed how
to make contacts in specific ways, but salespeople may also innovate
as well as copy outside sources. Although some overlap occurs, six
major sources of contacts can be delineated: the media, lists, referrals,
existing contacts, territories, and exhibits.

THE MEDIA

As noted in the preceding chapter on media promotions, vendors
sometimes use the media as a means of prospecting.

> The purpose of an ad is to get calls, not necessarily to sell a particular house,
> but to get calls, and from there, you've got to work that phone, ask enough
> questions and give enough information, inch your way into the individual, get
> their interest, get them as a client [real estate].

> The [advertised] introductory lessons included five class and five private
> lessons for $10. That was designed to get people interested in dancing, to
> recruit people. After that, it was $40 per hour for a private hour or $12 for a
> class hour [dance studio].

Not only may vendors advertise their products and/or services directly in attempts to get inquiries from prospects to whom presentations
can later be made, but they also may use the media to offer free products,
information, brochures, lectures, evaluations, and demonstrations, as
well as to announce contests, exhibits, and entertainment. It matters
little whether prospects come in person, write, or telephone for materials, or whether they attend vendor sponsored events, so long as they
respond to the offer. Although the success of any promotion is uncertain, these practices enable vendors to obtain lists of prospects and/or

provide them with immediate opportunities to make personal contacts, presentations, and sales.

> We'll put ads and mail-back cards in magazines such as _____ and _____ .
> You try to get them to send in for more information, maybe get some good
> leads through those inquires [manufacture—industrial].

> You can offer a "free appraisal" as an incentive to get people to call to list
> with you [real estate].

In addition to using the media to elicit leads, vendors sometimes screen the media in order to obtain names (and other information) on persons featured therein.

> Some of the real estate people, they're obituary watchers, so when someone
> dies, a few days later, they'll start making calls to the survivor. And some of
> them don't do it all that subtly, but they see it as a logical way of getting more
> listings [real estate].

> I'll often go through the papers and contact people you see there. That's a
> fairly common thing, but it's difficult to keep doing that, day in, day out.
> There, you look for people getting married, having children, getting promo-
> tions. Then it's a matter of following that up with a letter, or a phone call, or
> both. It's a good lead, "Congratulations on your . . ." [insurance].

LISTS

Lists provide a second avenue for prospecting. While lists of prospects may be developed by the vendors themselves, they also may be
purchased from other businesses, obtained from clubs and community
information centers, and derived from the alphabetized and commercial
listings in telephone books, trade directories, and the like.

> You try to get an idea of the companies in the area, and of the type of operation
> they have, where your product might be able to fit in. Then you go down there,
> and sometimes you're wrong, you don't have an application there. . . . Most
> cities have an industrial directory that you can buy for a couple of bucks, and
> from that you get an idea of their products, their staff size. There's a fair bit
> of information there. Then you pick the ones you think would be the most
> advantageous to call on [manufacture—industrial].

You can go through the yellow pages, see who's doing what, pick out some that seem more promising to approach. The addresses are there too, and often some other information from their ads that might be useful to you [manufacture—industrial].

In general, lists that are more up to date and provide more information about prospects are more valuable. Vendors may pursue prospects on lists through the mail or in person, but lists also signify a basic sales function of the telephone.

Using the Phone

While much field selling involves direct personal contact with prospects, those doing direct sales may also make extensive use of the telephone as a sales tool. Phone work may be used alone or in conjunction with other forms of prospecting.

We have a number of people on the phones. They dig up leads for us, for the salespeople. We connect on about 10% of those, but it saves you a lot of time and you'd be doing a lot of cold calls on people [manufacture—industrial].

On the phone, I will be calling both new people and people I've met before. The chances are greater when you're there in person, but you can call for appointments. Basically I introduce myself and tell them that I've got a really lovely line that I think would be of interest to them, try to put something really positive in, "I think you would find it worth your while to look at it. Could you give me 20 minutes of your time? When would be a convenient time . . . ?" And I also try selling to customers I already have, and I will get orders that way, but not nearly the size of orders I would get by going in person. So it's better to go in person, but to make the best use of your time, I think the phone is important. People like appointments, too, I've found [wholesale—giftware].

Although vendors on the phone may more innocently interrupt ongoing routines, they lack information more readily available to those calling in person.

If you're on the phone, you lose information. You can't relate to other things that are going on around the person. You don't know if the person is doodling, busy, or whatever [mixed sales].

The total reliance on auditory material also makes it more difficult for vendors and prospects to communicate by phone in reference to more complex products, illustrations, and product appearances. And, while some samples may be mailed out in advance, one loses the immediacy and impact of most demonstrations on the phone. Product qualities pertaining to sight, touch, smell, and taste are also lost.[2] As prospects often prefer to communicate more directly with vendors, the telephone also represents a more impersonal medium than does one's direct physical presence. Consequently, it is usually easier for prospects to refuse those phoning them than those calling in person.

> If you're calling on the phone, it's easier for them to put you off. They can do that in person too, but you're a lot more likely to get that on the phone. . . . The other way is to call ahead for an appointment, but even then, they want to know what it's all about, and it's just easier for them to refuse you on the phone. It's just much more impersonal [manufacture—industrial].

> We use the telephone a lot, but to be effective you have to go in person. . . .We use the telephone for prospecting, seeing who you have to see, but then it's a personal (in-person) call. Otherwise, it's too easy for them to put you off [manufacture—industrial].

Even with these shortcomings, telephone sales can be effective. This seems especially true when scripted in advance and pursued persistently.

> If you've got the DJ (disc jockey) voice, the right cadence, and the right choice of words, you can sell better over the phone. . . . You'll get people who are not interested and hang up on you, the people who are not interested, but will do you the courtesy of listening to the pitch, to someone who wasn't interested until you called, to someone who was interested and, "Funny you should call!" But the bottom line is percentages. You make a hundred calls and ten sales. It's a numbers game [mixed sales]!

> We had a track we read off the paper, with blanks to fill in along the way, depending on who you're talking to. But after a bit, you get it down pretty well. You can get pretty good at it after, to where you can make the sale in five minutes. . . . So you would call individuals who own a small business, managers. "Hi John, it's Sandy calling from _____ . It's published X times a year and goes out free of charge to businesses such as _____ and _____ , and although you are probably dealing with some of the larger companies in the area, we thought you would appreciate an opportunity to do

more business with the major firms. I'd like to get you into our magazine, at least start out with half a page, running for $800. I'd be happy to put your copy together for you. As a matter of fact, we could probably run your yellow pages ad." . . . You might also drop a line that so and so recommended him, flattering him, so it's more difficult for him to say no. On the phone, you tell the guy all the things you are going to do for them, so then it's, "Why don't we start you off with the half page. It's only $800, and you have the ad in the yellow pages, and we'll send the invoice to your account." And once he's said yes to that, you just go ahead and do it. . . . You say the price as though it's very nonchalant. And you might phone someone up, and you'll be saying, "It's only $800, and you get this and this and this." . . . And, if it's larger, you would be more likely to go and see them, maybe make a presentation to them. . . . With the presentations, you don't know what you're up against, whether it's to one person, a group, whatever. . . . Your job is to convince them that your product is better. So you'll try to convince them of that, in a matter of minutes. . . . You also use your features, your strong articles, show them how advertising will be interspersed with the feature articles [promotions—magazine].

Providing an option to physical, face-to-face interaction, the telephone may be incorporated into a vendor's routines in a number of ways. It should be noted, however, that compared to the costs of individual field calls, a major advantage of the telephone is it lessened cost per contact (not synonymous with sales). The telephone also represents a convenient device with which to maintain contacts, obtain basic orders, and to clarify uncertainties with existing customers.[3]

If you can use the telephone effectively, you can save a lot of money. Instead of running all around town to make a few calls, you can sit in the office and make a lot of calls in that nine-to-five workday. If you can use it as a marketing tool, which people who are very successful do, you can save a lot of money. And phoning long distance, you can really cut expenses, over what it would cost you to send people around. . . . You lose something by not being able to show the client the product, but you work on the percentages, so you can make it up that way [promotions—magazine].

We do very little cold calling. I think the statistics say that cold calls are successful one in seven times. But they are very expensive calls because it takes in the neighborhood of a $150-$200 minimum a day to keep an agent in the field, if you figure out their auto expenses and their rooms. And, how many calls are they going to get in a day? Two or three calls, perhaps, in that area. So it's quite expensive, and there isn't enough time to make it worth your while, so we will set up more appointments on the phone. That will help to cut down on the overhead because when you are making calls, you have already got something established with the person. Also, if you are making more cold calls, you need a larger sales staff and that is something we just don't have [manufacture—industrial].

In general, phone work seems advantaged when the prospects have been first contacted in other ways (e.g., mail, trade shows, referrals). And these other routings need not be sufficient to make sales (in themselves) to provide a base for further dialogue.

We'll use letters and then call the people after, ask them if they received the letter yet, and they'll say, "Yes" or "No." And it doesn't even matter whether you've mailed the letter or not, because you get the same kind of responses. Then I'll say, "The letter I sent to you referred to some ideas on saving money. I'd be very interested in sitting down with you and explaining some of the ideas we have." And again, very general, very general. Otherwise they'll say, "I already have one of those." And there are all kinds of programs, so you have to be extremely general. . . . As soon as you mention anything specific, or if they ask you, "What exactly is this about?" I'll just say to them, "It's about saving income tax, and to be perfectly honest, I don't know exactly what it will be about. That's why I want to meet with you, because every case is different. Your situation is going to be different from the next person's so I can't really answer that question." And you're being honest with them, but you're also being very general. . . . But you try to keep it very general, because once you start giving them a lot of information, then you give them something to say, "No, I'm not interested." And you don't want that, because once you sit down with the individual, you know you are going to get your ratio of sales. So I'll usually ask them three times to see them. Now, if someone is getting angry the second time, I won't go on. But if they're "Well, I don't know," and you have to judge this on the phone. Then it's, "Well, fine, I'm sorry we couldn't get together now, but may I call you in six months time, in the spring, fall, whatever." They almost always say yes to that. Then I just record it in my book and call them later [investments].

If someone has come as a guest, but not signed up, you'd call them up, see if you could spark a little interest in them becoming members. . . . Or you would also call members who hadn't been there for a while, suggest that they come down and bring a friend along, a guest, no extra charge. If you get an inquiry, someone wants some information on the club, you want to make sure you get a name, a phone number. If you don't get that, you've probably lost them! They might phone back in six months, if they get around to it, but this way you can call them back. "Hi, I was talking with you last week. You were going to come in for a guest workout. Come on in, we'd love to see you!" [fitness center].

GETTING REFERRALS

The third major source of prospects involved referrals. Referrals may come from satisfied customers who recommend vendors to others; denote names customers have given vendors in attempts to secure better deals from vendors, a strategy routinely promoted by some companies; or reflect the activities of "bird dogs," who, in exchange for finder's fees, steer prospects in the direction of particular vendors.[4] While word of mouth advertising may result in better prospects (should these people subsequently approach vendors), most referrals can be seen to advantage salespeople over complete cold calls (unknown stranger to unknown stranger) by minimally providing a name of a prospect and a shared reference point (the third party).

There are some people in the community who are quite knowledgeable about what's coming and going. If you get to know a couple of these people, it can be a good source of listings [of houses to sell]. We call these people "bird dogs" and you pay them a small commission from what you make [real estate].

We did a fair bit of promotions work in the newspaper. Another thing we did was to get the students to bring other students. We tried to get the students to bring their friends. Try to get them involved that way. They could bring guests, for free, especially to the parties, and the guests would get a special deal on subsequent lessons, and the student would get a free private lesson if the person they brought signed up for lessons. It worked out fairly well, especially if the students were enthusiastic about their progress. But you would also get students who didn't want their friends to know that they were taking dance lessons. That seemed especially true with the men. They didn't seem to want to let other people know that they were just learning to dance, or maybe having problems learning to dance, so some of them wouldn't bring their friends. But some of them did, and that was nice, because then you could tap into that group of people. We would also have competitions between the studios, trying to show among staff from the different studios who's the best in getting new members. So there, you would try to get your students to go and get new members, to bring the people they knew, get them to become members. As a staff person, you would get more points if you could get your students to recruit more people, or if you could get the existing members to take more new programs [dance studio].

Vendors may also obtain referrals from one another. This may involve referrals from people working in the same company as well as from vendors in different areas of sales.

> If you ran out of listings [of houses to sell], you could go to someone else [in the office], ask them if you could hold an open house at one of their listings, and there were always people in the office who had more listings than they could handle [real estate].

> The bankers work out deals with the automobile dealer. [For his efforts] the dealer gets a percentage of every car loan they write out of that dealership. And if the dealer's not happy with what he's getting from one bank, he might look around, see what he can come up with that's better [auto].

It is also evident that more established vendors tend to get more than their share of referrals (as well as directly benefiting from repeat customers).

> That's the name of the game, to have listings [of properties to sell], but a lot of people will take listings which are money wasters. If you have small listings, you have small commissions. . . . Some people are very good at attracting listings. One of the keys is just being in the business for a longer time, and currying clients, keeping people you sold a house to happy, felt you dealt with them fairly. They may return to you, but they probably won't if you don't keep in contact with them, so you want to keep a file, a rotating file to drop them something in the mail, a card or something, "Hello, how are you?" Something like that. You can develop a clientele that way. . . . If you acquire a reputation for being a big mover, big producer, like _____ and _____ , they are incredible for attracting listings [real estate].

> If you want to succeed, you've got to develop your regular clientele. That's your money in the bank, almost. If you're new, it's easy to become disillusioned because of that. A new man is probably working harder than the more established guy, and they're probably not going to be doing as well. But that's the way it is in most commission sales [auto].

EXISTING CONTACTS

Vendors may also use their associates as "launching boards" for prospecting. These contacts may involve relatives, friends, neighbors, and previous acquaintances, but they may also include associations and clubs joined with the express purpose of generating contacts for one's business, as well as those that salespeople encounter on a day-to-day basis.

> A number of my family are clients. . . . I would say it's common. I don't know if it's the best thing, but when you're starting out, it's all a numbers thing, so if you see X number of people, you're going to do business with a certain percentage. So the more you see, the more business that you're going to do. And the first people that you're going to deal with are the ones you're comfortable with, supportive. It's not always a good idea to deal with members of your family, because afterwards, there can be a few problems. But I haven't had any problems, and my father was probably one of the hardest sales I had [investments].

> In the insurance business, one of the first things they do is to get all the family and friends involved. That'll more than pay for the cost of the training you get. The real test of whether you can make it or not in insurance is what you can do once you've gotten past that [insurance].

An interesting variant of existing contacts involves vendors who approach their own suppliers as prospects for the products they offer. Their ability to do so will vary by the products in which they deal, but their own purchases provide levers (as well as familiarity) for approaching these suppliers.

> A number of the people we deal with are our [company's] suppliers. You can call on them easier, they're not going to refuse to see you. With them, it's more, "We've been good to you. Don't you think you would like to look at this?" And they look at it that way, too. If they're doing anything like that, they'll give you a shot. So you've got an in there [promotions—travel].

> As you know, we're quite large and diversified. We have a lot of product applications. So for us, a lot of our suppliers are good prospects. And it's easy to get in to see them. So there's that angle to work with. They want our business [manufacture—industrial].

BY TERRITORY

Vendors may also prospect on a territorial (e.g., neighborhood, area, community) basis. A certain area of coverage may be used as a starting point when vendors are unable (or unwilling) to obtain satisfactory listings in other ways.[5] Every person encountered is then treated as a prospect until the agent decides otherwise.

Selling signs, that's direct sales. Going from one business to another trying
to sell them signs for their windows, doors. Mobile signs. They're standardized signs, or ones that you can replace the letters on them, not customized
signs. . . . As I'm driving along, I'll be looking at the signs in the stores, stop
and check out the malls, see what they might be able to use. . . . Usually, I'll
work one community or area for a week or few days at a time. Just go up and
down the streets, seeing what you can hit on. You just keep your eyes open,
see what kind of signs they're using, if any, how they might be able to use
our signs for their business or how our signs would be an improvement over
what they're using now [promotions—signs].

Whenever someone opens up a new business, you go in and ask them. Explain
who you are, and let them know what you have. And radio needs to be
explained, really. Audience statistics, rate cards, all that sort of stuff. So you
stop in first time, probably, on a cold call. Introduce yourself. Give them your
card. And ask them if they're interested in radio advertising at all, which as
a new business they should be. They've got to let people know that they're
around. . . . And you sit down and explain radio to them. And, hopefully, they
will say, "Let's give radio a try." . . . Hopefully, you're there before the
newspaper, because if you're not, then the newspaper is more likely to get
their advertising dollars. . . . When you're driving around to see your other
clients, you look around to see what things are going on, and if things are
going up, you ask around. Ask your other clients, too. Not competitors, of
course. They notice things [promotions—radio].

DOING EXHIBITS

Trade shows and public exhibits represent another way of making
contacts. These events are organized with the express purpose of bringing vendors and prospects together. Prospective buyers sometimes pay
entry fees, but the vendors' investments are typically much more extensive. Although some sales occur "on the spot," these events are often
used as a means of getting lists of prospects to pursue at later dates.
Trade shows will be examined as part of the next chapter on showrooms
and exhibitions, but they can have considerable importance for businesses engaged in field selling.

You do get some people at trade shows that you couldn't get otherwise. Like
earlier today, I had two people that I've been calling on, not able to get to see
them, coming in. Now, they're interested in what I've got [manufacture—
computers]!

The people at the trade show are good prospects. They've already been qualified by coming to the show. So for us, it's a good way of making new contacts [manufacture—industrial].

Screening Prospects

Regardless of the means by which prospects are accessed, vendors tend to find themselves selecting (from among their prospects) those they consider the most viable (and allocating their time and efforts accordingly). Vendors could define all prospects as having equal potential, but given choices, they tend to be selective in defining those on whom they will concentrate their efforts.

If it's just the little guy on the corner, we wouldn't bother calling him because he isn't likely to spend the money on the advertising with us. He might be better to just go to one of the local papers [promotions—newspaper].

Being in the business, you learn very quickly the majority of companies that do incentive programs. So then you can make a decision and either go after companies that have already been doing them, or you can make absolute cold calls and go after companies that may not have even thought of them. And we'll do both. With companies that are already involved in incentive travel, we'll try to research them, find out where they've been going and who they've been dealing with. If they've been dealing with a travel agent, we will normally go to the travel agent and tell them that we'd like to make up a proposal for them to submit to the company. It's their bread and butter. If they refuse to do that, we'll go direct. If they go along with our proposal, then they're like our middleman. But a lot of the companies prefer to deal direct with the wholesalers. And in that case, how we handle it is call the switchboard and find out who is handling their incentives and promotions. And the way to get in is to tell them that you are going to give them something that no one else will. . . . If it's a company that hasn't been involved in travel incentives, we'll try to find out who the marketing manager or sales manager is, and oftentimes start sending them literature, before I call them. We'll send them a few things along the line, enclose your business card, and later call them and mention the literature, tell them that you would like to meet to discuss the concept with them, show them what we can do for them. So there, I would try to tell them about incentive programs, what they are and how they work, their advantages, and their costs to them. From there, you try to extract information from them, what sort of product they're selling, how many salespeople they have. What their busier times are. And you have to determine who the incentive program is going to be directed towards. Sometimes it's directed from a company to their distributors, sometimes to their own sales people, sometimes it's everybody, sometimes administration. It could be any target group [promotions—travel].

As might be expected, notions of viable prospects vary by agents within businesses as well as across businesses.

A new rep, no matter who, will introduce things to the retailer that the other guy didn't. "Have you ever tried this?" "No, I haven't. Does your company carry that . . . ?" Now, sometimes, it's that the other person didn't think the guy would be interested, or he might have mentioned it to him and the retailer forgot it, and now you've mentioned it again, and now he might be interested. So bring a new person in the territory, you can pick up some business that the other person passed over. . . . At the same time, though, it takes time to learn your way around. When you switch reps in the field, you probably gain and lose at the same time [wholesale—giftware].

New salesmen in a territory that has been established by a previous salesman always bring in more sales, because the previous salesman becomes so rooted in his job. It's something that we all have to watch for. You become so rooted in your job that you miss a lot of things. It's not abnormal, and it's not a fault, but a good sales manager would try to pick up on that. That is why a new bright man, really geared up to go, will increase the sales in the territory. He may lose a few accounts that liked this other fellow better, but you will make up in the other area where you won't lose much and will show an increase in that territory. A new person will bring in an increase, things that the other fellow never thought was viable to bring in dollars and cents [manufacture—industrial].

Making Calls

Other concerns aside, salespeople in the field have three advantages over those operating in showrooms. They can approach prospects of their own choosing, at their own initiative, and in the prospect's home territory. Thus, not only can vendors in the field be more selective with regards to those with whom they do business, and when they do so, but they can also gather information on prospects prior to their encounters (as well as in the process of making calls). Not only does this help vendors screen out those who, for one reason or another, seem "undesirable," but this additional information can facilitate all aspects of the pending transaction (e.g., approach, qualification, developing interest). It might also be noted that this quest for information need not stop at this level. One of the advantages of calling on customers directly is to learn more about their operations and how one's products might better be defined in that context.

> The first time you call on someone, you try to get an idea of their store, what sorts of things they have, where your products might fit in. If you're smart, actually, you'll spend a bit of time studying the store before approaching the manger. How can you tell this guy what he should be carrying, if he's been there for 10 years, and you haven't even looked around? It's more difficult approaching people the first time. You don't have anything to build on. . . . The second time around, it's much easier. The third time around, it starts to get pretty well automatic. But you have to keep making the cold calls, because over time, you will lose customers. It's something that you just never get away from [wholesale—giftware].

> When you're calling on people cold, you're advantaged and you're disadvantaged. You can see their situations better, more applications, but you lack the credibility you get when they come to your showroom, or even at the trade show [manufacture—industrial].

Despite these advantages, those making calls in the field face a number of obstacles. It is in this sense that concerns with cold calls and organizational structures are most noteworthy.

COLD CALLS

Cold calls are encounters in which vendors approach prospects with whom they have had no prior contact. As situations wherein strangers are approaching strangers, cold calls denote ambiguous contexts fraught with potential rejection. However, cold calls put vendors in direct contact with prospects and are considered extremely valuable for this reason.

> I first encountered Tom and Dianne at a mall. They were making cold calls on merchants to sell their products. I explained my project to them, and we discussed our common strategy for getting prospects, albeit for quite different purposes [notes].

Vulnerability and Stage Fright

Although vendors making calls in the field may gain more information with which to qualify their prospects more fully, they are generally disadvantaged relative to presentations. Not only are the places in which they present products devoid of many of the resources (e.g., props, equipment, support staff) one typically finds in showrooms, but presentations are given in unfamiliar settings, and in places under the control of the people upon whose good will the vendors are dependent for sales. Insofar as they assume initiative for encounters, people making cold calls tend to feel more vulnerable than those involved in either media or showroom settings. These concerns are not felt uniformly from one person to the next, nor are they of equal relevance to the same person over time. Nevertheless, they are elements with which most agents in the field have to contend at some point(s) in their careers.

> I do quite well on cold calls once I'm out there, but I hate them. Once I'm there, I'll do them, but getting to the store, the business, that's the hard part. You feel so vulnerable.... I can usually talk to retail salespeople, given my experience in the store, but getting there, that's the hard part [insurance].

> I find that you are always a little jittery when you are dealing with new accounts or with people, say presidents or corporations, things of that nature. But at the same time, you want to get the sale, so you sort of get over it that way. It can also be exciting, especially if you can make a sale where there's a lot of competition or where you're dealing with a tough customer and you come through on top [promotions—magazine].

While most evident among novices, stage fright (Lyman and Scott, 1970) may also be experienced by veteran salespeople. When the contact is vendor-initiated and/or the anticipated acceptance of the company (product) represented is more limited, the vendor's sense of vulnerability tends to be further heightened.

> You have to realize that you're just going calling on other people. They're just people, just like you. But some of the girls get so frightened.... The people can't hurt you, all they can do is say, "No." And they can say, "Yes.".... It's a challenge where you try to sell to every house, and not necessarily today, but keeping with them. It's not hard. You don't need to be afraid of people. And I've had people shut the door in my face. And there, I'll ring again, ask them if I've offended them somehow. You have to be able to overcome those people too [in-home—household products].

Some salesmen are good at going around and dealing with the people who are their regular customers, talking with them, sometimes maybe spending too much time with them, but the same people might not be able to make it doing cold calls. To make the hard sell, or even to have to approach someone who might be reluctant to buy, that is something else. And we do have to approach customers. We are after new business. We do want to hang on to our customers and, hopefully, get them to become loyal customers, but we're after the people who don't know us. We've had some problems with staff that way. And unfortunately, there are not that many people who can handle cold calls [manufacture—industrial].

Similar apprehensions may be noted among those using the telephone as a sales tool.

Some people feel comfortable on the phone. I don't. It may take me longer, but I would rather go in person. . . . That's something I should get over, though [manufacture—industrial].

If someone puts you off, wants to postpone a meeting, you don't know if it's a genuine reason or if they're just trying to put you off. . . . You can make an appointment to go over. Fine, so you go over, no one home. So you call. "Oh, sorry, we had to go out." So you rebook the appointment, and you find that the same thing happens again, and you wonder, "Are they avoiding you?" And part of it is that they're not putting the interest in it that you are. It doesn't mean the same thing to them that it does to you. It's your bread and butter. . . ! To them, it's spending money, and they're going to avoid that as much as they can. . . . As a result of the number of phone calls I got turned down on yesterday, I didn't make one call today [insurance].

Reducing Vulnerability

Concerns with stage fright appear to diminish somewhat when salespeople are invited to make presentations, can define their company as having greater marketplace acceptance, and can anticipate that their products will be in greater demand. As the immediate and subsequent materials imply, one's sense of vulnerability is also decreased when vendors have prearranged appointments, do more extensive preparation, and use the practices of premailing literature and/or "gifting."

I booked appointments for salesmen. . . . It was usually so much per appointment, so you had to really move. You would call a number of people to get one appointment, and then if the call was successful, depending on who you were working for at the time, which company, you would get so much if they

made the sale. . . . You'd do one company for a while, until they went to
another area. . . . It's not an easy job, because you're calling cold, usually
from the telephone book, so you might get someone who can't speak English,
whatever. . . . You have a standardized spiel, "Good afternoon, Mrs. Brown,
I have a pleasant surprise for you if you can give us a half hour of your time.
If you'll allow us to show you whatever, you will receive a set of six lovely
steak knives or whatever." Something along that line, usually with some
special gift or deal for them. . . . You'll maybe work with one group for six
weeks, six months, however long they're in the area [or running that promo-
tion]. If it's like baby products, you might get their names out of the paper,
so you would have a gift for the new mother. Then, when the salesman takes
the gift to the mother, it's an opportunity for him to make a pitch. People
would say, "What's the gimmick?" "What's the catch?" "If you're selling
something, I'm not interested." It depends on what kind of mood they're in
too. . . . It's alright for a while, but it gets very, very boring, because you're
never coming face-to-face with the person, and you're just getting leads, and
you're not really selling. It's soliciting, that's what it is, setting people up, so
they're [salesmen] not hitting the people completely cold. You're giving them
a lead, an opening [mixed sales].

If you've sent out some literature before, a few days before you call, it
gives you a nice lead into your call, "Mr. So and So? It's Harry Jones from
_____ . We're involved in automated manufacturing. We sent you a bro-
chure on our products a few days ago. Do you recall receiving it?" And you
go from there, depending on how he answers, but it gives you something to
talk about [manufacture—industrial].

ENCOUNTERING ORGANIZATIONAL COMPLEXITY

When salespeople approach businesses, the organizational structure
of the businesses to be approached can assume considerable significance. Purchasing practices can vary considerably across industries and
across companies within. Further, the purchase of different product
lines in any given company may involve rather different functionaries
and/or combinations thereof. This means that each time vendors approach unfamiliar companies, they are faced with the task of sorting out
prevailing purchasing practices. And, salespeople selling products that
are new to the company are apt to find purchasing procedures even more
perplexing.[6]

The way I look at cold calls is this. The first time, you basically go to learn
more about the company, the people, to do some qualifying work. With the

first person, you can ask a lot of dumb questions, try to figure out how their operation works. So by the time you run into the second or third person, you're already more familiar with who they are and the overall operation. So to those people, now, you start to look a little smarter [manufacture—industrial].

Each company is different, you have to figure out how they buy. In some, the buying is centralized. One guy will order for everybody. In others, each department might get their own systems. There, you have to do more running around, but you might be able to get in, although not for as big an order [manufacture—computers].

In this respect, the lack of localized decision making can be also troublesome for vendors.

A home is more flexible than a factory is, in terms of money. If you're dealing with head office, the decisions are easier for the purchasing agent to make. In the other cases, they have to requisition through head office, and they've been turned down before, or head office doesn't see the need for it, so they're more hesitant to proceed, even to the point of putting in the requisition. So that makes it more difficult, dealing with the branches as opposed to head office [manufacture—industrial].

In our business, we deal with two groups of people, the agencies and the clients, so you have to be prepared to sell under both conditions. And with some of them, they want facts and figures. They're black and white people. With an agency, you have to sell the agency so that they can go and sell the client. It's usually easier to go directly to the client. The agency is more interested in the costs, circulation, things like that. . . . When you go directly to the company, dealing with the president, the director of purchasing, whatever, it's easier. They can understand more what you're doing for them. But if you're dealing with a larger company, they're more likely to have an agency working for them. And there, you have to sell twice, because you have to sell the agency on the idea and they or you have to then sell it to their client [promotions—magazine].

Given the complexity of much organizational purchasing, vendors become very concerned about getting to the right person(s).

I try to get to the right guy the first time. I want the guy to have enough authority to order the machine. I don't like having to go back and have to prove it to somebody else. It's my time, and your profit is reduced if you have to call on someone a couple times like that. . . . I've run into situations like

that, where they've liked the product and then had to have the higher-up see
it before they could do anything. I try to avoid that. Get to the person who
can make the decision [manufacture—industrial].

I can spend a lot of time going into a lot of detail and it doesn't seem to come
to anything. Maybe they were interested, maybe they weren't. Sometimes, it's
not even the right person that I should be speaking to. You think they will be,
and sometimes they say they are. Especially on a cold call you ask, "Who's
in charge of advertising?" "Oh, I am." And you sit down and talk to him and
you find out that it wasn't him at all. You may have wasted a lot of time. . . .
I've just gone through four lunches, that I bought, and a couple of other
meetings. I've had commercials done, put them on tape. And I've gone out
there and found that the person who said he was in charge of all their
advertising has been fired, and he probably wasn't the right person in the first
place. So now, I've got to go to the president of the company and explain how
I made that mistake, "Maybe I should have been talking to you in the first
place, but I was told that you were too busy with other matters and this was
your advertising manager." So I may look a bit foolish on that, but maybe I
can clear up matters that way. It's taken a good month and I've found out an
awfully lot about the business. So at least when I'm going in now, it's not a
total cold call. So I'll try to get to the right man, and, hopefully, I've learned
a little about what he's trying to achieve. If I'm wrong, then, hopefully, he'll
be able to put me on the right track. We shouldn't end up wasting much more
time. Hopefully [promotions—radio].

The task of getting to the right person is complicated, however, by
screening agents, purchasing agents, and matters of credibility.

Getting Screened

Although often taken for granted, secretaries and receptionists frequently represent the first significant contact vendors encounter. Not
unlike the buyers they represent, these individuals also operate as
screening agents or gatekeepers (Katz and Lazarsfeld, 1955). Thus in
addition to defining significant mail and phone calls to be forwarded,
they can be critical in providing information about purchasing routines
and facilitating access to specific others in the company.

When you are selling to wholesalers, one of your big problems is getting past
the secretary. She's often been instructed that they don't want to be bothered
by salespeople, so your first major problem is just getting past her [manufac-
ture—giftware].

In factories, it's a matter of going in, and seeing the receptionist, and there, when you step in, the first thing you've got to do is to get on the good side of the receptionist. That receptionist is the key! She's the very first block you run into. She is there to get rid of the people who are a nuisance, that'll hold up things. It's not just to say "Hello" and be nice to people. You have to get on her side. You have to make her realize that you are the person who needs to be looked after immediately at that point in time. The best way of doing that is to be pleasant to her, give her the respect she has to give out to other people. And most people don't give her what she thinks is due her. So, "Hello, how are you? Nice to see you. Looks like you're working hard today. . . . By the way, is _____ in from purchasing? I would like to talk to him." If you know the guy's name, that's an advantage, because then she thinks there is some kind of connection there and she doesn't want to stir something up, make waves. And, if you've been nice, she'll do what she can. . . . Now, a lot of times the purchasing agent is going to come out to you, and you'll be sitting in the receptionist area, which is fine, if you can get across to him what you want to in five or ten minutes, because that's all you're going to have. Now, if you can get into his office, you've got 15 or 20 minutes, and you've got a private situation. Probably about 80% of the people in the receptionist area are not going to get anywhere. You've got to get inside! . . . If you don't have the name, you have to rely on that receptionist. You've got to become almost instantaneous friends with her, any way you can, really, without making it too damn obvious. The more obvious you are, the less opportunity you are going to have. . . . The receptionist will tell you almost everything you want to know. They like to feel that they're useful. Most people don't think that the receptionists and the secretaries are all that useful, but the receptionists and the secretaries run the place. If you can get by them and get along with them, they'll help you. They'll buzz your man in a meeting if they're on your side. If they're not with you, it's harder than hell to get in there [manufacture—industrial].

Dealing with Purchasing Agents

In smaller companies, most of the purchasing decisions may be made by the manager or the owner, but larger companies typically employ purchasing agents (also procuring agents, buyers).[7] While these designations suggest a locus of purchasing power in a company, salespeople soon learn that these titles are not as helpful as might first seem. They still have to define each agent within the purchasing realms of the company (i.e., duties, areas, authority).[8]

Getting to the right person, showing them the product, that's a big part of sales. With us, we find the purchasing agent really doesn't know that much about running the company. They're okay for ordering supplies, but for a new system, you've got to be able to get to someone else, someone who knows the business, and who can make decisions that would affect the whole business. So higher-up engineers, people in charge of plant designs, these are the people we want to be able to access because they can make the decisions we need made [manufacture—computers].

Purchasing is set up as little empires to themselves in a lot of cases. And you'll maybe be calling them, or you'll be there at the receptionist's desk, and she's saying, "So and so is here from such and such a company." "Oh, we don't need any of that." And they don't even know what you sell, but they don't need any. . . . Now, there are some salesmen who probably make it bad for everyone else, with their persistence, the high pressure bit. That'll turn off a lot of people in purchasing. But whatever's happened, whether they're on a little power trip or they've just gotten upset at another rep, they're shooing you away without even knowing anything about your product. And that's bad for their company too, because there could be people in their own company who have been looking for that very product [manufacture— industrial].

Should the purchasing agent seem central to the sale, attempts may be made to further access this person with regards to potential resistance(s) and operating style(s).

The customers are all different. Some just want to know "How much?" He doesn't want to go through the whole presentation. He just wants to know "How much?" Then you'll have the other person, someone who wants to be taken out for dinner, the whole thing. He's not doing the company any good, and the company would be better off without him, but there is that type of person. The salesman has to recognize that the purchasing agent is not a set unit. He's a variety of people, as multiple as the person on the street. And you must try to pick out what kind of person the buyer is, and work with that aspect. He may be a guy who just wants to be a Joe Blow friendly type. He might be a purchasing agent who would be far better off being an accountant. Or you might have someone who'd be much happier off working on a road crew. But you've got to figure out what he's like. . . . Sometimes you'll come to the realization that you don't need him, and go to the marketing manager, the vice-president, the president if you have to, because in a lot of cases the purchasing people are useless in their jobs. They've been misplaced. . . . Then you get those who are afraid. They live in terror. Some can make a purchase say up to $100,000 without the president's signature, but if they blow that money, they may get shafted right out the door. And he may be making only $25,000 per year, and his mortgage is due, and he can be very, very scared. So there, you would have to make him feel ten times more secure than someone else who knows what he's doing, who's more secure in himself. Someone who figures he can do well elsewhere, if they decide to fire him, it's different. But for the person who sees his future dependent on that one company, it can be more terrifying. He's scared, "I'll have to take this up with Mr. So and So, and Mr. So and So. And then I better check with Mr. So and So," and so on. And this person is running scared, and this is the worst type of person to deal with. And he's justly scared, but it gets tricky [manufacture—industrial].

The purchasing agent is not really interested in anything, but something that's going to save money. So if you can do that, that's the very first thing you bring up. If you can show him a cheaper way of doing what the's already doing, you can make a lot of ground with them. If you know what he's doing, the sort of equipment, supplies he's working with, what his needs are, you've put yourself ahead. So before making a cold call, you've maybe spent several hours on this company, so that you know where it's going. If you don't know their situation, he's going to realize that in a few seconds and that you're just poking around, not knowing at all what they need or don't need. Then it's more likely to be, "Thank you very much. Leave your card. If we need you, we'll call you." At this point, you know you haven't done your job, because you know that he needs you. And if he doesn't think that he needs you, you haven't done your job. And you better start doing better than that, or you'll starve to death . . .! Now if he gets to discussing his operations, you've got your next opening, and there you want to be able to tell him how your products will be of value to him. Then, it's a matter of getting together and discussing more specifically how we can get together to help him, the particular items he'll need, work out prices, set delivery times. So you make an appointment at that time. You don't leave it! You can't expect to get a call back on it. He's going to see 25 or 30 salespeople every day who are going to be offering competing products, so you've got to be able to make that appointment, "Can we get together next week? How's Monday afternoon? It's good for me, how about for you? When are you going to be available?" And there, you'll get everything from "Monday at 2:00" to "Well, I'm kind of busy, I'll give you a call." Don't go for that! It's not going to happen [manufacture—industrial].

Establishing Credibility

The matter of generating trust is considered in greater detail in *Making Sales* (Prus, 1989), but some differences between showroom and field settings should be noted here. Although credibility can be a problem for anyone engaged in sales, it is especially acute for those involved in field selling. As only a small percentage of companies are very well known in any area of direct sales, most vendors are apt to be unknown entities to new prospects. And, unlike those involved in showroom selling, vendors in the field generally have less accessible locations with which to be associated. Lacking both the props and the staff support generally available at showrooms, field agents face the task of establishing credibility much more on their own. Media support programs can also generate profile and reduce the number of calls agents make, but another common way salespeople attempt to build confidence is through repeated direct contact.[9]

> Some of the places, they will buy from you, not on the first or the second call, but on the third or fourth. They want you to keep coming back, to see that you're going to be around for a while.... So you keep calling on them. [manufacture—giftware].

> In selling computer systems, it might take you six to eight months to develop an account. . . . There, the first few calls would just be to find out more about the people and who makes decisions and what your existing systems are. Things like that. Basically, the first few calls you are doing involve a lot of fact finding about their operations. You will also want to meet the president or who would be making their decisions and try to qualify them. And, if you could, you would like to talk to the people in all the different departments that might in any way be connected with your product.... What I found in that situation was that what you actually sold were results, not the actual product! We had a lot of standardized programs that people could use, but what they wanted to know was, "What can it do for us, given that we have these situations and these problems?" Once you had become more familiar with them and developed their interests a little, what we would do is give them demonstrations. And there we would either bring them to our office or, even better, if you could arrange it, would be to take them to another customer with a similar system to what they would want to use. That would be more effective. We also had written-up portfolios indicating all the advantages and such about the system. But a big thing in selling is establishing trust. They have to believe in you and your product and that it will give the kinds of results that you said it would [manufacture—computers].

Maintaining Consistency in the Field

So far, attention has been given to (1) the uncertainties and forms of prospecting, (2) the sense of vulnerability people in the field tend to experience while making cold calls, and (3) the organizational resistances salespeople encounter. The focus now shifts to (4) the problematics of maintaining consistency of effort as this pertains to concerns with performing under pressure and the more solitary nature of traveling sales work.

PERFORMING UNDER PRESSURE

Constrained by mutually convenient and prospect-consented openings, vendors in the field face the task of achieving peak performance within specific time limits. With cold calls especially, there is the possibility that "one chance is all you get." Similar pressures may be noted in showroom settings, as when vendors perceive prospects to be rushed for time. However, insofar as vendors in the field infringe on the others' time, and are more apt to be explicitly informed of time limits, they tend to be more sensitive to the demands of performing under pressure.

> The hardest thing is to stay "up" [be enthusiastic]. If you go to see a client, you have to be up! You can't be dragging yourself around. You have to be up! They're doing the right thing! And if you look negative, it may be nothing to do with their program, maybe you're just having a bad day, they'll get doubts. And when they get doubts, you're in trouble, because then they start questioning what's going on, and they get nervous, and that creates bad effects, all around. So every time a client calls you, or you go out to see somebody, you really have to be up. You have to be enthusiastic. You have to feel good about what you're talking about. You have to look good, you have to look presentable. And they expect a certain image. . . . As their travel person, they expect you to look classy, and they don't want to deal with just anyone, so you've got to create that sort of image. And that gets difficult, because it's virtually impossible for anyone to be that way every day, all day. . . . You have to convince them, "Yes, this is a good idea." And you're not talking about a $1,000 advertising bill. You're maybe talking about $100,000, or more. So you can't show any doubts, any reservations. It can be bad, even if you lose a little of your initial enthusiasm. You've got to be on the upbeat [promotions—travel]!

> There are times when every place you hit, "click, click, click," you sell at every place. Really something! Then other times, you can go half the day and nothing turns up. . . . But you have to look successful. You can't walk in, looking like you're desperate. You have to make them feel like they need your product, not like you need their business [promotions—signs].

Given the dependence of field vendors on the time tracks of their prospects, and the problems associated with travel, one finds the work-

ing hours of those selling in the field much more "open" than most
vendors in other settings. Evening and weekend work may be entailed,
and management may find it difficult (or consider it impractical) to
achieve high levels of time accountability.[10] Under these conditions,
salespeople may become extensively involved in nonproductive and
time-consuming side activities. The mobile and uncertain aspects of
field sales tend to be wearying and destructive to effort in sales work

> Sales has more ups and downs than probably any other job, although I can't
> say for sure, because I've not done every other job. But you've got more ups
> and downs in sales, than say in the office [manufacture—industrial].

The following statements on failure and success illustrate some of
the difficulties vendors have maintaining consistency (and enthusiasm)
in the field.

Handling Failure

As agents in the field have to "make it happen" more on their own
than do those in showrooms, and face failure more directly than those
selling through the media, notions of withdrawal and persistence become central in dealing with failures in the field.

To the extent that vendors in the field work by themselves and do not
have prospects approaching them, withdrawal from action becomes a
common (if only temporary) option.

> If you're having a bad day, get the hell off the road! Make up an excuse what-
> ever it takes to cover yourself.... If you're having a good day, don't quit.
> Keep moving! You're up, and you can head right into it [manufacture—industrial].

> It's easy to keep going when you're on a roll. But if you're not having much
> luck, you start spending more time in the coffee shops, quitting earlier. You
> know you shouldn't be doing that, but it's hard to keep going when you face
> one setback after another [wholesale—giftware].

Recognizing the problems emerging from withdrawal, some salespeople (and managers) stress the value of goals, discipline, and persistence as a means of attaining success in the face of failure.

> There's a lot of pressure in the insurance business, and a lot of self-pressure
> too. If you can't discipline yourself, if you can't deal with a lot of rejections
> and keep going as if they never happened. If you can't keep from spending a

lot of time socializing in the office. In the office, you can sit down for a coffee, and that ten minutes can stretch into an hour and a half. And you figure that hour is costing you, how much money? So the ones that do really well do not socialize much with the other agents that way. They're very disciplined. And you figure the law of averages. If you make so many calls, you are going to have more successes, regardless of your style [insurance].

If it's slow, you just get out and go through your routine. You get dressed, get your book, and get out on the road, and start making calls. You can't sit around with the guys and grumble about the depressed market or the low sales. You just get out there and work. You just keep at it.... If you're working on commission, you just have to keep working away even if you aren't making the sales. So even if that commission is not coming in, you have to take the point of view that you are building up the business. And even if it isn't paying off immediately, it will pay off in the long run. I've been on commission in a number of businesses long enough to know that's the case! It's not something I read in a book. It's something I have experienced in a number of businesses. So I would say, just keep working away, and think in terms of building the business. The sales will come if you work [manufacture—appliances].

Managing Success

The setting of smaller, short-term goals may be beneficial in staving off failure, but the realization of these same objectives suggests a problem area for some salespeople. Generally lacking the immediate support of team members in the face of rejection, agents in the field also find themselves proportionately less accountable to others for the ways in which they spend their time. This is particularly true when they experience success.

If you're on your own, you can have a real problem getting yourself going, especially in the morning. You've got your own time to schedule, so it's easy to get away from making those calls and opening those doors.... I find with myself, I more or less live one day at a time, and if I've made a good buck today, I'll take it a little easier tomorrow. But that's the secret. Just because you've had a good day today, you can't relax tomorrow. You have to be consistent! But with me, it's from one damn thing to another! A gypsy! Don't want to make a fortune, just enough to go from day to day. You need to be on the go every day.... I'm the type that if I make a $100 (commission) in the morning, I'll sit on my rear in the afternoon. I don't have that consistency [promotions—signs].

You can't take time off to celebrate your sales. You will have days where you realize you have made more in the last day or the last few days than you have in the last month or couple of months and it is really tempting to say, "Well, I deserve it. Let's go relax." Take the afternoon off, and have a couple of beers. Just unwind, and sort of celebrate. That is a real mistake if you are in the commission part of sales. What you really need is consistency! And, whether you are having a good day or a bad day, you should just work through the whole day, just keep going with it. You really can't take time off to celebrate. . . . Another trap is where you get into the habit of only booking appointments at certain times. Say between 10 and 11:30 in the morning and between 2 o'clock and 3:30 in the afternoon. You might say, "Before 10 o'clock, it's too early, the person is not ready. They have to straighten things up or get their work in order." Then around 11:00 or 11:30, you might say, "Well, they are getting ready to go to lunch and that's not too good a time." Then you say, "Well, they might be taking a longer lunch, so they're not actually back until 2 o'clock." Then, around 3:30 you say, "Well, they'll be wrapping it up." . . . What you have done is limit yourself to the amount of time you can make calls. You have given yourself only two or three hours where you can call on people, so you have limited your chances of sales very much, because if you make so many calls, you just are going to make the sales. . . . Now, you don't know, when someone falls into this pattern, whether it is an accidental thing that just happens, or whether they have just gotten lazy, but it is pretty fatal! It's something that you should try to steer a new salesman away from. You can make calls at 9 o'clock in the morning or 6 o'clock in the evening, or after supper, and you can do business at noon and such, but it is easy to get into that, because it is easier to make calls between 10:00 and 11:30 and between 2:00 and 3:30 [manufacture—industrial].

In general, successes are much easier to handle than failures. Thus even those who define sales as a matter of averages and persistence tend to subscribe to the notion of success perpetuating success (i.e., "When you're hot, you're hot!").

When you make a good sale, the best thing you can do is to just keep going. But not everyone sees it that way. Some people, if they hit a good one, they'll say, "Well, 300 [commission], that'll carry me for a few days!" But you've got to set goals. It's good to keep going, even if you're not doing well. You have to work on the law of averages. For me, it's easier to keep going if I've just had a sale. But as I say, not everyone looks at it that way [promotions—magazine].

If I'm going well, I'll stick with it. . . . When you're up, you go in with a different attitude. It's like, "I don't give a damn! I just made a sale and nothing you can do is going to spoil that!" So I'll try to use that high to carry me along [manufacture—pharmaceutical].

ON THE ROAD

Though far from uniform across the realm of field selling, travel adds another very significant element to the lives of most of those involved. Overnight and longer sales trips are generally the most demanding, but even those fighting city traffic may find field sales a wearying experience.

> Your time is important, because you have to be places, you have to make appointments. . . . You have to time everything. You're going to be in this city, in that city, you're relying on the weather, the traffic, a big accident, there goes your schedule. You're screwed up [wholesale—giftware].

> That's one of the problems with appointments. It's hard to tell how long you will be at any one place, by the time they get around to seeing you or talking with you. Then you have to rush through city traffic. And if you're late, and they've been waiting around for you, that's not going to put you in their good books. Or they might not be able to see you if you get there too late. . . . If you leave too much time in between, you might be spending time twiddling your thumbs, but if you don't, the traffic can be murder for you [manufacture—computers].

Some veteran salespeople indicate that they enjoy traveling, especially on certain routes and in certain seasons, but extensive travel is generally interpreted less positively by those so involved.

> If a guy's been out and around in sales, he wants to know how much time he's going to have to spend on the road, away from home. And that's one of the things management will talk about very openly. . . . Now, if the guy is getting into sales, It might sound good, "If you have to fly there, we pay for your flight." "Hey, a flight, wow!" But what the hell is there to do once you get there? And the guy doesn't stop to think about that. And he's quite happy to go, the first few trips, and then after that it gets to be a little drudgery. If you talk to the guys who travel a lot, it's not a pleasure. They've been all over the world and they get the same thing on the other side of the world. Another _____ or _____ , something like that, one hotel room's much the same as another. And what is there that you can really do by yourself? So you ate in Vienna, had venison steak there. Everyone drools, "Oh, you lucky stiff!" Meanwhile, you've been on the airplane for umpteen hours, trying to get somewhere, and then you're beat when you get there and then the time change, and you've got to walk in as fresh as a daisy, on the upbeat [manufacture—industrial].

> The job [district manager] had a lot of glamour to start off with. Initially, the travel was fun, different. It's something that sort of wears off quite rapidly. . . .

You find it difficult, especially with a young family, being away from home for the amount of time you are. I guess, as a result of that, you start, you probably learn to cut corners, learn to delegate more and use your resources, probably, to your better advantage as you learn the job [department store].

Being Alone

All of the preceding elements tend to be intensified by the solitary nature of most field sales activity. Not only do vendors working more extensively by themselves have to do it all themselves in the process of making sales, but they often lack the opportunity to share dilemmas, frustrations, and strategies with others. Operating in somewhat distant and distrusting environments, solitary field agents tend to be more vulnerable to self-doubts than those involved in either media or showroom selling.[11]

If you've got problems at home and you're in sales, it can really be a problem, because in sales, you're dealing with people on a one-to-one basis. And on the road, you really don't have the opportunity to build up a relationship with these people, at least not the same way you would, say in an office, where you see the same people day after day. In sales, your main objective is to sell, and you might see that person once, or maybe six times a year, something like that. And you just can't build a personal relationship on that sort of contact. Now you might get along well with the odd person, but it's still basically a one-way street, where you're there to sell. You might find a little niche where you have a bit of a conversation for a couple of minutes, maybe lunch sometimes, but they have different ways of wanting to do business, so you try to adjust to their styles. So you finish with one, and get in your car and it's off to the next one. You're by yourself in the car, so you've got time to think about not only your last call and your next call, but what happened? And you'll get to thinking about your problems at home. And you don't have anyone really to talk with. And that's the worst part of sales. You really don't have anyone to talk to [manufacture—pharmaceutical].

What I don't like about sales is all the travel. Because when you are on the road you do get pretty lonely and there is a lot of pressure on you too. You have to eat by yourself, so you have supper and breakfast and lunch, usually by yourself, with no one really to talk to. You might have the odd person you are doing business with, but more likely than not, you're eating by yourself. . . . Then, of course, if you are in a slump, there is more pressure and so that is a problem too. But it can also turn around, so it certainly has its ups and downs. . . . Life on the road is not all that it is made out to be. It's not just a bundle of good times. And if you are into that, you get a bad reputation with the company, so it's a lonely kind of life. You're by yourself and when you're driving around, you especially experience that pressure. . . . And it's also hard to sell if you need the money because then there is more pressure on you. And then when you get a customer, someone who wants to buy your lines, you tend to sell them all that you can. And, as a result, you bury the prospect in your products. And that's not good, because you then kill your future sales, and that person won't be too happy to see you next time [wholesale—giftware].

Dealing with Repeat Customers

While a central task of many field sales positions is that of developing new accounts, a considerable amount of many salespeople's time may be spent servicing regular customers. Without going into great detail at this point,[12] it is evident that salespeople having more regular customers with whom to do business avoid some of the pressure field sales entails. Not only do repeat customers generally signify easier sales, and situations in which the vendors generally feel less vulnerable to rejection, but they typically ensure a more stable income for those on commission.

Most of the accounts we will be servicing will be regular accounts. Usually, what I will do is phone first and set up an appointment, because you don't want to be in a situation where you are just driving around town all day, just no time to do that. . . . And I will usually call all of my appointments by phone before I go and see them. That way you don't have to wait around for half an hour at this place and that place. You will never get any work done. And I would rather spend that half hour working with them, helping them out with their ad or working on it instead of sitting there waiting for them. So if they are ready to see me, I will come in and see them, and it works out very well [promotions—newspaper].

I do all my repeats, try to see them all, but some people, they buy more, so you try to see them more often. If they don't buy too much, you don't see them as often. You take the easy way out [wholesale—giftware].

In Perspective

With this job, you just never know what the next account will be like. Like you will see one account, a big one and the next one might be very small, somebody or some company just starting out. So you just never really know what you are going to encounter in a given day [manufacture—appliances].

Focusing on field sales practices, we find vendors (1) prospecting with and without the aid of the media, (2) screening prospects, (3) making calls, and (4) attempting to maintain consistency in the field. Calls in the field advantage vendors in some respects, but the obstacles experienced by people directly reaching out for sales include: vulnerability and stage fright, the problem of being "up," the uneven nature of success, and the wearying effects of travel and isolation.

Those involved in media promotions may also initiate contact with strangers, and endeavor to generate interest and credibility in the process. However, people in the field direct their communications toward specific others and these people have immediate opportunities to "talk back." Those working by phone may be seen to maintain some of the back region safety and autonomy that the media people enjoy, but they too are subject to the immediate displeasures of the prospects upon whose time they impinge. Those engaged in direct, "eye-to-eye," "belly-to-belly" selling are even more vulnerable. They more completely put their identities on the line with each call they make. They are particularly susceptible to rejection in making cold calls, but whenever they call on others they directly open themselves to their prospects' concerns, problems, and animosities. Although far from uniform, these pressures tend to diminish when vendors anticipate greater receptivity of their companies, products, and selves. Likewise, pressure is dissipated when vendors are financially less dependent on particular sales, are less involved in travel, and engage in team selling. Noteworthy as well are more extensive support systems in the forms of training; literature, samples, gifts; prearranged contacts; and opportunities to discuss success and frustration with co-workers and family members. Finally, those who develop a proportionately larger regular (repeat) clientele seem advantaged over those dealing more extensively with strangers.

The following quote is somewhat industry-specific, but it addresses a number of themes explored in this chapter. It also nicely depicts the sorts of resistances salespeople encounter in dealing with businesses that have already established particular routines.[13]

> The smaller the company, the easier the opportunity to talk to the decision makers. And the bigger the company, the more removed they are from the scene. Which is probably one of the Achilles' heels of all large business, that the decision makers sometimes remove themselves a little bit too far from information that can be made available to them from the outside, specifically for their business and for better efficiency in their business. They become very insulated. . . . What happens is that you start to talk to people at lower

levels. Good people to talk to because they are, in many cases, handling the nuts and bolts, but not the people who can make the decision. And, unfortunately, sometimes your ideas are passed between two or three hands. When that happens, the similarity between the original and the end delivery leaves something to be desired. . . . But there is something about dealing with the larger companies, and it is the bureaucracy which exists within the company, and there are some very large companies that are very frustrating. Large companies tend to have a lot of built-in roadblocks. . . . Take the situation of a large department store which, over the years, has depended upon print to communicate. Now print is certainly not eclipsed in the marketplace, but print has and must be understood to have taken on a different role in the marketplace. No longer are they the complete communicating instrument, really far from it. These things all come to play when we're talking about this problem within a company. That company very likely has set up quite a large advertising department, but that advertising department is geared for print and is staffed with people who can work with print and, indeed, their very existence depends upon, in some cases, the continued existence of print because that's all they can do. They may be layout people, they may be design people, they may be artists, they may be photographers, they may be people planning the purchase of media and they understand print and they don't understand very much else because they haven't had to work with it. So here is this very large group of people who, as I say, their very existence depends on the continued use of print. Now along comes a person who is selling television to say to them, "Look, you have to read this thing a little bit differently. You must start to understand the marketplace from the point of view that no longer is print able to do the total marketing job for you. Therefore, you should begin to take a fresh approach. At least take the time to give it an honest assessment because, if you do, you're going to find that your business is going to improve and indeed that your print efficiency is going to improve because television is one of the great catalysts of improving the efficiency of print." The first thing we are is a threat to this bureaucracy because they can't handle it. Therefore, it means a reduction in print, therefore, it could mean a reduction of jobs. So here is this person, or people, you're talking to, whether it be a manager or this group of people, whose very existence, to some degree, is threatened by this new ingredient that somebody would like to put into their mix. It can be a very different problem. Now the first thing you have to do is get above that man to his superior after you've done all the presentation. This will happen by itself, sometimes, where the amount of business or share of market is shrinking and where their growth is not adequate. But as long as their growth is adequate, they tend to continue to worship at the status quo. Where that may slip is when we in the broadcast industry have an opportunity to get our foot in the door [promotions television].

Notes

1. In some cases, of which real estate is perhaps most noteworthy, agents may define both buyers and sellers as *prospects*. While agents require buyers to make purchases, they also need listings of properties to sell. In general, vendors become more important and sought-after to the extent they are seen as having more desirable goods; and in some cases, vendors may be sought more eagerly than prospects when they are thought to have goods for which a market seems certain.

2. The telephone also poses significant obstacles in reference to both contracts and deposits. Although these concerns are not insurmountable, some sales are lost as a consequence. An alternative to these latter concerns is to operate honor systems allowing for some loss and/or pursuing delinquents as much as legally possible without contracts.

3. Vendors may use the telephone in any or all aspects of selling, from getting leads and completing sales to collecting debts.

4. For another discussion of the role of "bird dogs," see Miller's (1954) discussion of auto sales.

5. Stets-Kealey (1984) provides an insider account of door-to-door book sales (and prospecting) activity.

6. Regular suppliers are considerably advantaged over those seeking entry. They will have to make adjustments to personnel changes and to alterations in purchasing policies, but their earlier dealings provide these representatives with both easier access to company personnel and a better understanding of the working order of purchasing activity in that setting.

7. Advertising agencies operate in capacities somewhat parallel to purchasing agents vis-à-vis those involved in selling advertising. Not only do agencies tend to have particular medium preferences with which media representatives have to contend, but agencies are also concerned about being circumvented by the other two parties.

8. For two valuable statements on the relations of purchasing agents with others in their companies, see Strauss (1962, 1964).

9. It should be noted that the timing of one's calls relative to buyer problems may be no less critical for one's credibility.

> They usually won't buy on the first call. Not the big accounts. You can go for years to get a big account and it can still be worth it. . . . If they're having problems, though, and you're there at the right time, that can really make a difference [wholesale—industrial].

10. While time charts may be of use to agents (and companies), their value to both reflects the accuracy and regularity with which they are kept.

11. Some interesting (and strong!) parallels can be found between the experiences of people selling in the field and people involved in check forgery (Lemert, 1953) and card and dice hustling (Prus and Sharper, 1977) on a solitary (as opposed to a group) basis.

12. Chapter 4 ("Purchasing Products") of the present volume and Chapter 7 ("Developing Loyalty") of *Making Sales* (Prus, 1989) provide more insight on the significance of repeat customers to vendors and the processes by which repeat patronage may be developed (as well as the practical limitations of vendors' efforts in this direction).

13. As Lemert (1972) suggests in his analysis of secondary deviation, the more general message is as follows: To the extent people organize their lives (or businesses) around particular activities, it becomes more difficult for them to become disengaged from these practices even should they so desire.

Chapter 8
EXHIBITING PRODUCTS

The downtown association or the mall management can work their buns off to get the people to their area, but it's still up to you to get them into your door to sell them something. And that's where good displays are so important. Then, once you've got them in the door, it's up to you to sell them. Prove that you've got the right product for them, and sell it to them. And get them to be happy walking out the door, "I'm glad I stopped here." . . . And a good location is important, because you've got to get the people to come by before they can see your display [giftware].

What roles do showrooms and exhibits play in the sales process? What forms do they assume? How do more firmly situated showrooms differ from temporary exhibits? What are the central features of each? Often combined with media and field promotions, showrooms and exhibits denote settings in which prospects enter into vendors' "home territories." While highly dependent on those entering their arenas, vendors in these settings face prospects who appear to be more receptive overall than those encountered by vendors in the field. At the same time, however, vendors relying more exclusively on displays face the task of "making it happen" largely in these settings.

Showroom Promotions

As fixed locations in which customers may seek out vendors, show-room selling is further distinguished from field selling by an emphasis on displays. All sales take place within settings and involve some display (if only the vendor's personal appearance and the background of the immediate setting), but location and display tend to be especially

277

significant for those operating in showrooms. While this statement on showrooms largely addresses retail settings, the subsequent material on exhibits illustrates the general applicability of this material to other levels of trade (and vice versa). In what immediately follows, attention is given to location, display work, and clerking activities.

LOCATION

All vendors using showrooms are apt to be judged by their choice of settings and styles of display. However, location is especially consequential for those engaged in retail trade. Vendors dealing in larger (e.g., wholesale, industrial) purchases generally find that their customers are more willing to endure inconveniences of travel. Similarly, businesses engaged in media or field selling may locate anywhere that is convenient in reference to their required levels of services, labor, and travel. But those involved in retail showroom sales are particularly dependent on traffic flows.[1]

Location is everything. You'll see dealerships in poor traffic areas and they just don't make it. They're closed! Some of the areas might be great areas in five or six years' time, with development, but right now, they can be pretty dry. You've got to be where they get a lot of traffic [auto].

People like to go places that they can get to easily, park easily. So location, that way, is important, but especially parking! Also, they don't like places that are hard to get to, maybe where there aren't traffic lights, things like that [discount catalogue].

In discussing location, it is also important to contrast isolated businesses with those located within shopping centers (enclosed malls especially).

A [busy] mall merchant is paying a big dollar, but he's buying traffic. The fellow that's operating on [secondary] Street, he doesn't have the same traffic available to him, so he's got to buy it on his own [promotions—television].

Many years ago, all the shopping was done downtown, and eventually the downtown area became a little congested. And someone came along with the bright idea of setting up a whole bunch of businesses on the edge of town. Parking's cheap, the land, the taxes are minimal. And there are a lot of people in the areas, the cities were growing. . . . But what the malls did too, was to increase the retail base, the number of stores, so they drained off a lot of customers from downtown. . . . Now the downtown businesses are getting upset, but in the meantime, they've lost a lot of ground, expertise, and all the chains to the outlying areas, the malls [giftware].

Clearly not all malls are equally trafficked, and even within the "best malls," individual locations can significantly affect vendors' sales.

A store in the mall, everything else being equal, will do better than a street-level store. And then location, if it's a bigger mall, you'll do better than in a small mall, and then some malls are better located than others. If you're better located for major intersections, you are going to get more traffic. Some places have a very wide draw, so that can make a big difference, too [mixed clothing].

What counts most in looking for a location for a store in a mall is your anchor stores, and if you don't have a good, big anchor store, then generally you have a poor or mediocre type mall. Our stores that are in the malls that have good, big, strong anchor stores are the stores that do the best. Now this mall does not have a strong anchor store, so it's a mediocre mall [jewelry].

Given the ways in which people (especially retail shoppers) shop, a "well-trafficked location" is a valuable asset for providing product exposure to prospective buyers. Once prospects are in the vicinity, however, display plays an increasingly central role.

DISPLAY WORK

Showrooms may be best viewed as large display cases with everything that prospects associate with particular showrooms shaping their images of that store (and by inclusion, the products featured therein).[2] Thus, in addition to the "images" suggested by the media, one can also consider store settings and exteriors, decor and general internal appearance, and the appearances and manner of staff, as constituting the "display cases" experienced by buyers. The presentation (and packaging) of particular items within display areas is thusly contextualized within the more general showcase. Customers are not uniformly concerned with (or sensitive to) the "framing" of particular products within the larger contexts of showrooms, but display work has a number of features central to sales promotions.

A good display will do a great deal for you. That's where merchandising really comes into play. Will it get their attention? Will it get them interested in your product? Will it show them some feature that they might have missed otherwise? The more the display does, the easier it is for your staff to make the sale. . . . Many shoppers are leery of salespeople, but the same people will spend time studying the display if there's something there for them. . . . It's a silent salesman, if you want to think of it that way [department store].

Your display space, that's your bread and butter. That's why you want to stock them [buyers] with products that will move. If your line doesn't move, you'll get replaced with something else. You'll lose your space. That's part of the reason we have our restocking program. Most of the companies in our industry do that. If it's not moving, we will replace it with something that will move, hopefully [manufacture—cosmetics].

Displays are limited more by vendors' imaginations than by the products being featured. All sorts of materials—plastic, rubber, wood, cloth, paper, lighting, wire, string, wax, adhesives, glass, metal, and others—can be used in creating displays. Displays may be stationary or mobile, assume a great variety of shapes and sizes, and involve an assortment of colors and graphic designs. They may be situated on floors, walls, hung from ceilings, stood on counters, and used as packaging material. And, like other promotional efforts, displays may be used alone and/or in conjunction with other sales programs. Displays may even be used to consummate sales (i.e., vending machines). In addition to drawing attention to products and providing exposure, displays may also be used to provide favorable product definitions by making products appear more desirable, valuable, useful, unique, of better quality, more convenient, more economical, and so on.

What you do with your store, how you merchandise it, how much your store says, "This is a great place to be in!" makes a difference. You're selling these people the shell of your store before you're selling them the product. So making it attractive, the displays and all, that's a big part of it. The way you hang our purses, geometrically, or in colors. The same thing with your shoes, you can build pyramids with your boxes, the angles you put your shoes at. If you ever walked into a store where the shoes were all flat, and then you see another store where shoes are at angles, got some style to it, that's the one you're going to pick. . . . You get ideas [for displays] from other managers, your staff, from your competition, wherever you can [shoes].

> In doing displays, you're trying to give an image to your products. You want to make them more interesting, and more attractive. Make them seem more valuable [department store].

To the extent displays arouse interest, enhance products, and otherwise "educate" customers on the desirability of those products, they can be seen to facilitate all aspects of sales in that setting. However, it should be appreciated that like all promotional activity, display work is subject to interpretation. One may speak of displays that are considered attractive or unattractive more generally across populations, but persons with different perspectives may define the same displays quite differently.

> We know that we're going to lose some people because they feel our displays are too "tacky." At the same time, though, we're trying to create the image of a discount store. So we need the big "sales" signs and the bins with things dumped in them. That's part of our image [discount department store].

> The suppliers send you quite a few displays. You can get more too, if you order things in certain packages, or combinations. But what are you going to do with all of them? You only have so much space, and it all has to fit in, somehow. . . . If it's bulkier, or it means that I have to dismantle another part of our display, I'm probably not going to use it. Some of them are pretty complicated. And some really get in the way of other things. A lot just never get opened up [hardware].

Considering display work more generally, one finds that displays can significantly shape first impressions and generate product value. One may also note the relevance of product location, variety, staff and patrons vis-à-vis display.

First Impressions

Like other areas of promotion, first impressions of displays can be very consequential. Not only are vendors apt to have more difficulty completing a sale when buyers have developed initial unfavorable definitions of showroom displays, but buyers may not even look past displays they initially find uninteresting or displeasing.

> You have a lot of people who come in the front door. They look at one piece, another piece and out they go. That happens quite a lot. They take a look at the price, and they figure, "That's not for me." . . . We are known for a

higher-priced, more expensive line of furniture, and the people who can't afford it, they're not likely to even come in here. They might just open the doors and look at one or two pieces and go out again. [furniture].

Where you put things can really make a difference. The display may be the same size, but maybe you make it more visible, more apparent to another group of shoppers. That can make a big difference. Like we have had men walk right by our shop before, and because of the way our display was set up at the front, from what they could see from the front, they figured we had only ladies' shoes. Now we draw in a lot more men than before. Some of them will ask if we just started carrying men's shoes. They were missing it before [shoes].

Although prospects need not interpret displays as vendors intend, vendors doing display work may explicitly attempt to generate auras for their products or to otherwise define settings conducive to purchasing activity.

I try to create an atmosphere through the displays that I set up, one that is pleasing to the eye, soft colors, and yet which have some contrasts. It is a place I want people to come and relax, and feel comfortable. But it is also a place that I want them to get a little excitement and make purchases [women's clothing].

When we started out, we wanted a store that was different from the others, we were really going after a new look. Our store is unique, we feel, and we've tried to create a comfortable atmosphere, almost a homelike atmosphere [appliances].

Generating Product Value

Vendors generally assume that buyers' assessments of the worth of the products being featured are affected somewhat by the overall images buyers have of their showrooms. They also anticipate that product valuing will be affected by the immediate settings in which prospects locate products.

He [retailer] may not have the product in the right location. He may have it on a wooden shelf instead of a glass shelf, which could make all the difference in the world for selling it. A certain type of product does not sell well on wood. You put it on a glass shelf and it will whistle out of there! . . . It's how it looks on wood versus glass. That's the problem. . . . Also, he may have it too low. The best sales of a product is on a shelf between your eyes to your belt on you when you are standing there. Anything above or anything below is slower. . . .

That's what you call prime shelf space. That's where you want your product. Everybody does [wants their products there]. . . . If you get a small product and you only put out three or four pieces out of an order of 72 pieces, and it is a hot selling item in most stores, but he doesn't sell it, why? You only put our four of it. Spread it out! Give it the necessary show. Put it on the proper display shelf, and give it this level, between the eyes and the belt. That will show you the true level of sale. That is the testing area, but do it properly. Then move inventory around your store. Something that you may not have sold for a long time, change its location, and out it goes! It will move like you never have seen before. And even at a higher retail price than it was originally, and they [customers] will never remember it [wholesale—giftware].

If I want something to sell, I'll bring it into the showroom. Give it some exposure. The customer figures, "Must be something good, if they're featuring it in their showroom!" I've had cars sitting around here [in the lot] for months, not moving, costing us money. Then put them in the showroom, cleaned up and all, and the next day, a few days later, boom, it's gone! The showroom is powerful! We put our attractive cars in the showroom, but it's also good in terms of moving problem cars [auto].

Representing opportunities to feature items in integrated themes or combinations, displays may also be used to generate multiple sales.

Things don't sell as well when they're stuck in showcases. They need to be more visible. Visibility is really important. If you want to push a certain line of merchandise, you might put them at eye level. . . . You can get fantastic combination [multiple] sales if you put things out in sets. Like with the colognes and that, you would put them out with the bath powder, the body lotion, the bath gel, the perfume. Put out the whole set. You can get a lot of extra sales that way. . . . Another thing with displays is to have things that people can touch. They like to handle things. They really do! It's nice when it's out and they can see it. . . . They want to see it. They want to feel it. [department store].

You have to display things in different contrasts and colors to get people's attention so they look at it. That helps a lot. Because when they come into the store and look around and see the displays, that makes it more fun than just looking through the racks. When you coordinate things, like you put up a display and put a necklace on it and a skirt and blouse, and a sweater, sometimes they will buy the whole outfit. It gives us good ideas too, for when people are trying stuff on, you can coordinate outfits better [women's clothing].

Product Location as Display

The ways in which objects are featured within showrooms can affect their valuing, but the attention items receive (and their turnover) also reflects the locations in which these products are situated in showrooms. The following extracts further indicate the impact of location and some of its uses as display.

> We don't let anything sit on the ends (of display units) for more than a couple of days. It means a lot of work for the employees, because you're always moving things around, but things move so much better on the ends of the shelves, the displays. And then you get a lot of repeat customers, so you always want to have something to appeal to them, and this way, with the new merchandise coming in and the things on the ends moving around, there's always something happening in the store. . . . New tickets also fool them. We have different styles of price tickets, and there, a bigger ticket, a different color, will fool them. It can be the same price, but now they think it's on "sale," bigger tickets, different colors. So you're into all these games [discount department store].

> You have good display areas and not so good areas. The outside aisles are usually good because a lot of people start there, on one side or the other. The ends are good because most people pass by them. The inside aisles are not so good. . . . Then it depends on the height of the items. Eye level to waist level are better than lower down, say. Then it's how big is your display, because that's important too. . . . We also mix our "specials" in throughout the regular merchandise. We want people to go through all the aisles, because that way they're more likely to see something else they could use [grocery].

Variety as Display

Recognizing that both repeat customers and first-time prospects may be attracted by something "new and exciting," vendors may also strive for variety in their displays.[3] A sense of greater selection may be achieved by offering larger assortments of goods, but somewhat similar effects can be attained by simply moving goods around.

> Some people wouldn't agree, but I suggest that people get a bigger assortment of merchandise rather than a larger number of a few pieces. The bigger assortment will make their display more interesting, and sell more, so even if you never sell all of them, it'll be worthwhile to go for the larger selection [wholesale—giftware].

I like to move things around in the store. Then, your regular customers take the store less for granted. It might be the same thing, but now that it's in a new place, they see it for the first time. Otherwise, things get lost in the other merchandise [giftware].

Staff as Display

Display is not limited to inanimate objects. Vendors also serve as "displays" when they wear or otherwise use the products being promoted.

Head Office encourages us to do that. If there's a particular diamond ring that's on special, then they say, have the staff put them on and wear them. . . . We do encourage them if there's a particular thing that's on special, or even if they have an outfit on and some of the colored jewelry would go with it, then wear it because you are going to sell it from there. I've sold rings off my finger. I've sold beads from around my neck [jewelry].

A man with a scrunched up cowboy hat came by the booth. He noticed the hats and started trying them on. I tried to explain that it was best to determine his size, and then consider color and the style, but he wanted to go for color and style first. As it turned out, he wanted a hat that was the same style, color, and shape as mine with the same type of hatband, but he never came right out and said that until we found a hat that he liked and I was shaping it for him. . . . Although this person was less direct than many others, it is not uncommon for people to ask for a belt, a buckle, or a hat, "like the one you're wearing." [notes].

Patrons as Display

Existing customers sometimes serve as "displays." This is most readily noted when customers say they want an item like the one another person purchased or that they saw in someone else's possession. However, vendors may also refer prospects to existing customers' purchases (thereby using other customers as models).

Often, people watch what other people are buying. It doesn't always work that way, but they seem more likely to buy the same things I guess they take greater notice of the item, or maybe it just seems better if other people are buying it. And I'll do the same thing at the grocery store. You'll see things in other people's carts and think you might like that, or you better go back and get this other thing that you need [men's clothing].

Our equipment is large, and there's so much you can get, that I find our customers' offices are the best showrooms of all. Some of our customers have more of our equipment at their offices than we have at our showroom. So there, you make arrangements to take the prospect to one of your satisfied customers [manufacture—industrial].

Other Aspects of Display

Little attention in the immediate discussion has been given to pricing, presentations, or sales (specials). In a general sense, all images that vendors convey, including those generated through vendor "warranties," "service," and the like, can quite properly be considered to be part of product displays for they also shape the ways in which products are defined. The subsequent discussion of trade shows depicts a number of other features of displays and illustrates how displays may be combined with other forms of promotional activity.

Other Exhibits

Relying heavily on display work, other exhibits differ from showrooms largely by virtue of their temporary locations. While exhibitors may return to the same locations with some regularity, their presence is less predictable than those using fixed showrooms. Additionally, given greater time spans between appearances, prospects are not only apt to find more changes on the part of any exhibitor from one time to another, but exhibitors are also likely to encounter less continuity among those with whom they deal than are vendors employing showrooms. Exhibits may encompass both a wide variety of products (e.g., from produce to industrial products) and prospects (e.g., consumers, retailers, manufacturers), but the parallels across these markets (e.g., farmers' markets, craft shows, and trade shows) are rather striking. However, to provide greater continuity with the other material contained herein, the immediate emphasis is on trade shows. While very much display-oriented, the following discussion of trade exhibitions provides a particularly valuable synthesis of themes emerging in the media, field, and showroom modes of sales activity.

TRADE SHOWS

An assembly of often hundreds of exhibitors, trade shows operate as temporary showrooms in which vendors collectively reach out to the prospects the organizers have attracted to the show. While somewhat akin to consumer shows (and craft exhibitions), trade shows cater to those involved in manufacturing as well as those in retail, wholesaler, and commercial trade. Bringing buyers and suppliers together in focused settings, these events are generally located in large exhibition halls. The size of these exhibits are limited only by available facilities and the number of suppliers willing to pay for space to exhibit their products. While sometimes constrained by one setting, the organizers may also rent space in neighboring halls, hotels, and the like.

There are thousands of trade shows in North America (and Europe) every year, and suppliers may elect to attend one or more of these in an attempt to promote their goods. Some large corporations may exhibit in several hundred shows, but it is not uncommon to find many smaller companies involved in several shows per year, depending on their products and their applicability across trade areas.

There seems no limit to the product areas in which trade shows may be held.[4] Thus one can find trade shows in areas such as clothing, giftware, hardware, advertising, shoes, luggage, home building supplies, computers, industrial products, food stuffs, and office equipment. Exhibitors pay the organizers a fee for renting their space for the show's duration (e.g., 3-7 days). Presently, space tends to run between $3 and $20 per square foot for the show. While 10' × 10' displays tend to be the minimum spaces available, some exhibitors will rent larger blocks of space (e.g., 10' × 60', 20' × 80'). Rates will reflect the length of the show, its location, its popularity, and the prestige the organizers associate with the show. In addition to space rentals, exhibitors typically provide (rent or buy) display material and staff their booths during the show.

Exhibitors commonly use trade shows as a means of introducing new products, getting leads on new prospects, obtaining orders on the spot, visiting with existing accounts, and reviving former accounts. For buyers, it is a chance to examine the market, discover new products and suppliers, and discuss business with existing suppliers. As a result of the assemblage gathered therein, trade shows tend to be action spots.

Action Spots

Trade exhibits are big business! Not only may big businesses be involved in developing trade shows (organizing, advertising, renting equipment and staff),[5] but these exhibits are trading centers. While trade shows are often used to supplement other forms of marketing, a fair bit of business may take place at the trade show itself. Suppliers endeavor to make their booths attractive, but buyers may have an opportunity to survey a very large segment of their suppliers in a way that facilitates more exact comparison. In addition to seeing "what's new and exciting," buyers can also comparison shop more readily, discover some new sources of supply, and learn of trends taking place in their product areas,[6] as well as fraternize with suppliers in a relatively open setting.

> The trade shows are good because there's so much going on there. You can spend a day or a few days there and see so much. You have a better idea of what's new, what's coming out. What this supplier has, and this one, and this one, and these other ones here. You can run back and forth and compare prices and products, and find the new and exciting things for your store.... And there's all the tinsel and glitter, and bright lights, but there's just such a great selection. Sort of like the average shopper going to a mall as opposed to the corner store. There's so much there, and you want the best you can get for your store. Everybody does! That's why I like it much better than having a salesman call on you. This way, you can plan and compare, and it's pretty well all there [giftware].

> We have developed suppliers in other ways, but I like going to the industrial shows. Most things may not be too relevant to you, but you never know what you're going to find there.... It's a place with a lot going on and, of course, the exhibitors change somewhat from show to show too, which makes it more interesting, too. Disappointing sometimes. But if you get a line on one or two good suppliers, the show can be well worth your while.... You also get a better idea of what your competitors are buying, and what they're paying for things. So it's good there, too [manufacture—industrial].

In addition to orders placed directly at trade shows, these events can also represent noteworthy sources of leads for suppliers.

> These shows run a good bit of money. You've got your space at $10 per square foot, so figure 40 by 20 by $10, for this space here. Plus your travel and meals and shipping all this stuff both ways, and your booth too. This booth cost us over $100,000, so it's a big investment. But, if you make a few good contacts, it'll all be worthwhile [manufacture—industrial].

The show was very good for us this year, but I think a big part of it is us being out there, talking to people, "Hello, how are you?" and all the razzle dazzle. . . . A lot of the people at the trade show are companies who are involved in or interested in travel. So we did a lot of mailing from the show. Standing in the middle of the crowd is not the place to sell. You use the show as a place to get some exposure, getting your face known, lining up prospects, interviews. There's too much confusion at the show, and you have all your competitors standing around you, so you don't want to open up all that much [promotions—travel].

In what follows, consideration is given to (A) vendors' involvements in and preparations for trade exhibits; (B) the ways in which exhibitors make contact with those attending these events; and (C) exhibitors' attempts to assess the relative viability of trade shows as modes of marketing their products.

Getting Involved

Although the existence of trade shows is often taken for granted by long-term exhibitors, new exhibitors learn about these events in trade magazines, newspapers, and through contacts with organizers, buyers, suppliers, and even competitors. Once aware of these marketplaces, prospective exhibitors may seek out organizers, should the latter not endeavor to recruit them.

We'd been in business for some time, and we'd heard of some trade shows, where people in retail outlets go to do the buying. And a lot of people that we talked to asked, "Well, are you going to be in the show?" And I said, "We hadn't planned on it, but do you think it would be worthwhile for us to do that?" And everybody said, "For sure, go in it. You've got a new product." So we did, and it turned out well for us. That's what really got our business going [manufacture—giftware]!

Some of the trade show organizers have booths in which they promote forthcoming shows to those in attendance at the present one. While not all "visitors" would have goods they could promote at the same show or others the organizers assemble, a number of people attending any show (it seems) are people who are interested in ascertaining the feasibility of their goods for trade shows. . . . Some trade show organizers also send promotional literature on trade shows to anyone on their registration list (or other listings) that they think might be a prospective exhibitor at their shows [notes].

Once involved, exhibitors find themselves facing the tasks of setting up and staffing their booths.

Setting Up

Somewhat like nomads setting up camp in the desert, exhibitors at trade shows face the problem of assembling exhibits on a temporary basis. Those doing more shows tend to develop more extensive routines and more elaborate props (e.g., mobile display units), but each show must be dealt with on its own. While some products and/or display units are more fragile, all are to be ready for the show amidst the congestion and confusion of other exhibitors and the frustrations they experience.

One of the things I don't like of the shows is all the setup and all the dismantling work. We have spent hours and hours and hours, just packing and unpacking, because you have your glass shelving, your items, like glass that might break. So you have all the packing and all the crates, and you pay shippers to move it around to all the different shows. And you pay your staff overtime too, so it certainly adds to the cost of the overall show. And then we pay a nice little bit of money for the show, the electricity, and everything else that goes with it. I think you really have to be here when we are setting up and dismantling to realize all that is involved. . . . When you get here, you and the other people just find the bare floors. Then you set up an artificial little world. It's just unreal in a way. You set up your booths and displays, and when you step outside, it is just another world! But it does take a lot of time and you have to pack things carefully and set up your displays in certain ways, so that is a big part of doing a show [manufacture—giftware].

They're confusing. Everyone gets there more or less at the same time, depending on how much time they think they need to set up their booths. And you're there, trying to find your space and get electricity, and set up and unpack all your things, and move everything back and forth, because you've only got so much room to maneuver around. And the other people are doing the same thing. So it's congested. It can be a real struggle just to get it all together [manufacture—industrial].

Although constrained by the space rented, exhibitors have a wide range of options concerning the ways in which they set up their booths.

One finds all sorts of booth arrangements at the trade shows. The same vendor may also occupy one or more booths on an adjacent or isolated basis. Subsidiaries may be featured together, or in separate booths. One may also find both the manufacturer and the wholesaler for the manufacturer's line in the same or in distinct booths. While some of the scattering of booths reflects attempts of show managers to best accommodate the preferences of [especially long-term] participants, other instances reflect exhibitor preferences [possibly in an attempt to gain greater exposure]. . . . It might be noted that space charges are relatively minor compared to the overall costs commonly associated with travel, shipping, staffing, and the like [notes].

I prefer the gift shows [to field selling], because they're there to buy. We'll have some of our regulars there, but you get a lot of new people. . . . When you're an agent for several companies, it can get a little tricky, because you're in all these booths, and some of them [owners/managers] don't like you going back and forth like that [wholesale—giftware].

Despite the investments trade shows entail, one finds that some vendors at almost all shows are ill-prepared for encounters with their prospects.

Even though the items featured might be few in number and easy to assemble, it seems difficult for some of the vendors to be set up in time for show openings—even for the second and subsequent days [notes].

A surprising number of exhibitors (if one assumes a business sense of organization) do not have basic literature on their products at these shows. Although most companies at the trade shows I've attended have had catalogues and/or brochures on their products and price lists, perhaps 10-25% (varying somewhat by shows) of the vendors seem unprepared in one of these respects. Some claim that their prices are too variable. Many others have to "send material" to you. . . . Also, some of the materials one receives clearly have been prepared for other audiences and are now being used because the exhibitors had nothing else. While some of these "ill-prepared" vendors have small operations and may be in the the show for the first time, others are large companies and/or frequent show participants [notes].

Staffing. Once set up, exhibitors face the problem of staffing their booths. Since these shows often run 3-4 days, for about 10 hours a day, it is very demanding for one person to attend even a small booth for that period of time. Larger booths may require several people per day. Exhibitors based in the immediate area of the trade show are advantaged, as other staff people are more readily available for rotation.

A number of apparent "salespeople" at trade shows are not salespeople, but rather secretaries or office personnel who are filling in, and whose knowledge of their particular products may be quite limited. In part, this seems a function of the difficulty of having sufficient personnel to adequately handle the number of hours these shows entail on particular days and over the course of the show [notes].

For other exhibitors, it means that the costs of travel and accommodations add considerably to the costs of the show. There are some other options exhibitors may consider as well however.

Some vendors share booths in an attempt to reduce the overall costs of the show. While some savings will result from shared space rentals and staffing, one loses exhibit space. And buyers may encounter staff who know little about the other products being featured [notes].

In addition to renting display units, exhibitors can also rent staff from agencies in areas holding frequent trade shows. I hadn't realized how extensive the latter was until I kept encountering some of the same people at different shows (in very different product areas). Some people will, however, work for certain exhibitors each time particular trade shows are held. These people tend to become more familiar with those products. In other cases, however, leased staff do little more than provide brochures, take names [for future contact] and such [notes].

Making Contact

To appreciate better the nature of trade shows promotions, four aspects of making contact are outlined. Whereas much material in *Making Sales* (Prus, 1989) is also relevant to trade show promotions, immediate attention is given to attracting prospects, qualifying prospects, presenting products, and managing slow times at trade shows.

Attracting prospects. Give the usually wide assortment of products (and services) featured at most events, prospects entering most trade shows would likely be overwhelmed were they to attempt to become familiar with all that is about to be presented to them. Those who have attended the same show on previous occasions and/or those who are interested in very narrow lines of merchandise are advantaged, as are those who have had an opportunity to acquaint themselves with show literature in advance (some organizers provide rather extensive program material). However, the general hustle and bustle of trade shows makes it different for prospects to be as attentive to the exhibitors and their products as exhibitors would like.

It's an exhausting day. You're all up because you're seeing people that you haven't seen in a long time. And if you have a good rapport with these people, then they're happy to see you. But also you have the responsibility of your company money in your purse, so to speak. You've got the Christmas season coming up, you've got figures to do for your store, so you want to be as wise and responsible with this money that the company has entrusted you with. So that's a strain. You want to know that you're doing the right thing with their money, that you're going to make a profit on the money they've given you and you're not always right, of course, so all these things are going through your mind as you're there. Should I buy this, should I buy that. Am I going to make money? Am I going to be stuck with this? So it is exhausting. . . . By the end of the day at the gift show, my mind is just going in a thousand ways because there's so much to see, there's so much variety and so many suppliers have very similar products. So you have to juggle all the similarities, you have to juggle all the prices and go with either the suppliers that you trust and you're loyal to or somebody new that you think maybe they've got a better price and you're going to get a better deal there. You have a lot of things to weigh. That's tiring! That goes in with making it a very tiring experience, going to the gift show, because you've got a lot of responsibility and a lot of decisions to make in a very short time [jewelry].

I've noticed that my ability to concentrate diminishes sharply after several hours at a trade show. In addition to all the pitches, hustles, and products you encounter, you tend to become drained from the bright lights and the general intensity of interaction characterizing these events. While this can vary with the type of exhibit and people's concerns while there, both the exhibitors and the buyers with whom I've discussed this phenomenon report somewhat similar problems with fatigue [notes].

In light of this potentially distracting assortment of displays, products, and pitches, and prospects' tendencies toward product familiarity, a key task for exhibitors is that of obtaining visitors' attention. Some of the ways vendors attempt to attract prospects are indicated next.

Giveaways represent one of the best "drawing cards" at trade shows. Not all traffic denotes good prospects, and not all prospects appreciate the gifts they receive, but overall, people are more likely to seek out exhibitors offering freebees. . . . Ironically, a number of companies who sell "premium" items as manufacturers and/or wholesalers, do not themselves give out these items, even though they have inexpensive products in their own line. This is despite their particular relevance and apparent effectiveness. . . . I've asked these vendors about this on several occasions, but most of the people I've talked to directly in this regard have failed to see the irony of the situation (e.g., not doing the very thing they are promoting at shows featuring these very products). Some have rooted around to find me a freebee, seemingly insensitive to the more fundamental issue being raised [notes].

Since most of the buyers at trade shows are males, one means of attracting prospects is by having an attractive female at the booth. This seems part of the "display case." One of the companies involved in computer systems used a woman as a "steerer." She was to attract prospects and then refer these people over to the salesmen who would then pitch their product. . . . Although I've noticed such people on other occasions, this particular woman was pointed out to me by one of the vendors in a neighboring booth who contended that this was probably the most effective aspect of the other display [notes].

Some attempts to attract crowds appear self-defeating and/or disruptive to one's own staff (as well as those in neighboring booths).

The vendors at _____ had a videotape presentation. It was sufficiently loud that it made conversation difficult not only in that booth, but also in the neighboring booths [notes].

I stopped to talk with a salesman at an industrial show, commenting on how noisy these shows sometimes get. He was saying that he noticed he had become quite hoarse from the preceding day of the show. Then he turned on an air compressor to run his own equipment. The end result was that he made quite a bit of noise with his display and I could see where it had become more difficult for him to talk over the roar of his own equipment, never mind that of the other exhibitors. . . . I've noticed that a number of people in the industrial shows use noise to try and attract a crowd. . . . While these people drew some attention to their booths, many prospects also seemed to shy away from the larger areas in which these booths were located. . . . The exhibitors in the neighboring booths were quite unhappy with the result. Although they indicated that they were getting used to it, it was apparent that the overall effect was disquieting for both the buyers and the exhibitors. In some cases, the noise clearly startled people, adding an element of edginess to the whole show, particularly in the booths around that area [notes].

While not intending to provide a recipe for how to do trade shows, it is evident that displays can vary greatly in overall effectiveness. In general, displays seem more effective as promotional devices when characterized by

Bright lighting: Displays appear dull if they are not well lit (especially in comparison to others in the area). Also, lighting is more effective when concentrated on the display items, signs, and so forth, rather than on either the salespeople or the guests.

Physical prominence: Displays seem more effective when they have some height or depth; some object protruding or sticking out, as opposed to being "flat."

Color: A color-coordinated display with stronger color contrasts seems most effective (i.e., colorful, but not disconcerting to prospects).

Identity: Displays appear more effective when the names of companies and/or products are more prominently displayed. Some displays do very little of that, and they remain very obscure.

Items: Some displays have a virtual lack of "items." Although they need not be directly related, any items that people can handle or look at adds interest to the display.

Motion: Any motion (circular, horizontal, vertical movement) within a booth is more likely to attract the notice of prospects than stationary objects.

Size: While larger booths are more likely to be noticed, it seems important that the size of the booth match the items on display. Displays featuring many items may look cluttered if presented within a small area, but displays featuring a few (or smaller) items may look empty in even smaller spaces. Booths with fewer and smaller items seem more effective when their material (including the backdrop, if they have their own) is moved toward the aisle (thereby creating a greater sense of immediacy).

Staff: Booths seem more effective when they are staffed by attractive people. Given the greater proportion of males to females at trade shows, this seems especially true when staff are female, provided that they are familiar with the products being featured. The prospects seem to like talking with pleasant looking people, and if they're more knowledgeable, then their presence is not so likely to be seen as denoting a "sham."

Gifting: Vendors using specialty items (with their names on them) are able to attract customers, as well as facilitate recall of their booth with these items. Products with names on them are much more effective than other items given away [e.g., foodstuffs] as a result of their recall function. Also, if these premiums are more obvious (e.g., something to be worn as opposed to being tucked away), vendors gain more impact from them at the show as an advertising item.[7]

Draws: Companies sometimes have draws for prizes. These are good for getting business cards or names of people the vendors might be able to contact later. Not all the desired prospects will engage in draws and many "nonprospects" may participate, but the vendors can do some sorting afterwards. In contrast to the giveaways, draws require names and addresses. While many participate, others avoid participation for this very reason (i.e., they envision this to represent a route to a forthcoming sales call).

Literature: Displays tend to be more effective when the exhibitors provide some literature for the visitors. When this literature includes "product information" (this is not always the case!), it helps keep the exhibitor and their capabilities in mind. And, since the literature may be studied at length at the visitor's convenience, it may be used to provide fuller explanations than that feasible during the show.

Price lists and catalogues: As with the other literature, this material is apt to have more impact after the show than before it. It is valuable, however, in that it more readily enables prospects to make ordering decisions.

Simplicity: Given the fleeting nature of trade show encounters, exhibitors able to present their products more simply seem more effective. Exhibitors able to provide visitors with a basic idea of what their products can do, and prepared to provide prospects with more information if they're interested at that level (either at the show or at a later date, as the prospect prefers) seem more effective.

Qualifying prospects. In addition to the problem of getting attention, vendors generally find that the openness of trade shows represents an obstacle to qualifying prospects. Just as the prospects define each exhibit and the personnel they encounter therein, so do vendors attempt to establish working definitions of the prospects they encounter. Both parties are apt to be wearing name tags, but this information may be of limited value in knowing about those whom one encounters.

It's difficult to qualify people at the trade shows. They don't want to tell you much. They sort of feel you're pressuring them if you ask them more about their business [manufacture—industrial].

Selling at a gift show, it is quite different than selling in their store because at the show, you can't see their store. . . . You can't see what they have. You don't know how it is set up. You don't know what their display area is like. It is harder to make suggestions because of that, so it's more difficult for you to help the customer, to help yourself in that way. The big advantage of the show is that they can see the items, they can handle it, smell it, or whatever it is, feel it. On the road, it's different, because you'll have a few samples, but mostly you are selling from a catalogue, so they can just go by how it looks in the book [wholesale—giftware].

Presenting products. As with the other aspects of the encounter, exhibitors typically find themselves competing with the many distractions the show entails in making presentations. This means that presentations tend to be subject to considerable interruption and diversion.

I find that you have to really hustle at the gift show. It's a nice cordial atmosphere, but if you want to do well, you have to hustle. You don't have that much time for all the people around you. If you want to do well, you have to concentrate on the customers. So you do everything you possibly can to get them into the booth. Then, once you get them in there, get them all the information you can on why they should buy from you [manufacture—giftware].

You can't close [complete sales] as well at trade shows. A lot of the people go to the show to shop around. It may be a little different at some of the other shows, but with us, it seems that for the clients, it's a place where they can get all the information on some product that they want at one place. You'll also get people who are not making spot decisions, but they're going back and consulting with their people. . . . We sold a fair amount of equipment at the show, but the show sales are only a fraction of what we would be selling on the road. . . . They want to know what your warranties are, what the features of your machines are, how much energy they consume, and they go to the different booths collecting the literature, the brochures, getting prices, and then they leave. . . . You try to follow up on them, or sometimes they'll get back in touch with you. . . . You collect as many [business] cards as you can, get something to go on when you're calling on them [manufacture—appliances].

Slow times at trade shows. While some trade shows are busier than others, the traffic at individual booths tends to be erratic. There will be times when vendors find themselves overwhelmed by the number of prospects at their booths, but other times are very slow. The unevenness and unpredictability of traffic flows, along with the long hours and a concern with "being on," means that trade show work is a wearying experience.

When shows are slower, some of the vendors become more extensively caught up in side activities. For some, the telephone in their booth represents a distraction. While they may attempt to make better use of their time by using the phone, it also means that they may have been less responsive to prospective customers than otherwise would have been the case. In other instances, people may be talking with prospective customers and then leave them when the telephone rings. At that point, it is very easy for the prospect to say, "I'll be back later," and the person with the phone in their hand is really at a disadvantage. . . . Some people become involved in bookkeeping and letter writing, occasionally so distracted that they seem oblivious to prospects in their booths [notes].

The trade shows can be good, but they are tiring. You're on your feet all day, and you've always got to be in a state of readiness. Well, you don't have to, but if you're not, it's going to cost you. . . . You can't really relax, because you don't know when the next one will come along, or which one is the good prospect you really have to be on your toes for. So sometimes, you're run off your feet, and other times, it's a real drag [manufacture—industrial]!

Assessing Trade Shows

Like other marketing effects, trade shows are difficult to assess directly. One way of attempting to do this is to total all the costs associated with the trade show and divide these by the number of prospects/orders obtained from the show.[8] This could then be compared with similar material on the costs of calls in the field, media programs, and the like. However, since each marketing endeavor (e.g., media, salespeople, trade shows) may make other efforts more effective for people exposed to these combinations, and one cannot accurately ascertain the origins of many orders, it becomes increasingly difficult to sort out the effect of each promotion (and other effects, such as client referrals). Additionally, insofar as trade shows provide "changes of pace" from other sales programs, they may offer vendors more returns than the eventual sales they generate.

Given these elements, one finds that those doing shows have conflicting notions of their worth. A good portion of the exhibitors consider trade shows to be clearly beneficial. In support of this position, they typically cite good leads, greater buyer receptivity to ordering products, and higher levels of product feedback, exposure, and credibility.

What happens in the field, for me anyways, and probably others too, is that you get so caught up in servicing your existing accounts that you neglect the new ones. So the trade show is good for us, in helping get new accounts [manufacture—clothing].

What I like about the trade shows is that they're a good source for leads. The leads you get from the trade show are actually quite a bit better than those you would get in other ways. . . . Another good thing about the trade shows is the feedback you get from the retailers about your products. You get that to some extent from your people in the field, but you get more of that at the trade shows, so it's good for you that way too [manufacture—industrial].

At the other pole, some exhibitors have become strikingly disenchanted with their trade show pursuits.

Did you see the location they gave us? It's the pits! We've been going to that show for four years, and every year they promise us something better. Well, it has gotten a little better overall, but still a lousy location. It's been costing a good buck to be there every fall and spring, and it's reached the point where we feel it would be better for us to market our products in other ways [wholesale—giftware].

[organizer] does a lot of shows, and some of them are tie-ins where if you do this one, you have to do that one. So you have some that are good, like at [city], and others like at [city] that are losing propositions. And you figure, by the time you haul all your equipment and your staff back and forth, that the good shows have to be really good just to offset the others. It's just not worth it. We're going to get out of the trade shows. Concentrate more on the salespeople and the media. There you have a little more control over what you're doing [manufacture—industrial].

While still participating, some exhibitors are also fairly negative about the value of trade shows as a marketing tool. Many of these vendors contend that "image concerns" are more central to continuity than are resulting sales.

If you don't go to the trade show, the customers think that you've gone belly up! So you want to put in an appearance, even though you don't know exactly how much good it will do for you [manufacture—giftware].

I don't know how much good it does, but it keeps up your profile in the marketplace. The trade shows give you exposure that way. So even if you're not selling much at the show, you still get that exposure [wholesale—office equipment].

Other continued involvements reflect a lack of clearly more desirable alternatives. Accordingly, these vendors' trade show involvements assume shifting and sporadic qualities.

We do a lot of shows. Some we have stopped doing altogether because we didn't feel we were getting sufficient response. Some you can tell are good, because you get a lot of orders on the spot. Those are the ones we wouldn't want to pass up. But others don't do that much for you. And it's the old thing of, "Where do you want to put your money?" . . . Over time, you sort them out, the good shows and the not so good shows. But a lot are iffy too. You don't really know which way to go. Or with some, you know they would be better if you had a better location at the show. So that's something else, the position at these shows. If you can swing a better spot for the next time, that might be the deciding thing in your return. There really are good locations and deadly locations [manufacture—industrial].

It's hard to tell just how much the trade shows are worth to you. But how much is advertising worth to a company? You really can't put a dollar figure on it. The research suggests that it is worthwhile to advertise, that there's a certain cumulative effect. It increases product awareness. But when your business goes up overall, you don't really know what is responsible for it. Is it doing the trade shows? Your salesmen on the road? The service you're providing existing customers? Your developing products? Your new lines? It's really difficult to sort it all out [manufacture—giftware].

In Perspective

Focusing on showrooms and exhibits, this chapter has considered two major variants of display-oriented marketing activity.[9] While showroom selling may be combined with media and/or field marketing programs, vendors in showrooms face some unique concerns. Vendors working in showrooms avoid some of the demands of the field, but issues of location (for retailers especially) and display become strikingly prominent. In contrast to those buying larger amounts and/or more specialized goods, retail customers dramatically support visible and convenient enterprises. Viewing showrooms as "large display cases" serving to define the desirability and worth of objects, consideration was given to elements such as the significance of first impressions, strategies for creating value, and the roles that variety and staff (as models) may play in defining attractive displays.

Combining elements of media, field, and (especially) showroom selling, an examination of trade shows rounds out the chapter. Trade shows not only represent "action spots" for buyer-seller encounters, but they also provide valuable parallels with merchandising practices in retail settings. In addition to considering initial involvements of exhibitors in trade shows and their basic concerns with preparations, attention was given to the problematics of customer contact, and evaluating the worth of trade shows.

Although this chapter has revealed much about the background preparations involved in display-based sales, it is evident that we still have much to learn regarding the social construction of display work and of vendors' involvements and continuities in particular styles and themes of display. Particularly important in this regard is a continued recognition of the dilemmas vendors face in this realm of their marketing programs. As noted in earlier discussions of purchasing products, pricing, and media and field promotions, vendor marketing practices (including the use of showrooms and other exhibits) very much represent ongoing sets of gambles pitched at the "generalized other" (Mead, 1934). In all of these areas, we find much definitional recasting of the situations on the part of vendors and extensive use of hedging strategies as these tacticians strive for the (elusive) "best" marketing mix (package) amidst the ongoing, reflective adjustments of their competitors and the shifting interpretations and lines of action invoked by prospective customers.

Notes

1. One witnesses a somewhat parallel valuing of location in reference to residence (i.e., convenience, prestige).

The three most important things in buying a house are location, location, location! That's standard. That's gospel in real estate [real estate]!

2. Although only minimal immediate reference is made to the role that suppliers play (via packaging, display cases, and attempts to obtain better positions within merchants' showrooms), this should not negate supplier importance in shaping the eventual displays shoppers encounter.

3. Concerns with uniformity and other head office policies may prevent those in chain outlets from benefiting from variety in those displays.

> Generally, we try to keep our stores looking the same as much as possible so the customer that is in shopping can identify easily, get to know where the merchandise is in the store, feel comfortable with it, not having to know, "Where's the men's wear?" "Where's the children's wear?" [department store].

4. Sampson's (1977: 1-5) description of a "weapons" exhibit coincides highly with the trade shows depicted herein.

5. While trade (or public) exhibits may be organized by any group or organization, one also finds major show exhibitors who produce a number of diverse shows in the same area(s) and/or similar shows across the continent.

6. In addition to vendors featuring goods central to the show's theme, those involved in related goods and services are often in attendance. Thus, for instance, one frequently finds secretarial services, travel bureaus, print groups, banks, security agencies, and insurance companies at industrial shows. Even though these groups need not be involved in manufacture themselves, they may wish to reach some of the same audiences. Likewise, a number of clubs and associations in some way related to particular trade shows can often be found at the trade shows, as can people promoting magazines (subscriptions and advertising) in those areas. Further, one often finds a variety of government and community agencies at many trade shows, especially those involving industry. They tend to be concerned with promoting export programs, attracting businesses to their regions, and the like.

7. Gifting seems more effective when vendors use handouts (premiums, literature, and so on) as tools for engaging people in conversation and explaining the products offered. This is more difficult to do, but it results in more effective use of the material. Vendors will often shift back to giving things away without much dialogue, upon encountering a number of people who pick things up with no particular interest or application for the products. Gifting can still be valuable at that level, but it seems more effective when used to develop contacts. It's also more effective when the items given to prospects are accompanied by catalogues, brochures, and such, indicating the products (services) featured.

8. I have been getting a lot of different estimates on the costs of the "average sale call" from show organizers and sales managers. It is very difficult to define (i.e., standardize and compare) what they mean by a "call," and also what they mean by a "customer contact." . . . Industrial sales calls probably have a higher cost rate overall than do sales calls in other areas. Industrial customers are more likely to be further apart than customers in gift areas, cosmetics, signs, and other commercial products. That may be one reason for some discrepancy I have been getting in terms of actual costs. It should also be noted that the cost of calls may also be related to the complexity of the item being discussed, the overall size of the sale, and the bureaucracy involved in buying decisions (notes).

9. Vending machine operations (also worthy of further study) fall into a more general notion of display marketing practices.

Chapter 9
IN PERSPECTIVE

Insofar as human beings enter into economic processes, the final word about those processes, whether they are production, distribution, or consumption must be said from the standpoint of the relations of those processes to all human beings concerned. In short, the processes must be considered only provisionally impersonal, and as always ultimately personal. [Small, 1914: 725].

While one often hears the expression that business is simply a matter of supply and demand, this backstage inquiry into the experiences of those doing business strongly suggests otherwise. By focusing on the ways in which those involved in marketing and sales endeavor to work out their activities with others, we arrive at a fuller appreciation of the fundamentally social nature of the marketplace. Regardless of whether vendors are getting prepared for encounters (setting up businesses, doing management, buying goods, pricing, or promoting products via media, field or showroom sales) or attempting to deal with customers on a more interpersonal level (making presentations, generating trust, seeking commitments, pacifying customers, developing loyalty, holding "sales," and maintaining enthusiasm), it becomes strikingly apparent that business is "socially constructed activity." [1] It is in the preparations and dilemmas, the risks and gambles, the ongoing reflections and assessments, the encounters and relationships, the strategies and negotiations, and the frustrations and anticipations that business takes place.

In sales, everything is a gamble. Everything is a risk. You don't know if they are going to buy until you've got the money in the drawer, and even then, with checks, or returns, you don't know for sure. It's such a gamble! And in a way, it's kind of exciting. Every customer is different. Like if you push too much, you can lose your credibility. And you only have a few minutes to try to do the whole thing, figure out the people and all. You never know what will happen [cosmetics]!

The marketplace epitomizes social behavior. Not only is it characterized by (1) a plurality of diverse and shifting perspectives (and meanings) on the part of the participants, it also denotes (2) much ongoing reflectivity as participants anticipate, assess, and otherwise attempt to take the role of the other in developing potential lines of action, (3) widesweeping realms of negotiation (attempts to shape the behaviors of others and selectively resist their proposals for action), (4) a highly diverse set of relationships (varying greatly in intensity, importance, and longevity), and (5) a set of activities that, while possessing some senses of historical continuity, are continually being constituted and reconstituted over time as the parties involved work out the facets of their lives in conjunction with one another.

Some Common Questions

As a means of further putting the preceding chapters in perspective, it may be useful to consider two questions often encountered while doing this research. The first question typically assumed the form, "What surprised you the most in this study?" [2] The second was, "How will your book make salespeople (businesses) more effective?" While the study was clearly a major learning experience and is apt to result in some valuable realizations for all (vendors and buyers) who take the time to examine this material, careful readers will appreciate that both questions miss the central thrust of the study. Nonetheless, they afford some opportunity for further clarification.

WHAT SURPRISES?

What I have learned from sales is that it is a crazy world, and that nothing would surprise me any more. Nothing! I have met a lot of people and I have traveled around a lot in sales, and it is incredible just how different people can be. It just seems that you never have three people who are the same. It is really interesting, and maybe I should be a sociologist too [promotions—newspaper]!

In addressing the first question, "What surprised you?", it should be first noted that this research wasn't begun to uncover "shocking revelations." Nevertheless, I found the study of the marketplace a project fascinating from its inception. It has been intriguing, enlightening, and challenging.[3] However, rather than pursue the sort of exposés for which journalists are noted, the emphasis was on arriving at a careful, thorough, and intimate understanding of marketplace exchanges as experienced by vendors. The result was truly a major education, and one not attainable through existing textbooks or programs of study in marketing departments. In addressing matters of surprises, however, three realizations assume particular prominence.

A first, and still puzzling, realization pertains to the lack of literature on marketplace interaction on the part of both sociologists and researchers in marketing. At the outset, I had assumed that sociologists (as students of urban society) would have made much greater strides in analyzing marketplace exchanges. But despite some scattered probes into this area, sociologists have largely overlooked a most intriguing and valuable area of study.[4] I had also anticipated (with some trepidation) that the marketing literature would have been of great assistance,[5] possibly even making this study redundant. This was not the case. Some material was helpful, but the great bulk of the marketing literature was directed toward the search for causes, factors, formulae, and prescriptions on how to run businesses. Despite the intensive efforts of a great many capable researchers, scant attention had been paid to actual vendor behavior.

In some ways, a second surprise was even more ironic. While suspecting that business was much more a social activity than seemed commonly acknowledged, I wasn't able to anticipate just how extensively and fundamentally the marketplace constituted a social arena. Perhaps I had been influenced by the "marketing mystique," but inquiries into each realm of activity in the study (e.g., setting up businesses, managing, pricing, doing exhibits) impressed upon the study the inescapable conclusion that business is in all respects a socially constructed activity. Marketplace exchanges (and all that they entail) are inexorably bound by the perspectival, reflective, processual, negotiable, and relational nature of group life. Anyone who overlooks the symbolic, minded, dynamic, mediated, or associational features of exchanges (be these in reference to preparations, promotions, or sustained involvements) will miss much of the rich interactional contexts characterizing the marketplace.

A third surprise, and an especially pleasant one, reflected the willingness of the vendors encountered to assist me with this project. One often hears adages such as "Time is money." And while such utterances have been heard from some of those interviewed, the interest and support these people have shown in this project has been somewhat overwhelming. As with the recognition that business is a fundamentally social activity, I hadn't anticipated the extent of their generosity in sharing their experiences with others.

SUGGESTIONS FOR SUCCESS?

It's been interesting talking about sales because you spend over half of your life in the job, like 40 hours or more, and yet you don't actually sit back and think about it very much. It's just something you're doing, sort of day by day, just going through the routines a lot of time. And you're not likely to talk to other people, people who aren't in sales, because they don't think there is very much involved. They just don't realize what all there is to it. And I guess you, yourself, just don't think you are doing anything important, worth talking about with other people. . . . I think one of the reasons people change companies is because they only see so much challenge in sales and you get to know your product and you would like to try something else. And then, of course, in any area it gets to be a little discouraging because you aren't making all the sales you want to, and the customer is "always right!", so you have to cater to them [wholesale—jewelry].

However surprised inquirers may be to the answers to the first question, they tend to be even further puzzled at my responses to the second ("What makes for success?"). This study was not intended to find ways of making people more effective in their marketing endeavors. The inquiry was designed to see how people deal with their day-to-day situations and work them out with the others involved therein. The central objective was to examine marketplace activity as a subset of human activity, trying to see what we could learn about group life more generally from this inquiry. Salespeople, managers, and others may benefit by reflecting upon the contents with regards to their own situations,[6] but no magic formula for success is proposed. Business is a people activity and it needs to be recognized as such by researchers; as a complex set of symbolic interactions. Accordingly (and at the risk of appearing prosaic), it appears that vendors who attend more fully to all aspects of their relationships will likely do better in the long run. Effectively, this means that success reflects the consideration given to all the features (processes) of customer contact outlined in this monograph, as well as to all aspects of relationships with suppliers, staff, and the others with whom vendors do business. Success cannot be reduced to technique, however. Regardless of how well businesses (products) are set up, managed, and stocked, or products are priced, presented, and so on, the success of any business is contingent upon the ongoing social affirmation of those in the community setting in which that business is located. We live in a social world. As individuals we can endeavor to shape the lines of action that we (and others) experience. However, our very success in doing so is very much contingent on the enterprises of all of those whose lives intersect (some more directly, more centrally) with our own. Vendors can strive for buyer cooperation, but cooperation is precarious and is made even more so by the existence of competition and the opportunities afforded buyers therein.

To be sure, a wide set of strategies can be developed and implemented with some degree of success. However, all formulae, ideas, and concepts are subject to ever-shifting, competitive contexts. If they appear successful, marketing concepts are likely to be copied and integrated into the programs of others. This seems especially true for matters of technology, policy, advertising, and easily defined routines. In fact, the more readily concepts can be implemented and maintained in any particular setting, the greater their likelihood of becoming successfully adopted by others (i.e., becoming more common). Although not exactly their own undoing, as more and more vendors incorporate particular concepts into their programs, the originators become increasingly vulnerable to competition from other "clever ideas." The originators may benefit from the concept for some time relative to the emergence of clones, but should these vendors organize their routines (and investments) more extensively around these same concepts, they may have more difficulty than the later adapters should they decide changes are in order to remain competitive. This drawback also denotes another practical limitation to more extensive borrowing. To the extent vendors develop particular game plans and organize their activities around them, they tend to be less receptive (states of desperation aside) to practices they consider incompatible with the traditions they have established to date. Otherwise, we may expect to witness faster versions of musical chairs as vendors (re)discover, copy, and subsequently discard "hot" concepts over time.[7]

> In marketing, these things like contests, trading stamps, coupons, specialty advertising, they have these popularity peaks. You don't hear much of them for a few years, and then all of a sudden, they're the hottest things going. It's a reinvention, but it catches on [promotions—agency].

Vendor Activities in Context

In developing this study, an attempt was made to examine the activities constituting marketing and sales with minimal regard to the products being promoted. It was anticipated that this tactic would generate a broader appreciation of the forms these activities assumed as well as a base for assessing their generalizability across business contexts. A few people have been critical of this tactic, suggesting that it would have been easier and more instructive to concentrate on one business or one industry (e.g., shoes, real estate). While projects so defined would indeed be valuable and would involve less shifting of frames of reference (e.g., giftware to insurance; candy to real estate), some alternative strengths of this study might be noted.

By focusing on the more "generic" features of business activities, this treatment encourages comparisons across business and industries. Allowing for variations within and across businesses or industries, it eliminates some of the company and product mystique people may hold. It thus encourages comparisons with an eventual goal of better understanding marketplace exchanges.[8] Further, realizing that much work remains to be done, it is hoped that this material will not only sensitize other researchers to a wide range of marketplace issues for future inquiry, but that it will serve as an integrating focus for what otherwise would be relatively isolated studies of the marketplace.

The organization of the study around activities proved a productive strategy in facilitating a grounded inquiry of the marketplace experiences of vendors. However, as much vendor activity has been directed toward their customers (i.e., the preparations discussed in this volume, and the interpersonal encounters examined in *Making Sales*), it may be useful to reflect upon some more general aspects of vendor roles that cut across these realms of activity. Particularly noteworthy in this regard are the concepts of (1) image work, (2) vendor commitments,

(3) recruitment, and (4) careers. By indicating the implications of these other features of vendor roles for the businesses, products, and the people involved therein, it is hoped that we might not only gain a fuller appreciation of the vendors' situation, but of the problematics of gaining cooperation and shaping other people's lines of action more generally.

IMAGE WORK

Operating in the necessarily symbolic realities of the marketplace, vendors are the "products" as well as the "producers" of the images that abound therein.[9] These images revolve around (a) trading entities (e.g., companies, stores), (b) products offered for trade, and (c) the individual representatives of trading entities (e.g., managers, staff). While these three sets of images are intertwined (affecting one another, though unevenly from instance to instance), it seems valuable to be mindful of each throughout the discussion. In reference to each of these features, vendors may not only attempt to promote certain images of self, but are also targets of the qualities imputed to them by others. In addition to their own efforts, vendors find themselves subject to, and affected by, the images held of their companies, products, and representatives by suppliers, investors, competitors, other businesses, and customers (prospective, current, and former patrons).

Although vendors may be constrained from promoting certain images by virtue of images they have promoted earlier (e.g., exclusive versus discount operations, higher versus lower prices, distant versus friendly styles), their opportunities for success are greatly affected by the images others in the marketplace attribute to them. These images not only signify expectations associated with them by others, but also suggest concrete lines of action others may assume in reference to them.

Beyond the images vendors would like to promote, they may also attempt to resist unwanted identities originating from other sources. Images are problematic not only initially; they also assume dynamic qualities as vendors and others promote, challenge, and otherwise make adjustments to both their perceptions of the targets (trading entities, products, representatives) and the definitions those targets receive from others. Additionally, the role of any source can vary immensely relative to vendor-related images, both across and within subsets of audiences and over time. As the subject of these images, the vendors involved are typically more sensitive to the images surrounding the various facets of their enterprise than are most other audiences. Nonetheless, despite the significance of buyer images of businesses for the eventual viability of those businesses, vendor participation in the image shaping process appears to be sporadic and uneven in emphasis over time.

Trader Images

Image concerns regarding "trading entities" pertain not only to vendor attempts to become known as traders in certain commodity areas, but reflect all aspects of their marketing programs. This would include marketing organizational schemes, concerns with products carried, prices, promotions, prospecting formats, presentations, and modes of dealing with resistance, as well as practices pertaining to troublesome customers and customer loyalty. Focusing on product promotions, Chapters 6, 7, and 8 may more clearly illustrate the image dilemmas vendors experience vis-à-vis prospective customers than do some others, but all aspects of vendors' marketing (and sales) programs can affect people's (prospective and existing buyers, suppliers, investors, and staff) images of vendors and their willingness to be associated with particular vendors.[10]

Extensive use of the media can generate powerful sets of product and/or vendor images, but it is important to recognize that images of vendors are not limited to media promotions. Thus all forms of display work, as well as interpersonal contact and customer recommendations, may serve to promote "vendor mystique" as well as qualify images generated on other bases.

Product Mystique

Just as the support that particular vendors receive seems contingent on the images they achieve, so do purchases of particular products reflect the "magic" that customers associate with these products. People do not simply buy objects, they purchase symbols or images, which only incidentally may have this or that physical quality associated with them. For instance, in buying shoes, people may obtain "X" amount of leather, rubber, plastic, cloth, and so on, in the process, but they are (variously, but effectively) purchasing comfort, style, esteem, "savings," manufacture warranties, personalized fittings, or whatever else they associate with those shoes in each particular instance of acquisition. Like the mystique attributed to trading entities, that attributed to products is a function of audience definitions. Not only are variations apt to occur across audiences, but product mystique is in every case problematic and precarious. Despite the best efforts of vendors (and their agents), product images are subject to ongoing sets of interpretations, assessments, and resistances.

In part, buyer reservations about products reflect the efforts of vendors to promote the sales of their products. To the extent two or more vendors promote similar products, offer functional alternatives, or represent expenditure alternatives, they tend to raise questions about the desirability of each others' products. Further, in addition to the direct product comparisons vendors may make in attempts to gain advantages over their competitors, buyers may have much occasion for casual comparison as they contemplate purchases and/or discuss products with other interested parties.

Some products may enjoy extended periods of image receptivity, but any contemplation of inadequacies or alternatives appears to jeopardize the product images vendors desire. And to the extent these concerns are conveyed to others, a set of product images may emerge quite independent of those promoted by the vendors involved. Vendors may attempt to resist these alternative definitions, but they may also incorporate these images into subsequent product and/or promotional adjustments. Clearly, all members (or segments) of audiences are not equally concerned about particular product images. But it may be feasible to consider the "bantering" if not the "battle" of images pertaining to trading entities and the particular products they feature. Individual vendors and products may enter and exit from the marketplace with little overall recognition, but their fate appears no less sealed in the images they did or did not achieve with reference to prospective audiences.

Personal Identities

A third set of images pertains to the identities of the individuals involved in trading enterprises. These reputations often assume background roles relative to the trading entities these people represent and the products they promote. They do, however, denote important career dimensions for the individuals (whether owners, managers, or salespeople) involved. Other people (e.g., suppliers, customers) may prefer to engage in trade with certain representatives over others, but these identities also affect people's personal orientations to work (e.g., desires for more training, sense of dedication, levels of enthusiasm), and on their opportunities to move within existing, to other, trading entities. Consequently, beyond identities pertaining to trading entities, and the products featured in particular contexts, we may want to further delineate people's self-identities as traders and their more general reputations as traders within the marketplace community.

On another level, as representatives of businesses, products, and their own self-identities, salespeople are apt to experience some dilemmas regarding the particular sets of images they promote (or protect). While all three sets of images may coexist compatibly in many circumstances, situations become more complicated when one element conflicts with images of the others. For instance, on encountering setbacks, representatives may opt to blame the companies they represent, their products, or themselves. Different impressions of each may be given depending on the option selected.

VENDOR COMMITMENTS

A second major set of vendor dilemmas pertains to the investments vendors make with regards to their own businesses. Although vendors may be seen to request commitments on the part of prospective customers,[11] vendors themselves face a great many commitment points in their own ventures. Thus, in addition to concerns about becoming owners of businesses, it should be noted that all features of doing business entail ambiguity and risk.

Vendors may encounter dilemmas in reference to modes of marketing organization (e.g., chain versus solitary outlet, use of multiple fronts, pursuing franchise options), management (staffing programs and procedures), products (lines, inventory, diversification, suppliers), prices (proposed, adjustments, private brands), promotional formats (media, field sales, showrooms, trade shows).[12] The extensiveness of vendor commitments in each area may vary immensely, as may their abilities to shift particular investments to other realms. In each case, however, and despite attempts to "act rationally," vendors find themselves making commitments to the future. Like their customers, they are buying (investing in) images. Vendors can make informed guesses about the future, but in addition to their reliance on others to implement and support these visions through their actions, they are also in shifting competitive contexts and they face significant uncontrollables (e.g., general economy, emergence of alternatives, shifts in audience preferences).

Viewed thusly, each business involves a series of ongoing and often interrelated gambles. However, it would be highly inaccurate to reduce these gambles to matters of pure chance. While some players display a propensity for "long shots" and "high rolls," three elements significantly intervene. They are the reflective (reasoned, interpretive) nature of ventures, the dependencies of vendors on others for affirming the wisdom of moves they have made, and the mystique associated with success.

In the first instance, and even among the greater adventurers, one encounters selective risk taking in that most commitments represent "hedges" of various sorts. Six general strategies of hedging bets were articulated in Chapter 4 ("Purchasing Products"). These included (1) seeking consensus from others, (2) concentrating on basic patterns, (3) "testing the ice," (4) going with established (identified) winners, (5) diversifying investments, and (6) cultivating relationships with suppliers. If, for example, one casts the material in Chapter 2 ("Setting Up Businesses") in a somewhat parallel fashion, we find that prospective owners may hedge their bets with regards to many aspects of their businesses. Considered as indicative preliminary consultations with associates, "experts," and others; partnerships and corporations as alternatives to proprietorships; or the use of chains, chains with multiple fronts or franchises as alternatives to single outlets. Vendors may hedge their bets in somewhat parallel ways in reference to staffing decisions, pricing, media promotions, and so forth. Each single feature of vendors' marketing programs represents a series of options of which the selection of particular lines of action seems contingent on the "handicapping systems" with which players have come to feel comfortable over time. Like gamblers at the race track (Lesieur, 1977), each win serves to confirm the strategy selected; each loss becomes a lesson for the future.

It should also be appreciated that in contrast to the laboratory rolling of dice, for example, in which overall probabilities can be established with much confidence, gambling endeavors involving people (e.g., card and dice games, race tracks, businesses) are much more variable. They involve human intervention and all that accompanies it. The successes of business ventures are contingent on all the roles that the other players invoke in the process. Should the intended parties not cooperate with the vendor in anticipated ways, any marketing concept may be jeopardized. Vendors may hedge their bets in diverse manners but they are inevitably reliant upon the emerging practices of human interactors among whom quality control and prediction remains elusive. Further, while some commitments generate irrevocable positions (e.g., long-term contracts; irretrievable investments), other commitments assume a more tentative quality. These "exit opportunities" raise further dilemmas pertaining to the most opportune times to stay with winning (or even presently losing) propositions. This can be problematic under any circumstances, but the precarious dependence of businesses on human interaction makes these pursuits more uncertain than many other endeavors.

When vendors are accorded a "success mystique" by those with whom they do business, they are likely to find that their chances of winning have been strengthened even though their decisions may be no more (and possibly much less) astute than those of their competitors. As long as others act toward particular vendors as though they were winners (consider customers making purchases of name brands, suppliers extending credit lines, investors buying more stock), these images increase the likelihood that these vendors will have made the right decisions (whatever these were). Suggesting a longer life for any enterprise, the element of mystique speaks to the earlier mentioned formula for success and may help to explain the statement, "Nothing succeeds like success!"[13]

RECRUITMENT AS SOCIAL ACTIVITY

A theme exceedingly central to the preceding discussions of marketing and sales, "recruitment" emerges as a natural topic with which to move this chapter toward conclusion. Our understanding of recruitment would have been strengthened considerably had more material on prospective buyers been included, but much insight into this activity is afforded by the present study. However, I have drawn upon materials from *Making Sales* (Prus, 1989) in developing this statement on recruitment. The result is a more holistic statement of recruitment than that attainable from either volume alone. While *Making Sales* focuses on influence processes in interpersonal encounters, the concept of recruitment is quite properly rooted in the anticipations, preparations, and promotions discussed in *Pursuing Customers*.

Though suggesting somewhat one-sided initiative, recruitment powerfully addresses Blumer's (1969) notion of "joint activity."[14] In discussing an interactionist conceptualization of society, Blumer (1969: 16:20) suggests that joint activity, the "societal organization of conduct of different acts of diverse participants," is the core phenomena with which social scientists must come to terms.

As an area of investigation, Blumer says, "Joint action has a distinctive character in its own right, a character that lies in the articulation or linkage, as apart from that to be articulated or linked" (p. 17). He also envisions joint action as ongoing and problematic, "Joint action always has to undergo a process of formation; even though it may be a well established and repetitive form of social action, each instance of it has to be formed anew" (p. 17). A fuller appreciation of the concept of joint action emerges through this discussion of recruitment.

The Concept of Recruitment

For our purposes, the concept of recruitment denotes attempts on the part of people to: (1) initially involve others ("targets") in particular situations; (2) promote (and intensify) people's ongoing participation in particular situations; (3) discourage people's disinvolvements from particular situations; and (4) reinvolve people in particular situations should they become disinvolved from these settings.[15]

In assuming this view of recruitment, some general conceptual qualifications are in order. First, people promoting the involvements of others in particular situations need not envision their roles in the more comprehensive sense just outlined. For instance, they may attend only to initial involvements, or perhaps concentrate more heavily on the reinvolvement process.

Second, people may recruit others with varying degrees of explicitness and intensity of effort. Even when actively endeavoring to involve others in situations, people need not define themselves as recruiters or their targets as prospects. They also may encourage these involvements with wide variations in enthusiasm. For example, some prospects may be reluctantly pursued or may be passed over altogether.

Third, some recruitment endeavors are focused on a wide variety of targets (or may entail attempts to involve targets in multiple settings) and represent ongoing pursuits on the part of tacticians, but other instances of recruitment may assume highly selective targets or denote only occasional attempts to involve targets in specific situations.

Fourth, although many instances of recruitment may be intended to benefit those (tacticians) promoting target involvements, other efforts may reflect quite different interests. Thus recruitment may signify anticipated target benefits, group sympathies, noble causes, and the like.

Fifth, while recruiters are generally presumed more active in involving targets in situations than are the targets in involving recruiters,[16] it is critical to recognize that targets may pursue particular involvements with considerable persistence and intensity. People's success in recruiting others is contingent upon the extent to which targets define their interests as consistent with the lines of action proposed by recruiters. However, the targets may also actively try to involve the recruiters in these same situations.

A sixth and related qualification hinges on the general preparedness of targets and recruiters for mutual encounters. Recruiters may seem more prepared for encounters than are their prospects, but targets can "shop around," acquire experience as "the pursued," and use elements such as choice, skepticism, and distancing to their advantage in obtaining commitments from the recruiters!

Seventh, to the extent analysts focus on the coming together of recruiters and targets, they may neglect the other involvements in which these two sets of players find themselves. Thus, although recruiters may be diverted from attending as fully to prospects as they might like, targets may also find that other involvements preclude the sorts of commitments they may desire.

Finally, while we would expect each involvement to hold different meanings for each prospect, people may also redefine the significance of any and all of their involvements over time. From the recruiter's perspective, this implies not only moving targets but ones shifting in composition across time frames.

Viewed in these manners, recruitment merits extensive attention as "cooperative behavior." Like other instances of social behavior, recruitment may entail multiple and shifting interests, tactics, and commitments on the part of both parties.

Targets and Tacticians

Focusing on vendor activity, this project is very much an examination of customer-oriented recruitment tactics. However, while consumers and company buyers are most readily identified as targets for marketplace involvements, other targets of recruitment endeavors in the marketplace include prospective owners (also partners, stockholders, franchisees), managers, salespeople, and suppliers. Each of these latter parties may be seen to engage in attempts to involve other people in particular situations, but they also constitute targets in the involvements of others. Thus, while the material following is organized around vendor concerns with preparations and interpersonal influences, vendors' roles as targets are also quite noteworthy.

Getting prepared (setting the stage). Vendor preparations encompass people's involvements in setting up businesses, management practices, and the purchasing, pricing, and promotion of goods to be offered for sale. Each aspect of preparation allows us to reflect upon vendors' dual involvements as tacticians and targets.

People entering businesses as owners illustrate these dual features of recruitment. Not only may they find that they have been recruited into particular ventures by others, but they commonly face the task of having to sell others on the viability of their enterprises. Thus, while prospective owners may be pursued by people wishing to involve them in existing businesses, franchises, land, and so on, they generally find themselves promoting business concepts to bankers, family members, and other associates in attempts to gain the financial support or any other resources they require to start their businesses.

Owner-managers may be freer from the recruitment efforts of head office than those operating franchises or managing businesses for others, but all involved in management are subject to suggestions from others about ways in which to run their businesses. Beyond head office directives, managers commonly find that staff, suppliers, customers, and others actively encourage them to pursue particular lines of action. For their part, managers typically assume a plurality of recruitment roles. Although presumably with orientations toward the eventual recruitment of customers, managers also face the tasks of involving staff people in all aspects of their operations and maintaining their commitments on an ongoing basis. And, depending on their circumstances, managers may have to spend a considerable amount of time and effort "selling" head office, stock holders, or their suppliers on the viability of their practices. Each area of marketing activity thus denotes a particular realm of recruitment activity for those involved in management.

An examination of buyer-supplier relations (partners in trade) provides crystallized testimony to the two-way nature of recruitment activity. Although uneven, tentative, and cast against ever-shifting fields and the gambles implied therein, one notes tendencies toward pursuit and continuity on the part of both buyers and suppliers. This material also speaks to the "ambiguity of recruitment." While suppliers may be uncertain about the extent to which they want particular buyers as customers, buyers typically exhibit uncertainty regarding the desirability of dealing with certain suppliers, carrying certain lines, and so on. Denoting a more particular subset of activities than that commonly encompassed by management, one notes further attempts on the part of buyers to prepare for encounters with their suppliers. Their willingness to pursue or resist particular involvements with suppliers reflects their anticipations of their effectiveness in recruiting their customers on both a short-run and long-term basis. Even when buyers attempt to make adjustments to their (own) customers' preferences, it is difficult to predict what form these will assume in the future—ergo, the practice of "hedging involvements" with suppliers.

Reflecting both the products carried and the suppliers with whom they have become involved, the pricing practices of vendors draws further attention to the preparatory, reactive, and competitive nature of recruitment. Thus, even when blending customer preparations with expediency (e.g., standardized prices for items, standardized margins) dimensions of recruitment, vendors are affected by customer receptivity to pricing practices. Prices not "objectified" by purchases are typically readjusted in attempts to approximate more closely target perceptions and preferences. Partially signifying the general ambiguity of recruitment ("What is the 'best price' to promote desired levels of purchasing activity?"), tendencies on the part of vendors to compare their prices with those of competitors also alert us to the role that prospects' alternatives may play in the recruitment process.

The material on media, field, and showroom promotions fits most comfortably with conventional notions of recruitment. However, this apparent emphasis on customer-directed recruitment may obscure some other dimensions of involvement. For instance, while promotions are directed toward a business's customers, those implementing these promotional tactics may have to be sold on the viability of using these tactics by others (initially and/or on an ongoing basis). Likewise, those encouraging vendors to use particular promotional formats (e.g., media) may themselves rely heavily on alternative promotional formats (e.g., other media, agents in the field, trade shows) in their own search for new and continuing accounts.

Media promotions more readily represent one-way communications than do other modes of customer contact. But insofar as those involved in media programs attempt to adjust to feedback from customers or attend to the practices of their competitors, they provide us with further indication of the tentative, reactive (versus initiatory), and competitive nature of recruitment.[17]

The discussion of field sales pointedly alerts us to the outgoing nature of interpersonal recruitment programs. Whereas those initiating media programs are generally somewhat removed from those receiving their messages, people in the field (media salespeople included) face more direct risks of rejection. Thus, while media messages may be directed toward particular populations and individuals (e.g., personalized mailings), the elements of stage fright, self doubt, and direct resistance emerge prominently in field settings. Denoting levels of prospect access and vendor resourcefulness seemingly unattainable in media promotions, one nevertheless finds attempts on the part of businesses operating in the field to sell their agents on the desirability of doing field sales.

Showroom promotions are often buttressed by media and/or field sales activity; but in serving as "display cases," showrooms assume higher levels of prospect initiative (and receptivity) than that characterizing field sales. Although those involved in showroom sales avoid some of the dilemmas and frustrations associated with field sales, once prospects have entered the vendor's space the range of interaction tends to approximate that of the field sales setting. Embodying elements of media, field, and showroom promotions, trade exhibits denote some of the more fleeting forms of recruitment. While parallel in many respects to retail mall settings, public exhibits, farmers' markets, craft shows, and the like, trade shows provide particularly valuable views of the meshing of on-stage promotional activity on the part of suppliers and backstage preparations activity on the part of the buyers (also see Chapter 4 on buyer-supplier encounters). Like with other realms of promotion, one finds a number of businesses involved in the production and servicing of trade shows, with the exhibitors emerging as major targets for these enterprises.

Achieving interpersonal influence. When one looks ahead to the material in the companion volume, *Making Sales,* still other aspects of recruitment become prominent. Chapters 2 and 3 on making presentations and generating trust provide detailed accounts of the ways in which vendors approach and consolidate themselves with prospective buyers. Some sales will likely occur regardless of vendor initiatives, but matters pertaining to approaches and first impressions, qualifications, interest, and trust reflect active participation of the vendors involved in their roles as tacticians. While noting both the preparations (and training) vendor contact with prospects may entail and the standardized, repetitive forms recruitment endeavors may assume, attention here is also drawn to the problematic, symbolic, and creative nature of the relationship work in which vendors engage.

Should prospects seem reluctant to make the investments vendors desire, vendors are faced with the options of discontinuing their pursuits or attempting alternative tactics (Chapters 4 and 5 of *Making Sales*). As with other features of the encounter, earlier endeavors (successful or otherwise) may provide vendors with lessons for subsequent efforts. Consequently, as with the presentations just discussed, resistance often engenders prepared, standardized, and repetitive lines of action from vendors. Implementation of these tactics, however, remains problematic. Given the uncertain, situated, and emergent nature of prospect encounters, vendors may not only have considerable difficulty uncovering prospect reservations but typically face the task of resolving these within short time frames and in manners that prospects would find palatable. Additionally, while only sometimes aware of the evaluative contexts (e.g., comparison shopping, tight budgets, concerns for third party approval) their prospects are employing at given points in their encounters, vendors are often subjected to tactics that prospects have developed from their earlier contacts with vendors.

The discussion of troublesome encounters (*Making Sales*, Chapter 6) speaks to tactician concerns with maintaining organizational order and personal integrating in the process of recruiting prospects. Perceiving themselves to be dependent upon the prospects for both short- and long-term involvements, referrals of vendors to others, and image maintenance more broadly, vendors generally exercise some diplomacy in their attempts to align the behaviors of the disrupters they encounter. In the process of managing trouble, however, the emphasis may be diverted from that of recruiting prospects for product purchases to that of achieving order (and noninterference) in the setting.

The discussion of loyalty (Chapter 7 in *Making Sales*) draws particular attention to the long-term dimensions of recruitment. Effectively dependent on all aspects of the situations experienced by existing customers (as well as some consistency in the buyers' own situations), vendors nevertheless may make specific efforts to ensure continuity. To this end, tacticians may promote buyer perspectives, identities, activities, commitments, and relationships consistent with ongoing vendor involvements. However, and despite the major consequences of repeat purchases for the well-being of both the businesses and the individual salespeople involved, this realm of recruitment seems much more taken for granted than are others. Disinvolvement is often overlooked, and "loyalty work" is often only vaguely defined. As well, the attention given to new prospects, immediate purchasing commitments, and "trouble" frequently detracts from the development of long-term relationships with existing customers.

Still other features of recruitment (and continuity) are portrayed in the analysis of "sales" (Chapter 8 in *Making Sales*). As action-oriented events, "sales" are among the most intense and most fleeting encounters vendors have with buyers. Combined with preparations (of which price-cutting is especially evident), promotions, anticipation and uncertainty, are elements of skepticism, pressure, loyalty, and the competition. Frequently characterized by time limitations and competition between prospects, "sales" draw attention to the impact of both urgency and "collective atmospheres" on prospects' willingness to become involved in particular settings. Noteworthy also, are vendors' tendencies to become drawn into "sales" as recruitment devices on both a short-term and long-run basis. While vendors may enter into these events in an attempt to recruit prospects, they sometimes find they receive extensive encouragements from customers to continue these involvements.

Chapter 9 of *Making Sales* attends to the situated and long-term aspects of enthusiasm. It depicts some of the problems tacticians face in sustaining their own involvements. Hence, attention shifts to the wearying aspects of recruitment, the unpredictability of success, as well as the unpleasantries and disrespect recruiters may experience. Since it affirms the vitality of their involvements, increasing levels of success seem especially likely to promote people's continuity as tacticians. However, in the relative absence of more obvious prospect commitments, we note the role that self-reflectivity and the support tacticians receive from families, companies, peers, and outsiders may play in maintaining their enthusiasm in both situated and long-term respects. Like the involvements of customers in vendors' products, vendor enthusiasm emerges as a social process.

In sum, this consideration of the activities of those involved in recruitment not only indicates the initiative joint activity entails on the part of the tacticians, but it also depicts the tentative, reactive, competitive and negotiable nature of involvements. As well, insofar as tacticians are themselves targets of the recruitment endeavors of others, this statement has provided us with yet other opportunities to reflect upon recruitment.

CAREERS

As just indicated, recruitment centrally addresses the interactive elements of buyer-seller encounters. The concept of "careers" and the related notion of "interwoven involvements" foster a further appreciation of people's involvements over time and their interlinkages with one another. Thus, while the term *career* provides continuity over individuals' involvements in particular settings, the concept of interwoven involvements is especially valuable in highlighting the affiliational nature of people's participation in buying and selling roles. Like the notions of image work, commitments as social processes, and recruitment, these concepts help summarize central themes in this monograph.

Introduced at length in Chapter 1, the concept of career contingencies has been used throughout this study (in both this volume and in *Making Sales*). A major organizing concept throughout, the notion of careers was used extensively to explore people's participation in the marketplace as owners, salespeople, and buyers. Alerting us to the processes entailed in people's initial involvements, continuities, disinvolvements, and reinvolvements in situations, this concept generates a valuable natural history perspective on people's involvements in particular settings.

People's participation in the marketplace (and in the other settings cited in the introductory chapter) appears to revolve around their perspectives, identities, activities, commitments, and relationships. Each of these elements tends to affect the others, but the extent of people's participation in situations can vary immensely over time with regards to each of these aspects of their roles. Thus, rather than view people's involvements in singular terms, it seems more instructive to attend to the multifaceted, uneven, and shifting nature of these elements. It seems almost inevitable that people will be differentially involved in each of these components of their roles at any given point in time. For instance, participants may largely accept the perspectives or identities given roles represent at particular points in time, but find that they are having difficulties performing the associated activities, that they have made only minimal commitments in that role to date, or that the relationships they have formed with the other participants are far from satisfactory. Hence, a more complete and accurate picture emerges when we attend to the variations of intensity with which people may experience each of these subcomponents of their involvements over time.

As Lemert (1967) has suggested, people's continuity in particular roles is enhanced to the extent that they more completely organize their lives around these roles. Here, however, we have begun to specify five elements central to this process and to indicate the implications of each of these realms of involvement for people's overall participation in particular situations. Rather than discuss the global roles of those involved in the marketplace as buyers or vendors, we would want to consider buyers' and sellers' careers with respect to the acquisition of perspectives, the development of identities, the doing of activities, the shaping of commitments, and the formation of relationships in those contexts. By sorting out these dimensions we may achieve a sharper image of the dynamics of marketplace involvements.

Interwoven Involvements

Part of the difficulty in following and comprehending people's individual careers in particular settings is that each individual career can be understood only within the context of the other people who interact with persons in these settings.[18] We may try to distinguish each person's involvements from those of the others, but each person is both affected by and affects the other people with whom that person has dealings in a setting. Consider as illustrative the interlinkages of a group of co-workers or two parties engaging in trade or members of a club. People's exchanges with one another may prominently affect both their short-term experiences and their long-term involvements in those settings. In all cases, people's careers entail these interactive components.

Reflecting occasions for the sharing of perspectives, the affirmations of identities, the facilitation of activities, the interdependencies of commitment, and the development of relationships, the concept of interwoven careers spans as well as signifies people's involvements in the marketplace. Not only do other people influence individuals' initial involvements, continuities, disinvolvements, and reinvolvements, but those others also define the prominence and success those individuals experience in those settings.

The importance of the concept of interwoven careers may be further illustrated by the webs of associations the marketplace engenders. Striking in this regard are not only the interlinkages of manufacturer to manufacturer, or manufacturer to wholesaler, or wholesaler to retailer, or retailer to consumer, but also the parallel sets of activities in which these people find themselves engaged. The relationships of retailers and consumers parallel those of suppliers and retailers or advertising agencies and their clients, for instance. Indeed, the concept of interwoven careers cuts across all levels of "distribution" and assumes significance within each realm of exchange. This notion also accounts for the enduring sense of community experienced by those participating more fully in the marketplace. It encompasses people's experiences with the past, their anticipations with the future, and the immediate situations in which they find themselves. It provides continuity amidst the inevitable uncertainty of group life. This volume, *Pursing Customers*, generates only a partial picture of the range of activities in which vendors engage in pursuing and developing customer encounters.[19] Nevertheless, it is hoped that this monograph indicates not only the necessity of studying action as situated accomplishment, but also draws attention to the temporal (career) and the interdependent (interwoven careers) essences of human activity.

From Here . . .

In concluding this statement, I am keenly reminded that the larger project from which both the present text and its companion volume *(Making Sales)* are derived much more represents a starting point than a definitive inquiry into the marketplace. While the complexity of the marketplace made it difficult to establish closure on the parameters of this project, the study has been a humbling experience more generally. Despite the intensity with which each realm of vendor activity has been pursued, new and exciting areas of inquiry have (almost embarrassingly) continued to present themselves throughout. Perhaps most obviously, the study of consumer behavior offers some very exciting prospects.[20] Here, ethnographic inquiries into buyer involvements would add invaluable depth to our understanding of concepts such as images and interpretation, commitment processes, and recruitment, as well as provide further balance to this study. One could also apply the general model developed herein to international trade or the marketing of other "products," such as political parties, trade unions, sports teams, festivals, and community land development, or to medical, pollution, volunteer, education, and welfare programs, for instance,[21] and could add greatly to our understanding of group life in the process. However, and within the general confines of the immediate project, it is as though Pandora's box has been opened with vengeance. Each reworking of the present manuscript has suggested additional opportunities for research on the dynamics of the marketplace. Viable prospects for field research exist in abundance in every area of activity considered herein, from the involvements of newcomers in the business world and all aspects of vendor preparation to the processes of product promotion, and elements affecting continuity on the part of all involved in the marketplace. While I can only anticipate the eventual richness of subsequent ethnographic inquiry for understanding both marketplace behavior and group life more generally, it has been most rewarding to have been part of the process.

Before I started, I thought, "That's an easy job, working in a store." ... It's tough! You're dealing with people [appliances]!

Notes

1. I had quite anticipated this to be the case for interpersonal encounters (see *Making Sales*), but the material on vendor preparations (especially on pricing, which I had assumed to be least amenable to social process) was what most convinced me of the fundamentally and thoroughly social essence of business.

2. A colleague once suggested that, like children opening up a box of Cracker Jack, academics (and other readers) liked to get a surprise in every study. While noting that one's writing style could affect the process, he indicated that this was a relative advantage of hypotheses testing (did it or didn't it hold true, and why) over ethnographies of this sort in which the facets of the study are laid bare throughout. In a somewhat related vein, another colleague aptly noted that a major dilemma one encounters in trying to summarize ethnographic research is that the data assume an expansive quality rather than result in highly simplified findings. Accordingly, those doing ethnographic research quickly realize that "the world of human interaction simply doesn't fit into nice, neat little boxes!"

3. In some respects the term *overwhelming* is much more appropriate. The marketplace is just much more complex and dynamic than I had envisioned it to be.

4. Ironically, the Yellow Pages in most city telephone directories are about twice the size of the white pages. Studies of directory advertising and sales aside, it seems that social scientists have been missing a lot of the action! A drive (or walk) down any major downtown street should be no less revealing of this omission.

5. Discussions with social scientists suggest that while they commonly view the field of marketing as crass and commercial, they nevertheless imbue it with some mystique. This appears to reflect presumptions of esoteric knowledge and/or perceived powers of influence ("They must know what they're doing!") attributed to those involved in marketing.

6. Most people interviewed indicated that they appreciated the opportunity to reflect upon their situations in this more focused sense. Some also found that they had worked out solutions to some of their dilemmas in the process of articulating aspects of their situations for the study.

7. These "popularity" shifts are also addressed in Chapter 8 (Holding Sales) of *Making Sales* (Prus, 1989).

8. This is a point frequently made by my students, who especially appreciate the extended quotations as a means of understanding abstract notions within a variety of settings.

9. Readers should recognize my indebtedness to the exceedingly rich "image work" provided by Orrin Klapp's (1962, 1964, 1969, 1971) discussions of "social types" and Erving Goffman's (1959, 1963, 1967, 1971) material on "impression management." Lemert (1951, 1972), Becker (1963), Berger and Luckmann (1966), Lyman and Scott (1970), Hewitt and Stokes (1975) and Prus (1975a, 1975b, 1982) also address themes pertinent to the immediate analysis.

10. The discussion of "sales" (Chapter 8) in *Making Sales* (Prus, 1989) sheds further light on the interrelationship of vendor images and vendor marketing practices.

11. The pursuit of commitments (along with the neutralization of buyer resistances) is dealt with more fully in *Making Sales* (Prus, 1989).

12. As is evident in *Making Sales* (Prus, 1989), other major marketing dilemmas pertain to presentational styles, persuasion tactics, practices for dealing with troublesome customers, loyalty, and matters of sustaining enthusiasm.

13. Ultimately too, since, "Nothing gets copied like success!", it would seem that these winning forms may eventually lead to these vendors' own demise (i.e., "getting beat at their own games."). For an indication of the "price of popularity," readers are referred to Prus and Frisby's (1989) consideration of home party plans and the vulnerability of the originators of earlier versions of party plans to those subsequently copying these winning concepts.

14. Blumer uses this term rather synonymously with Mead's (1934) concept of "social action." However, the concept of joint activity more readily draws attention to the problematic and processual features of people "fitting their lines of action together." Social action is not simply other-directed behavior, it is a jointly constructed (interactive) process.

15. Readers will recognize these processes from the earlier statement (in Chapter 1) of the career contingency model. Here, however, we consider the careers of targets from the viewpoints of those (i.e., the agents) encouraging their involvements (throughout the career process). While we are clearly discussing "influence processes," the concept of recruitment as used herein allows us to attend to both the sequencing of relatively distinct influence processes and the relationship contexts in which influence takes place.

16. This holds true almost by definition. In a broader sense, it may be instructive to consider the processes by which people are defined as recruiters (or tacticians), versus targets, in situations.

17. Additionally, to the extent producers/users are "sold" on one variation of a media concept (e.g., one advertisement or slogan) versus another, we may further appreciate the pervasive nature of recruitment.

18. With regards to people's involvement in "deviance," this theme is especially evident in Miller (1978) and Prus and Irini (1988).

19. This theme is pursued in greater detail in *Making Sales* (Prus, 1989), wherein the emphasis is on "influence as interpersonal accomplishment."

20. Although far from completed at this writing, a study of shopping behavior (representing a natural sequel) was begun in the midst of the present project.

21. While an extension of marketing models to nonprofit settings is not a unique suggestion (see Fine, 1981), the approach introduced herein is significantly different from that characterizing the marketing literature.

REFERENCES

Abolafia, Mitchel (1982) Self-Regulation in Market Maintenance: An Organizational Perspective. Working paper, University of California-Davis, School of Administration.

Adler, Patricia (1985) Wheeling and Dealing. New York: Columbia University Press.

Adler, Patricia and Peter Adler (1983) "Relationships between dealers: the social organization of illicit drug transactions." Sociology and Social Research 67: 260-278.

Adler, Patricia and Peter Adler (1984) The Social Dynamics of Financial Markets. Greenwich, CT: JAI.

Adler, Peter (1981) Momentum. Beverly Hills, CA: Sage.

Anderson, Paul (1983) "Marketing, scientific progress, and scientific method." Journal of Marketing 47 (4): 18-31.

Andrews, John W. (1950) "U.S. vs. A&P: battle of titans." Harper's Magazine September: 64-73.

Angrist, Shirley (1955) "Real estate salesmen." Master's thesis, McGill University, Montreal.

Angrist, Shirley (1984) "Selling real estate: reflections and persuasion," pp. 132-145 in Audrey Wipper (ed.) The Sociology of Work in Canada. Toronto: Carleton Library.

Bagozzi, Richard (1979) "Opening statement," pp. 6-10 in O. C. Ferrel, S. W. Brown, and C. W. Lane Jr. (eds.) Conceptual and Theoretical Statements in Marketing. Proceedings of the American Marketing Association Conference. Chicago: American Marketing Association.

Bain, Robert K. (1959) "The process of professionalization: life-insurance sales." Ph.D. dissertation, University of Chicago.

Bass, Jay (1983) "Dunners and defaulters: collectors' work as a context for meaning." Urban Life 12: 49-73.

Becker, Howard S. (1963) Outsiders. New York: Free Press.

Becker, Howard S. (1982) Art Worlds. Berkeley: University of California Press.

Berger, Peter and Thomas Luckmann (1966) The Social Construction of Reality. New York: Anchor.

Bigus, Odis (1972) "The milkman and his customers." Urban Life and Culture 1: 131-165.

Bittner, Egon (1965) "The concept of organization." Social Research 32: 230-255.

Bittner, Egon (1967) "The police on skid row: a study of peace-keeping." American Sociological Review (32): 699-715.

327

Black, Donald J. and Albert J. Reiss (1970) "Police control of juveniles." American Sociological Review (35): 63-77.

Blau, Peter (1964) Exchange and Power in Social Life. New York: John Wiley.

Blumer, Herbert (1969) Symbolic Interactionism. Englewood Cliffs, NJ: Prentice-Hall.

Bogdan, Robert (1972) "Learning to sell door to door: teaching as persuasion." American Behavioral Scientist 16: 55-65.

Bohannan, Paul and George Dalton (1962) Markets in Africa. Chicago: Northwestern University Press.

Bonoma, Thomas V. and Gerald Zaltman (1978) "Introduction," pp. 1-30 in Thomas V. Bonoma and Gerald Zaltman (eds.) Organizational Buying Behavior. Chicago: American Marketing Association.

Borden, Neil (1964) "The concept of marketing mix." Journal of Advertising Research 4 (2): 2-7.

Brookfield, H. C. (1969) Pacific Market-Places. Canberra: Australian National University Press.

Browne, Joy (1973) The Used-Car Game: The Sociology of the Bargain. Lexington, MA: Lexington Books.

Caplovitz, David (1963) The Poor Pay More. New York: Free Press.

Caplovitz, David (1973) Merchants of Harlem. Beverly Hills, CA: Sage.

Caplovitz, David (1974) Consumers in Trouble. New York: Free Press.

Caplovitz, David (1979) Making Ends Meet: How Families Cope with Recession and Inflation. Beverly Hills, CA: Sage.

Carey, James (1968) The College Drug Scene. Englewood Cliffs, NJ: Prentice-Hall.

Cavan, Sherri (1972) "The class structure of hippie culture." Urban Life 1: 211-237.

Clark, Robert E. and Larry J. Halford (1978) "Going . . . going . . . gone: preliminary observations on 'deals' at auctions." Urban Life 7: 285-307.

Clinard, Marshall B. (1969) The Black Market: A Study of White Collar Crime. New York: Holt, Rinehart & Winston.

Clinard, Marshall B. and Peter C. Yeager (1980) Corporate Crime. New York: Free Press.

Collins, Oris and D. G. Moore, with D. B. Unwalla (1970) The Enterprising Man: A Behavioral Study of Independent Enterprise. East Lansing: Michigan State University Press.

Cressey, Donald (1953) Other People's Money. New York: Free Press.

Cressey, Paul (1932) The Taxi-Dance Hall. Chicago: University of Chicago Press.

Dalton, Melville (1959) Men Who Manage. New York: John Wiley.

Darden, Donna, William Darden, and G. E. Keiser (1981) "The marketing of legal services." Journal of Marketing 45 (Spring): 122-134.

Davis, Fred (1959) "The cab driver and his fare." American Journal of Sociology 65: 158-165.

Davis, Robert (1957) Performance and Development of Field Sales. Cambridge, MA: Harvard University.

Dean, Joel (1976) "Pricing policies for new products." Harvard Business Review Vol. 54 (November-December): 141-153.

Dempsey, William F., A. Bushman, and R. E. Plank (1980) "Personal inducements of industrial buyers." Industrial Marketing Management 9: 281-289.

Dingwall, Robert and Phil Strong (1985) "The interactional study of organizations." Urban Life 14: 205-231.

Ditton, Jason (1977) Part-Time Crime: An Ethnography of Fiddling and Pilferage. London: Macmillan.

Ditz, Gerhard (1967) "Status problems of the salesman." Michigan State University Business Topics 15 (1): 68=80.

Donovan, Frances R. (1929) The Saleslady. Chicago: University of Chicago Press.

Drucker, Peter F. (1964) The Concept of Corporation. New York: Mentor.

Eaton, Marian (1980) "The Better Business Bureau: the voice of the people in the marketplace," pp. 233-281 in Laura Nader (ed.) No Access to the Law. New York: Academic Press.

Edwards, W. (1954) "The theory of decision making." Psychological Bulletin 51: 381-417.

Emerson, Robert M. and Sheldon L. Messinger (1977) "The micro-politics of trouble." Social Problems 25: 121-134.

Enis, Ben M. (1979) "Opening statement," pp. 1-3 in O. C. Ferrel, S. W. Brown, and C. W. Lane Jr. (eds.) Conceptual and Theoretical Statements in Marketing. Proceedings of the American Marketing Association Conference. Chicago: American Marketing Association.

Ermarth, Michael (1978) Wilhelm Dilthey: The Critique of Historical Reason. Chicago: University of Chicago Press.

Evans, Franklin B. (1963) "Selling as a dyadic relationship: a new approach." American Behavioral Scientist 6: 76-79.

Fairlie, Robin (1979) Direct Mail. London: Kegan Paul.

Farberman, Harvey A. (1975) "A criminogenic market structure: the automobile industry." Sociological Quarterly (16): 438-457.

Ferman, Louis, Stuart Henry, and Michele Hoyman [eds.] (1987) The Informal Economy. The Annals of the American Academy of Political and Social Sciences 493 (September).

Festinger, Leon (1954) "A theory of social comparison." Human Relations 7: 117-140.

Festinger, Leon (1957) A Theory of Cognitive Dissonance. Evanston, IL: Row, Peterson.

Fields, Allen B. (1984) "Slinging weed: the social organization of streetcorner marijuana sales." Urban Life 13: 247-270.

Fine, Seymour H. (1981) The Marketing of Ideas and Social Issues. New York: Praeger.

Foxall, G. R. (1974) "Sociology and the study of consumer behavior." American Journal of Economics and Sociology 33: 127-135.

French, Cecil L. (1958) "The interrelationship of norms, social structure and productivity in a competitive retail sales group." Ph.D. dissertation, Washington University, St. Louis.

French, Cecil L. (1960) "Correlates of success in retail selling." American Journal of Sociology 66: 128-134.

Frisby, David (1984) Georg Simmel. New York: Tavistock.

Garfinkel, Harold (1967) Studies in Ethnomethodology. Englewood Cliffs, NJ: Prentice-Hall.

Gilderbloom, John I. (1985) "Social factors affecting landlords in the determination of rent." Urban Life 14: 155-179.

Glaser, Barney (1972) The Patsy and the Subcontractor: A Study of the Expert-Layman Relationship. Mill Valley, CA: Sociology Press.

Glaser, Barney and Anselm Strauss (1967) The Discovery of Grounded Theory: Strategies for Qualitative Research. Chicago: Aldine.

Glick, Ira O. (1957) "A social psychological study of futures marketing." Ph.D. dissertation, University of Chicago.

Glock, C. Y. and F. M. Nicosa (1964) "Uses of sociology in studying 'consumption' behavior." Journal of Marketing 28: 51-54.

Goffman, Erving (1959) Presentation of Self in Everyday Life. New York: Anchor.

Goffman, Erving (1963) Stigma. Englewood Cliffs, NJ: Prentice-Hall.

Goffman, Erving (1971) Relations in Public. New York: Harper.

Greenberg, David (1980) "Easy terms, hard times: complaint handling in the ghetto." pp. 379-415 in Laura Nader (ed.) No Access to the Law. New York: Academic Press.

Haring, Albert (1935) Retail Price-Cutting and Its Control by Manufacturers. New York: Arno Press.

Hayano, David (1982) Poker Faces: The Life and Work of Professional Card Players. Berkeley: University of California.

Hayes-Bautista, David (1976) "Termination of the patient-doctor practitioner relationship." Journal of Health and Social Behavior 17: 12-21.

Henry, Stuart (1978) The Hidden Economy: The Context and Control of Borderline Crime. Oxford: Martin Robertson.

Henslin, James (1968) "Trust and the cab driver," pp. 138-155 in Marcello Truzzi (ed.) Sociology and Everyday Life. Englewood Cliffs, NJ: Prentice-Hall.

Hewitt, John P. and Randall Stokes (1975) "Disclaimers." American Sociological Review 40: 1-11.

Hindelang, Michael (1971) "Bookies and bookmaking: a descriptive analysis." Crime and Delinquency 17: 245-255.

Hodgson, Richard (1974) The Dartnell Direct Mail and Mail Order Handbook. Chicago: Dartnell.

Homans, George C. (1958) "Social behavior as exchange." American Journal of Sociology 63: 597-606.

Hong, Lawrence, William Darrough, and Robert Duff (1975) "The sensuous rip-off: consumer fraud turns blue." Urban Life and Culture 3: 464-470.

House, J. D. (1977) Contemporary Entrepreneurs: The Sociology of Residential Real Estate Agents. Westport, CT: Greenwood Press.

Howton, F. William and Bernard Rosenberg (1965) "The salesman: ideology and self-imagery in prototypic occupations." Social Research 32: 277-298.

Hughes, Everett (1979) The Growth of an Institution: The Chicago Real Estate Board. New York: Adorno Press. (Original work published 1931.)

Hyman, H. H. (1960) "Reflections on reference groups." Public Opinion Quarterly 24: 383-396.

Jacobs, Jerry (1979) " 'Burp seltzer? I never use it': an in-depth look at market research," pp. 133-142 in H. Schwartz and J. Jacobs (eds.) Qualitative Sociology. New York: Free Press.

Jacobs, Jerry (1984) The Mall: The Attempted Escape from Everyday Life. Prospect Heights, IL: Waveland Press.

Kaiser, Susan (1985) The Social Psychology of Clothing. New York: Macmillan.

Karsh, Bernard, Joel Seidman, and D. M. Lilienthal (1953) "The union organizer and his tactics." American Journal of Sociology 59: 113-122.

Karikas, Angel and Rena Rosenwassen (1980) "Department store complaint management," pp. 283-316 in Laura Nader (ed.) No Access to the Law. New York: Academic Press.

Kasteller, Josephene, R. Kane, D. M. Olsen, and C. Thetford (1976) "Issues underlying prevalence of 'doctor-shopping' behavior." Journal of Health and Social Behavior 17: 328-339.

Katovich, Michael and Ron L. Diamond (1986) "Selling time: situated transactions in a noninstitutional environment." Sociological Quarterly 27: 253-271.

Katz, Elihu and Paul F. Lazarsfeld (1955) Personal Influence. New York: Free Press.

Klapp, Orrin (1962) Heroes, Villains, and Fools. Englewood Cliffs, NJ: Prentice-Hall.

Klapp, Orrin (1964) Symbolic Leaders: Public Dramas and Public Men. New York: Irvington.

Klapp, Orrin (1969) Collective Search for Identity. New York: Holt, Rinehart & Winston.

Klapp, Orrin (1971) Social Types: Process, Structure and Ethos. San Diego: Aegis.

Klockers, Carl B. (1975) The Professional Fence. New York: Free Press.

Kotler, Phillip (1972) "A generic concept of marketing." Journal of Marketing 36 (April): 46-54.

Kotter, John P. (1982) The General Manager. New York: Free Press.

Kreisberg, Louis (1956) "Occupational controls among steel distributors." American Journal of Sociology 61: 203-212.

LaBarre, Weston (1947) "The cultural basis of emotions and gestures." Journal of Personality 16: 49-68.

Lambert, David R. (1981) "Price as a duality cue in industrial buying." Journal of the Academy of Marketing Science 9 (3): 227-238.

Lazarsfeld, Paul (1959) "Reflections on business." American Journal of Sociology 65: 1-31.

Lemert, Edwin (1951) Social Pathology. New York: McGraw-Hill.

Lemert, Edwin (1953) "An isolation and closure theory of naive check forgery." Journal of Criminal Law, Criminology and Police Science 44: 296-307.

Lemert, Edwin (1972) Human Deviance, Social Problems and Social Control. Englewood Cliffs, NJ: Prentice-Hall. (Original work published 1967.)

Leonard, William N. and Marvin G. Weber (1970) "Automakers and dealers: a study of criminogenic market forces." Law and Society Review 4: 407-424.

Lesieur, Henry (1977) The Chase. New York: Anchor.

Levine, Donald (1971) Georg Simmel: On Individuality and Social Forms. Chicago: University of Chicago Press.

Levine, Edward M. (1972) "Chicago's art world: the influence of status interests on its social and distribution systems." Urban Life and Culture 1: 293-322.

Levy, Sidney J. (1978) Marketplace Behavior. Chicago: American Marketing Association.

Lilly, Robert and Richard Ball (1979) "Bidding and betting: the definitions of a good race horse and a closed community." Presented at the Mid-South Sociological Association meetings.

Lofland, John and Rodney Stark (1965) "Becoming a world saver: a theory of conversion to a deviant perspective." American Sociological Review 30: 862-875.

Lombard, George F. (1955) Behavior in a Selling Group. Cambridge, MA: Harvard University Press.

Luckenbill, David F. (1984) "Dynamics of the deviant sale." Deviant Behavior 5: 337-353.

Lutz, Richard J. (1979) "Opening statement," pp. 3-6 in O. C. Ferrel, S. W. Brown, and C. W. Lane Jr. (eds.) Conceptual and Theoretical Statements in Marketing. Proceedings of the American Marketing Association Conference. Chicago: American Marketing Association.

Lyman, Stanford M. and Marvin B. Scott (1970) A Sociology of the Absurd. New York: Appleton-Century-Crofts.

Lynn, Robert A. (1976) Pricing Policies and Market Management. Homewood, IL: Irwin.

Macaulay, Stewart (1963) "Non-contractual relations in business: a preliminary study." American Sociological Review 28: 55-67.

MacAndrew, C. and R. B. Edgerton (1969) Drunken Comportment. Chicago: Aldine.

MacLean, Annie M. (1899) "Two weeks in department stores." American Journal of Sociology 4: 721-741.

Maisel, Robert (1974) "The flea market as an action scene." Urban Life and Culture 2: 488-505.

Maisel, Roberta (1966) "The antique trade." Master's thesis, University of California, Berkeley.

Malinowski, Bronislaw (1987) The Sexual Life of Savages in North Western Melanesia. New York: Methuen. (Original work published 1929.)

Marx, Karl (1967) Capital: A Critique of Political Economy (Samuel Moore and Edward Areling, trans.) New York: International Publishers. (Original work published 1887.)

Maslow, A. H. (1954) Motivation and Personality. New York: Harper.

Matza, David (1964) Delinquency and Drift. New York: John Wiley.

Matza, David (1969) Becoming Deviant. Englewood Cliffs, NJ: Prentice-Hall.

McCall, Michal M. (1977) "Art without a market: creating artistic value in a provincial art world." Symbolic Interaction 1: 32-43.

McKendrik, Neil, John Brewer, and J. H. Plumb (1982) The Birth of a Consumer Society: The Commercialization of Nineteenth Century England. London: Europa.

Mead, George H. (1934) Mind, Self and Society. Chicago: University of Chicago Press.

Mead, Margaret (1950) Sex and Temperament. New York: Mentor.

Merton, Robert K. (1957) Social Structure and Social Theory. New York: Free Press.

Miller, Gale (1978) Odd Jobs: The World of Deviant Work. Englewood Cliffs, NJ: Prentice-Hall.

Miller, Stephen J. (1964) "The social base of sales behavior." Social Problems 2: 15-24.

Mintzberg, Henry (1973) The Nature of Organizational Work. New York: Harper & Row.

Moskovitz, Milton, Michael Katz, and Robert Levering (1980) Everybody's Business. New York: Harper & Row.

Nicosa, Francesco M. and Robert N. Mayer (1976) "Toward a sociology of consumption." Journal of Consumer Research 3 (Sept): 65-75.

Olmstead, A. D. (1986) "What will you give me? Buying and selling at public auctions." Presented at the conference, Ethnographic Research: An Interactionist/Interpretative Inquiry, Waterloo, Ontario.

Oxenfedt, Alfred K. (1975) Pricing Strategies. New York: Amacon.

Peven, Dorothy (1968) "The use of religious revival techniques to indoctrinate personnel: the home-party organizations." Sociological Quarterly 9: 97-106.

Phillips, L. W. and L. W. Stern (1977) "Limit pricing theory as a basis for anti-merger policy." Journal of Marketing 41: 91-97.

Pinch, Trevor and Colin Clark (1986) "The hard sell: patter merchandising and the strategic (re)production and local management of economic reasoning in the sales routine of market pitchers." Sociology 20 (2): 169-191.

Pope, Daniel (1983) The Making of Modern Advertising. New York: Basic Books.

Prus, Robert (1975a) "Labeling theory: a reconceptualization and a propositional statement on typing." Sociological Focus 8: 79-96.

Prus, Robert (1975b) "Resisting designations: an extension of attribution theory into a negotiated context." Sociological Inquiry 45: 3-14.

Prus, Robert (1976) "Religious recruitment and the management of dissonance: a sociological perspective." Sociological Inquiry 46: 127-134.

Prus, Robert (1978) "From barrooms to bedrooms: towards a theory of interpersonal violence," pp. 51-73 in M. A. B. Gammon (ed.) Violence in Canada. Toronto: Methuen.

Prus, Robert (1982) "Designating discretion and openness: the problematics of truthfulness in everyday life." Canadian Review of Sociology and Anthropology 19: 70-91.

Prus, Robert (1983) "Making purchases: careers of involvement in the marketplace," pp. 123-126 in P. E. Murphy, C. E. Lazniak, P. F. Anderson et al. (eds.) AMA Educators' Conference Proceedings. Chicago: American Marketing Association.

Prus, Robert (1987) "Generic social processes: maximizing conceptual development in ethnographic research." Journal of Contemporary Ethnography 16: 250-293.

Prus, Robert (1989) Making Sales: Influence as Interpersonal Accomplishment. Newbury Park, CA: Sage.

Prus, Robert and Augie Fleras (1987) "Corporate site location as social process: towards an interactionist analysis of industry location activity." Presented at the Canadian Sociology and Anthropology Association meetings, Hamilton, Ontario.

Prus, Robert and Wendy Frisby (1989) "Persuasion as practical accomplishment: tactical maneuverings at home party plans." In Helena Znanecki Lopata (ed.) Current Research on Occupations and Professions. Greenwich, CT: Jai.

Prus, Robert and Styllianoss Irini (1988) Hookers, Rounders, and Desk Clerks: The Social Organization of the Hotel Community. Salem, WI: Sheffield. (Original work published 1980.)

Prus, Robert and C. R. D. Sharper (1977) Road Hustler: The Career Contingencies of Professional Card and Dice Hustlers. Lexington, MA: Lexington Books.

Quinney, Richard (1963) "Occupational structure and criminal behavior: prescription violation by retail pharmacists." Social Problems 11: 179-185.

Ralph, Jack (1950) "Junk business and the junk peddler." Master's thesis, University of Chicago.

Rasmussen, Paul and Laurence Kuhn (1967) "The new masseuse: play for pay." Urban Life 5: 271-292.

Reingen, Peter H. and Arch G. Woodside (1981) Buyer-Seller Interactions. Chicago: American Marketing Association.

Riesz, Peta C. (1978) "Price versus quality in the marketplace." Journal of Retailing 54 (Winter): 15-28.

Rock, Paul (1973) Making People Pay. London: Routledge & Kegan Paul.

Ross, H. Lawrence (1970) Settled Out of Court. Chicago: Aldine.

Roth, Julius (1965) "Who's complaining? The inhibitions of the dissatisfied customer." Transaction 2 (5): 12-16.

Rubinstein, Jonathon (1973) City Police. New York: Ballantine.

Sampson, Anthony (1977) The Arms Bazaar. New York: Viking.

Sanders, Clint (1985) "Tattoo consumption: risk and regret in the purchase of a socially marginal service," pp. 17-22 in E. Hirshman and M. Holbrook (eds.) Advances in Consumer Research (XII). New York: Association for Consumer Research.

Sanders, Clint (1988) "Marks of mischief: the process of becoming and experience of being a tattooed person." Journal of Contemporary Ethnography 16: 395-432.

Sayles, Leonard (1964) Managerial Behavior: Administration in Complex Organizations. New York: McGraw-Hill.

M. Scherer, F. M. (1970) Industrial Purchasing. Chicago: Rand-McNally.

Schudson, Michael (1984) Advertising, the Uneasy Persuasion. New York: Basic Books.

Schutz, Alfred (1943) "The problem of rationality in the social world." Economica 10: 130-149.

Schutz, Alfred (1971) Collected Papers I: The Problem of Social Reality. The Hague: Martinus Nijhoff.

Scott, Marvin (1968) The Racing Game. Chicago: Aldine.

Shapiro, B. P. (1968) "The psychology of pricing." Harvard Business Review 46 (4): 14-25, 160.

Shibutani, Tamotsu (1961) Society and Personality. Englewood Cliffs, NJ: Prentice-Hall.

Shover, Neal (1975) "Tarnished goods and services in the marketplace." Urban Life and Culture 3: 471-488.

Simmel, Georg (1900) "A chapter in the philosophy of money." American Journal of Sociology 5: 577-603.

Simmel, Georg (1950) The Sociology of Georg Simmel (Kurt Wolff, trans. and ed.). New York: Macmillan.

Simmel, Georg (1978) The Philosophy of Money (Tom Bottomore and David Frisby, trans.). London: Routledge and Kegan Paul. (Original work published 1900.)

Siporin, Max (1967) "Bankrupt debtors and their families." Social Work 12: 51-62.

Sklar, Fred (1973) "Franchises, independence, and action: a study in the sociology of entrepreneurship." Ph.D. dissertation, University of California.

Sklar, Fred (1977) "Franchises and independence: interorganizational power relations in a contractual context." Urban Life 6: 33-52.

Small, Albion (1914) "The social gradation of capital." American Journal of Sociology 19: 721-752.

Smith, Charles W. (1981) The Mind of the Market: A Study of Stock Market Philosophies, Their Uses, and Their Implications. Totowa, NJ: Rowman & Littlefield.

Smith, Charles W. (1986) "The auction: A sociological process!?!" Presented at the conference, Ethnographic Research: An Interactionist/Interpretative Inquiry, Waterloo, Ontario.

Smith, Robert H. T. (1978) Periodic Markets, Hawkers, and Traders in Africa, Asia, and Latin America. Vancouver: Centre for Transportation Studies.

Sofer, Cyril (1965) "Buying and selling: a study in the sociology of distribution." Sociological Review 13: 183-209.

Solomon, Michael (1985) The Psychology of Fashion. Lexington, MA: Lexington Books.

Stets-Kealey, Jan (1984) "Selling as an act of control." Presented at the North Central Sociological Association meetings.

Stone, Gregory P. (1954) "City shoppers and urban identification: observations of the social psychology of city life." American Journal of Sociology 60: 36-45.

Strauss, George (1962) "Tactics of lateral relationship: the purchasing agents." Administrative Science Quarterly 7: 161-186.

Strauss, George (1964) "Work-flow frictions, interfunctional rivalry, and professionalism: a case study of purchasing agents." Human Organization 23: 137-149.

Strodtbeck, Fred and Marvin Sussman (1956) "Of time, the city, and the one-year guarantee: the relations between watch owners and repairers." American Journal of Sociology 61: 602-609.

Sturdivant, Frederick D. (1969) The Ghetto Marketplace. New York: Free Press.

Sutherland, Edwin (1949) White Collar Crime. New York: Dryden.

Swan, John (1986) "Trust building by medical salespeople." Presented at the conference, Ethnographic Research: An Interactionist/Interpretative Inquiry, Waterloo, Ontario.

Tucker, W. T. (1964) The Social Context of Economic Behavior. New York: Holt, Rinehart & Winston.

Valdez, Alvaredo (1984) "Chicano used car dealers." Urban Life 13: 229-246.

Veblen, Thorstein (1953) The Theory of the Leisure Class. New York: Mentor. (Original work published 1899.)

Velarde, Albert J. and Mark Warlick (1973) "Massage parlors: the sensuality business." Society 11: 63-74.

Wallendorf, Melanie (1978) "Social roles in a marketing context." American Behavioral Scientist 21: 571-582.

Walsh, Marilyn E. (1977) The Fence. Westport, CT: Greenwood Press.

Warner, W. L. and P. S. Lunt (1941) The Social Life of a Modern Community. New Haven, CT: Yale University Press.

Warner, W. L., M. Meeker, and K. Eels (1949) Social Class in America: A Manual of Procedures for the Measurement of Social Status. Chicago: Science Research Associates.

Wasson, Chester and David McConaughy (1968) Buying Behavior and Marketing Decisions. New York: Appleton-Century-Crofts.

Weber, Max (1947) The Theory of Social and Economic Organization (A. M. Henderson and Talcott Parsons, trans.). New York: Free Press.

Weigand, Robert E. (1980) "'Buying in' to market control." Harvard Business Review 58 (November-December): 141-149.

Wheatley, John J., J. S. Y. Chiu, and Arich Goldman (1981) "Physical quality, price, and perceptions of product quality: implications for retailers." Journal of Retailing 57 (2): 100-116.

Wiseman, Jacqueline (1979) "Close encounters of the quasi-primary kind: sociability in a second-hand clothing store." Urban Life 8: 23-51.

Wrighter, Carl P. (1972) I Can Sell You Anything. New York: Ballantine.

Zakuta, Leo (1970) "On filthy lucre," pp. 260-270 in Tamotsu Shibutani (ed.) Human Nature and Collective Behavior: Papers in Honor of Herbert Blumer. Englewood Cliffs, NJ: Prentice-Hall.

ABOUT THE AUTHOR

Viewing humans as living, thinking, interacting beings, Robert Prus (a sociologist at the University of Waterloo) has been extensively involved in developing a social science attuned to people's lived experiences. He has examined a number of social worlds, finding that an intimate understanding of each realm of human enterprise helps to better understand people's interchanges in other settings.

Following some graduate school work on revocation decision making by parole officers, Dr. Prus embarked on a study of the recruitment practices of clergymen. The insights gained from these inquiries were to lay some of the foundations for the present study, as was an examination of the careers and pursuits of some confidence operators (*Road Hustler,* Prus and Sharper, 1977). The conceptual materials developed in this study, along with the tutelage in fieldwork technique provided by C. R. D. Sharper, readily lent themselves to a detailed investigation of the careers, activities, and entanglements of the people whose lives intersect in the bar/hotel community (*Hookers, Rounders and Desk Clerks,* Prus and Irini, 1988). It was from this study that much of the substantive and conceptual impetus for the present inquiry into the marketplace developed.

The present volume is one of two books generated by a larger study of marketing and sales activity. *Pursuing Customers* concentrates on vendor preparations and the pursuit of customer contact, while *Making Sales* is very much a study of influence as interpersonal accomplishment. Dr. Prus hopes to extend the knowledge of both the marketplace and the interpretive analysis of social action by incorporating insights and concepts developed from the present study into ongoing research on consumer behavior and the corporate site-selection process.